THIRD EDITION

■

SPORTS CONDITIONING AND WEIGHT TRAINING

PROGRAMS FOR ATHLETIC COMPETITION

WILLIAM J. STONE

Department of Exercise Science and Physical Education
Arizona State University

WILLIAM A. KROLL

President, Strength Training, Inc.

 WCB Wm. C. Brown Publishers

Book Team

Editor *Chris Rogers*
Developmental Editor *Cindy Kuhrasch*
Production Coordinator *Carla D. Arnold*

 Wm. C. Brown Publishers

President *G. Franklin Lewis*
Vice President, Publisher *George Wm. Bergquist*
Vice President, Publisher *Thomas E. Doran*
Vice President, Operations and Production *Beverly Kolz*
National Sales Manager *Virginia S. Moffat*
Advertising Manager *Ann M. Knepper*
Marketing Manager *Kathy Law Laube*
Managing Editor, Production *Colleen A. Yonda*
Production Editorial Manager *Julie A. Kennedy*
Production Editorial Manager *Ann Fuerste*
Publishing Services Manager *Karen J. Slaght*
Manager of Visuals and Design *Faye M. Schilling*

Cover photo © David Madison, 1989
Cover design by Jeanne Marie Regan

Figures 5.16, 5.32, 8.4: © George McGlynn

Library of Congress Catalog Card Number: 89–81829

ISBN 0–697–10974–7

Printed in the United States of America by Wm. C. Brown Publishers, 2460 Kerper Boulevard, Dubuque, IA 52001

10 9 8 7 6 5 4 3 2 1

CONTENTS

Contents

PREFACE

Since the publication of the second edition, the explosion of interest in sports conditioning continues. Several publications, including the *National Strength & Conditioning Association Journal,* regularly publish up-to-date information and research on sports conditioning. The authors are gratified to see that many of the concepts we proposed in the first edition in the 1970s are currently endorsed by conditioning experts. The authors believe this third edition is a significant improvement over the second edition, and are appreciative of comments and suggestions, both from reviewers and readers.

In addition to bringing the material up-to-date, the authors have added several new features. Chapter 8, Putting It All Together, has been moved to Part One and expanded. That places it in a more logical position to summarize the foundation material. The triathlon event has been added to Chapter 18, Individual Sports, because of its explosive growth during the past decade. A new section (Part Three) has been added with the purpose of building a better strength program. The strength and weight training exercises have been moved from Chapter 4 to a newly developed Chapter 19 in Part Three. Also, Chapter 20, Facility Development, has been added for those who wish to develop a strength and conditioning facility. In response to current needs, it is anticipated that this third edition will better serve the needs of athletes, coaches, or students of sports conditioning.

This book is designed to offer sound, systematic training programs for those who wish to *apply* strength and conditioning techniques to *specific* sports. It should be, by design, a practical volume for the coach or athlete who wishes to use it in his or her sport. The programs offered in this volume are *basic* and simple, in order to meet the needs of *men* and *women* athletes in a wide age range.

The widespread use of supplementary training of men for sports is not of recent origin. However, female athletes and coaches are, for the most part, relative newcomers to highly competitive athletic programs and intense training regimens. Many athletes and coaches of both sexes are influenced by the training regimens of high-level performers in their sport. The major considerations in the adoption of a training program are whether the program is scientifically sound, and whether it is appropriate to the age and sex of the athlete or team. The authors have made a major effort to describe the scientific bases of sports conditioning in readable fashion and then to outline easily followed conditioning programs for specific sports.

Part One of this volume is designed to furnish the scientific foundations of conditioning and strength building. It outlines the rationale for supplementary training for athletes and describes the exercises and techniques used in Part Two. The programs described in Part Two are geared to specific sports and can easily be used by the novice with guidance from Part One. **Those athletes with no prior weight training experience are cautioned to seek help from coaches or experienced weight trainers before attempting unfamiliar weight exercises. Athletes should not use high-intensity conditioning programs if they have cardiorespiratory problems that limit their physical activity.**

The authors are very cognizant of the need for a practical source for conditioning men and women. They have extensively studied the theoretical bases of conditioning and have tested the techniques offered here under practical conditions. Perhaps of more importance to many readers, they also combine many years of experience in the conditioning of topflight professional, college, and high school athletes. They envision that the book will be a valuable aid to coaches and athletes who strive for excellence in their sport.

Acknowledgments

We would like to thank the following people for their reviews: Claudia Blackman, Southern Illinois University; Philip L. Henson, Indiana University; Renata Maiorino, University of Missouri; Robert Symons, University of North Florida; and Anne Tuite, Bowling Green State University.

William J. Stone
William A. Kroll

PART ONE

FOUNDATIONS OF CONDITIONING AND STRENGTH BUILDING

Chapter 1 deals with the rationale for supplementary training for sports and the scientific bases of conditioning and strength building. The second chapter describes the structure and content of the muscles and cardiorespiratory systems, and what happens to those systems as a result of training. In Chapters 3 and 4, attention is drawn to the basic techniques of conditioning and strength development. In the fifth chapter the distinction is drawn between flexibility, warm-up, and stretching. Injury prevention and rehabilitation techniques are discussed in Chapter 6. Chapter 7 deals with sports nutrition and explores a number of questions frequently asked by coaches and athletes. The final chapter in this section is designed to bring together the many concepts developed in Part One. It offers practical suggestions to the coach for employing conditioning programs off-season, pre-season, and in-season, as well as within the regular practice session. It also gives guidelines on how to identify or to avoid overtraining.

ONE

SPORTS CONDITIONING

This book is written for YOU, the athlete or coach. Part One is designed to aid you in using the conditioning programs listed in Part Two. Part Three is designed to help you build a better program, and lists specific strength exercises as well as information on facility development. The background information is intended to give you a basic understanding of the scientific principles involved in training. The specific techniques should enable the novice to initiate a conditioning program that is scientifically sound and easy to follow. This chapter will discuss the need for physical conditioning in sports and will define some of the basic goals of sports conditioning.

SPORTS CONDITIONING: THE RATIONALE

Recent decades have shown a vast improvement in sports performances, and numerous performance records have been set. While that statement could be made at any point in the history of sport, there has been a noticeable acceleration in the rate at which records have been broken.[10] Those sports in which records are kept and can be compared over time, primarily include track and field and swimming.

Recorded performances improve over time for many reasons—bigger athletes, better nutrition, improved coaching techniques, technological improvements, better sports medicine, and more scientific conditioning programs. It is frequently pointed out that men's gold medal winners of past Olympic swimming events would be hard pressed to place in a respectable position in current Olympic Games, in the women's division! Obviously, training and conditioning programs have played a major role in the improved performances in sport. It is impractical to compare teams and athletes in many other sports with their counterparts from the past, but the indications are that their increased size, speed, power, and conditioning have resulted in superior performances.

Olson and Hunter found that major college football players increased measurably in size, strength, and speed between 1974 and 1984.[13] Between 1947–48 and 1985–86 the average player in the NBA increased in size from 6′3′′ and 186 pounds to 6′7′′ and 214 pounds. McClellan and Stone report the results of a survey of major college football teams.[8] Those responding had invested heavily in equipment, facilities, and staff. Although a statistical analysis was not appropriate, there was an obvious relationship between the quantitative investment and a two-year comparison of media ranking and bowl appearances.

Professional sports teams and most major college athletic programs have strength and conditioning coaches and training facilities. Elite amateur athletes are also trained under the most scientific conditions.[14] Many high schools have weight rooms and off-season programs for young athletes, and most age group sports programs approach conditioning very seriously. Exercise and sports science has contributed in a variety of ways to improved performance in sport. Exercise physiologists, biomechanists, and sports psychologists have tested or filmed athletes. Data from those evaluations have led to improvements in training, performance, and mental attitudes.[4,10,14]

Much of the impetus for improved conditioning techniques and better performance emerged from the decade of the 1950s. During that time interval training was being introduced into this country on a widespread basis, Roger Bannister broke the four-minute mile barrier in England, and a number of other performance barriers were cracked. Bannister's accomplishment came as a result of a careful and scientific approach to conditioning on the part of a pre-med student with a great deal of knowledge about exercise physiology. Strength training began to become a part of the preparation and conditioning of a number of outstanding amateur and professional athletes.

It may be difficult for younger athletes and coaches to imagine the earlier resistance to some of the techniques that are now commonplace in sports conditioning. Strength training was shunned by many athletes and coaches three decades ago. As already indicated, most professional and many college teams now have a strength and/or conditioning coach. Scientific conditioning programs have become a standard practice from high school athletes to professionals. For most athletes and coaches, the conditioning results alone justify the time spent in sports conditioning. Sports scientists require a more stringent order of proof, and a significant amount of research data supports many of the current conditioning approaches. Some practices are less well documented and will require additional investigation before sports scientists are satisfied that they are effective. The authors take the position that sports conditioning promoters cannot take sole credit for improved performance, but that a scientifically devised program can contribute to performance. A major objective in this text is to review the scientific bases of conditioning and their application to sports conditioning programs.

Perhaps one of the most dramatic examples of the importance of conditioning in sport occurred during the 1970s. For many years the Soviet ice hockey team had made regular visits to the United States to challenge college hockey teams. The Soviets were almost always victorious. When a series of games with "Team Canada" was started in the 1970s, the Soviets were given little chance to win against the National Hockey League professionals who made up the Canadian group. The first series proved to be eye opening for United States and Canadian hockey observers. The highly disciplined Soviets, skating relentlessly, were able to win several games primarily on the basis of superior physical conditioning. Games that were close in the first period became a rout in the third period as the better-conditioned Soviets outskated the NHL professionals. The Soviet team was subject to a highly scientific training program, which paid dividends on the ice.

SPORTS VS. CONDITIONING REQUIREMENTS OF SPORT

It has long been recognized that actual practice of a sport is the best means of preparing for the skills and strategies needed for the game. Some sports, however, do not make sufficient demands upon all of the physiological systems supporting the performance. Thus there is the need to spend time in developing top physical condition. Conditioning exercises are necessary to increase the capacity of the supporting systems and, in many cases, the muscles directly involved.[9]

The amount of time spent in practice in order to develop skills and strategy versus physical conditioning will vary according to the physical demands of the sport. Runners and swimmers are constantly practicing their skills as they work out, but their performance will be determined primarily by their physical condition. Volleyball and basketball players probably do not require the high degree of physical conditioning needed by swimmers and runners, but conditioning is still an important component of their game. On the other side of the continuum from the highly physical sports are activities that require a great deal of attention to skills development (golf), but less concern for physical conditioning (fig. 1.1). This spectrum of sports is best viewed as a continuum, with both skills-strategy development and physical conditioning as basic preparation for all sports.

Hence, the baseball player strengthens his arms, wrists, and shoulders by performing weight training exercises rather than relying on the weight of the bat alone to furnish increased strength. The pitcher runs in order to increase his general endurance as well as the local muscular endurance in his legs, knowing that there may be only limited opportunity for him to run during a game. Both of these conditioning factors are necessary for the baseball player, but skills practice alone will usually not develop them sufficiently. The same rationale applies to a wide range of sports, including many that are far more vigorous than baseball. The platoon system in football reduces the amount of time actually spent in the game, yet the player on either offense or defense must be prepared for rigorous physical activity. The football player requires considerable endurance despite the fact that the ball is in play for only a few seconds at a time.

Although the use of weight training and physical conditioning programs has become very widespread in athletics, it should also be noted that practice does not automatically ensure better performance. The key element in making supplementary training a valuable contribution to the total program of preparing the athlete for competition is *specificity of training*.

SPECIFICITY IN ATHLETIC PERFORMANCE AND CONDITIONING

The most dominant characteristic of sports skills performance is a high degree of specificity. *Specificity* means that sports skills are highly unique; that no matter how much "alike" they appear, there are usually a number of minor differences that make it difficult to perform many skills well without a great deal of practice. Furthermore, one cannot carry over athletic performance from one sport to another unless the two are nearly identical.

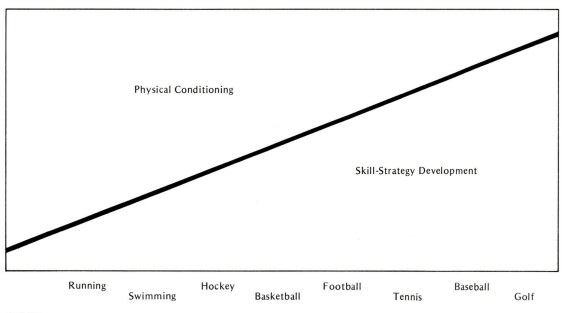

Physical Conditioning

Skill-Strategy Development

Running   Swimming   Hockey   Basketball   Football   Tennis   Baseball   Golf

SPORT

Figure 1.1   Skill vs. Conditioning Requirements of Sports

The concept of specificity is sometimes difficult to comprehend because of a number of multiskilled individuals who tend to excel in several sports. There is considerable evidence that such rare individuals are probably blessed with many specific skills and have practiced those skills a great deal. They are also highly motivated.

The staggering number of physical factors, such as arm speed, leg power, reaction time, and balance, that might be involved in various combinations in a single sports skill makes specificity quite logical. The fact that many psychological factors also play a role in athletic performance adds to the uniqueness of each sports skill and performance. The astute coach or athlete pays heed to the specificity of sports skills development by concentrating primarily on the actual practice of the sport. It should not be surprising that the same principle must be applied to sports conditioning. Specificity in training refers, then, to matching the conditioning or strength demands of the sport to the training techniques.

Physical conditioning for any sport should match the physiological demands of the activity. Basketball, for example, requires a high level of general endurance, but also includes brief periods of all-out activity such as occur during a fast break. Football, on the other hand, represents a series of all-out bursts of energy followed by brief recovery period. Recent work in muscle physiology lends support not only to sports conditioning, but to specificity when preparing for sports performance. Research on muscle fiber typing indicates that endurance training affects one muscle fiber type while anaerobic training affects another fiber type. This suggests strongly that if both qualities are needed in a sport, training must be designed for both. (Fiber typing is discussed in more detail in Chapter 2.) Of even greater concern to coaches and athletes is evidence that training systems are not complementary and may even be detrimental to the other training quality. Thus it becomes extremely important for the coach or athlete to weigh the amount of general endurance versus all-out power required in the sport. This factor is discussed in detail in Part Two, wherein training programs are designed relative to the physical demands of each sport.

DEFINITIONS

A few descriptive definitions are in order here to prepare the reader for terms that will be used frequently throughout the book. The terms are briefly defined, synonymous terms are used, and brief explanations are given of their importance to athletic performance.

Aerobic Power

Aerobic power is the ability to take oxygen into the tissues and to maintain high work loads continuously for prolonged periods of time without becoming unduly fatigued. In sports terminology, this refers to the ability of an athlete to operate at high levels of activity during the game and to continue "putting out" without becoming prematurely "winded." Most team sports require a good-to-excellent aerobic capacity on the part

Aerobic Power

of the athlete. Aerobic capacity is literally the basis of good athletic performance, as most sports require moving the body almost continuously.

Sports medicine experts and exercise physiologists recognize aerobic power as the major index of general endurance or physical fitness. Aerobic capacity depends upon the ability of the heart and lungs to supply oxygen to the working muscles and is developed usually by large muscle, whole body movements like running, swimming, and cycling.

Anaerobic Power

Anaerobic power is the ability to work explosively in excess of the body's capacity to take oxygen into the tissues, resulting in an oxygen debt. This type of work in sports is characterized by the performer going all out for brief periods of time, such as in a series of fast breaks in basketball. The capacity to operate anaerobically is limited to brief periods even in the most highly trained athlete. Anaerobic training can increase the athlete's capacity to operate at intense levels, and the training effect is brought about from physiological and

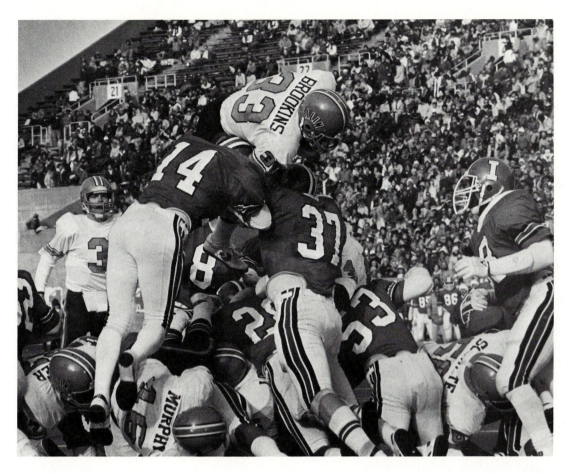

Anaerobic Power

psychological factors. The latter factor is an important one, since it involves a willingness to withstand the discomfort of going all out repeatedly.

If aerobic capacity is the basis of most performances, anaerobic capacity can be considered the frosting on the cake. At the highest levels of athletic competition, where the range of skill is narrow, willingness to tolerate anaerobic effort may provide the margin necessary to win or to succeed.

Muscular Strength

Strength or *1 RM* (one repetition maximum) refers to the maximum amount of tension the muscle or muscle group can apply in a single effort. Strength can be subdivided into two components: 1) *static strength,* meaning the maximum amount of tension the muscle can apply against resistance, involving little or no movement in the muscle, and 2) *dynamic strength,* referring to the application of great force through a full range of motion. **Nearly all applications of strength in athletics are of this type.** The athlete applies force through nearly a full range of motion and very rapidly, as is evident in throwing, jumping, running, kicking, and striking.

One of the major factors distinguishing the skilled performer from the less skilled one is strength. It has been clearly established in a number of studies that strength training has a beneficial effect on motor skills and sports performance.[5] While it should not be inferred that strength is the cause of skill, that relationship held through all the age groups studied. Increased strength could be a prerequisite to better athletic performance. The same might be said of aerobic capacity. Better performance cannot be expected unless the athlete has sufficient strength and aerobic power to maintain lengthy practice sessions or game situations without undue fatigue. Strength training is anaerobic in nature, and it affects the same fibers as anaerobic training.

Muscular Endurance

Muscular endurance refers to the capacity to continue submaximal muscle contractions repeatedly. It is associated with local areas of the body, such as the legs in running, swimming, or bicycling. Most athletic events require **local muscular endurance** in one or more areas of the body, and this endurance is developed by weight training with light resistance or aerobic training. Although muscular endurance is on the opposite end of

Power/Explosive Strength

Speed

the continuum from strength, it can be greatly influenced by the strength of the local muscle group. If two athletes are applying force against the same resistance repeatedly, then the stronger of the two should fatigue less because he or she will be using a smaller percentage of maximal strength with each effort. That is an illustration of *absolute endurance*. If the two athletes were applying force relative to their strength, it would be an example of *relative endurance*. Muscular endurance is an important facet of athletic performance simply because actions are repeated over and over in a game.

Power

Power refers to work (force × distance) per unit of time. This is the application of great force in a very brief time span. In athletics, *explosive strength* is often used synonymously with the term *power*. The football lineman, basketball rebounder, and shot-putter come

to mind most readily when describing explosive strength or power.

There is perhaps no other cluster of performances in athletics wherein strength building has greater potential to contribute toward better performance than those events requiring explosive strength. The great increase in dynamic strength that accrues from weight training can be utilized directly when applying force rapidly. Some of the earliest efforts to use supplementary weight training were designed to increase athletic power. Leading exercise scientists and strength and conditioning coaches view power as the most important dimension of sports conditioning.

Speed

Speed refers to the rapidity with which one contracts a muscle or group of muscles. Running speed in sports is thus a series of rapid muscle contractions. The time that it takes the athlete to move from one place to an-

Acceleration

other is a measure of his or her speed, but there is another component of movement time, and that is *acceleration*.

Acceleration

Acceleration refers to increasing the velocity (speed), such as the sprinter leaving the starting blocks or the golf club accelerating as it approaches the ball. These same examples also involve explosive strength, which points out the interrelationship of strength-speed-power.

The importance of speed and acceleration in athletics is obvious, whether they involve the athlete moving his body quickly or accelerating light objects such as rackets, clubs, bats, or balls. The strength-speed relationship is not nearly as clear, however, as that of strength and power. The relationship between strength and speed of limb movement is not particularly high when there is little resistance. With greater resistance, the contribution of strength to speed becomes greater.

Thus, the contribution of additional strength to limb speed may be greater for the shot-putter than for the baseball pitcher. The pitcher may still benefit, although gains in speed may not be proportional to gains in strength. The same principles may be said to apply to running speed. Since acceleration is a major factor in running short distances, the increased strength derived from training may be of greater importance when overcoming inertia than at later stages when top running speed has been attained.

Flexibility

Flexibility refers to the range of motion in a joint or series of joints. Most athletic events require a dynamic range of motion. Flexibility can also be measured in the static mode by having the athlete reach slowly through a full range of motion. The importance of flexibility is very evident in those sports events that are judged aesthetically, such as gymnastics, diving, and figure skating. Flexibility is also important in the majority of sports that value performance strictly on effect rather than form.

Agility

Agility involves rapid change of body direction or limb position. Greater acceleration of the body and greater speed of limb movement contribute to increased agility. The interrelationships of factors in sport performance should be evident. Control of the body can be dependent upon the strength of the supporting muscles in the arms, legs, or trunk. Most sports require a great deal of agility—for example, volleyball, basketball, baseball, football, and tennis.

THE DIMENSIONS OF ATHLETIC PERFORMANCE

Many factors contribute to athletic performance, some of which were defined here. It is not surprising then that there is as much specificity to both athletic performance and conditioning as there is, given the variety of ways those factors can contribute to different sport skills. In figure 1.2 the authors have reduced a variety of factors into three dimensions: physical endowment, specific skill, and psychological endowment.

Figure 1.2 is intended to illustrate the importance of practicing the specific sports skill for improvement in athletic performance. The other dimensions are also important in determining the quality of the athletic performance. Physical endowment is highly important in athletic performance and many physical endowment factors can be improved by sports conditioning. While the athlete may not be able to influence height or body

Flexibility

Agility

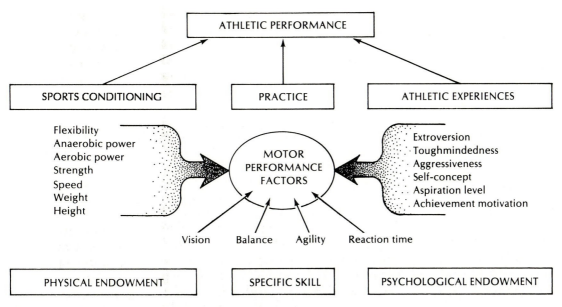

Figure 1.2 The Dimensions of Athletic Performance

type, he or she can increase strength, speed, aerobic power, anaerobic power, and flexibility, among other factors. Those factors influence not only athletic performance in general, but also specific sports skills. Psychological endowment, while also very important in athletic performance, is considerably more difficult for the coach, in particular, to influence. There is greater variability among athletes in behavioral response to athletic experiences than in physical conditioning.

In preparing for a sport, it is evident that the coach or athlete must be concerned with all three dimensions which contribute to athletic performance. It is fair to state that most of the time spent in preparation for sport goes into the development of skills and strategies. This is as it should be—that is what sports are all about. One of the objectives of this text is to encourage athletes and coaches to give more careful consideration to the physical dimension through sports conditioning.

SPORTS CONDITIONING

The authors identify the major areas of sports conditioning as aerobic power, anaerobic power, flexibility, and strength. Many factors targeted for sports conditioning can be included in those four major headings. Anaerobic power can also include the development of speed, power, and acceleration. Aerobic power as well as strength will influence muscular endurance. Nearly every sport requires some level of conditioning in each of those four areas, although the emphasis on each may vary.

Another area of conditioning and motor skill development is agility development. Specificity research tells us that agility development is highly specific to the sport or a specific position within the sport. The authors recommend that coaches or athletes develop their own specific agility drills which are highly related to the sports skill to be practiced.

Sports Conditioning
Aerobic Power
Anaerobic Power
Flexibility
Strength

POSITION STATEMENTS

Not every effort to improve sports performance through science and technology has been met with universal acceptance. Attempts to mold the minds and bodies of athletes through high-level technology is not desirable in the views of some sports observers. The view suggests that the athlete is being demeaned, and takes on a robot-like characteristic. Some aspects of training and performance enhancement have drawn much stronger criticism or debate. Two areas in the latter category involve the intense training of children and youths, and the widespread use of performance-enhancing drugs, particularly the use of androgenic, anabolic steroids.

AEROBIC AND STRENGTH TRAINING FOR PREPUBESCENTS

In the early 1980s, the American Academy of Pediatrics (AAP) issued two position statements concerning the risks of distance running and weight training for children.[1,2] Both position statements suggested an increased risk of injury for children, and others have questioned the trainability of children either for aerobic power or strength.

Aerobic Training

Some early studies on high intensity training with children and youths left some confusion regarding the trainability of their aerobic capacity. Stone has reported, however, that two large-scale and longitudinal studies of elementary aged children have left little doubt that functional aerobic power can be significantly improved in children.[17] A key factor in such studies is the use of a training prescription which meets threshold requirements. It has also been noted that there is no apparent detrimental effect on normal growth and development from aerobic training.

There is little documentation of injury to children from aerobic training. The most likely injury would involve the overuse syndrome, and children, like adults, can be susceptible to overuse. Such injuries have been reported in children and youths from baseball (elbow), swimming (shoulder), and running (stress fracture). Rules which limit the number of innings pitched by youngsters are designed to avoid such problems. The potential for overuse injury in children is real, and they should be protected from overtraining just as any other athlete.

Strength Training

The major question concerning the trainability of prepubescents for strength gains involves the hormone testosterone. Since prepubescent males are lacking in the hormone, and females never develop androgens, it has been hypothesized that neither group could benefit from strength training. Several studies specifically involving prepubescents have clearly demonstrated increases in strength.[11] Strength gains have also been reported in the longitudinal studies previously cited.[17]

Over half of the injuries reported for weight training involve those age nineteen or under and, usually, those unsupervised. The major concern with prepubescent children is the potential for injury to the epiphyseal area, or growth plate. While growth plate injuries have occurred, they are a very small percentage of all sports injuries, and variation in growth is extremely rare.

The National Strength and Conditioning Association (NSCA) has issued a position paper on prepubescent strength training.[11] That paper has outlined both the benefits and risks of strength training. The NSCA has concluded that benefits such as strength gain, injury protection, and knowledge of proper technique far outweigh the risks. NSCA has gone on to issue guidelines for safe and effective strength training programs for prepubescents.

THE USE OF ANABOLIC STEROIDS IN SPORTS

Androgenic anabolic steroids have been used in strength building efforts and sport for over thirty years.[20] Both public knowledge and the widespread use of androgenic agents are of more recent origins. The early use was secretive and not widespread beyond the strength building or football communities. Because of the iceberg nature of that use, and the limitations on medically prescribed dosages, it has taken the exercise science and sports medicine communities some time to gather sufficient facts about the full effects. The public became very aware of the steroid problem in the 1980s, especially as it affected the Olympic Games. Coaches, exercise scientists, and sports medicine experts are justifiably alarmed at the potential widening use of steroids by both high school athletes and nonathletes. The latter group is seeking body building effects.

The androgenic anabolic steroid is a derivative of the male hormone testosterone, and it aids in protein synthesis in the muscle. Numerous studies have left some question about its effect on performance.[20] It can be expected to produce weight gain through added muscle tissue, but the major contribution to performance appears to be restricted to a combination with weight training. Greater body weight in muscle can be an advantage in sports that rely on mass and strength to a great extent.

In addition to the ethical objections of steroid use, sports authorities are greatly concerned with the welfare of users. There are a number of undesirable side effects associated with steroid use, and some serious health risks. Users are frequently found to be using ten to one hundred times the medical dosage. The list of adverse effects includes elevated blood lipids and blood pressure, increasing the risk of heart disease; greater risk of liver cancer; premature closing of the growth plate in prepubescents; mood swings and increased hostility; sterility, baldness, and acne in males; and masculinization in females.[20]

The international sports governing bodies and sports medicine communities uniformly reject the use of steroids as both unfair competition and a risk to the user. Both the American College of Sports Medicine and the National Strength and Conditioning Association have issued position statements against their use.[3,12] Strength coaches and exercise scientists throughout the country reject the use of steroids and have encouraged drug-free sport and strength competition. The authors take the same position and add the following request. **If you know of someone who is using steroids, it is your obligation to warn them of the risks involved.** If you, yourself, are involved, at the very least, seek the care of a knowledgeable sports medicine physician and insist on blood testing for liver or heart disease risk.

SUMMARY

There are many factors involved in successful athletic performance. The authors of this book have focused entirely on the physical conditioning involved in preparing for a sport. Athletes and coaches can greatly increase such abilities as aerobic and anaerobic power, muscular strength and endurance, and athletic power-speed-flexibility. The techniques can be used by athletes of both sexes and by a wide range of age groups.

The authors have defined the various terms to be used in the book and have outlined the four major areas of sports conditioning. In addition, the positions of the major sports medicine, strength and conditioning, and sports organizations are cited in regard to conditioning for children, and the use of anabolic steroids.

For a more detailed description of the concepts introduced in this chapter, the reader is referred to the annotated references. In Chapter 2 we will deal with the scientific bases of athletic conditioning.

REFERENCES

1. American Academy of Pediatrics. 1982. "Risks in Long-Distance Running for Children," *News and Comments* 33:11 (June).

2. American Academy of Pediatrics. 1982. "Weight Training and Weight Lifting: Information for the Pediatrician," *News and Comments* 33:7–8 (July).

3. American College of Sports Medicine. 1984. "Position Stand on the Use of Anabolic-Androgenic Steroids in Sports," *Sports Medicine Bulletin* 19:13–18.

4. Burke, Edmund J., ed. 1980. *Toward an Understanding of Human Performance.* 2d ed. Ithaca, NY: Mouvement Publications.

5. Clarke, H. Harrison, ed. 1974. "Strength Development and Motor-Sports Improvement," *Physical Fitness Research Digest* 4:1–17.

6. Clarke, David H., and Helen M. Eckert, eds. 1985. *Limits of Human Performance.* American Academy of Physical Education. Champaign, IL: Human Kinetics Publishers, Inc.

7. Fox, Edward L. 1984. *Sports Physiology.* 2d ed. Philadelphia: W. B. Saunders Co.

8. McClellan, Tim, and William J. Stone. 1986. "A survey of Division 1A strength and conditioning programs," *NSCA Journal* 8(2):34–36.

9. Morehouse, Lawrence E. 1962. "Athletic Physiology," *Proceedings of the 4th National Conference on Medical Aspects of Sports.* American Medical Association.

10. Murphy, Patrick. 1986. "Longer, Higher, Faster: Athletes Continue to Reach New Heights," *Physician & Sportsmedicine* 14:140–149.

11. National Strength and Conditioning Association. 1985. "Position Paper on Prepubescent Strength Training," *NSCA Journal* 7(4):27–31.

12. National Strength and Conditioning Association. 1985. "Position Statement: Use and Abuse of Anabolic Steroids," *NSCA Journal* 7(5):44–59.

13. Olson, John R., and Gary R. Hunter. 1985. "A Comparison of 1974 and 1984 Player Sizes, Maximal Strength and Speed Efforts for Division I NCAA Universities," *NSCA Journal* 6(6):26–28.

14. Reynolds, Gretchen. 1986. "Scientific Sweat," *Superfit* 2:33–73.

15. Sharkey, Brain J. 1986. *Coaches Guide to Sport Physiology.* Champaign, IL: Human Kinetics.

16. Stone, William J. 1981. "Sports Conditioning," *Osteopathic Annals* 9:12–18.

17. Stone, William J. 1985. "Aerobic and Strength Training for Elementary Aged Children," *Proceedings of the International Pre-Olympic Symposium,* 42–46.

18. Wilmore, Jack H., ed. 1973. *Exercise and Sports Sciences Reviews,* Vol. 1. New York: Academic Press.

19. Wilmore, Jack H., and David L. Costill. 1988. *Training for Sport and Activity: The Physiological Basis of the Conditioning Process,* 3d ed. Dubuque, IA: Wm. C. Brown Publishers.

20. Windsor, Robert E., and Daniel Dumitru. 1988. "Anabolic Steroid Use by Athletes: How Serious Are the Health Hazards?" *Postgraduate Medicine* 84:37–48.

CHAPTER
TWO

PHYSIOLOGY OF FITNESS AND STRENGTH FOR SPORTS

In order to understand better the scientific bases of training and conditioning, a brief review of some physiological aspects of athletic performance is presented here. Special focus is aimed at the muscular system because the muscles are ultimately responsible for the movement and performance of the athlete. The descriptions are succinct so that the reader can move rapidly to succeeding chapters that make application of this information to training and conditioning techniques. Readers who require more detailed information should consult the references.

SPORTS FITNESS: AEROBIC AND ANAEROBIC MECHANISMS

Each time an athlete moves—whether to run, jump, throw, kick, or produce any sports movement—the immediate source of energy at the muscle level is the high-energy phosphate compound adenosine triphosphate (ATP). The two major metabolic systems responsible for supplying ATP to the muscles are the aerobic and anaerobic pathways. The aerobic system supplies energy through a complex series of steps involving the Krebs cycle, the electron transport system, and the utilization of oxygen at the mitochondrial level in the muscle cell (fiber). The major sources of energy for the aerobic system include free fatty acids and carbohydrates. The anaerobic system bypasses the Krebs cycle in the absence of sufficient oxygen and utilizes carbohydrates as an energy source. The anaerobic system has the additional flexibility of releasing ATP through two different substrate mechanisms. One of these mechanisms relies on stored creatine phosphate (CP), while the others involve the production of high levels of lactic acid (LA).

Although ATP is the direct source of contraction energy in the muscle, the calorie-containing foods are also involved in energy metabolism. It should be noted that the only calorie-containing foodstuffs are fats, car-

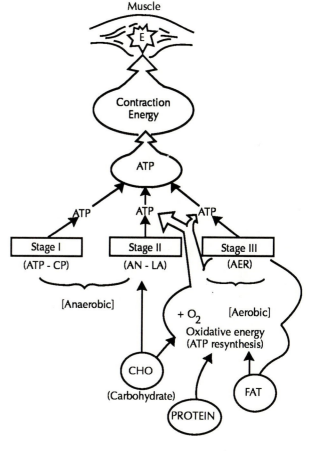

Figure 2.1 ATP Yield from Three Stages of Metabolism

bohydrates, and proteins. Although those nutrients help supply energy for the body, they do so indirectly. Since ATP is the true source of energy at the muscle level, carbohydrate and fat are used primarily to rebuild ATP. Protein is not considered to be of major significance in that process. Figure 2.1 is a graphic illustration of the working relationship between the three energy yielding stages and the role of the calorie-containing nutrients.

Table 2.1 Three Energy Mechanisms for Muscular Contraction

(A) Energy Capacity, Power, and Limitations.

Stage	Energy System	ATP (units) Capacity	Max Power Output	Time Limit @ Max Power	ATP Delivery/Yield
I	ATP-CP	0.6	3.6/min.	up to 15 secs.	High rate/very limited
II	AN-LA	1.2	1.6/min.	30–60 secs.	High rate/limited
III	AER	"Theoretically unlimited"	1.0/min.	over 2 mins.	Low rate/unlimited

(B) Sports Utilizations

Stage	Sports Activity
I	Brief, explosive bursts—e.g., 50m dash, jumping, throwing, tackling (most sports skills)
II	"All-out," exhaustive efforts—e.g., 400m run, 100m swim, repeated fast breaks, etc.
III	Continuous, endurance efforts—e.g., marathon, triathlon, X-country, soccer (low- to high-level effort)

It should also be noted that carbohydrate, fat, and protein do not break down into ATP, but supply the energy for the resynthesis of ATP.

Carbohydrate is the major energy-supplying food for exercise and sport, and is the sole supply when anaerobic metabolism is under way (Stages I and II). Fat is a significant source of energy during aerobic exercise and sport. In all cases, the early minutes of exercise utilize carbohydrate as the predominate fuel. During a two-hour bout of aerobic exercise, the fuel supply will shift from almost entirely carbohydrate in the early minutes, to 60 or 70 percent of the energy derived from fat at the end. It is estimated that the crossover (50 percent of the energy coming from carbohydrate and fat, respectively) occurs at approximately 20 minutes of continuous exercise. Over the entire two-hour period, carbohydrate will still supply the majority of the energy calories. About 75 percent of the energy used to resupply ATP was already stored in the muscle cells in the form of carbohydrates and fats.

During aerobic exercise and sport, energy can be derived from a mixture of fats and carbohydrates. Carbohydrates are stored in the body in a limited amount compared to fats. In an intense, two-hour bout of exercise, it is possible to deplete the stored carbohydrate (glycogen) in the muscle. This effect is commonly referred to as "running into the wall" and will most often occur at approximately 20 miles of hard running. The athlete who can effectively use fat for fuel will be able to avoid such problems. This is referred to as "glycogen sparing" metabolism. By comparison to the two anaerobic stages of energy metabolism, the aerobic energy stage is virtually limitless.

Stage I. ATP-CP

Exercise physiologists have identified three energy-yielding mechanisms that encompass all sports activities. The three mechanisms differ in the amount or limits of ATP energy they can supply. Those limits are converted from quantitative amounts to time limits at maximal utilization rates for ease in discussing sports activities. The anaerobic (AN) Stage I mechanism comes into play in brief bursts of activity extending from fractions of a second to 15 seconds (table 2.1). Most sports skills are performed within that time span: bursting out of the blocks in a dash, throwing a ball, jumping for a rebound, and making a block or tackle. The energy is supplied by the ATP-CP mechanism at a very high rate for a very brief period. The ATP for this activity is readily stored in the muscle and is rapidly resynthesized with the aid of CP after use—thus the ability to repeat the act quickly or to repeat it after a brief rest.

Stage II. AN-LA

There are times when the athlete must extend himself or herself at a high rate for more than just a few seconds. As the athlete races around the quarter-mile track or engages in a series of fast breaks in basketball, an additional source of ATP can be supplied for a longer but definitely limited period (30–60 seconds). By utilizing carbohydrates directly, the AN-lactic-acid (LA) mechanism can produce larger amounts of ATP at a relatively high rate. The Stage II mechanism can be used at critical times in sport, but it has an extremely high after-cost. The by-product of the AN-LA mechanism is lactic acid and it is accompanied by a high level of oxygen debt if carried to its limit. Indeed, the athlete who has "burned it" in wind sprints or other Stage II activities can be left exhausted and require considerable time to recover. While metabolic recovery from Stage I activities will be nearly complete in three minutes, recovery from an all-out, Stage II effort may require an hour or more. All sports activities involve some aspect of AN Stage I, and anaerobic activity is certainly associated with the more exciting aspects of sport. Anaerobic activity cannot continue for long, however, without the involvement of the aerobic system (AER).

Stage III. AER

Most sports entail fairly continuous periods of action punctuated with anaerobic bursts. When activity continues beyond two minutes up to two hours or more, the Stage III mechanism is employed. Although the AER mechanism produces ATP energy at a very low rate, it is "theoretically unlimited."[6] The anaerobic mechanisms have finite limits (Stage I) or LA tolerance limits (Stage II). The AER mechanism is a continuous cycle of ATP production and resynthesis. It is capable of tapping copious supplies of stored muscle glycogen and triglycerides as well as free fatty acids. The endurance activities, such as distance running and swimming and cross-country skiing, are usually associated with Stage III. The "cruising," dribbling, and constant movement in sports often make them very aerobic in nature. Soccer and basketball are excellent examples of sports with a large aerobic ingredient and significant anaerobic action. Aerobic power has been designated as the foundation of athletic conditioning. The ability to continue practicing or playing without undue fatigue and the ability to recover from vigorous activity are determined by the AER system. The ability to delay fatigue is also a significant factor in injury prevention.

As long as there are sufficient fuel (glycogen and free fatty acids) and oxygen available, the athlete can perform in a steady state. Steady state exercise means that the oxygen uptake meets the oxygen demands of the activity and little or no lactic acid buildup occurs in the muscles.

The authors referred earlier to the "theoretically unlimited" nature of aerobic exercise and sport. As long as there is sufficient fuel and water provided, and brief rest periods allowed, the human appears to have almost limitless physical endurance in the aerobic mode of exercise. A few vivid examples are in order. Great feats of endurance have challenged athletes for many centuries. Runners who have mastered the 26-mile marathon have attempted, and completed, double marathons. Some have then moved on to 100-mile endurance runs. In the last decade, the triathlon has emerged as a new challenge for serious endurance competitors, and even for recreational athletes. The Ironman triathlon in Hawaii requires a 2.4-mile ocean swim and a 112-mile bike ride, then completes the day with the standard 26-mile marathon. The present record is under eight and one-half hours. Most performers require more time to complete the event. Hawaii is also the site of the Great Hawaiian Foot Race. That event involves ten consecutive days of running, averaging 28 kilometers per day. The athletes rest for two days before resuming the race with eight more days of running— a total of 500 kilometers in twenty days.

In 1982 the first Great American Bike Race was attempted, from Santa Monica to New York City. The event drew a total of four competitors and the winner covered the more than 3,000 miles in just under ten days. In order to cover the necessary 300 plus miles per day, the competitors were forced to cycle over 20 hours each day. The accounts of the first race make rather fascinating reading, with performers consuming more than 12,000 calories of food daily, suffering fatigue and blisters, and fighting to remain awake. In such efforts the body is a far more willing participant than the mind, which tends to want to leave the scene, suggesting that the body is not smart enough to quit!

Two walkers, one male and one female, have traversed the perimeter of the United States, traveling nearly 11,000 miles. Perhaps the most amazing aerobic effort was completed by Stan Cottrell, who **ran** across the country in forty-eight days. He covered the distance between New York City and San Francisco by averaging an incredible 64.5 miles per day!

All of these endurance efforts are evidence of the nearly unlimited capacity of humans to work in the aerobic mode. It is also evidence of the magnitude of the human spirit to overcome great physical challenges. Most of the performers described were not highly paid professional athletes, but amateurs who trained hard to achieve a new aerobic endurance record.

In the preceding chapter the *aerobic* power system was described as the ability of the athlete to continue performance without becoming prematurely fatigued. The aerobic capacity is determined by the ability of the body to deliver and take up oxygen into the tissue. This means a step-by-step process of 1) getting oxygen into the lungs (ventilation); 2) having the oxygen pass the membrane between the lungs and the blood to combine with hemoglobin, an O_2 carrying agent; 3) having the oxygenated blood pumped out to the muscles by the heart (cardiac output); and 4) getting the oxygen into the muscle tissues where it is needed (oxygen uptake). The last step involves sufficient blood vessels (capillaries) to carry oxygenated blood to the muscle fiber and then to the energy powerhouses (mitochondria) within the muscle tissue where oxygen is absorbed. All of these processes are improved by aerobic training.

The foregoing discussion relates to the three mechanisms for supplying energy for muscle contraction. The three mechanisms will supply ATP either aerobically or anaerobically. The mechanisms are described graphically in figure 2.1 and table 2.1.

AER-AN TRAINING EFFECTS

Aerobic Training Effects

Repeated overload of the aerobic system results in numerous adaptations or training effects within the various physiological systems. *Overload* simply means subjecting the systems or muscles to activity loads

Table 2.2	Aerobic Demands of Sports
High	Running—Swimming—Basketball
Medium	Hockey—Football—Tennis—Volleyball
Low	Baseball—Archery—Golf

MUSCLE STRUCTURE AND CONTRACTION

The internal structure of the muscle can best be described by likening it to a huge telephone cable with thousands of wires packed tightly together but individually insulated and combined in clusters. In viewing the cross section of a muscle, it is apparent that there are thousands of fibers bound together by connective tissue, each with its individual insulation and nerve innervation. As few as ten and as many as several hundred fibers can contract together to form a *motor unit*. The motor unit is the smallest functioning unit of contraction within the muscle; i.e., the muscle tends to contract in units, a few or many, depending upon the demands on the muscle. The motor unit is composed of the motor nerve fiber, its branches, and all the muscle fibers they innervate. All of the fibers in a motor unit respond when the threshold is reached. Some motor units contract readily (low threshold), while others will contract only under vigorous stimulation from the nervous system (high threshold). Stimulation is carried from the brain to the muscle by the nervous system.

The method the nervous system uses to increase or decrease the strength of the contraction involves changes in the frequency of stimulation messages to the muscle. This results in the contraction of few or many motor units as the case may demand. Thus the athlete can produce maximum effort or fine movements with the same muscle or muscle groups.

greater than those to which they are normally accustomed. Training effects are usually increased in the functional capacity or magnitude of the various systems that contribute to physical output. In the circulatory system the heart and blood vessels are very much affected by training. The heart muscle becomes stronger and capable of greater output per minute (cardiac output). More blood vessels (capillaries) become available within the muscle, making easier the delivery of oxygen to the tissues. The blood volume and oxygen-carrying capacity (hemoglobin) increases, thus adding to the effect of more capillaries. The number and density of mitochondria increase in the cell, also increasing the oxygen uptake.

The respiratory system is also influenced by training and greater amounts of oxygenated air can be brought into the lungs (ventilation). The exchange of oxygen from the lungs to the blood and from the blood to the tissues is enhanced. The oxygen uptake increases, forestalling oxygen debt in the athlete. At less than maximum effort the athlete is capable of faster recovery when better trained. The combined result of increasing the capacity of the various systems operating in aerobic work is rather dramatic, resulting in the athlete's ability to perform at higher levels.

The aerobic demands of various sports are listed in table 2.2.

Anaerobic Training Effects

The anaerobic mechanisms are also affected by training, but the exact scientific explanation of this phenomenon is not clear and may, in part, be due to psychological factors. ATP concentration, anaerobic enzymes, and myofibril density within the muscle are increased by anaerobic training. Athletes who undergo severe training programs have considerably greater tolerance for pain and discomfort than nonathletes. This indeed may be the hallmark of many champion athletes, i.e., their willingness to persevere at intense training levels and to give maximal effort in the latter stages of the game. The effects of anaerobic training have not been as thoroughly studied as those of aerobic training.

Muscle Fiber and Fiber Type

The basic element or cell of the muscle is called a *muscle fiber*. To gain some perspective of internal structure, it should be noted that the largest muscle fibers are about the size of a human hair. The fiber may run the entire length of the muscle, but it is more likely to be linked in series within the belly of the muscle (fig. 2.2).

One of the most fascinating discoveries relating to muscle physiology in athletes involves fiber typing work from muscle biopsies. Sections of muscle tissue are removed to determine the percentage of fast (white) or slow (red) twitch fibers within the muscle. Fast twitch fibers (FT) are high in glycogen (sugar), ATP supply, and predominate in high-speed and power activities. The FT fibers contract with great force, rapidly, but also fatigue quickly. The slow twitch fibers (ST) have a much greater blood vessel supply, oxidative capacity, and predominate in aerobic or endurance activities. ST fibers do not contract with great force, but can sustain contractions for long periods. The type of fiber is apparently determined by the nervous system innervation, and some athletes will have a greater abundance of one type of fiber than of the other (table 2.3).

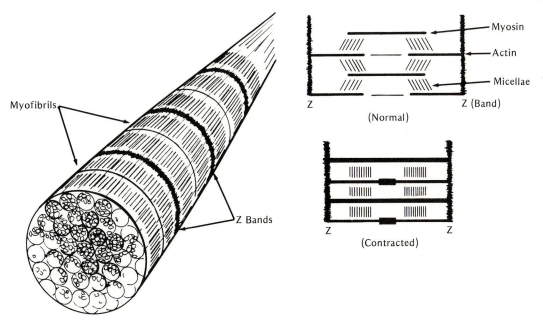

Figure 2.2 Muscle Fiber

Table 2.3 Fiber Type and Sports

Predominant Fiber Type	Sport Demands	Athletes
Fast Twitch (White)	Speed and power	Sprinters, weight lifters
Slow Twitch (Red)	Endurance activities	Distance runners, swimmers

The FT fiber could also be described as an *anaerobic* fiber, while the ST fiber is predominately *aerobic*. Research suggests that the percentage of FT or ST fibers is genetically determined.[13]

A major concern for coaches and athletes is that aerobic training *does not* significantly train the fast twitch fibers and anaerobic training *does not* significantly train the slow twitch fibers. There is a tendency for some FT fibers to become more oxidative with endurance training. Those fibers are known as fast oxidative fibers. Concentration on only one type of training may be sufficient if the sport requires only aerobic or anaerobic output, but most team sports do not fall into only one category. Most team sports will require training of *both aerobic and anaerobic mechanisms*, but in proportions that specifically match the demands.

Muscle Contraction

To understand how the muscle contracts, it is necessary to focus on the minute structures within the muscle fiber responsible for shortening the fiber. The myofibril is composed of alternating strips of myosin, a heavy protein filament, and actin, a thin, segmented protein filament. Columns of myofibrils pack the muscle fiber, running parallel with it. When the muscle is stimulated

to contract, tiny hooks or "fingers" located on the myosin element reach across, link up with, and pull the actin strips past the myosin strips. This causes the fiber, and thus the muscle, to shorten. These "cross-bridges" are known as *micellae,* and their action produces a sliding effect as the actin filaments are drawn past the myosin filaments.

ATP has previously been described as the energy source for muscle contraction. Briefly, the muscle contracts after a message has come down from the brain via the nervous system and triggers ATP within the myofibril by a complex biochemical process. This ATP triggering results in myosin and actin coming together (muscle contraction).

Strength Training Effects

A number of physiological changes take place in the muscle when it is repeatedly subjected to an overload such as occurs with strength training. These changes involve the nervous pathways from the brain to the muscle, the tendonous attachments of the muscle, and the muscle itself. The combination of these changes can produce dramatic increases in strength and muscular endurance over a period of time.

Perhaps the earliest and yet most lasting effect of overloading the muscle involves the nervous system. During specific strength-building exercises, the motor nerve pathways carrying messages from the brain to the muscle become so frequently and vigorously bombarded that there is an increase in the efficiency of travel along those routes. In motor skill development this change is associated with learning, and strength-building exercises are subject to the same changes. The strength builder "learns" the skill and mechanics of the strength-building exercise, and the increased efficiency results in a more effective use of force. Perhaps a large portion of early strength gains result from learning, a greater efficiency in the application of force and nervous stimulations of high-threshold motor units not generally called upon to work.

Hypertrophy, or increase in size, occurs as the muscle is trained. The covering of the individual muscle fiber thickens and toughens as do the tendons supporting the muscle. This yields greater protection for the muscle and makes it less susceptible to injury. The increase in size is in no way proportional to increases in strength and muscular endurance. Barely measurable increases in size may accompany very great increases in strength and endurance. This effect needs to be emphasized, because many athletes, both men and women, do not desire noticeable increases in muscle size.

As the muscle hypertrophies, the fibers grow larger rather than increasing in number. Much of the increase in size can be accounted for by increase in muscle sarcoplasm or fluid in the fiber. Increases in the total amount of stored glycogen and other chemicals involved in ATP production accompany the increase in fluid. The number and size of myofibrils (contractile protein) increase. Many small changes in the muscle and nervous system add up to a dramatic increase in muscular strength.

SUMMARY

The physiology of fitness and strength is far more complex than is suggested in this brief chapter. Those who desire to gain more information regarding the physiology of exercise and sports are referred to the bibliography. A great deal is known about the physiology of exercise and especially training effects. In Chapter 3 we will describe some of the basic techniques used in conditioning for sports.

REFERENCES

1. Astrand, Per-Olaf, and Kaare Rodahl. 1986. *Textbook of Work Physiology,* 3d ed. New York: McGraw-Hill.

2. Armstrong, Robert B. 1976. "Energy Release in the Extra-Fusal Muscle Fiber," *Neuromuscular Mechanisms for Therapeutic and Conditioning Exercises.* Baltimore: University Park Press.

3. Burke, Edmund J. 1980. "Work Physiology and the Components of Physical Fitness in the Analysis of Human Performance," *Toward an Understanding of Human Performance,* 2d ed. Ithaca, NY: Mouvement Publications.

4. Clarke, David H., and Helen M. Eckert, eds. 1985. *Limits of Human Performance.* American Academy of Physical Education. Champaign, IL: Human Kinetics Publishers, Inc.

5. deVries, Herbert A. 1986. *Physiology of Exercise for Physical Education and Athletics,* 4th ed. Dubuque, IA: Wm. C. Brown Publishers.

6. Fox, Edward L. 1984. *Sports Physiology,* 2d ed. Philadelphia: W. B. Saunders Co.

7. Fox, Edward L., Richard W. Bowers, and Merle L. Foss. 1988. *The Physiological Basis of Physical Education and Athletics,* 4th ed. Philadelphia: W. B. Saunders College Publishing.

8. Goldsmith, A. L., et al. 1975. "Mechanism of Work-Induced Hypertrophy in Skeletal Muscle," *Medicine and Science in Sports and Exercise* 7:185–198.

9. Gollnick, P. D., and L. Hermanson. 1973. "Biochemical Adaptations to Exercise: Anaerobic Metabolism," *Exercise and Sports Sciences Reviews,* Vol. 1. New York: Academic Press.

10. Holloszy, John O. 1973. "Biochemical Adaptations to Exercise: Aerobic Metabolism," *Exercise and Sports Sciences Reviews,* Vol. 1. New York: Academic Press.

11. Ianuzzo, C. David. 1976. "The Cellular Composition of Human Skeletal Muscle," *Neuromuscular Mechanisms for Therapeutic and Conditioning Exercises.* Baltimore: University Park Press.

12. Karlson, Jan. 1979. "Localized Muscular Fatigue: Role of Muscle Metabolism and Substrate Depletion," *Exercise and Sports Sciences Reviews,* Vol. 7. Franklin Institute Press.

13. Krahenbuhl, Gary S. 1976. "Muscle Biopsy Research: Implications for Competitive Athletics," *Arizona Journal of HPERD* 20:8–12.

14. McDougall, J. D., et al. 1979. "Mitochondrial Volume Density in Human Skeletal Muscle Following Heavy Resistance Training," *Medicine and Science in Sports and Exercise* 11:164–166.

15. Noble, Bruce J. 1986. *Physiology of Exercise and Sport*. St. Louis: Times Mirror/Mosby College Publishing.

16. Stone, William J. 1981. "Sports Conditioning," *Osteopathic Annals* 9:12–18.

17. Taylor, A. W. 1975. "Endurance Training— Scientific Application," *The Scientific Aspects of Sports Training*. Springfield, IL: Charles C Thomas.

18. Thorstensson, Alf, et al. 1977. "Muscle Strength and Fiber Composition in Athletes and Sedentary Men," *Medicine and Science in Sports and Exercise* 9:26–30.

19. Vrbova, Gerta. 1979. "Influence of Activity on Some Characteristic Properties of Slow and Fast Mammalian Muscles," *Exercise and Sports Sciences Reviews,* Vol. 7. Franklin Institute Press.

20. Wenger, H. A. 1975. "The Physiology of Endurance Training," *The Scientific Aspects of Sports Training*. Springfield, IL: Charles C Thomas.

CHAPTER
THREE

AEROBIC AND ANAEROBIC CONDITIONING

Training techniques for aerobic and anaerobic conditioning have reached a high level of sophistication. Some basic elements are essential for any training program if the program is to be effective. Those elements, along with the ones discussed in Chapter 4, form the basis for the programs offered in Part Two for specific sports. There are several effective ways of training for aerobic and anaerobic conditioning. As long as the basic elements and the requirements of specificity are met, the training program will be effective.

A major contributor to the effectiveness of endurance and strength training is *overload,* which simply means continuously subjecting the athlete to work loads greater than those to which he or she is normally accustomed. In strength training, overload is accomplished primarily by increasing the resistance (weight). By progressively applying the basic elements of training, the aerobic and anaerobic systems are overloaded. The concept of *progression* is discussed in more detail later in this chapter.

Chapters 3 (Aerobic and Anaerobic Conditioning), 4 (Strength Training for Sports), and 5 (Flexibility, Warm-Up, and Stretching) are intended to be used as detailed references for coaches and athletes using the programs enumerated in Part Two. They describe the techniques involved in the programs designed by the authors for specific sports. Additional suggestions for implementing training programs are offered in Chapter 8 (The Conditioning Program: Putting It All Together). All aspects of sports conditioning could be included under the heading of either aerobic or anaerobic conditioning. Of the four target areas identified in Chapter 1 (anaerobic power, aerobic power, strength, and flexibility), both strength and flexibility training could be labeled anaerobic conditioning. Those two areas, however, have been treated in separate chapters and in some detail (Chapters 4 and 5).

BASIC ELEMENTS OF CONDITIONING

Several elements determine the effectiveness of sports fitness conditioning programs: 1) mode, 2) intensity, 3) duration, 4) frequency, 5) interaction, 6) progression, and 7) rest. By applying all of these elements, the coach

---

Table 3.1 The Basic Elements of Conditioning

Mode: Sport-specific training

Intensity: 60–100% max

Duration: Amount of time actually spent in exercise, resulting in the total work done

Frequency: 3–4✕/week (building)
5–6✕/week (peaking)
1–2✕/week (maintaining)

Interaction: Intensity, duration, and frequency can be manipulated to achieve the same amount of total work done!

Progression: All training programs should utilize a gradual application of overload.

Rest: All training regimens require the proper rest necessary to build adaptation in the athlete.

---

or athlete can be assured that optimal training will result, regardless of the genetic characteristics of the athlete. Table 3.1 lists the basic elements of sports conditioning.

Mode

The fitness seeker has the luxury of selecting the kind of aerobic exercise or strength training he or she prefers, provided that it trains the basic elements of fitness. The athlete does not have that choice, and sport-specific training is essential. The hockey player must train on ice, the swimmer in the water, and the skier on snow. The vast majority of athletes, however, train both aerobically and anaerobically by running.

The whole body exercise most often used for training athletes in a wide variety of sports is running. There is good reason for this. Running does not require "learning," it can be done with a minimum expenditure of time, and it is more specific to most sports than other training modes. Most sports or games require the athlete to move around on the ground, so running is an easily adapted training technique. Naturally, swimmers, skaters, or cyclists would not train by running, since they can select the more specific training modes that suit their sports. Athletes occasionally resent the time spent in this type of conditioning, but running is really the most logical training mode for aerobic and anaerobic conditioning for a wide range of sports.

Intensity

In sports conditioning the degree to which the athlete works physically is a measure of the intensity of training. More intense training causes a more extreme response on the part of the body: the heart rate is higher, breathing is faster, oxygen debt is incurred earlier, and exhaustion occurs sooner. In running, swimming, or cycling, the *rate* at which one runs, swims, or cycles determines the intensity of training.

The two simplest means of gauging the intensity of sports conditioning are measuring the *time* it takes to run or swim a distance, and determining the athlete's HR (heart rate) at the conclusion of the activity. An example of two training bouts at different intensities for the same athlete would be:

Athlete	Training Mode	Distance	Time	HR	Relative Intensity
"A"	Running	¼ mi.	1:30	150	Lower
"A"	Running	¼ mi.	1:15	175	Higher

Similar examples could be given for many training modes—swimming, cycling, stair stepping, or other whole body activities. An important concept to note is that intensity will be *relative*. This means that for each athlete the work load imposed will lie on a continuum from low to high. It also means that another athlete, "B," might be better conditioned and respond with a *lower* HR for running the same distances at the same rate (time) as athlete "A." Although the two training bouts are less intense for athlete "B," one bout is still more intense than the other.

Athlete	Training Mode	Distance	Time	HR	Relative Intensity
"B"	Running	¼ mi.	1:30	125	Lower
"B"	Running	¼ mi.	1:15	150	Higher

The use of HR as a measure of intensity is based upon the concept that each athlete has a maximum heart rate (Max HR). To estimate Max HR, the following formula is used:

	Example
220	220
− Age	− 20 (Age)
Max HR	200 (Max HR estimated)

Table 3.2 THR (Training Heart Rate)*

% Max	THR	Predicted Max HR	Adjusted THR
95%	190	200	193
90	180	200	186
80	160	200	172
70	140	200	158
60	120	200	144

*Based upon a Predicted Maximal HR for a 20-year-old athlete, and adjusted by the Karvonen formula.

Thus, an eighteen-year-old athlete would have a *predicted* Max HR of 202. It should be noted that this is only an estimate and the true Max HR might vary by ± ten beats. To determine the HR necessary for training effect to take place, a percentage of the Max HR is used to determine the training heart rate (THR). Two techniques can be used and they are illustrated in table 3.2. For a training effect to take place, the THR must reach 50–60 percent of Max HR. Athletes, who require intense training, will usually train at 80–95 percent of Max HR. The simplest technique would be to take a HR of 80–90 percent of the predicted Max HR, e.g., 90 percent of Max HR 200 = THR 180. An adjusted formula can also be used based upon the difference between the resting HR and the Max HR. The adjusted formula was developed by Karvonen.[9] The difference between these two is multiplied by 60–80 percent and *added* to the resting HR, e.g.,

Step 1.	Max HR 200	
	− 60	(Rest HR)
	140	
	× 80%	
	112	(80% of difference)
Step 2.	112	
	+ 60	(Rest HR)
	172	THR adjusted

This technique is more commonly used for determining THR for well-trained athletes (table 3.2).

The intensity of an exercise can be quickly determined by palpating the carotid artery at the neck (just under the back corner of the jaw). The pulse will be very strong at that point after exercise and a *ten-second count immediately as exercise ends* will closely estimate the exercise HR. The ten-second HR count is multiplied by six to convert to a one-minute count. (See table 3.3 for easy conversion.)

PRINCIPLE: The more intense the training (whether aerobic or anaerobic), the greater the training effect. Duration can compensate for less intensity in aerobic conditioning.

Table 3.3 Heart Rate Counts

10-sec. Count	HR (min.)	10-sec. Count	HR (min.)
35	210	25	150
34	204	24	144
33	198	23	138
32	192	22	132
31	186	21	126
30	180	20	120
29	174		
28	168		
27	162		
26	156		

Duration

Although intensity is a major element in training athletes, the duration of training will also influence the training effect. The *duration* of training refers to the length of time the athlete actually works during a training session. For example, an athlete may run for three minutes, rest for five minutes, and run again for three minutes. The duration of training is actually six minutes. In another session, an athlete may run continuously for six minutes duration, but at a different intensity.

The objective of the training (aerobic or anaerobic) will determine the duration. Aerobic training is conducted at lower intensities but greater duration than anaerobic training. Since anaerobic training is of high intensity for brief periods, duration is accomplished by repeated bouts of activity in a training session.

Since duration also has a major influence on the total work done, it is an important factor in training. There is, however, a point of diminishing returns for duration training. For example, doubling the running time from 30 to 60 minutes will result in a proportionally smaller improvement in aerobic capacity. It has been estimated that the maximum training effect will occur between 6,000 and 10,000 calories per week, or approximately 60 to 100 miles run.[17] There will be exceptions to those estimates. Some athletes can tolerate less training, and some significantly more. Duration training also leads to a performance plateau, which may require increased intensity and intervals to break through.

PRINCIPLE: The greater the duration of training (whether aerobic or anaerobic), the greater the training effect.

Frequency

The number of times per week that the athlete trains is the measure of frequency. Most school athletic teams practice five days per week. This is based on the five-day school week with weekends off. Some athletes may practice six, or possibly seven, days per week, while others may practice only three or four days per week. The practice referred to is primarily skills and strategy practice.

Physical conditioning also varies from team to team or athlete to athlete in terms of frequency. Conditioning frequency is greater in the early stages of training than in the later stages. For example, a team may be conditioned daily in the pre-season period, but use only one to three days per week for maintaining condition during the season. Studies on training effects indicate that significant levels of conditioning can be accomplished in the frequency range of two to four times per week. Less physically demanding sports may require only twice-a-week training sessions, while more physically demanding sports may require five or six training sessions per week.

A training program with a frequency of two to three times per week over a period of six to eight weeks is usually sufficient to produce significant training effects. Greater training effects require more frequency over a longer period of time. *Maintaining* sports fitness levels does not require as much frequency as it does to attain them. As few as one or two training sessions per week will maintain high percentages of sports fitness and strength over a sports season.

PRINCIPLE: The frequency of physical training must fall in the two-to-four times per week range to produce training effects of value to the athlete.

Progression

Progression is also an important aspect of effective training. Progression is accomplished by gradually increasing the intensity and duration of training as the athlete becomes more physically fit. In strength training, "progressive resistance" describes the overload on the muscles and there is a "progressive overload" for whole body conditioning. Over a period of time the athlete is able to tolerate higher work intensities for longer periods of time (duration). An example of a progressive increase for intensity could come from an earlier example.

Date	Athlete	Training Mode	Distance	Time
9/1	"A"	Running	¼ mi.	1:30
9/15	"A"	Running	¼ mi.	1:15

The example shows that athlete "A" was capable of running ¼ mi. fifteen seconds faster on 9/15. The second bout of training was more intense, thus the example illustrates progression in training. A similar example could be given for progression in duration. The athlete may have run for a total of six minutes on 9/1 and ten minutes on 9/15.

In the early stages of training the athlete will not be able to tolerate the intensity and duration that can be handled later in the training season. The wise use of progression by the athlete or coach enables the athlete to reach an optimum level of condition for the sport in the most efficient way.

PRINCIPLE: The intensity and duration of physical training should be gradually and continually increased to reach optimum levels of sports fitness.

Interaction

There is an *interaction* between intensity, duration, and frequency, especially in aerobic training. This means that although intensity may be the primary overload factor, overload (and training effect) can also be achieved by increasing the duration and/or the frequency. The total amount of work done by the athlete may be the ultimate determinant of training. Greater amounts of work are accomplished by athletes in modern training programs. This is one of the most significant factors to account for better performance in track and swimming today when compared to past performances.

Athletes can compensate for training at lower intensity by working longer (duration) or more often (frequency). It should also be noted, however, that even endurance athletes, who focus on great duration and total work for a training effect, will also engage in high-intensity training. The reason for this is to train also the high-threshold anaerobic fibers (FT), which can contribute to high-level aerobic performance.

Rest

It may seem rather obvious that the athlete must rest between bouts of exercise, and between days of training. Rest is essential between repetitions of either aerobic or anaerobic training to allow the muscles to recover from fatigue. Resting, or training lightly, between days of intense training is also essential to allow the body to recover and the muscles to rebuild. It has been found in laboratory studies that simulating marathon performance produces enzymes usually associated with a heart attack. Intense efforts leading to prolonged muscular soreness (like a marathon) may require weeks for full recovery from muscular damage. Training adaptation comes about through stressing the system, depleting energy stores, and then resting to allow the stored energy to become resynthesized. It also occurs as the muscle, or physiological systems stressed, become functionally stronger as a result of adapting to the training stress.

Perhaps no other cause is associated with poor performance as often as overtraining. Athletes and coaches frequently take the attitude that the opponents must be training and preparing night and day, hence they must do the same to keep up. The topic of overtraining is discussed in greater detail in Chapter 8, but the concept of rest is an important part of optimizing training effects. Proper rest is the first line of defense against the problem of overtraining.

CONTINUOUS TRAINING (AEROBIC)

The basic technique for developing aerobic fitness is low intensity *continuous* activity for periods of twenty minutes or longer. The duration of activity may begin with five minutes and is progressively increased to ten to fifteen to twenty minutes or longer. The intensity is also progressively increased so that the athlete covers greater distances in the same time. Dr. Kenneth Cooper popularized aerobic training for adults by the publication of his best-selling book on aerobics.[4] The beneficial effects of aerobic training are detailed in Chapter 2. As the capacities of circulatory, respiratory, and muscular systems increase, the ability to deliver oxygen to the muscle tissues increases. Anaerobic (lactic acid) energy use is delayed and fatigue is postponed as the athlete increases his or her aerobic power.

LSD

Continuous training has also been identified as long-slow-distance (LSD). This variation of continuous training involves greater *duration* and less intensity as a means of developing aerobic power. It is very effective in producing greater aerobic power. It is a classic example of the use of *duration* in training to compensate for lower intensity as previously discussed.

An example of a continuous (aerobic) training regimen for one month might look like this:

July	Training Mode	Distance	Goal/ Min.	Times/ Week
Week 1	Run	1.0 mi.	8:00	3
Week 2	Run	1.5 mi.	12:00	3
Week 3	Run	1.5 mi.	11:30	3
Week 4	Run	2.0 mi.	15:00	3

In the example the duration of training has increased from 1.0 mi. to 2.0 mi. and from 8:00 to 15:00 min. The *intensity* has also increased because the rate of running the first week was 8:00 min. for 1.0 mi., while in week 4 the rate has increased to 7:30 min. for 1.0 mi. The latter figure is based on running 2.0 mi. in 15:00 min.

Over a period of time endurance athletes will develop great duration in their training until they are running twice a day and covering more than 100 miles in training per week. This means that they will run at least six miles in each session. Marathon runners may run as much as 150 miles per week in preparation for an event which is estimated to be 99 percent aerobic.

Fartlek

Another variation of continuous training is called *Fartlek*. The athlete runs continuously to train aerobic capacity, but varies the intensity during the training session. As the athlete feels the need to rest, the intensity is reduced, and when the athlete feels recovered, the intensity is increased for a period of time.

There is relatively little technique to be learned when running for continuous training. Perhaps the major exception for most athletes is concentrating on running "flat-footed." This means that an athlete who is used to landing on the sole of the foot when running must remember to land on the heel, then sole.

Fartlek training points out the variation in intensity that can occur in aerobic training. Aerobic training can progress from very light activity to high-intensity aerobic training which also involves the anaerobic system, specifically Stage II or AN-LA. This implies that, at some point, the athlete has crossed over from totally aerobic work to a "mixture" of aerobic and anaerobic work.

THE ANAEROBIC THRESHOLD

In Chapter 2 the various energy systems are discussed and treated as independent entities. That concept implies that the athlete works either in aerobic metabolism or in anaerobic metabolism. Although most sports movements require energy predominately from Stage I (ATP-CP), Stage II (AN-LA), or Stage III (AER), there can be some overlap. Aerobic and anaerobic metabolism can be going on at the same time. In running 400m all out, the athlete is working primarily in Stage II (AN-LA), but Stage III (AER) is also engaged. The athlete is taking in oxygen, although not enough, during the period of the race. Conversely, a middle distance runner, who is performing a predominately AER effort, can be producing some LA because the intensity of the work has crossed over the anaerobic threshold (AT).

The concept of AT suggests that at some point, LA (lactic acid) begins to accumulate in the muscle tissue and then in the blood. That point is generally identified as a certain percentage of the athlete's maximum oxygen uptake or maximal AER power. The concept is illustrated in figure 3.1. Traditionally it has been assumed that the AT occurs between 50 and 70 percent of $\dot{V}O_2$ max.

A considerable research effort has been made to determine the AT. Training appears to raise the AT for the athlete, and well-trained athletes have a higher AT. Skinner has suggested there may be three phases in the

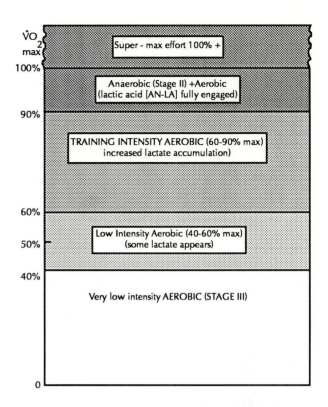

Figure 3.1 Anaerobic Threshold (AT) and Maximal Oxygen Uptake ($\dot{V}O_2$)

transition from AER to AN work.[15] These phases would include: 1) a period from low level to moderate AER work which is truly AER, 2) a second phase (40–60 percent of maximum oxygen uptake) when a small amount of LA begins to appear and has been labeled AT by some, and 3) a third phase from 65–90 percent of maximal oxygen uptake when LA increases significantly, but the athlete can continue to work for prolonged periods. Above this level the AN-LA system is fully engaged and the athlete will exhaust in a very short time, probably less than a minute.

As the AT is crossed, the onset of blood lactate (OBLA) leads to an increased accumulation of lactate in the blood, interference with fat metabolism, and the use of more glycogen as an energy source. This leads to the accumulation of more lactate and, eventually, exhaustion. The athlete needs to train at a level close to the OBLA to optimize training. The percentage of maximal oxygen uptake ($\dot{V}O_2$ max) used in training or performance is called the fractional utilization. The athlete who has good training efficiency can operate at a higher fractional utilization prior to the OBLA. Such efficiency is improved with training, and performance in many sports can also be improved by increasing $\dot{V}O_2$ max.

As the $\dot{V}O_2$ max is increased by 25 percent through training, the athlete can exercise at higher levels for

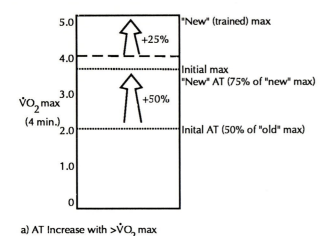

a) AT Increase with >$\dot{V}O_2$ max

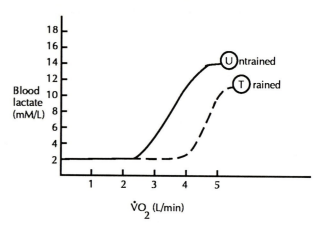

b) OBLA Increase with Training (>$\dot{V}O_2$ max)

Figure 3.2 Increased $\dot{V}O_2$max and Increased AT (a) and OBLA (b)

longer periods of time. That is one advantage of increased $\dot{V}O_2$ max. Another is the increase that also occurs in the AT. The anaerobic threshold might increase from 50 to 70 percent of $\dot{V}O_2$ max with training. The most important aspect to note is that the increase represents 70 percent of the new max, resulting in a 50 percent increase in the AT. In brief, the OBLA is pushed higher with aerobic training leading to increased $\dot{V}O_2$ max. Both concepts are illustrated in figure 3.2 a and b.

It is important for coaches and athletes to know that many sports and many athletic efforts involve both the aerobic and the anaerobic systems. Often the athlete must work for prolonged periods in the third phase of the AT (65–90 percent maximum). When the athlete must train for such an energy expenditure, or for some mixture of aerobic and anaerobic effort, the training often involves the use of the interval technique.

INTERVAL TRAINING

Over the past several decades interval training has had a major impact on sports training. *Interval training* is alternating work and rest periods during a training session. Continuous training involves continuous work, which concludes the training session when it comes to an end. In interval training a work bout is followed by a rest period, then another work bout, and so on. The technique is credited to Dr. Woldemer Gerschler of Germany.[17] He introduced the technique about 1930 and it began to appear in the United States in the 1950s. A Finnish athlete named Pihkala used interval training in the early 1900s, but the great Czech, Emil Zatopek, was the first to employ interval training seriously.[13]

Interval training rests on the very sound physiological fact that the athlete can produce a much greater total work load in a training session if the bouts of exercise are spaced. Åstrand found that a pace (intensity) that caused exhaustion in nine minutes could be continued for an hour, and much more work could be done if rest intervals were included.[1]

Continuous	*Interval*
9 min. = 1,940 kg (work done)	1 hour = 64,800 kg
Max HR = 204	Max HR = 150
LA = 150 mg	LA = 20 mg

In this example the total work done in over an hour (on a bicycle) was *thirty-three times greater* than the continuous activity that caused exhaustion in nine minutes, yet the rate of work was the same. The Max HR reached in nine minutes of continuous activity was 204 and the lactic acid level (LA) was 150 mg. Both of these figures signal the approach of exhaustion for persons exercising. The heart rate (150) and LA level (20 mg) for the interval technique are in the training zone but not close to the exhaustion level. An indication of how the HR responds during continuous and interval training is described in figure 3.3.

It is possible to manipulate several factors in an interval training program to produce an overload. A basic interval training program might be designed as follows:

Distance	Rate	Rest	No. of Reps	Frequency
440 yds.	75 secs.	90 secs.	10	4 days

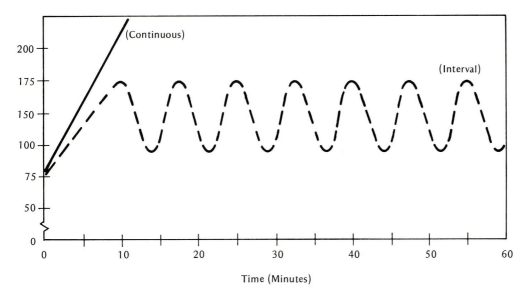

Figure 3.3 Continuous vs. Interval Training

In this example the athlete runs 440 yards in 75 seconds, then rests for 90 seconds. At each training session this work-rest ratio is repeated ten times (ten reps), and there are four training sessions per week. An overload could be applied to the athlete by increasing the rate (from 75 to 70 sec.), by decreasing the rest (from 90 to 80 sec.), or by increasing the number of repeat intervals (ten to twelve reps). Thus, a later version of the interval program would be as follows:

Distance	Rate	Rest	No. of Reps	Frequency
440 yds.	70 secs.	80 secs.	12	4 days

Another interval training technique used by some coaches and athletes involves HR as a measure of intensity. A training HR (THR) is set at 160–180 (fig. 3.2). When this rate is reached, the athlete maintains the THR for a set period, then begins a rest interval until the HR recovers to 120–140. Recovery is not "complete" but the athlete is sufficiently recovered to work again soon at a high rate without reaching exhaustion such as occurs when training is carried on continuously to fatigue.

Another advantage of the interval training technique is that the athlete can work at very intense anaerobic rates (maximum) for brief periods of time. These repeated efforts produce an anaerobic training effect. Perhaps of even greater importance, these bouts of exercise exceed the intensity of play in most sports, but prepare the athlete for those intense periods when they do occur in competition.

There are many ways of manipulating the work and rest intervals in interval training. These variations of the internal technique have a variety of names aimed at developing quantity (many intervals at submaximal

effort) or quality (maximal effort intervals). There can be an interaction among work, rest, and repetitions in the interval technique just as was observed with intensity, duration, and frequency in continuous training.

Because there are so many ways of manipulating the interval to cause an overload, it is not possible to elaborate on all the possibilities. Basic aerobic and anaerobic intervals for the three stages of energy output follow in the next section. A system for establishing interval training intensities has been developed by Wilt.[18] The technique involves establishing a training interval intensity based upon best performance in shorter sprints, or best time in a 1,500m effort. The athlete adds 1.5 to 5.0 seconds to best time in distances from 50m to 200m. For distances above that (400m to 1,500m), 1.0 to 4.0 seconds is either subtracted or added to the average time for 400m, based upon a best effort in the 1,500m. Examples of the technique are found in table 3.4. The duration recommended for each interval workout is 2.0 miles.

Although the interval between work bouts is identified as REST, the athlete is actually active at a reduced rate. At a minimum output, athletes should continue walking between work bouts and most athletes can jog easily. The cardiovascular system is still under stress during the rest period. Recovery, especially from lactic acid accumulation, is hastened by mild activity. Coaches and athletes have known this fact instinctively by the use of walking or jogging after wind sprints or other vigorous activity.

Aerobic and Anaerobic Intervals

Some general guidelines should be kept in mind when training for aerobic or anaerobic intervals. If the reader will recall the three mechanisms for supplying energy (fig. 2.1), the kind of training interval should match as closely as possible the demands of the sport. Åstrand and others have recommended general training intervals for aerobic and anaerobic power.[2,3,6,13,16] The basic intervals for conditioning the three energy mechanisms are summarized in table 3.5. Intervals below 20 seconds of work result in little LA accumulation, quick recovery, and can be repeated many times. The ATP-CP system has very rapid recovery, approaching full recovery in three minutes. Intervals at 30 seconds will result in significant increases in LA, and as the interval reaches 60 seconds, LA accumulation will maximize and recovery is greatly prolonged. A rest interval of four to five minutes is necessary to yield sufficient recovery to sustain repeated AN-LA intervals. AN-LA training is very exhausting, both physically and mentally. The coach or athlete must "flirt" with the tolerance levels of this system or the training session can come to an abrupt halt at maximum oxygen debt. This means that the upper limits of LA tolerance have been achieved,

and the athlete is exhausted. A small reduction (3.3 percent) in running speed has been found to drop the percentage of effort in terms of maximal oxygen uptake from 100 percent to 90 percent.[13]

The reader should be aware that these intervals are guidelines and are not intended to apply to each specific sports training program. They are, however, effective in guiding the coach or athlete to select aerobic or anaerobic intervals that match the energy output demands of the sport.

It should also be noted that there are some "gaps" in the intervals suggested in table 3.5. Those areas represent transition areas between the various stages. For specific events or sports some intervals may need to be used within those transition areas.

The concept of AER intervals may appear at first to be a misnomer. Typically we consider continuous work to be the major technique for developing AER power, and intervals to be restricted to anaerobic training. The concept of AT (anaerobic threshold), however, suggests that some AER effort must be done at high work loads, which may also engage the AN system. Continuous AER training is usually carried on at 60–80 percent of maximum capacity. AER intervals, however, can train the athlete at 80 percent or above, which aids the athlete in peaking for AER power. AER intervals also fit more readily into the regular practice session than, for example, a 60-minute run. The highly conditioned endurance athlete will be capable of maintaining high-intensity (80–90 percent) activity for prolonged periods (30–60 minutes). Such work is really continuous, but at an intensity that most athletes could tolerate only in shorter intervals.

Interval training techniques can be used to train all three energy supply systems: ATP (anaerobic), aerobic, and anaerobic (lactic acid). By using interval training, athletes in running and swimming events pile up staggering amounts of work in each practice session. Athletes in many sports can also gain the benefits of systematic training specifically geared to the demands of their sport. Training programs for specific sports are described in detail in Part Two.

Table 3.4 Interval Training Intensities

Distance	Training Formula (Best Time +)	Interval Training Time
50m	50m time + 1.5 secs.	6.0 + 1.5 = 7.5 secs.
100m	100m time + 3.0 secs.	(example)
200m	200m time + 5.0 secs.	
400m	Average 400m for best 1,500m, −1.0 to 4.0 secs.	75.0 − 4.0 = 71.0 secs. (example)
800m–1,500m	Average 400m for best 1,500m, +3 to 4.0 secs.	75.0 + 4.0 = 79.0 secs. (example)

Sample Interval Workouts:
400m × 8 = 2.0 miles
800m × 4 = 2.0 miles
800m × 2 + 400m × 2 + 200m × 4 = 2.0 miles
(1.0 mi.) + (0.5 mi.) + (0.5 mi.)

Table 3.5 AN-AER Training Intervals

	Work	% Max	Rest	Reps
Anaerobic				
ATP-CP	5–15 secs.	100	15 secs.–2 mins.	5–20
AN-LA	30–60 secs.	90	4–5 mins.	5–10
Aerobic				
Continuous	10–60 mins.	60–80	NA	1
AER Interval	3–5 mins.	80	3–5 mins.	3–10

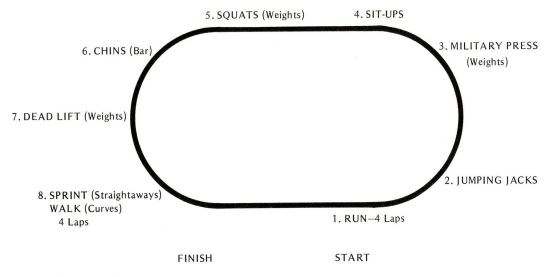

5. SQUATS (Weights)   4. SIT-UPS

6. CHINS (Bar)   3. MILITARY PRESS (Weights)

7. DEAD LIFT (Weights)

8. SPRINT (Straightaways)
WALK (Curves)
4 Laps

2. JUMPING JACKS

1. RUN—4 Laps

FINISH   START

Figure 3.4 Circuit Training: Set Up on a ¼-Mile Track

CIRCUIT TRAINING

Circuit training is a simple, efficient method of training that has been adopted by many coaches.[12] It is a series of exercises that can be easily designed for a specific sport. Circuits are also used in strength training, and strength training circuits are offered in Chapter 4. Perhaps the greatest advantage of circuit training for sports is that *all aspects of physical conditioning* can be built into the circuit. The circuit can be designed to condition for *muscular strength and endurance, aerobic power, anaerobic capacity* or *speed,* and *flexibility.*

A circuit can be set up indoors or outdoors with a series of exercises to be completed in as short a period of time as possible. An athlete could do a number of push-ups, then move on to the next station and do several sit-ups, continuing through the entire series of exercises. A circuit might contain from six to twelve stations according to the need of the coach or athlete. See figure 3.4 for an example of a general conditioning circuit.

Normally, a circuit is completed three times in a conditioning session, but it could be run only once or twice if time must be saved. An overload is applied by increasing the number of times each exercise is done or by adding weight for weight training exercises. The time allowed to complete the circuit can also be reduced to increase the intensity of the training.

It is evident from figure 3.4 that the coach or athlete can design circuits for a specific sport using as many exercises as time permits. The coach or athlete can concentrate the exercises on the specific needs of the sport, e.g., flexibility, arm strength, or leg power. Examples of specific circuits for various sports are described in Chapter 4 and included in the programs listed in Part Two.

SUMMARY

The basic elements of conditioning programs include mode, intensity, duration, frequency, progression, interaction, and rest. A progressive overload is applied to training by the use of the basic elements. Training goals can be accomplished through a variety of modes, such as running, swimming, cycling, or other whole body activities, but they should be sport-specific to be effective.

Continuous training is used primarily for aerobic conditioning, while interval training can be used to train both the aerobic and anaerobic systems. The AT is important in establishing training intensities. Circuit training is an efficient and effective technique for combining aerobic and anaerobic training, muscular strength and endurance, and flexibility.

REFERENCES

1. Åstrand, I., et al. 1960. "Intermittent Muscular Work," *Acta Physiol. Scand.* 48:448–453.

2. Åstrand, Per-Olaf, and Kaare Rodahl. 1986. *Textbook of Work Physiology,* 3d ed. New York: McGraw-Hill.

3. Christensen, E., et al. 1960. "Intermittent and Continuous Running," *Acta Physiol. Scand.* 50:269–287.

4. Cooper, Kenneth H. 1982. *The Aerobics Program for Total Well Being.* New York: M. Evans.

5. Costill, David L. 1986. *Inside Running: Basics of Sports Physiology.* Indianapolis: Benchmark Press, Inc.

6. Fox, Edward L., and Donald K. Mathews. 1974. *Interval Training: Conditioning for Sports and General Fitness.* Philadelphia: W. B. Saunders Co.

7. Fox, Edward L. 1984. *Sports Physiology,* 2d ed. Philadelphia: W. B. Saunders Co.

8. Fox, Edward L., Richard W. Bowers, and Merle L. Foss. 1988. *The Physiological Basis of Physical Education and Athletics,* 4th ed. Philadelphia: W. B. Saunders College Publishers.

9. Karvonen, Martti J., et al. 1957. "The Effects of Training on Heart Rate," *Annals of Medical Exp Fenn* 35:307–315.

10. Londeree, Ben R. 1980. "Anaerobic Threshold Training," *Toward an Understanding of Human Performance,* 2d ed. Ithaca, NY: Mouvement Publications.

11. Madsen, Oberjan. 1983. "Aerobic Training: Not So Fast, There," *Swimming Technique* 10:13–18.

12. Morgan, R. E., and G. T. Adamson. 1961. *Circuit Training.* London: Bell & Sons.

13. Peronnet, Francois, and Ronald J. Ferguson. 1975. "Interval Training," *The Scientific Aspects of Sports Training.* Springfield, IL: Charles C Thomas.

14. Pollack, Michael L. 1973. "The Quantification of Endurance Training Programs," *Exercise and Sports Sciences Reviews* Vol. 1. New York: Academic Press.

15. Skinner, James L. 1980. "The Transition from Aerobic to Anaerobic Metabolism," *Research Quarterly for Exercise and Sport* 51:234–248.

16. Stone, William J. 1981. "Sports Conditioning," *Osteopathic Annals* 9:12–18.

17. Wilmore, Jack H., and David L. Costill. 1988. *Training for Sport and Activity, The Physiological Basis of the Conditioning Process,* 3d ed. Dubuque, IA: Wm. C. Brown Publishers.

18. Wilt, Fred. 1968. "Training for Competitive Running," *Exercise Physiology.* New York: Academic Press.

CHAPTER
FOUR

Strength Training for Sports

This chapter provides the fundamental concepts and the specific information necessary to carry out a successful year-round strength training program for athletes. In order to do this, the reader must have a clear understanding of the difference between strength training for athletes and other types of weight training; some terminology used in strength training; the essentials of strength training for athletes; the practical methods of varying the elements of intensity, duration, and frequency in the strength program; and systems used in devising strength programs. The specific techniques of performing strength exercises can be found in Chapter 19, Strength Exercises.

Following the principles and guidelines outlined in this chapter should result in successfully developing strength in the athlete. There are many external factors, however, which can influence the development of strength. They include body type and metabolism, diet, rest and sleep, injury, and the motivational level of the individual to adhere to the strength training program.

To be successful, the strength training program should achieve two main objectives: 1) it must be effective in reducing the number of athletic injuries which could otherwise occur, and 2) it must be effective in improving athletic performance. The strength programs offered in Part II are based on the information developed in this chapter, and are directed toward achieving these two objectives.

TYPES OF WEIGHT TRAINING

The general subject of weight training has, in the past, been surrounded by misconceptions, inaccuracies, and misunderstanding. The reason for this is a general lack of knowledge about the use of weights in the specialized area of strength training for athletes. An understanding of the differences between strength training for athletes and the other types of weight training can help clarify the areas of misconception. Therefore, each of the various types of weight training will be defined.

Rehabilitation

Resistance training is used widely as a clinical means of rehabilitating people with injuries. Chapter 6 will discuss injury prevention and rehabilitation in detail.

Bodybuilding

This type of training is generally associated with the physique (as with Mr. America or Mr. Universe competitions). The goals of the bodybuilder are a massive musculature, with beautiful, well-proportioned, and well-defined muscles. There are many professional and amateur bodybuilding competitions. Strength, power, muscular, endurance, cardiovascular endurance, flexibility, agility, speed, or other athletic qualities are not essential for these competitions.

The bodybuilder uses many repetitions in the "super set" type of programs (p. 45). In some bodybuilding systems (blitz systems), circuits of several exercises on a single body part are performed over long periods of time. If flexibility and agility are not included in the bodybuilder's program, they are susceptible to reduced flexibility and athletic ability. However, if flexibility and athletic ability are maintained, the bodybuilder need not lose these qualities. There is no truth to the old misconception that bodybuilders are always muscle-bound. Many of the programs and techniques developed in the sport of bodybuilding have contributed greatly to the field of strength training for athletes.

There are two types of competitive weight lifting—Olympic Lifting and Power Lifting, with international and world competitions in both sports. The Olympic Lifts are included in the Olympic Games. In both Olympic Lifting and Power Lifting competition is conducted in the same manner. There are three judges for each event or "lift." Three attempts are allowed in each lift. One successful attempt in each lift is necessary to stay in the competition. The weight on the bar is increased in a manner similar to raising the high jump or pole vault bar. It is increased only once for each lift, until all lifters have made three attempts. If a lift is missed on the first or second attempt, the lifter may use the same weight for the next attempt. This attempt must be done within three minutes if no other lifters are going to attempt the same weight. The alternative is to attempt a heavier weight successfully in order to stay in the competition. The rules in both sports stipulate the strictest of form, and any variation is call for disqualifying the attempt. The winner is determined by the highest total poundage of the best attempt in each lift.

The *Olympic Lifts* are the "snatch" and the "clean and jerk." When done properly, they are extremely quick, athletic movements, unlike the Power Lifts. In the "snatch" the bar is lifted from the floor overhead in one movement. The "squat style" or "split style" may be used. The "clean and jerk" entails two movements—taking the bar from the floor to the shoulders (the clean), and thrusting it overhead, extending the arms (the jerk). The Military Press was one of the Olympic Lifts until the early 1970s.

Power Lifting consists of the Squat, the Bench Press, and the Dead Lift. More weight can be used in the Power Lifts; consequently they are done at slower speed than the very quick Olympic Lifts.

In the starting position for the *Squat,* the lifter has the barbell on his back and is standing erect. The line or midpoint of the thighs must drop until it breaks the imaginary plane parallel to the floor. The lifter then rises from this position again to the starting position. During the *Bench Press,* the bar is lowered to the chest, paused for one second, and raised again. The *Dead Lift* is performed by lifting the barbell from the floor until the body is standing completely erect, the weight held with the arms extended downward. The training for both Olympic and Power Lifting is extremely specialized and specific to the movements involved, and obviously concentrates mainly on developing maximum strength.

General Conditioning

Many persons use weight training as a means of keeping physically trim at every age. There are probably as many systems of training for this purpose as there are individuals participating in weight training to keep in shape. The public in the United States spends millions of dollars each year for spas, health clubs, YMCAs, and individually owned weights. With the acceptance of supplemental weight training programs for nearly every sport, many former athletes who used weight training for strength development continue to use it as a method of keeping physically trim. This is one of the side benefits offered the athlete by the inclusion of

weight training in the athletic program. Weight training for such purposes does not replace aerobic training for cardiovascular conditioning.

Strength Training for Athletes

The term *strength* training rather than *weight* training for athletes is used since the goal is to develop strength by many different methods, and in many cases various machines, pulleys, and devices are used that employ no weights. In recent years active scientific study and widespread practical application of strength training by athletes and coaches throughout the world have shown conclusively that strength training can be extremely effective in improving athletic performance and preventing athletic injuries, if the proper type of strength program is employed.

The correct strength training program can offer the athlete increased speed, quickness, muscular endurance, coordination, explosive power, and flexibility, as well as pure strength. The most important concept to remember is that the correct type of strength program must be used in order to receive the specific results desired.

One of the old misconceptions concerning weight training is that it caused "muscle-boundness" or loss of flexibility. Many scientific studies over a long period of time have shown that weight training does not impair flexibility and that it may, in fact, actually increase flexibility.[17,18,53] The proper training techniques, which nearly always include a full *"range of motion,"* are necessary to ensure that flexibility is maintained as a result of a weight training program.

Another misconception is that weight training causes slowed movement in the trained muscles. Studies conducted decades ago by Chui[9] and Karpovich and Zorbas[57] discounted this idea, and later research efforts have supported those results.[10] There is also evidence that an increase in muscular speed may accompany an increase in muscular strength.[10] The essential components and concepts of weight training for athletics are included in the following sections.

STRENGTH TRAINING TERMINOLOGY

Isometric Contraction

This type of muscle contraction involves no joint movement. Isometrics are usually done by applying pressure to an immovable object, but may be done by simply contracting the muscles while holding the limbs still. Isometric training was a popular form of strength building for sports during the early 1960s. The greatest amount of force can be achieved in an isometric contraction. The value of the strength developed is only effective in a narrow range close to the point at which it was developed. This major disadvantage has led to a limited use of isometrics for sports.

Isotonic Contraction

This type of muscle contraction involves limb or body movement. Although isotonic contraction for training is done against resistance, all movements of the body are technically isotonic movements, although some are not done against resistance. There are several types of isotonic contractions.

Concentric contraction involves shortening of the contracting muscle, which moves the resistance. The muscle overcomes the resistance, moving the limb through the motion by shortening itself.

Eccentric contraction entails lengthening of the muscle. This is done when a weight is lowered through the range of motion. The muscle slowly yields to the resistance, allowing itself to be stretched.

Isokinetic contraction is a special type of isotonic contraction. It is created by controlling the speed of the contraction mechanically. The purpose is to allow a maximal contraction to be achieved throughout the entire movement (range of motion). The maximal force that can be achieved at any one point in the movement varies. The speed of movement also influences force. The slower the isokinetic movement, the greater the amount of force that can be applied through the movement. It should be noted that during isokinetic movement the isokinetic device is set at a given speed. No matter how hard the individual attempts to force the device through the movement, the speed remains constant. The device includes a gauge that records the amount of force produced. With conventional isokinetic devices, this includes a "needle type" indicator showing the amount of force currently being produced. The final reading shows the maximum amount of force produced at the peak of the contraction.

The majority of muscular contractions used in athletics are "explosive" in nature. As discussed in Chapter 1, power is developed when acceleration of an object is occurring in a brief time span. The amount of force behind this acceleration also determines the amount of power generated. Some athletic movements are composed of a coordinated chain of muscular contractions. These movements can use the summation of the forces developed by each succeeding contraction to create a greater amount of power and/or velocity. To improve performance of such movements it is advantageous to be able to imitate natural athletic movements at slightly slower speed against resistance. This is often done with pulleys, isokinetic equipment, weights, or other specially designed devices.

Variable resistance refers to a type of isotonic strength training equipment that changes the amount of resistance offered throughout the range of motion. The equipment is normally designed to offer resistance that closely matches the strength available throughout the movement.

Repetition

Repetition is the completion of one entire cycle of an exercise. If an athlete does ten push-ups, he or she has done ten repetitions. (Repetitions is many times abbreviated "reps.") One repetition of the maximum weight that can be lifted is abbreviated 1RM (or 1 repetition maximum). It follows that "3RM" means "the highest weight with which three repetitions can be performed." The same is true for abbreviating any other repetition maximum. After the point where no more repetitions can be completed, momentary failure, or acute muscle fatigue (AMF) is experienced.[52]

Set

Set is the completion of one "turn" or "bout." It can also be defined as a consecutive series of reps. If an athlete does ten push-ups and then rests, and then does ten again, he or she has done two sets of ten repetitions.

ESSENTIALS OF STRENGTH TRAINING FOR ATHLETES

An understanding of the essentials of strength training for athletes represents the *first step* toward unraveling the misconceptions and confusion mentioned earlier. Each of the other four types of weight training is a separate "area of concentration." Each has its own goals, programs, exercises, training techniques, and methods. Ideas from each area have been successfully applied in athletes' strength programs but, despite this, some of the procedures and techniques used in each of these areas do not apply and should not be used in training athletes. It is necessary to be able to determine which ideas can be applied successfully to this type of training. The scientific research literature in physical education indicates at least seven essentials that should be present in an athlete's strength program. Each of the seven has a substantial amount of documentation supporting it. The existence of these essentials therefore forms a scientific basis upholding and giving validity to the field of strength training for athletics.

By ascertaining whether or not these essentials are present one can determine if the strength program is fundamentally sound. In this way they can serve as a guideline to the athlete and the coach in creating, adjusting, and administering strength programs for athletes. Most important, a working knowledge of the essentials can ensure (by scientific support) that the strength program will produce positive results in achieving the athletes' two major objectives: preventing injuries and improving athletic performance.

The following are considered "The Essentials of Strength Training for Athletes":

1. Total Body

Each major body part needs to be included in all strength programs for athletes. This is necessary in order to improve athletic performance and to help prevent injuries. The proportional development of the muscle groups throughout the body ensures that the newly acquired muscular strength can become "functional strength." This is mainly true of athletic movements that require the transfer of force from one body part to another (i.e., the application of the principle of the summation of forces or the conservation of angular momentum). Overall development gives the athlete the capability of learning new skills more easily. The strengthening of the total body also helps to prevent athletic injuries. This occurs in two ways, the first being that stronger body parts are less likely to be injured. Strengthening all of the body parts eliminates weak areas especially vulnerable in heavy contact sports like football. Second, strengthening the total body in the proper way helps to eliminate injuries caused by muscular imbalance.

2. Progressively Increasing Overload

In order to develop maximum strength the athlete must use progressively increasing resistance. Strength training is perhaps the best example of the application of the "Overload Principle." To develop maximum strength, this principle is applied in the following way:

1. There must be an organized method of gradually increasing the resistance used in the strength exercises.
2. The completion of the sets and repetitions in the strength program must require maximum efforts.
3. Maximum strength is best developed by training heavy repetitions of 1–8 RM.

3. Stretching

Stretching is an extremely important essential in strength training for athletes, if only for the purpose of developing and maintaining the flexibility necessary in athletics. This means that athletes who are involved in a strength training program need to be involved in stretching exercises for the whole body on a daily basis. Besides flexibility, stretching has many other benefits

(Chapter 5). In fact, stretching *is* strength training. Consider the following:

a) When a muscle is placed on stretch, it is at its strongest position. The farther it can be stretched, the stronger it is.
b) The strongest muscular contraction comes following a pre-stretch. Some strength training systems such as "The Jones System" make active use of this principle.
c) Since stretching increases flexibility, the range of motion through which the body part can be moved is lengthened. It is therefore capable of increasing velocity over a greater distance thereby creating greater force.

Considerable research confirms that stretching exercises increase flexibility. Research continues to present conflicting evidence as to whether or not weight training reduces or increases flexibility.[53] Some research studies indicate that, after 12 years of age, a person tends to become less flexible in some ways, unless he or she performs stretching exercises. There has never been a research study indicating that weight training, when combined with stretching exercises, reduces flexibility. In fact, studies have shown that strength training and stretching significantly increase sprint speed as well as flexibility.[17,18]

4. Practicing the Sports Skills

Athletes need to perform the skills in their particular sport on a year-round basis. This practice is particularly essential when the off-season strength program is being performed. The reason for this was expressed by Sparrow,[28] a specialist in motor learning at the University of Illinois.

It is often observed that following off-season weight training an athlete shows a falloff in sport skill performances. This may be due to interference[4] from weight training during the noncompetition period. To help reduce this performance decrement many athletes combine off-season conditioning with skill practice. Traditionally, due to the nature of the activity, team-sport athletes are unable to practice many of their particular skills during the off-season. Unfortunately, there is little experimental evidence that weight training itself produces physiological or psychological changes which actively inhibit skill performance. Typically, however, an athlete who does not follow a weight training or skill practice program during the off-season shows less reduction in performance than the regular weight trainer. Therefore, it seems likely that weight training is responsible for poor early season performance if not combined with skill practice. On the basis of these findings, it is strongly recommended that off-season weight training be combined with a program of specific sport skill practice whenever possible. (For other sources supporting this statement, see [16,26] and [33] in the bibliography.)

The skills should be performed in the normal way, that is, without any extra resistance. During the off-season strength program this should be done three or four days a week. A short five- to ten-minute period is all that is necessary to keep the skill pattern grooved.

Strength training for athletes utilizes the principle of specificity in terms of the application of two other essentials. These are applied mainly during the pre-season and in-season strength programs.

5. Specificity in Terms of Muscular Endurance

Strength training should be specific to the muscular endurance requirement of the sport. For example, a basketball player should generally do more repetitions in strength training than a shot-putter or even a football player because the amount of muscular endurance required in basketball is greater. Most sports require repeated bursts of activity, which challenge muscular endurance. The lower repetitions (1–8) used to develop maximum strength[5] in the off-season do not develop strength with the component of high endurance. The strength developed at low endurance can help the athlete perform with increased strength at high endurance. To accomplish this, the athlete must undergo a two- to three-week "adjustment phase" where lighter resistance is used at the desired endurance. This is usually done during the pre-season period.

6. Specificity in Terms of Range of Motion

The athlete's strength program during the pre-season and in-season periods should utilize, to a great extent, exercises that imitate the exact range of motion required in the sport. Exercises used to maintain strength in the large "power muscles" and exercises used to prevent injuries in key areas should also be utilized. However, all other strength exercises done at this time should be employed to improve performance through the specific range of motions that the activity requires. It has long been recognized in the area of motor learning that the specificity of a skill is distinct and peculiar to itself. Since the strength and power of athletic movements are developed specifically, having power in one movement does not guarantee having power in another.

In normal practice most coaches and athletes know that the exact range of motion must be used. Differences in ROM (range of motion) between training and actual performance in delicate, complex movements may result in no beneficial effects, and in fact may actually interfere with normal movement patterns. In strength training the greatest usable strength will be developed if the exact range of motion is followed. For example, if an athlete is training to strengthen the throwing motion, he needs to consider whether he is training to throw a football or to pitch a baseball. The

movement in his strength program is then constructed to match the exact range of movement of the athletic skill as closely as possible. In the case of the throwing motion, a wall pulley, Mini-Gym, or another similar device is often used.

7. Specificity in Terms of Speed of Movement

It is the opinion of the authors that specificity in terms of speed of movement should be employed in pre-season and in-season strength programs for athletes. We believe that the current scientific evidence supports this practice; however, there remains some controversy on this point within the field.

The major argument against strength training at fast speed involves the question of safety. Research on either side of the discussion remains scant. This is not to minimize the importance of safety—safety is definitely a factor that should be considered a major priority in the strength program and at all times. (See Safety, p. 219.)

In most athletic activities high speed is a critical factor. The authors believe that the research surrounding the principle of specificity, and in particular speed of movement, indicates that the strength training for athletics should be performed at high speed if the skill is performed at high speed. The slow speed strength developed by resistance training is best transferable to athletic movement after it has been trained at fast speed. High speed resistance training should be done in the pre-season program as a means of transferring the slow speed strength developed in the off-season to the high speed requirement of the sport.

THE VARIABLE ELEMENTS (INTENSITY, FREQUENCY, DURATION)

When discussing strength training for athletes, it should be remembered that strength training is one of four types of conditioning for athletes. Therefore, the same elements that apply to aerobic and anaerobic conditioning also apply to strength training. These elements (intensity, duration, and frequency) are discussed in Chapter 3 in relation to aerobic and anaerobic training. As mentioned earlier in this chapter, strength training and stretching are actually special types of anaerobic conditioning. Circuit strength training is sometimes used for the development of aerobic conditioning. There is rarely a clear-cut distinction between aerobic and anaerobic exercise, since most activities are a blend of both systems.[53] For this reason, one cannot state that strength training is not sometimes aerobic; however, few if any research studies have shown circuit strength training to produce a significant cardiovascular training effect. In any case, the effects produced by strength training are typically anaerobic in nature. (See Anaerobic Training Effect, p. 18 and Strength Training Effects, p. 19.)

The *major organizational step* involves the application of the elements of intensity, duration, and frequency. When strength training is first employed on a widespread basis in a particular sport, the ability of the coach to vary these three elements skillfully is not as critical as it is later. The competitive edge in simply employing a fundamentally sound strength program is proportionally greater in the first years. As time goes on and programs become more sophisticated, the importance of variation and control of the intensity, duration, and frequency in all sports will tend to increase. This has already occurred in football, the weight events in track, swimming, to some degree in college basketball, and baseball. In highly competitive situations these factors can influence winning or losing "the close ones."

The following statements are intended as guidelines to the reader. Few scientific studies offer precise answers to many of the factors involving the variation of intensity, frequency, and duration. The authors will therefore offer suggestions based upon surveys of the most successful strength programs for athletes used nationwide, as well as those developed through personal experience in the field. Wherever unbiased scientific research has illuminated a point of importance, it is documented to the readers' advantage.

Intensity

Intensity is the most important of the three elements of strength, just as it is in aerobic and anaerobic training. The term *intensity* has traditionally been used in the field of weight lifting or weight training to designate the amount of weight lifted in a single repetition. The authors have expanded the use of the term in order to keep it consistent with terminology used in sports conditioning, and with concepts related to strength training for athletics. As a result, the discussion of intensity will include the following factors:

1. particular exercises used
2. number of exercises per workout
3. amount of weight per set
4. number of sets per exercise
5. number of repetitions per set
6. time interval between sets
7. number of repetitions per unit of time.

Intensity factor #1: The particular exercises used. In selecting the exercises to be used, the purpose of each exercise must first be identified. For this reason the

strength exercises have been classified into four groups according to their function.

Major exercises are those that develop the large power muscles of the body. They are explosive muscles that are used as main movers in nearly all athletic movements. The major exercises are trained with emphasis toward maximum strength.

1. The Bench Press develops the large muscles of the chest, shoulders, and arms.
2. The Squat develops the muscles of the hips, thighs, and the lower back.
3. The Power Clean is a complex athletic movement that develops the muscles of the shoulders, arms, back, hips, thighs, calves, and forearms (or grip). The Power Clean should be used only when close supervision is available.

Assistant exercises are those that assist the development of maximum strength in the major exercises. The large muscles involved in the assistant exercises are the same as those involved in the major exercises. The angle of movement is changed so that the large muscle and some of the surrounding supporting muscles are developed to a greater extent.

1. Bar Dips assist the Bench Press.
2. Behind Neck Press assists the Bench Press.
3. Front Squat assists the Squat.
4. Incline Press assists the Bench Press.
5. Leg Press assists the Squat and Power Clean.
6. Military Press assists the Bench Press.
7. Back Squat assists the Squat.
8. Dead Lift assists the Power Clean. Some strength coaches consider the Dead Lift a major exercise. It is the authors' opinion, and the opinion of most, that the Dead Lift is an exercise that should not be trained for maximum efforts, for safety reasons. (See Dead Lift.)
9. High Pull assists the Power Clean.

Supplemental exercises are used to develop the many other muscles utilized in performing athletic movements and preventing athletic injuries. There are so many supplemental exercises that it is impractical to attempt to list them here. Among the exercises described in this chapter that are not previously listed as major or assistant exercises are the supplemental exercises. Supplemental exercises are generally designed for strength and muscular endurance. Despite this, the complex variations in repetitions, sets, and the weight used in most strength training systems are not usually applied to the supplemental exercises. Many times supplemental exercises isolate muscle groups rather than work several or many areas as major or assistant exercises do. The supplemental exercises selected for a program vary, based on the performance needs of the sport, the special areas of injury risk presented by the sport, and the weaknesses or injury history of the individual athlete. Some supplemental exercises such as those involving the neck and, in some cases, the shoulder girdle are trained mainly for hypertrophy to prevent injuries. Others, such as leg extensions, may be used to prevent injuries by pausing or overloading in the completely extended position, thus ensuring the development of fixator muscles (those which support the knee when the foot is planted). Still other supplemental exercises such as those working on the extremities (e.g. toe raises or wrist curls) are usually trained for higher repetitions (25 to 50 or more) because of their extremely high endurance capability and utilization in the sport.

Specialty exercises are those that have been created especially for a particular sport. They are usually designed to imitate the exact range of motion used in a specific sport skill. They may, however, be designed to isolate a particular muscle group used in a sport or to strengthen one in order to help prevent an injury common to a particular sport.

The specialty exercises for each sport included in this text can be found at the end of each chapter dealing with that sport in Part II. These classifications apply directly to the free weights. Most exercise machines and other equipment can be easily adjusted to this classification system when specific exercises are not available. This can be done by substituting an assistant or a supplemental exercise to work the same area at the same intensity as the "free weight" exercise listed on the program (e.g., the Leg Press for the Squat).

Intensity factor #2: The number of exercises per workout. In determining the number of exercises to be used in each workout, several criteria must be considered:

1. the time available for each workout
2. the period in the year-round program (off-season, pre-season, or in-season)
3. the strength training equipment available
4. the personal opinion of the athlete or coach as to which system of training best serves his needs

In the opinion of the authors, the optimal off-season strength program should involve each of the major exercises twice per week, with three or four assistant exercises done once or twice a week. This means that when the frequency of the off-season workouts is three per week, some combination of three of these exercises is contained in each workout (3 majors, or 2 majors and one assistant, or 3 assistants, etc.).

It normally requires four supplemental exercises to work on the neck, grip, calves, and abdomen in each workout. Sometimes two or more other supplemental exercises may be added to isolate areas, such as upper or lower back, knee, or ankle. These extra exercises can be alternated or rotated weekly, working them from one to three days per week. The athlete may also choose to work on one or more specialty exercises in the off-season workout, even though specialty exercises are stressed most in the pre-season and in-season.

A total of seven to twelve exercises or more can be included in the off-season program. The duration of this type of workout would be from 1½ to 2 hours or more. It is possible to shorten it to approximately an hour or less for young athletes or if time is limited. This is done by reducing the recommended number of sets, or the number of extra supplemental or specialty exercises.

The number of exercises is usually kept the same during the pre-season program, with the addition of several specialty and supplemental (injury prevention) exercises. The objective in the pre-season includes adjusting the muscular endurance to the level required in the sport. The number of exercises is therefore kept high in the pre-season to ensure the building of muscular endurance.

During in-season the number of exercises in each workout can usually be reduced. Concentration at this time is on injury prevention, specialty movements, and the overall maintenance of each of the major muscle groups.

Intensity factor #3: The amount of weight per set. In the off-season strength program the amount of weight per set is determined by considering the following:

1. the strength of the athlete
2. which type of exercise is being performed (i.e., major, assistant, supplemental, or specialty)
3. the exact purpose of the set being done
4. at what phase in the athlete's overall conditioning program the workout is to occur
5. the intensity level called for by the workout (light, medium, heavy, etc. See Cycle Systems)

A question nearly always asked by the athlete just beginning a strength program is, "What weight should I start with?" It is difficult to provide an exact answer, since the possible range of a beginner's strength is so wide. The best answer is to start with the empty bar or the lightest possible weight on the first workout, and proceed to increase the weight gradually, making sure that the proper form is maintained. After the first workout, the athlete or coach may be able to estimate or safely determine the athlete's maximum for one repetition (1RM). By knowing the "max," the starting warm-up weight can be determined by using Table 4.1.

Table 4.1 Selection of a Starting Weight Based on 1RM

Starting Weight	Maximum
20–30	40–50 lbs.
35–50	55–75
55–65	80–100
70–80	105–125
85–100	130–150
105–125	155–175
135	180–Up

A guideline for increasing the amount of weight in the off-season is: "Whenever repetitions are performed, increase the weight in the next workout!" This does not apply when the athlete is involved in a "cycle system" or a program that specifically calls for less than maximum resistance levels.

Another rule of thumb to aid in increasing the amount of weight used is: "Always make larger, or equal, increases first." The following example will help clarify this.

Example. Assume that the athlete is performing repetition series "A."

Reps.	10	10	8	8	6	6	4	4
A Wt.	135	135	145	145	155	155	165	165
B Wt.	135	135	150	150	160	160	170	170
C Wt.	135	135	150	150	165	165	175	175

When the repetitions are accomplished and the weight is to be increased from 165 to 170, it is necessary to increase all but the first two sets. This allows that the larger (15 lb.) increase will be made first. The resulting repetition series appears as shown in series "B." The next (5 lb.) increase from 170 to 175 produces repetition series "C," which shows the first two larger (15 lb.) poundage increases first.

The first two weeks of the off-season strength program are considered the preparatory period or "preparatory phase." At this time, light-to-medium weights are used, gradually increasing into the regular off-season workout.

The off-season strength programs in this text contain the following general pattern in terms of the purpose of each set in a series. The major and assistant exercises utilize the first two sets for warm-up. Supplemental and specialty exercises require only one warm-up set. A very light weight is used for the warm-up. It must be light enough to ensure that perfect movement form is used on each repetition and that there is no thought or sign of muscular strain by the performer.

The next two or three sets are generally done with a medium amount of weight. The purpose of the medium weight is to concentrate on form and gradually adjust to the heavier amounts of weight to be handled.

The final sets of the major, assistant, and supplemental exercises are usually done with maximum weights.[22] By this is meant that the repetitions are done at the repetition maximum level where the athlete is not able to do more repetitions than the program calls for in each set. (See Repetition, p. 35)

This example shows how such a repetition series appears in the text.

Bench Press

10	10	8	8	6	6	4	4
warm-ups		medium sets		sets for 6 RM		and 4 RM	

Maximum weights on the final sets can be used in nearly every workout for most off-season strength programs. The exception occurs when a cycle system is being utilized. In such cases, the program will specify the exact amount of weight to be used on a "percentage maximum" basis.

In the pre-season and in-season strength program the amount of weight can be adjusted in a more general way. During these periods the sets are very often at the same weight. An estimate of this amount is 50 percent of 1RM, which is light enough to be used for the warm-up as well as the remaining sets. As programs and strength equipment become more specialized, the variation of the amount of weight in the pre-season and in-season will be more sophisticated. The negative performance aspects of training with too much weight in-season deter the use of wide variations in the amount of weight at this time. This is especially true in the sports activities with delicate, complex skill involvement.

Another factor which influences the overall conditioning program in-season is the intensity of the other types of conditioning. The cumulative effect of the total amount of stress and fatigue on the athlete from practice and conditioning must be carefully controlled. This may mean reducing the amount of weight used.

Intensity factor #4: The number of sets per exercise. The number of sets per exercise is determined by considering the special characteristics of the exercise itself and the seasonal point in yearly training cycle (or the "phase" of the program).

In the "preparatory phase," or the first two weeks of the off-season program, each exercise can be started with three or four sets and increased by one set per workout until the full off-season complement for each exercise is attained. In the regular off-season program, the major and assistant exercises that use large amounts of weight involve from three to five warm-up and medium weight sets before reaching the sets of maximum intensity. With the supplemental and specialty exercises, maximum resistance is usually reached after one to three sets. Then all classifications of exercises from three to five sets are usually performed at the maximum intensity level. The exception to this is the Power Clean which, although it is a major exercise, normally involves only five or six sets. These might be one warm-up, one medium, three medium heavy (done with concentration on form), and one heavy.

The major and assistant exercises are normally trained for a larger number of sets because of the fact that more adjustment intervals are necessary to reach the heavier weights. The larger muscles trained in these exercises also respond well to more sets in terms of strength development. An even larger number of heavy sets, during certain periods of the program, can be beneficial to the development of maximum strength. As sets are added, the amount of benefit derived from the addition of each successive set is gradually decreased. Therefore, the costs to the athlete in terms of the additional time and energy must be weighed against his or her personal need for additional strength.

Few sets are used in the Power Clean because of the stress created by the impact of handling a heavy weight explosively, and the need for quickness and good form. Proper form and quickness decrease rapidly with fatigue.

During the pre-season and in-season strength program the number of sets per exercise usually remains constant throughout the workout. Three to five sets are recommended for the pre-season workouts and one to three sets for the in-season. This often entails a circuit training program. Exceptions to this include football linemen and linebackers who may train the upper body to develop maximum strength in season. Such workouts include Bench Presses, Incline Presses, and weighted Bar Dips. Another group of athletes who train maximally year round are the track weightmen.

The previously described tendencies represent the general pattern of sets used by the majority of collegiate and professional strength programs for athletes. The Jones System is the major exception, employing only one or two sets of each exercise year round.

Intensity factor #5: The number of repetitions per set. The number of repetitions that should be used is determined by the immediate objective of the strength program. The ultimate objective of the program in terms of strength is to develop the greatest amount of functional strength at the endurance level of the particular sport.

Maximum strength and maximum local muscular endurance lie on opposite ends of a continuum. Each sport corresponds to a certain point on the continuum where the combination of muscular endurance versus strength is at a specific level for that activity. This may even differ from position to position, even within a particular sport. If maximum muscular strength is desired, the training program will emphasize greater resistance with fewer reps. Conversely, if maximum local muscular endurance is desired, the strength program should emphasize many reps against less resistance (fig. 4.1). This effect is best illustrated by the work of Anderson and Kearney.[2]

Because of this continuum the athlete must train his or her muscles in-season at the endurance level of the particular sport. The question is "how can one develop more force (or strength) at high endurance levels?" The answer lies in the fact that maximum strength can be developed in such large amounts at low endurance. This is done during the off-season. The transition or adjustment of this maximum strength to local muscular endurance is done during the pre-season. Because of the effect of the maximum strength versus maximum muscular endurance continuum, not all of the strength will transfer. The amount that does transfer makes a significant difference in terms of functional strength at the necessary endurance level. The practical application of this fact has made strength training advantageous to athletes in nearly every sport. *More strength with endurance* can be achieved by training for maximum strength off-season, then transferring that strength to high endurance. This is much more effective in producing strength with "absolute" endurance than is training with lighter weights at high endurance year round. In this fact lies one of the key concepts in strength training for athletes.

Maximum strength is best developed by performing repetition maximums between 1RM and 8RMs. Beyond ten repetitions, increased muscular endurance becomes the dominant result. Significant strength gains have been produced at 60 percent of 1RM. Best results are achieved within the range of 80 to 100 percent of 1RM. Research directed toward this subject has shown that many variations of repetitions within the 1RM to 8RMs range are effective in producing maximum strength gains.[5,10,52]

Only a few exercises in an athlete's off-season program do *not* employ the one to eight "maximum strength reps." These usually include exercises for the extremities, the abdomen, and any specialty exercises involving complex movements, such as throwing or kicking. In the pre-season and in-season workouts the repetitions are adjusted as closely as is practical to the muscular endurance required by the sport.

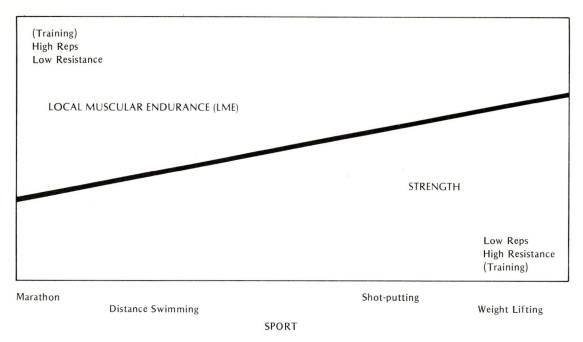

(Training)
High Reps
Low Resistance

LOCAL MUSCULAR ENDURANCE (LME)

STRENGTH

Low Reps
High Resistance
(Training)

Marathon

Distance Swimming

Shot-putting

Weight Lifting

SPORT

Figure 4.1 Muscular Strength–Muscular Endurance Relationship

Intensity factor #6. The time interval between sets. Controlling the time between sets is a very important part of controlling the intensity of any strength program. The criteria to be considered in varying the time intervals between sets are:

1. the amount of weight lifted
2. the objective of the program in terms of maximum strength versus maximum muscular endurance
3. the objective of the program in terms of increasing muscular size or muscular strength
4. the importance of muscular recovery to the performance of the exercise being trained
5. the amount of time available for the workout
6. the intensity of the other types of conditioning in which the athlete is involved

When a muscle reaches momentary failure, AMF, it takes approximately five minutes for the muscle to recover 99.9 percent. Of this recovery, 95 percent occurs within 2½ minutes, 75 percent within one minute, and 50 percent within 30 seconds.[52] For this reason, athletes lifting heavy weights for maximum efforts (RMs) must rest at least two or three minutes between sets.

In the off-season major and assistant exercises are usually trained in a "set system."[15] All of the sets of one exercise are completed before beginning another exercise. When this is done, the rest intervals between sets can be gradually increased in length as the sets get heavier: 1 minute intervals after warm-up sets, 1½–2 minute intervals after medium sets, and 3–5 minute intervals after heavy sets.

If the time available for the strength workout is limited, the shorter of the suggested rest intervals can be utilized. When training an exercise that requires quickness and good form in a complex athletic movement, the athlete may benefit by using the maximum allotted time for the rest interval. The Power Clean is an example of such an exercise.

The supplemental and specialty exercises in the off-season program can employ a "circuit" system, thereby reducing the time between sets. To accomplish this, two to five exercise stations are prepared. When maximum strength is the objective, the exercises can be arranged so that consecutive exercises do not work on the same muscle groups. As a result, a rest interval of between one and 30 seconds, or less, can be achieved. The athlete can go through such a circuit by working continuously until all the sets of each exercise are completed, or can take a rest interval after one set of each exercise is completed. If a rest period is taken after each round, the time can be used to adjust the amount of weight at the various stations. In some cases the athlete may wish to develop the size and muscular definition of a certain muscle or area of the body. To do this, a bodybuilding technique, "supersets," can be used. Supersets are done by performing different exercises that continuously place stress on the same muscle group. This helps to create a better "pump" by continually forcing the blood into the muscle. The capillaries in the tissue are kept expanded for a longer period of time, the result being larger increases in muscular size. An extension of the technique used by bodybuilders is called a "blitz system."[15]

The pre-season and in-season strength programs often employ a circuit training system. In such cases the time interval between sets is usually beween 3 and 10 seconds. When high intensity and the improvement of muscular endurance is desired, the athletes can run or move very quickly between stations in an attempt to get the time between sets as short as possible. If heavy weights are to be used, a "set system" is employed with the time intervals the same as those used for the major or assistant exercises in the off-season.

Intensity factor #7: The number of repetitions per unit time. As mentioned previously, opinions differ about the speed at which the strength repetitions should be performed. Information supporting fast-speed strength training was offered by Wilmore,[54] and Counsilman.[13] Information supporting slow-speed strength training is offered by Westcott.[52] The authors have concluded that the best method is to develop strength in the off-season with heavy resistance, and then transfer the strength to fast-speed in the pre-season and in-season. With heavy weights, the intensity of the exercise does not depend as much on movement speed as it does with lighter weights.

In the pre-season and in-season the program can be renderd ineffective if the repetitions with light weights are not done at a sufficiently high speed. For example, in a pre-season or in-season circuit a station is usually designed to last for a specific time interval. This might vary from 12 seconds to one minute. If the light repetitions are performed slowly, with pauses, very little work will be performed. It is possible that some minimal amount of strength maintenance will result in this situation, but there will likely be little benefit in terms of muscular endurance. A minimum number of repetitions for each timed station should be prescribed. It is also recommended that if high intensity and high muscular endurance are desired, constant fast-speed movement should be maintained throughout the interval. This means starting the first repetition at the very beginning of the interval and not allowing the bar or the force lever of the machine to pause until the very end of the interval. Discipline and enthusiasm are required if this is to be achieved. (See Strength Training Circuits, page 47.)

This method of circuit training results in an extremely high intensity level. If, as in the case of many college football programs, the pre-season entails two-a-day practices, an intense strength program of this type should be used discriminately.

Frequency

During the rest period between workouts the muscles rebuild. Waste products are eliminated from the tissues, and biochemical changes occur which cause the development of strength and/or muscular endurance. The level to which the muscle rebuilds is to a great degree dependent upon the length of the rest period and the intensity of the workout that preceded the rest period. For this reason, controlling the frequency of workouts properly has a great deal to do with the success of the strength program.

The frequency most often recommended in the off-season and pre-season is three days a week. Athletes just beginning strength training should stay on a three-day-per-week program for at least six to eight weeks, until an adjustment to the stress of strength training is made. Some athletes respond well to a regular program of four or five days per week.[54] Considering the amount of time dedicated to other areas of conditioning, it is usually advisable to wait until the second off-season program to extend beyond three days per week.

In advanced strength training programs even six- or seven-day-per-week programs are used by some individuals for limited periods of time. Programs with such high levels of stress are used to stimulate greater development by athletes who are acquainted with advanced strength training methods. To understand the value of such stressful training, it is necessary to understand the general pattern of strength development. Larger strength increases occur in the first few weeks and months of strength training. As time goes on, increases become smaller and so-called "plateaus" become longer. Some advanced individuals have found a method to help overcome such long plateaus. If the individual is in good condition, training three days a week, workouts are increased to seven days a week. This makes it impossible to recover fully between workouts. The experienced individual knows how to avoid injuries by using the proper exercises and by adjusting the weight and number of repetitions. After a number of these seven-day-per week sessions (usually 1½ to 2½ weeks), the fatigue level has increased to the point that much lighter weights must be used. By continuing at this frequency the body gradually permits the weight to be increased again. After four to six weeks from the beginning of the seven per week workouts the strength level is back to the point of the original plateau. The workout frequency can then be reduced to four, five, or six days per week, depending upon how long the individual can tolerate the work level. When the days are reduced, the body is able to recover fully, developing greater strength. This method works successfully for certain individuals and in some cases has been responsible for the development of the enormous strength of the world-class weight lifters. *Such high training frequencies are definitely NOT recommended for most athletes.* Because of the success of athletes such as former world record holder and National Powerlifting Champion John Kanter of Phoenix, Arizona, and many others, it is not possible to discount the advantage of extremely high workout frequencies to some individuals.

The frequency of pre-season workouts is usually three days per week. When an extremely intense pre-season program or training camp is administered, two days per week is sometimes used. In these instances, the athletes are on more of a maintenance strength program rather than one geared to develop explosive strength or high muscular endurance.

The in-season strength program normally entails a frequency of one or two days per week. This is the frequency recommended by the authors. However, three-day-per-week in-season strength programs are not uncommon in some sports. There should not be a mandatory strength workout on the day prior to an athletic competition. It has been observed that some athletes prefer performing a few light sets just prior to competition. This procedure helps reduce muscle tension and partially pumps and warms up the muscles, perhaps providing some psychological as well as physical benefit. The intensity of such a warm-up should obviously be kept at a minimum.

Duration

The duration of the off-season strength workout can vary from 45 minutes to four hours. These figures, of course, represent extremely short and extremely long off-season workouts. The optimal duration for the off-season workout depends upon the relative contribution that strength training makes toward the improvement of performance in that particular sport. For example, strength training affects performance a great deal more for football linemen, or the weight events in track, than it does in cross-country or golf.

The statement of this fact does not diminish the importance of strength training to success in any sport. It is rather a recognition that a higher degree of "functional strength" can be developed for certain types of athletic activities than for others. When the level of competition is so high that the margin of success is very slim, a small amount of functional strength can easily mean the difference between success and failure.

To determine the relative value of strength training versus the other types of conditioning (aerobic, anaerobic, skills, and flexibility training), a concept dealing with the economic use of time is necessary. A law of economics called The Law of Diminishing Return needs to be considered in this situation. This law states that when an investment is made in a productive area, a return results; however, as continuing investments in the same area are made, the return beomes progressively smaller.

In the case of strength training for a football lineman the return on the investment of time does not diminish as rapidly as it does for a complex skill activity such as golf. The first hour and a half of investment for the football lineman and for the golfer yield a great return in terms of improved performance. When a golfer's workout is extended beyond an hour and a half, the amount of beneficial return is reduced considerably. At this point it becomes more likely that the extra time would have been better spent on skills training. If the workouts were extended to 2½ or 3 hours, it is almost a certainty that an extra hour of practicing golf would have been a wiser use of the available time. The same cannot be said for the football lineman, since the strength training done during the third and even the fourth hours of his workout might benefit him more than extra hours of additional skills practice. The relative value of increasing the duration of the workout, in terms of the improved performance of the individual athlete, must be carefully considered when planning workouts.

At the junior high and high school levels there is often a "class period" limitation of the amount of time available for off-season strength training. In such situations the workout must be compressed. This can be done by 1) shortening the time between sets, 2) training the major exercises in a circuit, or 3) training five or six days per week on a "split routine" (upper body one day, lower body the next).

During the pre-season and in-season the duration of the workouts is greatly reduced. For most sports a 20–30 minute circuit can be employed effectively in the pre-season. The duration of an in-season workout is even shorter, usually ranging from 7 to 15 minutes. If a heavy workout is to be used during this period by a special group or individual such as a football lineman, an additional 20–30 minutes should be allowed.

DEVISING STRENGTH PROGRAMS

Any strength program for athletes that follows the principles, essentials, and elements previously described in this chapter should produce significant strength gains. As mentioned previously, large increases in strength will occur within the first six to eight weeks. Later the gains are smaller and generally occur more slowly. The tendency toward slower and smaller strength increases must be recognized and accepted. In the view of the authors, the existence of actual strength "plateaus" is questionable. The reason for the concept of the "strength plateau" is that in most cases the athlete has considered his strength based solely upon his 1RM. As was pointed out in the discussion concerning

Table 4.2 The Year-Round Variance of the Elements of Intensity, Frequency, and Duration

	Off-Season	Pre-Season	In-Season
INTENSITY			
Amount of Resistance	Heavy	Light	Lighter
Speed of Exercises	Slow	Fast	Faster
Total Number of Exercises	7 to 12	8 to 12	7 to 10
Number of Major Exercises	2–3	2–3	2–3
Sets	8–10	5	2–3
Reps	1–8	10–50	10–50
Number of Assistant Exercises	1–2	1–2	1–2
Sets	6–8	5	2–3
Reps	1–8	10–50	10–50
Number of Supplemental Exercises	3–5	3–5	3–5
Sets	3–5	5	2–5
Sets	3–5	5	2–3
Reps	8–30	10–50	10–50
Number of Specialty Exercises	1–3	1–3	1–3
Sets	3–5	5	2–3
Reps	10–50	10–50	10–50
Frequency			
Days/Week	3–5	3	1–2
Duration			
Workout Time	45 min.–4 hrs.	20–30 min.	7–15 min.

"number of repetitions," training with repetitions between 1RM and 8RMs produces strength increases that are not significantly different. Since the goal of the athlete is not the increase of the 1RM alone, the suggestion is made that within the range of 1RM to 8RMs, strength improvements can be occurring constantly. In order for this to occur, the athlete must know how to utilize the correct strength system (table 4.2).

The Set System

The "set system" is the most common method of strength training. Off-season strength training programs predominately utilize this system. The "set system" means that several sets of the same exercise are performed with rest periods (1 to 5 minutes) in-between.

The "circuit training" system, or "strength training circuit," is the other most frequently used method of strength training. It is contrary to the "set system," since a variety of different exercises are performed in a series with less time between sets (2½–10 seconds). Strength circuits are the most common form of strength training pre-season and in-season. In the circuit system, the exercises are usually arranged so that the same muscle group is not exercised on two consecutive stations. There are many intricate types of strength circuits and various methods for administering them.

"Super set" indicates that consecutive sets of different exercises which work the same muscles or muscle groups are performed. The sets are done with a min-

imum of rest between sets. The concept of *super sets* was developed by bodybuilders who use the method to increase muscular size. Blood flow to the local area is increased greatly as capillaries are forced open, and the bodybuilder experiences the "pump." Super sets normally appear as 3 or 4 station mini-circuits, but there are innumerable super set systems possible. Athletes in various sports can utilize variations of them to increase muscular size or local muscular endurance.

"Forced reps" is another technique that originated in bodybuilding. It is simply a matter of manually aiding in the completion of a repetition that would otherwise not be completed because of fatigue. The goal is to work the muscle as completely as possible. Some athletes and strength coaches prefer to use forced reps throughout their training whenever possible. The authors do not recommend this as a normal practice. It tends to create a psychological dependence on the spotter and eliminates objectivity as to how such work was actually done. In many programs, maximum efforts are not always desirable. "Forced reps" tend to put the strength program out of control. It can become maximum effort at any or all times. Even the spotters themselves, or the amount of resistance a particular spotter supplies, may change from set to set and workout to workout. For the purposes of this text, forced reps are not recommended, unless specified in the particular strength program itself.

The effectiveness of various types of strength training programs has been studied in recent years.

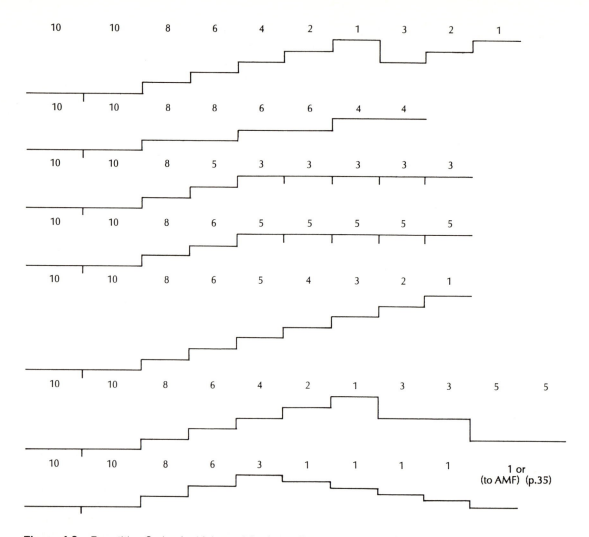

Figure 4.2 Repetition Series for Major and Assistant Exercises

Berger, DeLorme, and Watkins did classic early studies in this area. Numerous other persons have also contributed substantial research in this area.[54] Beyond the basic indications that heavy low repetitions (1–8 RM) are most effective in producing maximum strength gains, no repetition series or pattern of progressively increasing resistance has been found to be clearly superior. Most strength experts readily agree that the method that works best for one individual may not at all be best for another. In fact, the best program for an individual during a particular off-season may not be the best for the same individual the next off-season.

Figure 4.2 shows some commonly used repetition series with the resistance levels or increases indicated by the "step-like" lines.

A method of increasing strength while maintaining a repetition level that can be increased is as follows:

In one workout of a major or assistant exercise, the athlete finds his or her RM for two repetition levels (example 3RM and 5RM), in the next Monday workout the athlete performs the following repetition series: 10 10 8 5 3 3 3 3 3. The 3s are done at a resistance level of 3 RM minus 10 pounds. If three sets of three reps are performed successfully, the five sets of three reps are increased in the following Monday workout. The increase should be +5 pounds for upper body exercises and +10 pounds for lower body exercises. Do not exceed this amount of increase. If three sets of three repetitions are not performed successfully, the weight remains the same the following week. If at any time the repetitions are not performed successfully for three consecutive weeks, two options are offered: 1) the weight can be increased by the desired amounts (+5 or +10 pounds) and the repetitions decreased to 2s, or 2) a higher repetition, lower resistance level can be selected.

If the first option is selected, the following repetition series results: 10, 8, 6, 4, 2, 2, 2, 2, 2. In this case, three sets of the 5-set series must be accomplished the first time they are attempted. If the athlete is not able to accomplish this, option #2 is selected for the following week.

If the second option is selected, the higher repetition series to be used should not be the same as the one being performed in the same exercise on another day of the week. The amount of weight to be used is determined by the same method used at the beginning of the program. The amount of weight used is the RM - 10 lbs. In the example case, the repetition series resulting might be 10, 10, 8, 7, 7, 7, 7, 7.

When option #2 is selected, possible repetition series higher than 3s that could be chosen are 4s, 6s, 7s, and 8s.

This type of program is effective for programs 8 or up to 10 weeks in length, maximum. Longer programs require cycle systems. If this same program is to be used the following year, the athlete will probably need to use different repetitions for the five sets the second year. A common mistake is made when the athlete trains on a heavy program for a prolonged period of time. Continuously increasing the resistance to be lifted each day, on a daily and weekly basis on and on, produces overtraining, thereby creating an unnecessary plateau.

Cycle Systems

Cycle systems were developed to help avoid overtraining, eliminate guesswork, and ensure that "peaking out" occurs at the proper time. When strength programs are extended continuously throughout the months of the off-season, overtraining becomes a definite problem. The cycle programs allow for the necessary "recovery" as well as "overload." In junior high school and college level sports in the United States this type of program is not usually necessary. This is because the athlete's off-season strength program normally extends for only six to a maximum of ten weeks, after which a lengthy interruption occurs. When an athlete's strength program extends beyond ten weeks, including the two-week preparatory period, a cycle program of some type should be employed.

The sports situations in the United States in which cycle systems are most commonly used are in the weight events in track, where heavy strength training occurs throughout the in-season period, and in professional sports, where uninterrupted training occurs throughout the off-season, in college football—which would otherwise lend itself well to cycle programs—the placement of spring football permits only a six- to ten-week off-season strength program. These problems, along with others such as multiple sport high school situations, limit the effectiveness, and therefore the application, of cycle systems in this country.

Cycle systems are constructed using several different guidelines to adjust the amount of weight, the number of repetitions, and the spacing of the recovery period. Cycle systems are characterized by the utilization of a recovery (or light) week every three or four weeks. The amount of weight or the overall intensity of the program handled each week is varied. The training week is rated as follows: 1) heavy, 2) medium heavy, 3) medium, or 4) light. The individual workout intensity may also be rated in the same way.

In some cases the workout rating system is based upon the number of repetitions performed within a certain percentage (e.g., 50 percent) of the athlete's 1RM. This would include only repetitions done in the major or assistant exercises. Another method used in this text to present a cycle program for track weight events utilizes the percentage of a projected 1RM to rate the weekly and daily workouts. The details of this system are presented in Chapter 17. This program can easily be adapted to strength programs for any sport if extended off-season periods are available. To accomplish this, substitute the described cycle system into the major and assistant exercises recommended in the off-season program for the appropriate sport.

Strength Training Circuits

Strength training circuits, as mentioned earlier, generally consist of a number of strength exercises done in a series. The selection of the particular exercises used is based on the specific movement patterns of the sport and the needs of the individual athletes involved. Most circuits arrange the exercises to change the muscles or muscle groups exercised on consecutive stations. In some cases, however, super set stations may be employed in a circuit or in part of a circuit.

To administer the circuit, the program is selected and the pathway pattern or track of the circuit throughout the strength facility is planned. When the strength facility floor plan is arranged, it is suggested that consideration be given to the in-season and preseason circuits which will be employed by the staff. Some adjustments of the strength equipment are usually necessary, however, for each circuit that is to be performed. After the adjustments are made, the stations should be marked by placing numbered cards in sequence through the circuit. The circuit is then tested by the coach or an athlete. It is checked for time, resistance levels to be used, and movement efficiency. Strength circuits can vary in length from approximately 15 to 40 stations, depending on the size of the group. They can rotate through the circuit until the desired number of stations has been completed. A written record and diagram of the circuit should then be made so that it can be set up exactly the same way each time. The record is also kept for future reference.

Circuits are usually conducted using *timed intervals* or *designated repetition intervals*. In both cases, a whistle is sounded at the start and end of each station. The amount of resistance at each station is normally set by the coach and is not changed throughout the circuit. Exceptions to this will be discussed in the descriptions of the particular strength circuits. The amount of weight is determined by the repetition level, the endurance required by the length of the circuit, the speed of movement desired, and the training situation. (See *Intensity Factor #3.*)

When the strength circuit is taught, the expectations for the athlete should be described and demonstrated as completely as possible. This includes the precise movements which need to be made between stations as well as the techniques involved in each strength exercise. For most pre-season and in-season use, the athletes should be taught to do all repetitions without pausing. This means that the repetitions are done fluidly, with no stops at the bottom or top of the movement stroke. This is necessary to ensure that the work gets done when the stations are being performed for timed intervals.

The movement speed of the exercises and of the movements between stations (rotation intervals) should also be demonstrated. This enables the athlete to get a mental picture of how the circuit is to be performed. After the circuit is learned, if it is not being performed as it should be, repeating this demonstration can be an effective motivator.

1. The Walking Circuit (Learning Circuit)

When a circuit is first taught, it should be performed at slower speed until the movements are learned. It is particularly necessary that no speed be required during the rotation interval. If faster speed is to be required after the circuit is learned, the most efficient steps are emphasized. This includes beneficial hand movements and foot placements as well as any safety precaution which needs to be observed. The walking circuit can be administered using timed work intervals or a given number of repetitions. If timed intervals are used, they are usually 15–25 seconds in length. When a given number of repetitions is required, the repetition number can be displayed on the station number card. To ensure that is it not confused with the station number, it should be designated by the word REPS or printed in a different color.

Uses for the "Walking Circuit":

1. learning other types of circuits
2. 3 or 4 supplemental and/or specialty exercises performed in a "mini-walking circuit" in the off-season program
3. a light workout circuit

4. a warm-up to another circuit
5. an in-season football circuit. If a circuit is to be performed on the day after a football game, many team members may be sore, bruised, and slightly injured. In that case, a walking circuit may be advisable so that players can perform each station at the appropriate speed and intensity.

2. The Continuous Circuit

The continuous circuit is conducted in the situation where athletes are scheduled to perform at individual times or appointment times. This would usually occur in the in-season as a maintenance circuit. Several athletes can be scheduled at 15-minute intervals throughout the day or over any extended period. As they arrive, they can begin the circuit immediately since it is ongoing. The coach can have each athlete start at Station 1 or join the "back of the pack," i.e., the station just vacated by the last person in the group currently involved. Starting incoming individuals at the back of the pack keeps the group together, makes supervision easier, and ensures that no one skips a station. The continuous circuit can utilize timed intervals or designated repetition intervals and a whistle to start and rotate.

After the circuit is learned and the proper work habit is attained by all the athletes, it can be beneficial to administer with fewer restrictions. By designating the number of repetitions for each exercise and allowing athletes to rotate at will, without the whistle, individual attention can be given. Athletes with injuries or weak areas can concentrate on those areas and change the amount of weight to suit their needs.

3. The Speed Circuit

This circuit is utilized when speed of movement and explosiveness are to be emphasized. The speed circuit functions at a muscular endurance level optimal for football. It is also excellent as a light, fast basketball workout to be done as one of two in-season workouts each week. The other should be one which emphasizes endurance and is usually done earlier in the competition week.

The speed circuit is administered on a system which rewards speed. Top speed is usually possible for only 20 to 25 stations. It is emphasized that the movement must be as fast and explosive as possible, with completely fluid movement—i.e., no pauses. The circuit stations are 25 seconds in length. Rotation intervals are 5 seconds in length. The athletes should also be told the approximate number of reps to attempt per station. At the beginning of each speed circuit, it is recommended that 5 stations be performed at *walking* speed as a warm-up. Then after the faster stations have started, the speed reward system is put into effect. If the coach notices that every team member is working as hard and fast as possible, no one is seen to pause before any repetition at the top or the bottom, and everyone has begun the next station on or prior to the starting whistle, then the upcoming station interval is only 20 seconds in length and the rotation interval is cut to 4 seconds. After this is achieved, the same criteria are applied to the next station. Again, if it is an all-out effort, no pauses, and rotation is completed on or before the whistle, the station interval is 15 seconds and the rotation interval is 3 seconds. Any pause, slow rotation, or decreased movement speed on the exercise by a single team member bumps the station interval back up to 25 seconds. This has been known to cause groaning or a similar response on the first occasion, which can cause the next rotation interval to be slower and thus another 25-second work interval. Team sports require eliminating past errors and concentrating on quickly reacting with a correct response. For this reason, this circuit is excellent in developing great team attitude. Teams have been able to master an efficiently designed circuit, achieving 12-second stations and 2½-second rotations.

As mentioned, after the speed circuit has been practiced and perfected to some degree, the effects can be extremely positive in terms of the effort and enthusiasm produced. Since the work stations are timed intervals, the determination as to how hard an athlete is working is, to some degree, a subjective evaluation. In other words, it is possible to perform the work movements at slower speed without pausing and to move quickly on the rotation interval, to "beat the system." This usually occurs when the program is being learned or over a period of time the program has become boring. If this happens, the coach can switch the work station from timed to *designated repetition*. If this is to be done, the athletes should be advised of its likelihood prior to the circuit. At that time, the coach simply picks the slowest team member he can find and audibly counts the reps until the designated number, then blows the whistle to rotate. This can be done for a single station or for as many as needed, until the exercise speed increases sufficiently. The coach can also switch to designated intervals in the midst of a timed interval by simply picking up the count where he finds it: ". . . 7, 8, 9, 10, 11, 12, BEEP." *Warning:* Tempo or effort motivators such as this lose their effectiveness if they are overused.

4. The Variable Speed Circuit

The variable speed circuit is the same as the speed circuit in that timed intervals are used and speed is the main emphasis. In fact, an excellent way to teach it is to begin by first teaching the speed circuit. The advantage of the variable speed circuit is that it can be lengthened into a long endurance circuit. It was developed for long and intermediate distance events preseason and in-season, and can be used pre-season for other sports such as basketball, wrestling, soccer, or hockey.

After the regular speed circuit has been perfected down to 15- or 20-second timed intervals, the endurance factor of five additional stations per day is introduced. At this time, the speed factor is temporarily reduced. The athletes are told that exercise movements are to be at 75 percent speed, and to move briskly between stations, again at 3/4 speed. The circuit can be performed at this speed, adding 5 stations each workout until an optimal number is reached. If the program is being run three days per week starting with a 20-station base, it takes three weeks to increase it to 65 stations. Some teams have been known to increase this circuit up to a peak of 75 stations.

There are several variables which can be applied within this circuit so that an unlimited number of adaptions are possible. First, after the circuit is conducted for 2 or 3 weeks, some type of variation in intensity and duration is necessary. There will need to be light, medium, and heavy workouts. Speed can be varied; a 75 percent speed movement with brisk walking rotations has already been mentioned. Ninety percent speed movements with 4- or 5-second rotations and 100 percent super-fast movements with 2½- or 3-second rotations can be integrated. The following are other possibilities.

1. If the choice of 20 90% stations or 10 super-fast stations is offered, the athletes may be observed to achieve a new level of speed intensity.
2. Super-long stations, 30 to 35 seconds in length, can be used at the end of a circuit to help push the finish. Usually 3 to 5 of these are sufficient and they are particularly suited to long-distance athletes. This is particularly specific to the type of mental toughness required by these events. The continual pounding and discomfort are present and, just as in a race, the athletes cannot let up—in this case because a pause will cost the entire team an extra station. The fact that long-distance events use very light resistance also makes these long stations possible.
3. Fartlek-type training is also possible with this circuit. This simply means that the intensity is varied by the leader or the coach at random.
4. At some points, the strength aspect of the program can be increased by adding resistance throughout the circuit. In all cases, the strength program must be totally integrated into the overall program. With endurance athletes, increased resistance must be done judiciously and, obviously, accompanied by a decrease in the circuit duration.

5. The Station Elimination Circuit

The station elimination circuit is usually conducted with timed interval stations and timed rotations. A large number of stations, possibly 40 to 50, are scheduled, since the objective of the group is to eliminate the number to be performed. Each time the entire group performs a station and a rotation perfectly, a station is subtracted. *Perfectly,* of course, means that there are no pauses in the repetitions and that each athlete completes the rotation and begins the next station on or before the starting whistle. The coach calls out the number to be completed each time he approves a perfectly executed station. *Example:* In the beginning, "O.K., 40 stations to go, ready, set, BEEP." Then after a perfect station and rotation, the coach announces "39." This method requires that the athlete on Station 1 be designated as the "leader." When the leader reaches the coach's number, the circuit is over. The elimination circuit rewards improvement in speed, endurance, and teamwork. It is an excellent circuit to use for group competitions. Football groups—for instance, linemen, linebackers and tight ends, and backs and receivers—can compete during a pre-season camp. Awards can be given for the best single workout (fewest stations on one day) and/or best overall, strength circuit champs (fewest stations for the entire camp). The elimination circuit can be used for any sport, and is best utilized in the pre-season.

6. The Perfect Circuit

The perfect circuit is actually the opposite of the station elimination circuit. The team is required to perform a given number or *goal number* of perfect stations. The station intervals and the rotation intervals are timed, no pause is allowed, and the coach has the opportunity to switch to designated interval stations at any time. The number of perfect stations completed is announced by the coach when it is accepted. When the goal number is reached, the circuit is over.

The circuit is excellent for motivating athletes to perform at their very best from the very beginning of the workout, and to sustain the effort continuously until a goal is achieved. It is not as good for group competitions as the elimination circuit.

7. The Muscular Endurance Circuit

The muscular endurance circuit stations are those where maximum efforts of 10–20 RM are required. It should, therefore, be prefaced by an extended warm-up of approximately 15 to 20 stations. It also works best if no more than 15 to 20 athletes are involved at once. To administer this circuit, the athletes are arranged at the stations in order of strength—the strongest athlete first, the next strongest second, and so on down until the weakest athlete is last. A "designated competition station" is selected and given the station number *1* in the circuit. It should be a station where a maximum effort of 10 to 20 RM can be done safely and measured exactly. The bench press is an excellent example. If a maximum of 15 to 20 athletes are involved, the circuit can be designed so that one lap around it is 15 to 20 stations. In that case, the strongest athlete begins on the designated station and, after the first rotation, the next strongest athlete is on the designated station. The resistance is kept light for the warm-up lap and the rotation intervals are performed at 75% (brisk walking) or walking speed. After the warm-up lap, extra resistance is added to selected stations throughout the circuit. An assistant coach or the athletes themselves can quickly add the weight. On Station 1, the designated station, a resistance between 10 and 20 RM for the strongest athlete should be used. The station just prior to Station 1 *must not* exercise the same muscles as Station 1. When the muscular endurance lap of the circuit is begun, the strongest athlete does as many reps as possible on the designated station. At the same time, each athlete is simultaneously performing continuous, no-pause repetitions on the particular exercise wherever he or she is located. When the maximum RM is completed, the whistle blows and the team members walk to the next station. The maximum RM achieved on the designated station is recorded as the athlete's personal record, or PR.
Example:

Bench Press

	Weight		PR
1. Ken Norman	205 lbs.	×	14 reps

The weight is then reduced for the second strongest athlete. It is normal to give the athlete a few seconds to prepare. Ask the athlete if he or she is ready. Give the athlete a spot if needed. Start the rest of the team with a whistle on the designated athlete's movement.

Before the beginning of the circuit, the coach will need to prepare as follows:

1. Place the required plates near the stations that need additional weight for the muscular endurance lap.
2. Prepare a record chart for the PRs, with the athletes' names in descending order of strength.
3. Calculate the proper plates to be used on the designated station so the weights can be removed as quickly as possible as the circuit progresses. For instance, if the weights needed in descending order are 205, 185, 175, 155, and 135 pounds, each side of the Olympic bar is loaded from the

inside out as follows: a 45-pound plate, two 10-pound plates, one 5-pound plate, and one 10-pound plate. This amount equals 205 pounds for athlete #1. When the outside 10-pound plate is removed from each side, 185 pounds is ready for athlete #2, and so forth. If 205 pounds were loaded the usual way, with a 45-pound and a 35-pound plate on each side of the bar, the 35-pound plates would have to be removed from each side and replaced by 25-pound plates on each side.

As the circuit is repeated week after week, the athletes compete to improve their PR on station 1. When a player achieves 20 reps on a particular weight, his other competition weight for the designation is increased by 5 pounds for the next workout. In this way, the athlete can move up in the team strength order by increasing the weight he or she can handle at the designated station.

The muscular endurance circuit can be used in-season or pre-season for sports high in muscular endurance such as basketball, wrestling, and soccer. The circuit develops local muscular endurance in each area exercised since athletes at all stations are continuously moving while the designated athlete competes for his or her best effort. In-season, the muscular endurance circuit is used as the first of two strength workouts per week. There should be at least 48 hours allowed between the completion of this circuit and competition. The team members usually get very involved in cheering for the athlete at Station 1, and this creates a positive atmosphere during the circuit. Discipline rules are still applied, so if an individual gets so involved in cheering for his teammate that he stops or pauses a rep, the team performs an extra station after the endurance circuit is completed.

8. The Survival Super Set Circuit

The survival super set circuit is created by inserting a series of 4 to 8 super sets into a circuit. The station intervals in the entire circuit are timed and the rotation intervals should be timed and very fast. Spotters will be required at each super set station excluding the first one. The bar must be kept moving at all times during the station interval. The spotters should supply only as much help as is necessary to keep the resistance moving. To designate the super set area and the importance of each team member surviving it without giving up or pausing, it can be given a nickname, such as "Murderers' Row." This indicates its successful completion as the accomplishment of a formidable task, which it should be. The super set survival circuit increases local muscular endurance, tolerance to the type of discomfort experienced in strength training, and can be, as the

colloquialism states, "good gut check" for a pre-season camp. This circuit is excellent for wrestlers, football players, or any athlete where a combination of local muscular endurance, strength, and tolerance toward pain is required.

9. Alternating Activity—Strength Endurance Circuit

Alternating activity and strength endurance in a circuit is a technique very similar to the circuit training program described in Chapter 3. Athletes perform a series of circuit stations and proceed immediately into another activity. Nearly any type of athletic activity can be utilized. To be effective, the activity must be set up in close proximity to the strength circuit so only a few seconds elapse between the two.

During in-season, the activity will tend to be very sport-specific. The coach should be careful during in-season not to create such an overload that full recovery for an upcoming competition is not achieved. A good in-season strength workout for distance runners is to alternate running stadium steps and a variable speed circuit. In pre-season, progressively increasing overloads in areas most specific to the sport are beneficial. The alternating activity—a strength endurance circuit can also be utilized in a situation where a base level of conditioning is being established. For example, a sport characterized exclusively by anaerobic bursts needs to develop an aerobic base during off-season. This type of circuit utilizing 1- or 1½-mile runs alternating with a variable speed circuit can be integrated into a regular weekly schedule of aerobic workouts. This would provide for strength maintenance while the emphasis is placed on developing the aerobic base. The alternating activity—strength endurance circuit—can be organized with swimming, plyometrics, wrestling, sprints, or skating and is useful to supplement nearly any sport.

10. Discipline—Concentration Circuit

The discipline—concentration circuit was created for a specific situation in which the athletes are very stiff, sore, bruised, and physically lethargic. It also has other uses when, for whatever reason, discipline in the strength program becomes a problem. One advantage of the circuit is that it can be administered effectively to an extremely large group, which in some cases can be the cause of a discipline problem. The perfect example of the time to use this circuit is on the morning after a football game.

First, various stations are created with the idea that four athletes will be working at each station. There should be approximately 7 stations in one circuit. Two or more of these circuits can be conducted at one time. An example of the discipline—concentration circuit stations is offered in figure 4.3.

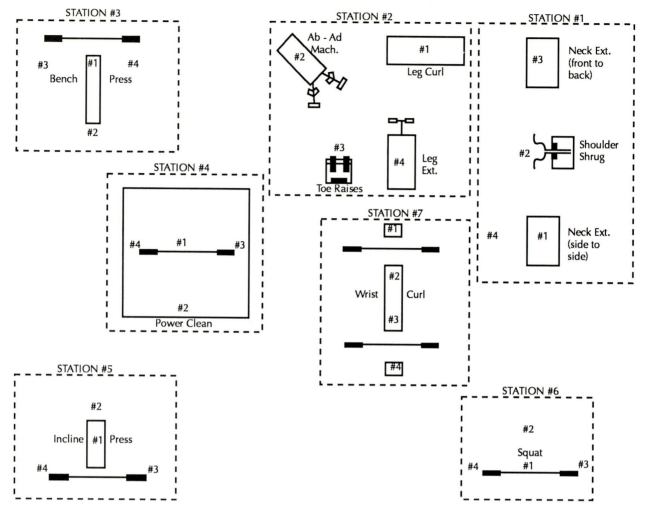

Figure 4.3 Strength Circuit 10
Discipline-Concentration Circuit

The athletes rotate through a four-position mini-circuit three times within each of the major stations before changing to the next major station. The unique element in the circuit is that free weights are used, and athletes are not permitted to allow the weights to touch the ground except when rotating major stations.

The stations operate with the following pattern.

1. The command is given, "bars up," on which command athletes #3 and #4 lift the bar into position for athlete #1 to perform the exercise.
2. The starting whistle blows and athlete #1 performs the movements of the exercise for the timed interval (25 seconds).
3. When the whistle is blown ending the work interval, athletes #3 and #4 take the bar from #1 and hold it in place until #2 is in place and ready to begin the exercise.
4. When all stations are ready, the starting whistle is blown.

5. After the work interval starts, athlete #1 changes places with athlete #3 and gets ready to be the spotter and take the bar from athlete #2. This frees athlete #3 to prepare to be the next worker.
6. When the groups complete 3 cycles, or 13 work intervals, the command "bars down" is given. All groups rotate to the next station and the cycle is repeated.

If at any time any bar in the room touches the ground during the 12-station mini-circuit, it will be audibly apparent to all. The penalty is normally that the group of four must repeat that 12-station circuit after the workout.

This system may seem to be too structured or deliberate. In reality it works well, and if it is to be used by a team involved in heavy contact the day after a competition, it need not be introduced as a discipline or punishment program. In such cases, the athletes who are stiff and sore should begin by jogging an easy ½ mile before the circuit. Some athletes may not be able to perform the strength exercises (even with very light weight) without a spotter. The circuit provides helpers who can aid the athlete by reducing some of the resistance, thus getting needed movement and circulation to sore muscles. Soreness here does not refer to injured (pulled, strained, or torn) muscles. There are no rules in the circuit concerning pauses or repetition number, so the athletes can move slowly if desired. Since the bars cannot touch the ground, they are dependent on each other for help, and forced to concentrate on a minimal level. The discipline-concentration circuit is a light, low intensity circuit in which athletes can chat about the previous day's or night's activities while getting the soreness out.

Some details to set up the stations:

1. Major stations can be numbered with larger numbers of a different color than mini-stations.
2. On stations where the on deck athlete is not involved in an exercise, an "X" with athletic tape on the floor can mark the best place to wait.
3. The bench press should be performed on a flat bench with no weight rack. This ensures that the athlete performing the exercise will not put the bar on the rack.
4. The power clean must be performed keeping the bar approximately 6" off the floor. If this becomes a problem, have the athletes do hang cleans. *Hang cleans* are performed by lowering the bar to just above the knees.
5. The incline press should be performed on an incline bench without a rack if possible. If the bar is set on the ground behind the incline, the workers can change places more quickly.
6. The squat should also be performed without a rack. Place the bar in front of the worker. The on deck athlete waits behind. Do *not* attempt to do heavy squats in this circuit.
7. Wrist curls are performed using 2 barbells, a flat bench, and 2 stools. A stool is placed at each end of the bench. An athlete sits on each stool, facing another athlete seated on the end of the bench. The athletes do not need to move on the mini-circuit rotations. They simply hand the bar to their teammate directly across from them. Each athlete gets 6 sets of wrist curls before changing stations.
8. The neck station requires two neck machines—one for side-to-side (right and left lateral flexion and extension), and one for back-to-front flexion and extension. A station for shoulder shrugs and a rest or on deck spot are also necessary.
9. The leg exercise station utilizes 4 machines: 1) leg extension machine, 2) leg curl machine, 3) calf machine, and 4) abduction-adduction machine.

Plyometric Training

Plyometrics is best described as a special type of strength training utilizing the myostatic reflex (stretch reflex) within the muscle to develop maximum explosiveness or explosive power.[40] It was first employed by Russian and German coaches and was proposed as an effective way of bridging the gap between pure strength and functional (usable) strength or explosive power. There are several ways in which the myostatic reflex can be utilized in athletics. One way is in PNF stretching (Chapter 5), as a response to an isometric contraction. Another way is to pre-stretch the muscle slowly to cause a more forceful contraction. A third technique is the quick concentric response to rapid eccentric contraction of the muscle as used in plyometric training. "The faster the muscle is forced to lengthen, the greater tension it exerts. The rate of stretch is more important than the magnitude of the stretch. In order to achieve high level results from the eccentric contraction (pre-stretching), the concentric contraction which follows must take place immediately."[21]

From this statement, it can be reasoned that plyometric training consists of quick concentric responses to rapid eccentric contractions. Therefore the method used in plyometrics is to jump, land, and jump again as quickly as possible. The athlete might pretend that he is landing on a hot plate. Plyometrics can be beneficial to any sport where explosive movements predominate. Examples are football, volleyball, sprinting, and the throwing and jumping events in track. *Caution:* Junior high or any athletes under 16 years of age should *not* do plyometrics. For depth jumps a maximum of 40 take-offs per workout is recommended for even the best conditioned athletes.[48] Twenty to thirty take-offs are maximum for less prepared athletes. In all plyometric exercises, begin at a low level (1 or 2 sets per workout) and increase very slowly on a day by day basis. Beginners start off-season with one day per week, 20–30 total reps per workout. Build up to 30–40 jump reps per workout, then twice a week. Some research has recommended 10–15 minutes rest between depth jumping exercises.

One-Leg Hopping

One-leg hopping is done at moderate speed for 20 yards on one leg, then 20 yards on the other. Attempts should be made to cover as much distance as possible on each hop.

Two-Leg Hopping

Two-leg hopping is done at moderate speed for twenty yards, using the arms as well as the legs to achieve maximum distance. These are standing broad jumps, done without falling forward upon landing.

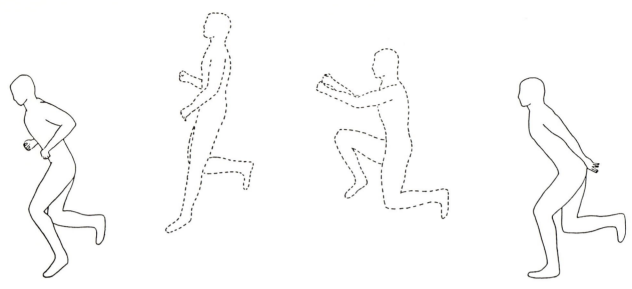

Figure 4.4 One-Leg Hopping (Plyometrics)

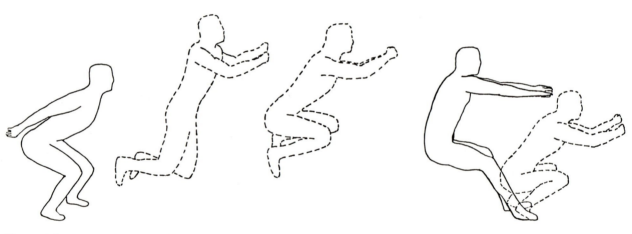

Figure 4.5 Two-Leg Hopping (Plyometrics)

Speed Hopping

Speed hopping is one- and two-leg hopping done at fast speed. Two-legged hops are done keeping the feet together. Continuous bursts are performed covering 20 yards, twice. The distance is gradually increased to 40 yards.

Alternating Sprinting and One-Leg Hopping

The athlete sprints 25 yards, then hops 25 yards on one leg at full speed, alternating the two activities for up to a mile. Hopping legs are alternated after each sprint.

Power Bounding

Power bounding is performed by jumping as high and as far as possible. Each bound is a maximum effort. The distance should be increased gradually from 30–100 yards. Athletes should not race each other, but should concentrate on each explosive effort. It is best if this is done on a soft landing area.

Depth Jumping

Depth jumping is performed by jumping (actually stepping) off a box onto a mat and then immediately exploding back onto a box, or simply into the air as high as possible. The first set of depth jumps should be done from a lower height (26″) as a warm-up. The following sets are done from a height of 44″, down to the mat, then up onto the 26″ box. Three or four sets of 10 repetitions are completed twice each week during off-season.

Figure 4.6 Power Bounding (Plyometrics)

SUMMARY

This chapter contains basic information on muscle contractions; types of weight training; the essentials of strength training for athletes; the elements of intensity, frequency, and duration as applied to strength training; and the methods used to devise strength programs. The strength training circuits to be used in specific sports programs (Part II) are described. The reader is encouraged to refer back to these descriptions in implementing specific conditioning programs for these sports.

REFERENCES

1. Allerheiligen, William. 1982. "A Basic Program Guide to Beginning, Intermediate, and Advanced Strength Cycling," *NSCA Journal* 4(5):33–34.

2. Anderson, Tim, and Jay T. Kearney. 1982. "Effects of Three Resistance Training Programs on Muscular Strength and Absolute and Relative Endurance," *Research Quarterly for Exercise and Sport* 53:1–7.

3. Ball, Russ. 1988. "Equipment Utilization and Construction: The Plyometric Box," *NSCA Journal* 9:79–80.

4. Battig, W. F. 1969. "Facilitation and Interference," *Acquisition of Skill*. New York: Academic Press.

5. Berger, Richard. 1962. "Effects of Varied Weight Training Programs on Strength," *Research Quarterly* 33:168–181.

6. Berger, Richard, and Billy Hardage. 1967. "Effects of Maximum Loads for Each of Ten Repetitions on Strength Improvement," *Research Quarterly* 38:715–718.

7. Calloway, William. 1978. "Plyometric Training for Greater Speed," *Scholastic Coach* 48:9–11.

8. Chu, Donald A. 1984–1989. "Jumping into Plyometrics," *NSCA Journal* (series of articles) 6(5):30–31 to 10:82.

9. Chui, Edward F. 1950. "The Effect of Systematic Weight Training on Athletic Power," *Research Quarterly* 21:188–194.

10. Clarke, David H. 1973. "Adaptations in Strength and Muscular Endurance Resulting from Exercise," *Exercise and Sports Sciences Reviews,* Vol. 1. New York: Academic Press.

11. Clarke, H. Harrison. 1974. "Strength Development and Motor-Sports Improvement," *Physical Fitness Research Digest* 4:1–17.

12. "Coaches Roundtable: The Squat and Its Application to Athletic Performance," 1984. *NSCA Journal* 6(3):10–60.

13. Counsilman, James E. 1976. "The Importance of Speed in Exercise," *Scholastic Coach* 46:94–99.

14. Darden, Ellington. 1972. "Misconceptions about Weight Training," *Muscular Development* 9:26–49.

15. Darden, Ellington, 1973. "Weight Training Systems in the USA," *Journal of Physical Education* 70:72–76.

16. Dickinson, J. A. 1976. *Behavioral Analysis in Sport*. London: Lepus.

17. Dintiman, George B. 1964. "Effects of Various Weight Training Programs on Running Speed," *Research Quarterly* 35:456–458.

18. Dintiman, George B. 1971. "Techniques and Methods of Developing Speed in Athletic Performance," *Proceedings: International Symposium on the Art and Science of Coaching*. Ontario, Canada: F. I. Productions.

19. Fleck, Steven J., and William J. Kraemer. 1988. *Designing Resistance Training Programs*. Champaign, IL: Human Kinetics.

20. Fleck, Steven J., and William J. Kraemer. 1988. "Resistance Training: Basic Principles," (part 1 of 4) *Physician and Sportsmedicine* 16:160–171.

21. Gambetta, Vern. 1978. "Plyometric Training," *Track and Field Quarterly Review* 78:58–61.

22. Hoolahan, Paul. 1980. "Strength and Conditioning for Basketball: The University of North Carolina Program," *NSCA Journal* 2(4):20–21.

23. Jacobsen, Bert. 1981. "Reach Failure to Gain Success," *NSCA Journal* 3:24–25.

24. Karpovich, Peter V. 1951. "Incidence of Injuries in Weight Lifting," *Journal of Physical Education* 48:71–72.

25. Klinzing, James. 1984. "Sprint Training: Improving Sprint Speed for All Athletes," *NSCA Journal* 6:32–33.

26. Knapp, B. 1963. *Skill in Sport*. London: Routledge & Kegan.

27. Kraemer, William J., et al. 1988. "A Review: Factors in Exercise Prescription of Resistance Training," *NSCA Journal* 10(5):36–41.

28. Kroll, William A. 1981. "Essentials for Strength Training for Athletes," *NSCA Journal* 3(4):32–33.

29. Kroll, William A., and Janet Kroll. 1981. *Strength Training Chart*. Champaign, IL: Kroll & Kroll.

30. Kroll, William A. 1982. "An Analysis of the Rate of Strength Development of the Predicted Strength Gain in Collegiate Football Players," *NSCA Journal* 4(4):34A.

31. Kroll, William A. 1983. "Conditioning for Basketball," *NSCA Journal* 5(2):24–26.

32. Kroll, William A. 1983. *Physical Conditioning for Winning Football*. Dubuque, IA: Wm. C. Brown Publishers.

33. Lilian, Gary L. 1976. "Optimal Weight Training," *Management Science in Sports,* Vol. 4. New York: North Holland Publishing.

34. Lundin, Phil. 1985. "A Review of Plyometric Training," *NSCA Journal* 7(3):69–74.

35. McFarlane, Brent 1985. "Plyometrics: Special Strength—Horizontal or Vertical," *NSCA Journal* 6:64–66.

36. Moffroid, Mary T., and Robert H. Wipple. 1970. "Specificity of Speed and Exercises," *Journal of American Physical Therapy Association* 50:1692–1699.

37. Murray, James, and Peter V. Karpovich. 1956. *Weight Training in Athletics*. Englewood Cliffs, NJ: Prentice-Hall.

38. O'Shea, Patrick J. 1976. *Scientific Principles and Methods of Strength Fitness,* 2d ed. Reading, MA: Addison-Wesley.

39. Pedemonte, James. 1981. "Training of General, Specific, and Special Strength: A Key to Improved Performance in Sport," *NSCA Journal* 3(6):54–55.

40. Radcliffe, James C. and Robert C. Farentino. 1985. *Plyometrics: Explosive Power Training*. Champaign, IL: Human Kinetics.

41. Rasch, Philip J. 1982. *Weight Training,* 4th ed. Dubuque, IA: Wm. C. Brown Publishers.

42. "Roundtable: Practical Considerations for Utilizing Plyometrics" (part 1). 1986. *NSCA Journal* 8(4):14–22.

43. "Roundtable: Practical Considerations for Utilizing Plyometrics" (part 2). 1986. *NSCA Journal* 8(4):14–24.

44. Stone, Michael H., et al. 1981. "Hypothetical Model for Strength Training," *Journal of Sports Medicine and Physical Fitness* 21:342–351.

45. "Specific Power in Jumping and Throwing—A Summary of Development in Plyometric Exercises." 1974. *Modern Athlete and Coach* 2:7–8.

46. Starck. A. 1982. "Abuse of the Overload Principle: A Physiological Basis for Cycling," *NSCA Journal* 4(1):36–38.

47. Verhowshansky, Yuri. 1969. "Perspectives in the Improvement of Speed-Strength Preparation of Jumpers," *Yessis Review of Soviet Physical Education and Sports* 4:28–29.

48. Verhowshansky, Yuri, and U. V. Chernousov. 1974. "Jumps in the Training of a Sprinter," *Yessis Review of Soviet Physical Education and Sports* 9:62–64.

49. Vermeil, Al, and Don Chu. 1982. "Periodization of Strength Training for Professional Football," *NSCA Journal* 4(3):54–55.

50. Walderyak, Paul E. 1984. "Training: Super Circuit Training," 67:38–40.

51. Westcott, Wayne L. 1974. "Effects of Varied Frequencies of Weight Training on the Development of Strength," Masters thesis. Penn State University.

52. Westcott, Wayne L. 1981. *Strength Fitness: Physiological Principles and Training Techniques*. Dubuque, IA: Wm. C. Brown Publishers.

53. Wickstrom, Ralph L. 1963. "Weight Training and Flexibility," *Johper* 34:61–62.

54. Wilmore, Jack H., and David L. Costill. 1988. *Training for Sport and Activity,* 2d ed. Dubuque, IA: Wm. C. Brown Publishers.

55. Wilt, Fred. 1976. "Plyometric Exercises," *Track Techniques* 64:2024–2025.

56. Young, Warren B. 1987. "Track and Field: The Triple Jump and Plyometrics," *NSCA Journal* 9:22–24.

57. Zorbas, William S., and Peter V. Karpovich. 1951. "The Effect of Weight Lifting Upon the Speed of Muscular Contraction," *Research Quarterly* 22:145–148.

CHAPTER
FIVE

FLEXIBILITY, WARM-UP, AND STRETCHING

In the first edition of this book the authors stressed the importance and necessity of stretching exercises for athletes. It was recommended that stretching be conducted both pre- and post-exercise, either in practice or in competition. Unfortunately, very little space was allotted to the concepts of flexibility, stretching, and warming-up. In the intervening years stretching exercises have become very much "in vogue" for athletes at all levels of competition. Stretching has become a very common pre-event ritual for the 10K weekend runner as well as for the professional athlete in team sports. Warming-up and stretching are not entirely new practices for athletes, but a serious examination of those techniques is fairly recent. deVries was one of the first exercise scientists to stress the importance of flexibility in sports conditioning.[8]

While it is gratifying to the authors to see increased attention to stretching as a part of preparation for sport, it is evident that confusion has developed concerning the relationships between warming-up, stretching exercises, and flexibility. A number of stretching and flexibility systems appears to be vying for prominence in sport. As so often occurs in scientific study, it may be that several systems are effective in developing flexibility. It is clear to the authors that there is a need to distinguish between the objectives of warming-up exercises versus stretching exercises, even when they are done together as was suggested in the earlier edition of this book. The authors have added this chapter in order to address the very questions and problems indicated here. Also included is a greatly expanded list of stretching exercises and some suggested stretching programs.

FLEXIBILITY

Flexibility is the range of motion in a joint or series of joints. Most interest in flexibility in the past has involved physical therapy or other medically related applications designed to rehabilitate patients. Flexibility has also been recognized recently as one of the components of physical fitness. Two kinds of flexibility have been distinguished—static flexibility and dynamic flexibility. Static flexibility is determined by measuring the range of motion (ROM) about a joint or series of joints. The body is not in motion, nor is there any effort to move quickly as the ROM of a joint is measured "statically." An example would be to reach slowly toward the toes with the knees straight, in a sitting position (the sit and reach). Dynamic flexibility, on the other hand, implies moving flexibility and may also involve high-speed action. The simultaneous leap and kick of the dancer is an example of dynamic flexibility. It should be evident that most athletic events involved dynamic ROM.

Flexibility is usually measured in the static mode and a variety of instruments have been used to measure it. The simplest instrument for measuring flexibility has been the goniometer, which measures the angle of the ROM. The elgon, or electrogoniometer, is a more sophisticated instrument that can also measure dynamic flexibility angles. The Leighton flexometer can be strapped onto a limb and can measure the ROM in slow or rapid movement.[15] Sit and reach-type tests, or floor-touch tests, have also been used as screening tests for flexibility, and require no sophisticated equipment.

The Nature of Flexibility

A number of anatomic factors determine flexibility. The most important factor, for stretching programs, is the muscles. Flexibility at a joint will be reduced if the muscles operating at the joint are tight or shortened. This can occur from lack of use or overuse and also from emotional anxiety, which can lead to muscular tension. The myotatic stretch reflex of the muscle also operates when the muscle is rapidly stretched, as in the knee jerk. The rapidly stretching muscle sends messages to the nervous system, which quickly signals the muscle to contract. In the tight or shortened muscle the stretch reflex will operate early as the muscle is stretched and thus inhibits stretch. The stretch reflex is responsible for possible tear or injury. When the stretch reflex is engaged early in the stretch, the stretched muscle contracts, and full stretch and relaxation are impossible. In this situation, the muscle is fighting against itself.

The connective tissue in and around the joint is also responsible for determining flexibility. In addition to the muscle, ligaments, the joint capsule itself and tendons are also influential in determining flexibility.[12] The more elastic the joint connective tissue is, the greater the ROM. It is important to note, however, that most efforts to increase flexibility through stretching are directed to the muscle. Ligaments and tendons do not have the elasticity of muscle tissue; hence it is undesirable to produce too much slack in them. If they become overstretched or injured, their ability to maintain the integrity of the joint is greatly reduced. Although there are no clear standards for optimal flexibility at this time, no particular advantage comes from possessing "excessive" flexibility. Excessive flexibility in the joint might even be associated with a higher potential for joint injury.

One of the proposed causes of muscle injuries is a lack of flexibility. The tight or shortened muscle that has not relaxed, or that is in a state of myotatic stretch reflex, may be more susceptible to injury or tear. It is frequently suggested that the unyielding antagonist, such as a thin hamstring, is overpowered and injured by the more powerful agonist, in this case the quadriceps group. In a cold or unrelaxed state the tight muscle would be more prone to injury. Unfortunately, there is not a great deal of clinical or experimental data to confirm the suggestion. It would certainly appear prudent at this time to maintain flexibility and avoid practices that tighten or shorten the muscle.

Certain factors associated with flexibility do give us additional information about its nature. For some time it has been known that flexibility tends to decrease with age, even in children. It has also been noted that females tend to be more flexible than males. The precise reasons for sex differences are unknown, but they could be attributed to different activity patterns. Body build, on the other hand, does not appear to contribute to differences in flexibility.

One of the most firmly established characteristics of flexibility is its specificity.[4] This means that in any individual, good shoulder flexibility may not be accompanied by good knee flexibility. The same joint on one side of the body may be more or less flexible than its counterpart on the other side of the body. This also implies that there is no general characteristic of flexibility. Level of activity has been associated with flexibility, and it may also contribute to some of the specific patterns of flexibility for individuals or groups. As a result, stretching will aid only the joints being stretched.

Efforts to increase flexibility through stretching programs have been successful. Greater ROM can result through systematic stretching programs.[4] Athletes generally are more flexible than nonathletic groups, but there are differences among sports groups. Baseball players and swimmers have been found to be very flexible, weight lifters are more flexible than normal, while wrestlers tend to be less flexible among athletic groups. Within sports groups, specific patterns of flexibility are related to frequent or unique joint movements in those sports.

The effects of increased flexibility on sports performance may range from obvious to subtle. There is face validity to the need for excellent flexibility in dance, gymnastics, diving, and swimming. Those sports have an aesthetic component, and increased flexibility obviously enhances performance since it is part of the scoring system. The contributions of flexibility to the performance in many team sports is less obvious. Athletes in baseball, basketball, football, and other team sports frequently exhibit excellent flexibility. Their performances may be aesthetically pleasing, especially in slow-motion instant replay, but they are judged solely on effect—did the player catch the ball or make the basket? A few efforts have been made to relate flexibility to physical performance, and they have generally been successful as long as the flexibility is specific to the sports event.[6]

Temperature, both environmental and internal, appears to have an effect on flexibility. Flexibility seems to be enhanced in a warm environment; most athletes have experienced that effect. In addition, some warm-up or prior stretch results in better flexibility when it is subsequently measured. The effects of warming-up and its relationship to stretching and flexibility are also important to understand.

WARM-UP

Stretching exercises do not necessarily warm up the athlete. Their purpose is to relax and lengthen the muscle through stretching and, eventually, to increase flexibility. Warming-up, on the other hand, serves to increase blood flow, elevate the temperature of the muscle, and lubricate the joints via joint fluids. In the whole body sense, warm-up also serves to elevate metabolism by increasing heart rate, respiratory rate, and oxygen uptake.[3] As indicated, warming-up also serves to increase flexibility, since flexibility is enhanced in heated muscles. Most stretching experts now agree that a warm-up period should be done *prior to* stretching.[17,18]

Warming-up exercises can consist of rhythmic calisthenics and jogging if the main purpose is to elevate metabolism and warm the muscles. Warming-up exercises can precede stretching or be combined with stretching. Warming-up exercises should gradually increase in vigor just as repeated stretching seeks to lengthen the muscle more with each effort. The value of warming-up is not without some controversy, and it is appropriate here to review the information available.

The effects of warm-up listed here are not controversial. The effects on muscles, joints, and metabolism are rather clear. The established benefits of reduced injury or greater safety for exercising adults are not well documented. The objectives of warming the muscles, based on physiological effects, are primarily related to reduced injury potential, increased flexibility, and better performance. Adults are also cautioned to undergo whole body warm-up to elevate metabolism and to prepare their cardiorespiratory systems for more intense activity. There are also questions to be raised about the nature of the warm-up and the subsequent performance, as well as injury and safety.

Many different warming-up techniques have been employed in studies of warm-up.[16] Nonspecific (unrelated) and even passive techniques have not proved effective in improving performance. They would include hot showers, massage, local heating, and mild calisthenics. Specific (related) and more vigorous types of warm-ups have generally had a positive effect on performance. They usually involve a vigorous period of actual practice of the sport skill. Much of the value of actual practice of a motor skill prior to competition involves a renewal of the psychomotor skill. This is evident in such things as the baseball pitcher's warm-up, batting practice, basketball pre-game shooting, and other related practice. For those events that require more strength, power, aerobic, or anaerobic effort than skill, the vigor of the warm-up appears to be important. In such cases the pre-event warm-up should be vigorous enough to produce the physiological effects mentioned. This means elevated muscle and/or body temperature. Perhaps no area of exercise science has been so thoroughly studied yet remains so controversial as the area of warm-up. Since the preponderance of evidence, both research and clinical, supports warm-up, the authors recommend that it follow the guidelines listed.

One last point to be discussed about warm-up involves the time sequence. Depending upon the environment, the effects of warming-up can be expected to last approximately one-half hour, and should be planned accordingly. A lengthy period of inactivity (sitting on the bench, or half-time rest) will result in a cooling-off. Additional warm-up and stretching are required in such instances. In very cold weather the warm-up effect may not last thirty minutes; in hot weather it may last much longer.

STRETCHING

Stretching has both a short-term and a long-term effect. The short-term effects include increased ROM, lengthening and relaxing the muscle, and reducing the soreness and/or injury potential. These are the reasons for stretching pre- and post-exercise. These objectives are related to flexibility, but increased flexibility does not permanently occur after a few stretching sessions. The long-term effect of repeated stretching sessions, done in relation to exercise or at other times, is an increase in flexibility. The evidence is discussed in greater detail, but it is important to note the distinction between the long-term and short-term effects of stretching. Both of those effects have potential for improved performance.

The renewed interest in stretching and flexibility has resulted in more research focused on stretching techniques. Several thorough reviews have covered the areas of warm-up, stretching, and flexibility.[6,10,18,20] The three major techniques of stretching are 1) ballistic, 2) static, and 3) partner-assisted. There is increasing evidence that partner-assisted stretching is the most effective means of increasing flexibility.[11] Despite the growing evidence, many stretching experts prefer static stretching because it does not require a trained partner, and can be easily learned. Although ballistic stretching is the least preferred because of the potential for injury, it is a necessary part of warming-up for most athletes.

Ballistic Stretching

Ballistic stretching includes those rapid stretching movements that are characterized as "bouncing" or "bobbing." Rapid bends to a toe touch are an example of ballistic stretching. Some vigorous warm-up calisthenics involve ballistic stretch. Preparation for vigorous activity, as has been established previously, requires a vigorous warm-up, often of the actual event. Flexibility programs that have used ballistic stretching have proved successful in increasing flexibility.[6] Despite that success, most sports scientists recommend static stretching programs because they are less likely to produce the myotatic stretch reflex.

Static Stretching

The term *static stretching* is usually associated with the work of deVries.[8,9] The technique involves a slow stretch and "hold" of the stretched position from several seconds to a minute. The major advantage of the static stretch technique is that it will not elicit the myotatic stretch reflex if done properly. A major reason for increasing the length of muscles—and hence flexibility—is to avoid the stretch reflex. The tight or shortened muscle will respond with contraction to rapid stretch. This suggests that ballistic stretching, although generally effective, is stretching a muscle in partial contraction. This is ineffective in producing a full ROM and totally ineffective in relaxing the muscle. The very technique employed (ballistic) to reduce injury could also lead to injury—and it has.

Most static stretching adherents emphasize the importance of *relaxing* the stretched muscle.[2,9,19] Relaxation enables the stretched muscle to cease stretch reflex impulses coming from the muscle spindles. Anderson recommends a technique that involves two parts.[2] First the muscle is stretched in the *easy* stage for 20 to 30 seconds. By this time the muscle should have relaxed and the stretch reflex halted. The easy stage is followed by a *developmental* stage, which involves an added stretch-and-hold for 30 seconds. At no time does the technique involve a drastic or painful stretch, and the entire period of stretch involves 50 to 60 seconds. Anderson's technique is highly applicable to sport, and he illustrates specialized stretching programs for specific sports.[2]

Partner-Assisted Stretching

The partner-assisted stretching techniques have come essentially from therapeutic applications in rehabilitation. Usually the therapist aided the patient in achieving full ROM following injury or surgery. The two major forms of assisted stretching are the Active Controlled Stretch (ACS) and PNF, the Proprioceptive Neuromuscular Facilitation.

ACS. While static stretching adherents agree on the use of the slow, relaxed stretch, they differ slightly on the application of the stretch. Shelton, a pioneer in developing flexibility programs for therapeutic as well as athletic purposes, recommends an Active Controlled Stretch (ACS).[19] The starting position is important in ACS, as the muscle to be stretched should be in a gravity-assisted position. When the biceps is contracted (flexion at the elbow) in the standing position, it is in an antigravity position and the triceps can be stretched and relaxed in a gravity-assisted position. In that same position it is difficult to stretch the biceps or get it to relax, since it is constantly counteracting gravity (antigravity).

Shelton maintains that the two-joint muscles are more susceptible to shortening and tightening. They include, among anothers, the hamstrings and the gastrocnemius (calf). Shelton also suggests the addition of

manual assistance if the contracting muscle is not strong enough to adequately stretch the tight muscle. A great deal of caution must be advised, since manual assistance is usually a therapeutic technique and too vigorous a push can trigger the stretch reflex or injure the muscle. The authors do not recommend the use of manual assistance when it is employed by young athletes with limited knowledge of anatomy. The person using manual assistance to stretch must be quick to reverse the movement when the stretched muscle produces a myotatic stretch reflex.

PNF. Proprioceptive Neuromuscular Facilitation (PNF) is primarily a therapeutic technique that has found its way into sport stretching programs.[7,13,18] The technique is credited to Knott and Voss.[14]

PNF technique follows a specific routine with a partner.

1. The muscle to be stretched (agonist) is placed on a stretch with the assistance of the partner, taking 5 seconds.

2. The muscle is then relaxed for 5 seconds.

3. The same muscle is contracted isometrically with resistance from the partner for 5 seconds.

4. The muscle is relaxed again for 5 seconds.

5. The opposing muscle (antagonist) is contracted against the partner's resistance.

6. The muscle is stretched with the assistance of the partner, and it should yield a greater ROM than the first stretch.

PNF has been found to be more effective than static stretching for increasing ROM.[11] The most effective PNF technique involves a contract-relax-antagonist contract sequence, which is similar to the technique just described. It is also the principle employed by Shelton in ACS. The use of partner-assisted stretching requires a partner who is trained in identifying the stretch reflex, and can avoid injury.

It should be noted that the purpose of increasing flexibility is to reduce the potential for sports injury, and to contribute to sports performance. Flexibility well in excess of the normal range has no particular advantage either in preventing injuries or in aiding sports performance. Joint laxity and extreme ROM may even be associated with an increased susceptibility to joint injury. Greatly reduced flexibility may be associated with a greater incidence of muscle strains.

STRETCHING PRINCIPLES

Other stretching techniques, including Yoga and Kung Fu, have been used in sports flexibility programs. The name of the stretching technique is less important than the application of sound stretching principles.

1. The purpose of stretching is to lengthen and relax the muscle and ultimately to increase flexibility. Like strength, there will always be individual differences in flexibility, thus flexibility training should not be a contest.[1] Stretching programs should be individualized as much as possible.
2. Slow, static stretching is recommended. When the stretch is held for 30 to 60 seconds, it gives time for the muscle to relax and the stretch reflex to dissipate, both pre- or post-activity.
3. Warming-up requires vigorous related activity to be effective. The purpose of warm-up is to elevate muscle and body temperature as well as metabolism. Vigorous ballistic activity may be part of the warm-up.
4. Since flexibility is specific, the application of stretching exercises, should include specific muscle groups used in your sport or event. Some general flexibility exercises should be done for each of the major areas of the body, starting from the head and working down: neck, upper body, trunk, back, and legs.

WARM-UP AND STRETCHING EXERCISES

Figure 5.1 Deep Breathing

WARM-UP EXERCISES

Warm-up exercises, as previously mentioned, are most effective if they are vigorous and actually related to the activity to follow. Several warm-up exercises are listed here, and they are designed to cover whole body warm-up. Specific, task-related warm-ups are suggested, just as the athlete should select stretching exercises that are aimed at specific joints and muscles involved in subsequent practice or competition.

Deep Breathing

Stand with the stomach in, pelvis tucked under, and knees slightly bent. From a standing position, inhale fully as the arms are raised in front to the overhead position. Exhale fully as the arms are lowered to the sides. Repeat 10 times.

Arm Circles

Extend arms to the side, shoulder height. Rotate arms in tight (6″) circles, reversing direction after 10 counts. Repeat twice.

Chest Stretcher

Extend arms forward, shoulder height. Pull arms back vigorously with bobbing motion and four counts. Extend arms to the front and repeat 5 to 10 times.

Burpee

Bend over and place hands on the floor directly in front of the feet. With weight on the hands, thrust legs straight out to the back. From this arm support position, thrust feet back to original position and stand erect. Repeat 5 to 10 times.

Figure 5.2 Arm Circles

Figure 5.3 Chest Stretcher

Chapter 5

Figure 5.4 Burpee

Figure 5.5 Running in Place

Jumping Jacks

From a standing position, jump up and bring arms overhead to the sides as the feet spread to the side. Return to starting position on the second count. This exercise should be done rapidly to a 1–2–3–4 count. Repeat 5 to 10 counts of 1–2–3–4.

Running in Place

Start with a slow jog in place, gradually increasing the speed and height of knee action. Running in place can continue for 1 to 3 minutes.

STRETCHING—WHOLE BODY

The stretching exercises have been organized into stretches for different areas of the body. The coach or athlete should select stretching exercises for all the major areas of the body, while also selecting specific stretches that work the muscles and joints involved in the specific sport.

Relaxation Stretch

Lying on the back, gradually relax all areas of the body. Begin by loosely shaking the hands, ankles, arms, and legs until the entire body is loosened and relaxed. All of the body parts should become limp and relaxed with a feeling of great heaviness. This is an excellent technique for getting complete relaxation prior to competition, as well as for relaxing the muscles and making them less resistant to stretching.

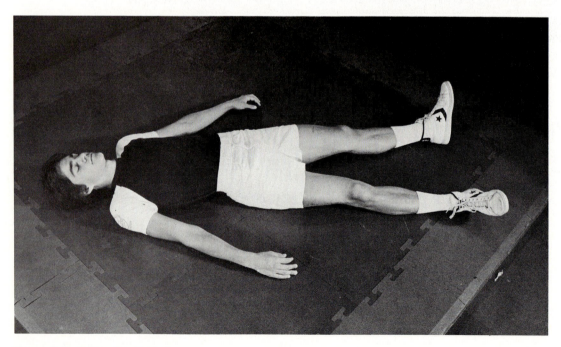

Figure 5.6 Relaxation Stretch

Figure 5.7 Neck Rotation

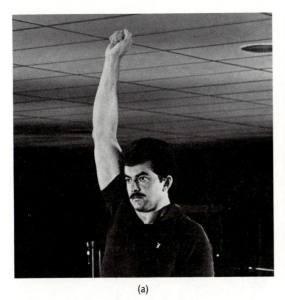

(a)   (b)

Figure 5.8 Tricep and Shoulder Stretch

STRETCHING—NECK AND UPPER BODY

Neck Rotation

From a standing position, rotate the head very slowly in one direction for 4 counts. Reverse direction for 4 counts. Repeat 2 to 3 times in each direction. Rotate head forward and side to side, but not backward.

Tricep and Shoulder Stretch

This stretch is done in the standing position. First, the arms are extended straight over head so that the inside of the elbow is next to the head (fig. 5.8a). Then reach across and grasp the elbow of the arm and shoulder to be stretched. The elbow is flexed and then slowly pulled behind the head until the shoulder and tricep stretch is felt (fig. 5.8b).

Figure 5.9 Shoulder and Side Stretch

Shoulder and Side Stretch

This stretch is done from the same position as the tricep and shoulder stretch. The upper arm is held against the head (fig. 5.9). The stretch is then done by bending sideways from the hip, stretching the muscles of the side and rib cage.

Shoulder and Chest Stretch

This exercise is done in the standing position by first interlocking the fingers behind the back (fig. 5.10a). Bend forward, keeping the knees slightly bent and the elbows straight, lifting the arms as high as possible (fig. 5.10b). This can be done with the palms either up or down (fig. 5.10c).

(a)   (b)   (c)

Figure 5.10 Shoulder and Chest Stretch

Figure 5.11 Assisted Chest and Shoulder Stretch

Assisted Chest and Shoulder Stretch

This stretch can also be performed from the sitting position with an assistant. The athlete's arms are extended behind him while the assistant holds the wrists and lifts them gently until the stretch is felt in the shoulders and/or chest. Keep the head as upright as possible.

Overhead Shoulder Stretch

From a standing position, extend the arms in front of the body, interlocking the fingers (fig. 5.12a) and turning the palms outward (fig. 5.12b). Raise the arms overhead until the stretch is felt.

(a)   (b)

Figure 5.12   Overhead Shoulder Stretch

Assisted PNF Shoulder and Chest Stretch

The athlete begins in the sitting position with the assistant standing behind him. The arms are extended behind him with the elbows kept straight and the thumbs pointed upward. The assistant grasps the athlete's wrists and applies "easy" pressure, pulling the arms together. The athlete attempts to move the arms in the opposite direction on the "flex" command. On "stretch" the assistant applies the inward pressure, repeating the stretch until the developmental stretch is felt.

STRETCHING—TRUNK AND GROIN

Side Bends

From a standing position, bend to the side with a *slow,* stretching motion as the arm reaches down the side of the leg. Hold position and relax. Alternate stretching one side and then the other. Repeat five times each side.

Trunk Rotation

Stand with knees slightly bent, pelvis tucked under. Standing with hands on hips, rotate slowly from the waist, with legs straight. Rotate four counts in one direction and then reverse for four counts or rotations. Repeat two to three full four counts on each side.

Kneeling Groin (Psoas) Stretch

Keeping the feet directly under the knee throughout exercise, press the back hip forward toward the heel of the front foot until stretch is felt in the front of hip. Body is in a straight line. Hold for 30 to 60 seconds. Repeat on other side.

The Yogi

This exercise is particularly good in preventing groin pulls and strains. It is done with the back straight in the sitting position by bringing the legs to a crossed position (Indian style), then placing the bottoms of the feet together. In this position the feet are kept close to the buttocks, and the stretch is done by pushing the knees down toward the floor. An advanced method is

Figure 5.13   Assisted PNF Shoulder and Chest Stretch

Figure 5.14   Side Bends

Figure 5.15 Trunk Rotation

Figure 5.16 Kneeling Groin (Psoas) Stretch

Figure 5.17 The Yogi

to have an assistant help develop flexibility in this area by placing a greater stretch on the area by pushing on the knees. This method is used by many high school and collegiate wrestlers and must be developed by slowly increasing the pressure over a number of training sessions.

Assisted PNF Lower Back and Groin Stretch

From the sitting position, with the legs as wide as possible, the athlete bends forward at the waist until an "easy" stretch is felt in the lower back and/or groin. The assistant then stands behind the athlete and places the hands just below the shoulder blades. On the "flex" command the athlete flexes the lower back by at-

Figure 5.18 Assisted PNF Lower Back and Groin Stretch

tempting to return the torso to the upright sitting position while the assistant provides resistance. The stretch is done by bending forward at the waist, the assistant adding the additional movement until the developmental stretch is achieved.

Assisted PNF Sitting Groin Stretch

The athlete takes the sitting position with the legs spread as wide as possible. A slight bend at the knee is permissible. The assistant places the hands inside the athlete's knees to provide resistance. The athlete attempts to push the legs together on the "flex" command. On the "stretch" command the assistant stretches the groin by placing pressure in the opposite direction.

Assisted PNF Lying Groin Stretch

The athlete performs this stretch by lying on the back with the legs extended straight upward and held apart. The assistant stands with the shins against the back of the athlete's thighs and places the hands on the inside of the athlete's knees. On "ready," the athlete attempts to spread the legs as far as possible. On the "flex" command the athlete attempts to bring the legs together.

The athlete is permitted only slight movement before the isometric contraction. The stretch is done by the athlete again, attempting to spread the legs as wide as possible while the assistant continues the movement until the developmental stretch is achieved.

Assisted PNF Hip Flexor Stretch

The athlete lies face down on the mat and bends the right leg at the knee so that the lower leg is perpendicular to the ground. The assistant kneels behind the athlete and places the athlete's ankle on the right shoulder and the right hand under the athlete's right knee. The assistant puts the left hand on the athlete's right buttock and holds it down while lifting the right knee so that the hip flexor receives an "easy" stretch. When the "flex" command is given, the athlete attempts to drive the right knee down to the ground. The assistant resists. On the "stretch" command the assistant lifts the knee again, holding the buttock down until the hip flexor receives a developmental stretch. The stretch is performed twice for each hip.

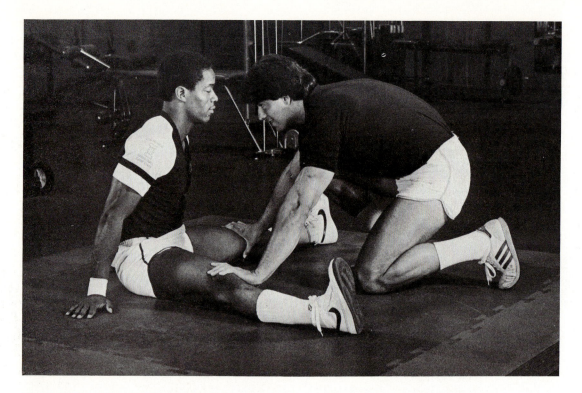

Figure 5.19   Assisted PNF Sitting Groin Stretch

Figure 5.20   Assisted PNF Lying Groin Stretch

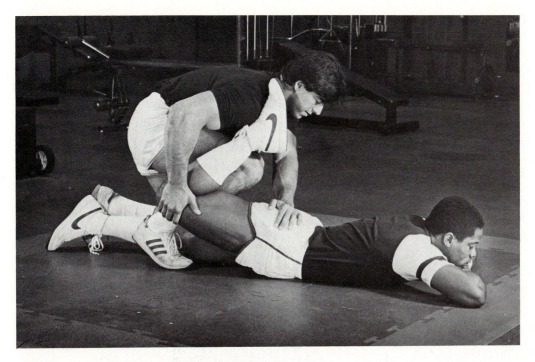

Figure 5.21 Assisted PNF Hip Flexor Stretch

Figure 5.22 Wide Straddle Stretch

Wide Straddle Stretch

From the seated position, with the head and back erect, the legs are spread as far as possible for the stretch. Keeping the torso erect, the athlete leans forward, stretching the groin and hamstring. The stretch is then held for 10 or more seconds, relaxed, and repeated.

STRETCHING—BACK AND LEGS

Head to Knee Stretch

This stretch is done from the sitting position. It stretches the lower back and hamstrings. The bottom of one foot is placed against the upper inside thigh of the opposite leg (fig. 5.23a). The foot of the extended leg is kept with the toe pointing straight up. The athlete sits up perfectly straight and then begins the stretch by bending forward at the waist. The athlete stretches by leaning forward at the waist only, not by lowering the head and reaching for the toe (fig. 5.23b).

Bending Forward Stretch

This exercise, which stretches the lower back and hamstrings, is done in the standing position. Variations are done with the legs together or apart. The head is lowered to the knees until tightness is felt. This position is held for 30 to 60 seconds. Return to the standing position and relax for several seconds; then repeat the exercise. The hands and arms may be used to help pull the head toward the knees. This should be done easily at first with light to moderately firm pressure. Keep knees slightly bent throughout the exercise.

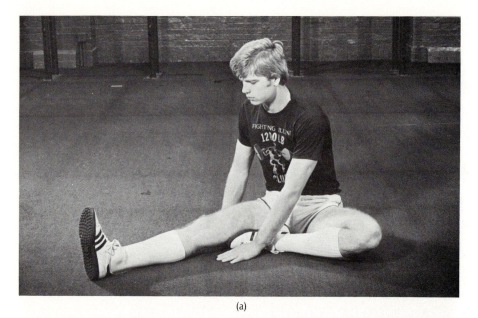

(a)

(b)

Figure 5.23 Head to Knee Stretch

Foot to Hand Stretch

This exercise stretches the muscles of the hips and lower back. It is done in the supine position with the arms extended perpendicular to the sides of the body. In the starting position the legs are together. Keeping the knees straight, one leg is moved diagonally across, flexing and rotating the hip until the foot touches the opposite hand. After the stretch the leg is returned to the starting position. After several seconds of rest the stretch is repeated with the other leg. As a variation, stretching slightly different muscles can be done by using both legs instead of only one. Bending the knee without attempting to touch the foot is another variation.

Lying Hamstring Stretch

Lying on the back, raise one leg as high as possible overhead with knee straight. Hold stretch. Repeat exercise with opposite leg and complete 5 reps with each leg. If the athlete encounters difficulty, bend the knee of the opposite leg.

Back Stretcher

Take position on hands and knees with back straight. Slide backward until sitting on heels with palms still on floor, arms straight, head down. Return to starting position while arching back slightly. Repeat 5 times.

Figure 5.24 Bending Forward Stretch

Figure 5.25 Foot to Hand Stretch

Flexibility, Warm-Up, and Stretching

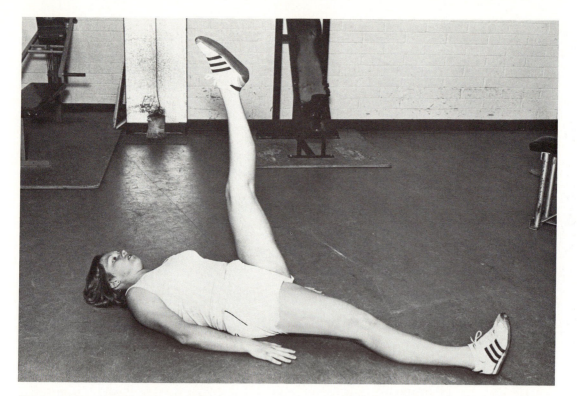

Figure 5.26 Lying Hamstring Stretch

Figure 5.27 Back Stretcher

Figure 5.28   Low-Back Stretch

Figure 5.29   Hanging Stretch

Figure 5.30   Head to Knee

Hanging Stretch

Many athletes, especially football linemen, can benefit from hanging from a bar. The time of the hang can be increased gradually from a few seconds up to one minute. This exercise helps stretch the vertebral joints. It relieves pressure on the discs between the vertebrae, and stretches the muscles of the back, the shoulders, the rib cage, and the sides.

Head to Knee (from the wide straddle seat position)

This exercise stretches the hamstrings and lower back. It is done with the seated straddle position as the starting point. Other variations are done with the legs together, or from the "hurdles" position.

Low-Back Stretch

Lying on back, grab below one knee with both hands. Bring knees to chest, holding 30 to 60 seconds. Repeat with other leg. Then bring both legs up to chest and hold again 30 to 60 seconds. Repeat 5 to 10 times.

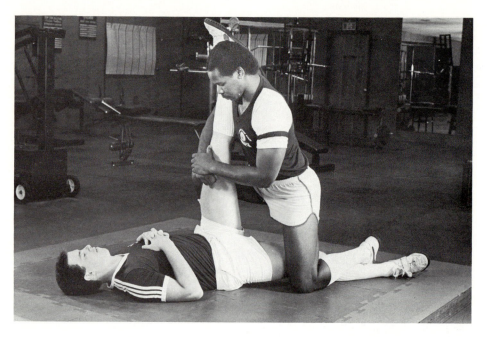

Figure 5.31   Assisted PNF Hamstring Stretch

Assisted PNF Hamstring Stretch

The athlete being stretched lies on the back and raises the right leg straight upward, perpendicular to the ground. The assistant kneels and puts the hands on the athlete's knee to be sure that it is kept straight during the stretch. The chest and shoulder are placed against the athlete's ankles and calf (fig. 5.31).

On the "ready" command the athlete locks the knee and flexes the hip as far as possible. On the "flex" command the athlete flexes the hamstring while the assistant resists, allowing only slight movement. On "stretch," the athlete flexes the hip while the assistant applies gradual pressure until the developmental stretch is achieved. The stretch is done twice on each hamstring.

Standing Quadricep Stretch

This stretch is done from the standing position; pulling the knee to the buttocks. Keep the pelvis tucked under and hold for 30 to 60 seconds. Repeat with opposite leg.

Prone Quadricep Stretch

Prone position, hips pushed into mat, face on the mat. Lying prone, the athlete bends the knee and grasps behind the ankle with the arm on the same side. Stretch slowly and hold for 30 to 60 seconds. Repeat with opposite leg after returning to original position. Repeat 3 to 5 times.

Figure 5.32   Standing Quadricep Stretch

STRETCHING—LOWER LEGS

Calf Stretch

This exercise is done by leaning against a wall, pole, or some other stationary object. From the standing position, approximately 3½ to 4½ feet from the wall, the athlete faces the wall and then leans against the wall, keeping the heels flat on the ground. The feet should be pointed straight ahead. One knee is then raised as

Figure 5.33 Prone Quadricep Stretch

Figure 5.34 Calf Stretch

close as possible toward the chest, placing a greater stretch on the calf muscles of the opposite leg. This is done with both legs and then repeated. Taller persons will need to stand farther from the wall. If an object to lean against is not available, this stretch can be done by placing one foot ahead of the other and then leaning forward, keeping the feet pointed straight ahead with the heel down (fig. 5.34).

Ankle Stretch

The ankle can be stretched in the sitting position by flexing the knee, grasping the foot, and then stretching the foot manually through each of its movements. They include rotation in both directions, flexion, extension, inversion, and eversion.

Figure 5.35 Ankle Stretch

Figure 5.36 Heel Cord Stretch

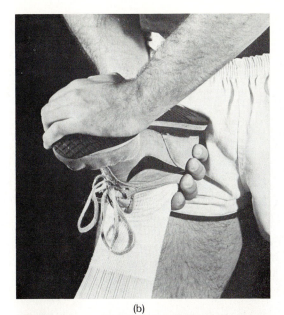
(b)

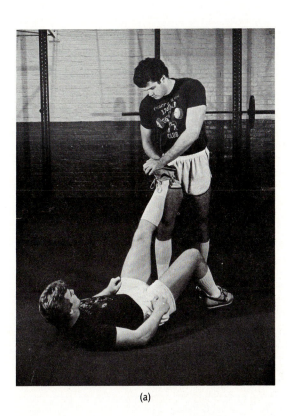
(a)

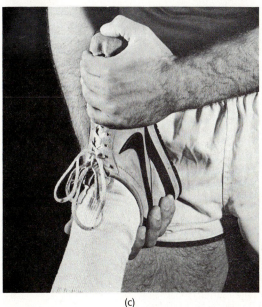
(c)

Figure 5.37 Assisted PNF Ankle Stretch

Heel Cord Stretch

In a sitting position with legs straight, curl toes toward body. Hold stretch for 30 to 60 seconds, maintaining straight legs. Repeat 3 to 5 times.

Assisted PNF Ankle Stretch

The ankle is stretched in four directions: flexion, extension, inversion, and eversion. This stretch is done with the athlete lying on the back while the assistant stands at the feet. The foot is grasped by the assistant and

placed in the stretched position. On the "flex" command the athlete attempts to straighten the ankle and the assistant offers resistance. When the "stretch" command is given, the assistant moves the ankle to the point where the developmental stretch is received. The stretch is done on each ankle twice for each of the four directions. This is the most time-consuming of the stretches and may be abbreviated by stretching in two of the directions per day on alternate days.

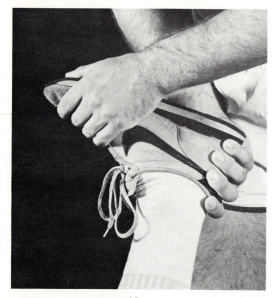

(d)

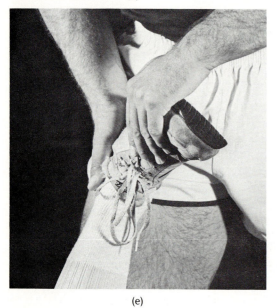

(e)

Figure 5.37 (Continued)

STRETCHING PROGRAMS

Several sample stretching programs follow. They are intended to be illustrative of whole body stretching and are related to the kind of conditioning anticipated or completed. Specialized programs for specific sports or specific events should be developed by the coach or the athlete. Examples of football and basketball stretching programs are included.

Table 5.1 Stretching Program for Pre- and Post-Aerobic Training

Warm-Up Exercises
Neck Rotation (5–7)
Overhead Shoulder Stretch (5–12)
Kneeling Groin Stretch (5–16)
Side Bends (5–14)
Head to Knee Stretch (5–23)
Bending Forward Stretch (5–24)
Hip Flexor Stretch (5–21)
Lying Hamstring Stretch (5–26)
Prone Quadriceps Stretch (5–33)
Calf Stretch (5–34)

Note: Other stretches may be included or substituted to satisfy individual needs.

Table 5.2 Stretching Program for Pre- and Post-Anaerobic Training

Warm-Up Exercises
Relaxation Stretch (5–6)
Shoulder and Side Stretch (5–9)
Shoulder and Chest Stretch (5–10)
Head to Knee Stretch (5–23)
Bending Forward Stretch (5–24)
The Yogi Stretch (5–17)
Kneeling Groin Stretch (5–16)
Sitting Groin Stretch (5–19)
Hamstring Stretch (5–31)
Calf Stretch (5–34)

Note: Other stretches may be included or substituted to satisfy individual needs.

Table 5.3 Stretching Program for Pre- and Post-Strength Training

Warm-Up Exercises
Relaxation Stretch (5–6)
Neck Rotation (5–7)
Assisted Shoulder and Chest Stretch (5–11)
Kneeling Groin Stretch (5–16)
Head to Knee Stretch (5–23)
The Yogi Stretch (5–17)
Foot to Hand Stretch (5–25)
Prone Quadricep Stretch (5–33)

Note: Other stretches may be included or substituted to satisfy individual needs.

Table 5.4 Stretching Program for Pre- and Post-Football Practice

Warm-Up Exercises
Relaxation Stretch (5–6)
Neck Rotation (5–7)
Overhead Shoulder Stretch (5–12)
Shoulder and Chest Stretch (5–10)
Head to Knee Stretch (5–23)
Bending Forward Stretch (5–24)
The Yogi Stretch (5–17)
Kneeling Groin Stretch (5–16)
Lying Hamstring Stretch (5–26)
Sitting and/or Lying Groin Stretch (5–19, 5–20)
Calf Stretch (5–34)
Ankle Stretch (5–37)
Prone Quadricep Stretch (5–33)
Relaxation Stretch or Hang on Bar

Note: Other stretches may be included or substituted to satisfy individual needs.

Table 5.5 Stretching Program for Pre- or Post-Basketball Practice

Warm-Up Exercises
Relaxation Stretch (5–6)
Neck Rotation (5–7)
Overhead Shoulder Stretch (5–12)
Trunk Rotation (5–15)
Sitting Groin Stretch (5–19)
Back Stretcher (5–27)
Low-Back Stretch (5–28)
Hamstring Stretch (5–31)
Lying Hamstring Stretch (5–26)
Calf Stretch (5–34)
Heel Cord Stretch (5–36)
Ankle Stretch (5–37)
Hang on Bar

Note: Other stretches may be included or substituted to satisfy individual needs.

SUMMARY

Stretching and flexibility exercises have become important aspects of preparing the athlete for practice and competition. Warming-up, which can precede stretching, is designed to elevate muscle temperature and body metabolism. Stretching exercises have the short-term effect of relaxing and lengthening the muscle. Habitual stretching leads to increased flexibility, and the preferred technique is the slow or static stretching routine. Stretching exercises should not only focus on the major areas of the body, but also involve sport-specific stretching to match the anticipated movements of the event.

REFERENCES

1. Alter, Michael J. 1988. *The Science of Stretching.* Champaign, IL: Human Kinetics.

2. Anderson, Robert A. 1984. *Stretching.* Bolinas, CA: Shelter Publications.

3. Beaulieu, John E. 1980. *Stretching for All Sports.* Pasadena, CA: The Athletic Press.

4. Clarke, H. Harrison. 1975. "Joint and Body Range of Movement," *Physical Fitness Research Digest* 5:1–22.

5. Croce, Pat. 1984. *Stretching for Athletics.* Champaign, IL: Human Kinetics.

6. Corbin, Charles B., and Larry Noble. 1980. "Flexibility: A Major Component of Physical Fitness," *JOPER* 51:23–60.

7. Cornelius, William L. 1985. "Flexibility: The Effective Way," *NSCA Journal* 7(3):62–64.

8. deVries, Herbert A. 1971. "Flexibility, an Overlooked But Vital Factor in Sports Conditioning," *Proceedings: International Symposium on the Art and Science of Coaching.* Ontario, CAN: F. I. Productions.

9. deVries, Herbert A. 1986. *Physiology of Exercise for Physical Education and Athletics,* 4th ed. Dubuque, IA: Wm. C. Brown Publishers.

10. Etnyre, Bruce R., and Eva J. Lee. 1987. "Comments on Proprioceptive Neuromuscular Facilitation," *Research Quarterly for Exercise and Sport* 58:184–188.

11. Etnyre, Bruce R., and Eva J. Lee. 1988. "Chronic and Acute Flexibility of Men and Women Using Three Different Stretching Techniques," *Research Quarterly for Exercise and Sport* 59:222–228.

12. Holland, George J. 1968. "The Physiology of Flexibility: A Review of Literature," *Kinesiology Review,* 49–62.

13. Knorty, Karen, and Chris Ringel. 1985. "PNF: Flexibility Techniques," *NSCA Journal* 7(2):50–53.

14. Knott, Margaret, and Dorothy Voss. 1968. *Proprioceptive Neuromuscular Facilitation,* 2d ed. New York: Harper & Row.

15. Leighton, Jack R. 1966. "The Leighton Flexometer and Flexibility Test," *J. Assn. Physical and Mental Rehabilitation* 20:86–88.

16. Neuberger, Tom. 1969. "What the Research Quarterly Says about Warm-Up," *JOPER* 40:75–77.

17. Roth, Peter, and E. Benjamin. 1979. "Warming-Up vs. Stretching," *Running Times* 11:15–20.

18. "Roundtable: Flexibility." 1984. *NSCA Journal* 6(4):10–22.

19. Shelton, Robert A., et al. 1983. *Basic Exercises: Pre-Conditioning, Re-Conditioning, Re-Habilitation.* Dubuque, IA: Eddie Bowers Publishing Co.

20. Wathen, Dan. 1987. "Flexibility: Its Place in Warm-Up Activities," *NSCA Journal* 9(5):26–27.

CHAPTER
SIX

SPORTSMEDICINE: CONDITIONING FOR INJURY PREVENTION AND REHABILITATION

When athletic trainers and sports medicine physicians discuss athletic injuries, they invariably emphasize the importance of preventive measures. Foremost among preventive recommendations has been the warning that many sports injuries are the result of inadequate physical conditioning.[2,8,11] Until recently there was very little documentation of the conventional wisdom that preconditioning is essential to prevent or reduce the chance of sports injuries.

Although overuse training can lead to injury, as detailed in Chapter 8, it is often the result of a previously inactive athlete moving too rapidly into intense training or competition.[5] Many sports medicine experts not only emphasize the importance of conditioning but also recommend specific exercises related to the particular type of joint stress the athlete will undergo. Olson[9] described the effectiveness of off-season conditioning as a deterrent to injury in high school football. Burkett's[3] classic work on hamstring injuries highlighted the importance of muscle strength balance. He found that a strength imbalance as small as 10 percent led to a 70 percent chance of injury to the *weaker* hamstring. Other studies[1,4] have also confirmed the effectiveness of reducing athletic injuries by preconditioning.

PREVENTION OF ATHLETIC INJURIES

Many precautions can be taken to prevent athletic injuries, including the use of quality equipment and facilities, proper medical care and athletic training and physical and psychological readiness for the sport. It has been recognized for some time that a large percentage of athletic injuries are caused by inadequate physical conditioning. The conditioning program should include the proper balance of aerobic and anaerobic training, flexibility, strength, and agility to meet the demands of the sport.

Conditioning for aerobic power has been described elsewhere as important in enabling the athlete to practice longer and harder with less fatigue and less susceptibility to injury. In most circumstances when the fatigue is a prevalent factor in injury, it is the general endurance of the athlete (aerobic power) that is found lacking. The athlete should be conditioned by gradual increases in the intensity of either practice or play. Anaerobic conditioning must precede vigorous anaerobic performance on the part of the athlete. Oftentimes injury is the result of a more forceful muscular contraction than the athlete is prepared to make. The proper mechanics of a new skill should be learned before the athlete attempts the skill under full speed or maximum force conditions.

Sufficient flexibility is necessary to reduce the potential of muscle, tendon, and ligament injuries. Strains, pulls, stretches, and tears may result from a lack of flexibility. Both general stretches for the entire body and special stretching exercises for specific movements of the sport are recommended. Athletes vary in the amount of stretching necessary to prepare them for competition and conditioning. Some have a greater tendency for muscle cramps, strains, and pulls while others may require additional stretching in particular areas of the body. Techniques for static stretching are discussed in Chapter 5 and are considered by the authors to be an integral part of any conditioning program.

The strength training programs offered in the text include strength exercises designed to reduce the potential of injury to the athlete. Some strength exercises are included to protect specific areas of the body susceptible to injury because of the nature of the particular sport.

The high incidence of certain injuries with particular sports could be described as sport-specific. The most frequently injured joint in sport is the knee. Football has a high rate of knee injury, as well as ankle, back, and neck injuries. Basketball is also stressful to ankles, knees, and the lower back. Knees are frequently injured in skiing, and the dagger-handled ski pole led to many thumb injuries during falls. Because certain joints or areas of the body are at higher risk of injury in specific sports, care should be taken to ensure that the muscles supporting those joints are strong, and that good flexibility is present. The neck, shoulder, wrist, knee, and ankle are joints that may need additional protection.

Some athletes will require strength exercises designed to reduce a personal weakness or a muscular imbalance, i.e., one muscle of a paired group being weaker than the other. There is evidence that muscular imbalance may be the cause of one of the most nagging sports injuries, the hamstring pull. As mentioned earlier, specificity also applies to preventive conditioning. If muscular endurance, speed, and range of motion are required of the sport, then the conditioning program must match those requirements. The human body (muscles and joints) is subjected to tremendous stresses and forces during athletic performance. If these stresses and forces are the result of high speed movement on the part of the limbs, then the muscles and joints should be prepared by high-speed conditioning.

Preventive conditioning is well worth the time and effort. Any athlete or coach who has had to deal with injuries will agree that prevention is preferable to rehabilitation.

TRAINING INJURIES

Fortunately, the rate of injury from sports conditioning is relatively small in comparison to sports competition. The athlete who is required to spend considerable time in endurance training can be susceptible to the overuse syndrome. Overuse is the most likely injury to be triggered by sports conditioning. If the same movements are also repetitive in the sport, such as track, the overuse potential is greater. Chapter 8 warns the athlete and coach about overtraining, and the conditioning programs offered in this text are designed to be used with adequate rest and recovery. The year-round program, cycle training systems, and alternating workout intensities are all intended to prevent overtraining and injury. It is also the responsibility of the coach and athlete to be aware of overtraining symptoms (Chapter 8), and to act accordingly—reduce training or rest.

Safety instructions and precautions are included for strength training, which can produce minor strains and sprains. A carefully planned strength program can, and should, be injury free. Proper lifting, careful supervision, and the use of progression can make strength training injury free. Detailed safety instructions are included with the strength exercises found in Chapter 19.

If minor injuries do occur, prompt attention can prevent them from becoming chronic or serious. The injury cycle follows a well-known path: injury (trauma)–hemorrhage–inflammation–scarring. Pain, swelling, redness, and heat may accompany the injury.

The most effective first aid for such injuries is RICE (rest–ice–compression–elevation).[2,8,11] In addition to resting the affected area, ice is the most important care to be given to the injury. Ice should be applied for 20 minutes **ON,** and one to two hours **OFF** during at least the first 24 to 48 hours. Application of ice (cryotherapy) is the first line of defense in sports medicine. Ice prevents or reduces the accumulation of fluids, which is known as inflammation. It is the inflammation that causes much of the pain in the joint or injured area. Ice also serves as a local pain killer. The application of ice should be limited to 30 minutes. After 30 minutes the body reverses the effect of the ice by dilating the area to prevent frostbite. Many professional athletes use ice routinely after performance to reduce joint trauma. Baseball pitchers will ice elbows and shoulders, while basketball players apply ice to their knees and lower back. Ice can be used chronically on joints which sustain heavy stress in training and performance.

Compression simply means a tight wrap to aid in the prevention of inflammation. Elevation allows gravity to aid in the further reduction of fluid from the area. Anti-inflammatory medication may also be added to the treatment when necessary. It is important to distinguish which medications have anti-inflammatory action. Aspirin and motrin (ibuprofen) are both over-the-counter anti-inflammatories, but some pain killers, such as tylenol, have no anti-inflammatory effect.

Treatment of minor conditioning injuries should not be confused with sports medicine care for most serious injuries. The athletic trainer or team physician should be consulted if there is any question as to how serious the injury is. Griffith has offered an excellent layman's source of sports injuries, and some basic information about making a decision about seeking sports medicine care or not.[7] The diagnosis, treatment, and rehabilitation of serious sports injuries should be under the direction of the sports medicine physician.

REHABILITATION

Extreme caution is urged in retraining an athlete after injury. Several steps should be taken before rehabilitation is attempted.

1. When an injury first occurs, it should be reported immediately to the team trainer—or to the coach if no trainer is available. This should be done regardless of how minor the injury may appear. If the injury is obviously serious or if it persists, a doctor should be consulted.
2. If there is a period of latency from the regular athletic activity, the physician should be consulted before activity or reconditioning is undertaken.

3. The advice and directions of the physician should be followed precisely. The physician may indicate medical implications that are not apparent to the trainer, coach, or athlete. The supply of good sports medicine doctors has increased significantly since the first edition of this book. The physician, coach, trainer, and athlete should work together to help rehabilitate the athlete. The physician should be expected to prescribe exercises after serious injury.

Several questions should be considered before initiating a rehabilitation program: What type or combination of exercises should be done, e.g., walking, stretching, running, swimming, weight training, or agility exercises? How intense should each type of exercise be? What is the purpose of each exercise prescribed by the physician? How can the athlete tell whether he or she is doing too much of any type of exercise? What is the expected length of the period of retraining before recovery is complete? How can the athlete tell when he or she is fully recovered?

It may be necessary to have someone assist the athlete in the early stages of rehabilitation. That individual may help the athlete perform the exercises, or even manually guide the athlete through the range of motion to reduce the effort on an injured limb. Rehabilitation of injuries must obviously be very individualized, but there are general guidelines to follow.

Guidelines for Reconditioning

1. The reconditioning program or exercises prescribed by the physician should be carefully followed.
2. Begin conditioning slowly and easily. Increase speed and intensity very gradually.
3. Be certain that movements are done smoothly, avoiding jerky or stressful movements of the joints.
4. Some discomfort is to be expected when performing exercises, especially as the amount of intensity increases. Sharp pain or increasing discomfort is the signal that the exercise must be discontinued or modified.
5. General conditioning or conditioning of specific parts of the body should be maintained, whenever feasible during the period of latency.
6. Low resistance and high repetition (fifteen to twenty-five reps) is usually the rule for rehabilitative exercises.
7. Rehabilitation should not result in the overdevelopment of one limb. It may be necessary to train the opposing muscle group or limb. If an injured limb is very heavily retrained, muscular imbalance may result.

Rehabilitative exercises may be done daily or even several times per day. In some circumstances greater rest may be required and rehabilitative sessions may be held less often. The concept of active rehabilitation is widely used in medicine and can hasten the recovery of the athlete. Impatience is probably the greatest danger to the athlete during the rehabilitative period.

INJURY PREVENTION AND REHABILITATION EXERCISES

The following are stretching, strength, and agility exercises that are particularly valuable in injury prevention and/or rehabilitation. Other exercises not described here can be found in either Chapter 5 or Chapter 19.

Foot, Ankle, and Calf Exercises

Calf Stretcher (See Chapter 5)
Toe Raises (See Chapter 19)

Ankle Rotation. This exercise is done by placing a towel (folded lengthwise) on the floor in front of a chair or bench. A weight (about ten pounds) is placed on the end of the towel. In the sitting position, the athlete then pulls the towel across by placing his foot on the towel and rotating the ankle. He then lifts the foot and reaches over and pulls more towel across. This can be done ten or fifteen times with each foot. To strengthen the antagonistic muscles, the movement may be done in the opposite direction.

Golf Ball Pick-Up with Toes. In this exercise a golf ball is lifted by the toes. It can be held for as long as possible, then placed back on the floor and repeated with the other foot. After the toes have exercised holding the ball, they can be stretched or spread while the other foot flexes.

Dorsiflexion of the Foot. This movement, which involves the muscles in the front of the calf, the foot, and the ankle, can be strengthened by having the athlete or a partner provide the resistance by hand. Static stretching can be done in each direction before and/or after the strength exercise. The resistance should be steady and should allow smooth movement through the entire range of motion.

Another method of strengthening this area involves hanging a weight from the end of the toe. A strap eighteen inches long and a high table on which to sit are necessary to perform this exercise. The strap is tied to the ankle with the end hanging over the toe. A weight (five to fifteen pounds) is then tied to the strap. It is helpful if the strap is taped to the shoe so that it will not slip off the toe. This method takes more time than

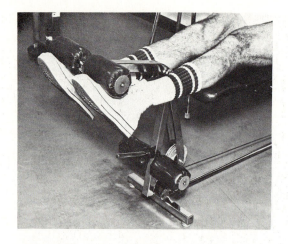

Figure 6.1   Dorsiflexion of Foot

Figure 6.2   Dorsiflexion of Foot (with Weight)

Chapter 6

the manual method, and for that reason is usually used for rehabilitation rather than as a preventive measure. In such cases, the dorsiflexion of the ankle should be accompanied by alternating inversion and eversion of the foot. This can be done every other set or every other rep. This movement may also be strengthened using a standard leg extension, leg curl machine.

Ankle Strengthener and Stretcher. This exercise is done to prevent ankle sprains. Some arc-shaped footing six to ten inches deep and approximately 3½' × 3½' is needed.

Jumping on either the convex or concave surface creates inversion and eversion of the feet, strengthening the feet and ankles. Approximately the same number of repetitions should be done on each type of surface so that balanced muscular development is ensured.

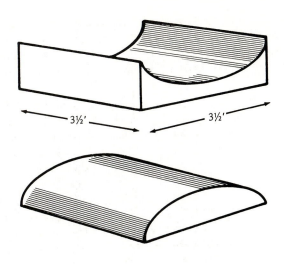

Knee and Thigh

Toe Raises (See Chapter 19)

Leg Extension. This exercise is done on a "quad" or leg extension machine by taking the resistance through a range of motion from where the knee is flexed to where it is fully extended.

Figure 6.3 Leg Extension

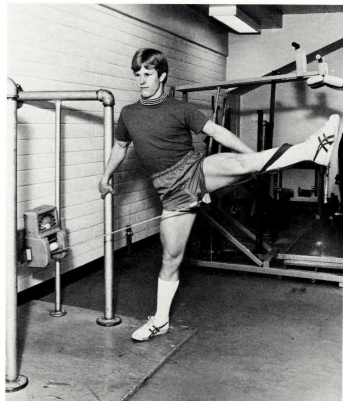

Figure 6.4 Lateral and/or Diagonal Leg Motion

Leg Curl (See Chapter 19
Half Squat (See Chapter 19

Lateral and/or Diagonal Leg Motion (with pulley or ankle weight). After the ankle is attached to a pulley, the leg, with the knee completely extended, is adducted or abducted so that resistance is applied laterally to the knee. See figure 6.4.

Single Leg Lifts. These are done as the initial rehabilitation exercise on the knee, especially when complete mobility cannot be or has not been restored.

Double Leg Lifts (See Chapter 5)
Head to Knees (See Chapter 5)
Wide Straddle Stretch (See Chapter 5)
"Good Morning" Exercise (See Chapter 19)
Hyperextension (See Chapter 19)
Half Squat (See Chapter 19)
Sit-Ups (See Chapter 19)
Single Leg Lifts (See Chapter 19)
High Knee Lift (See Chapter 19)

Lateral Leg Lift. This exercise is performed by lying on the side and raising one leg as high as possible, by abducting the hip then lowering the leg slowly. This can be done without resistance as a stretch or with ankle weights. A weighted boot or a floor pulley can be attached to the ankle.

Hip Extension (with pulley or weighted boot). This exercise is done in the prone position by attaching a high pulley to the ankle. The range of motion is basically the same as the Single Leg Lift except that the resistance is in the opposite direction, thus exercising the muscles of the hips and lower back.

Hip Circumduction (with angle weight or weighted boot). This movement is done by moving the foot through a circular pattern while abducting and adducting the hip.

Head to Knee Stretch (See Chapter 5)
Yogi (See Chapter 5)
Foot to Hand Stretch (See Chapter 5)
Wide Straddle Stretch (See Chapter 5)
Stiff-Legged Dead Lift Stretch (See Chapter 19)

Hand and Wrist

Wrist Curl (See Chapter 19)
Wrist Roller (See Chapter 19)
Reverse Curl (See Chapter 19)
Squeezing Rubber Ball

Figure 6.5 Arm Circles

Wrist Flexion and Extension (with dumbbell). This exercise is done with a light dumbbell by flexing and extending the wrist so that the largest and smallest joint angles are alternately opposed to the thumb and fifth finger.

Wrist Rotation (or supination and pronation with dumbbell). This exercise is done by simply rotating the wrist back and forth while holding a dumbbell.

Finger and Hand Flexion and Extension. This is done as a stretch by simply alternating the spreading of the fingers (complete extension) and clenching of the fist.

Elbow

Curl (with dumbbell or pulley for rehabilitation)
   (See Chapter 19)
Reverse Curl (with dumbbell or pulley for
   rehabilitation) (See Chapter 19)
Tricep Extension (lying, sitting, or standing with
   dumbbell) (See Chapter 19)

Arm Circles. These are done with the elbows extended and the arms straight out to the sides, making small circles in either or both directions. They may be done with no weight or with a light (five to fifteen pound) dumbbell.

Forearm Circles. These are done by holding the elbow at the side, contacting the body. The hand is then moved in a circular motion. This should be done in both directions. A dumbbell is usually used, but the exercise may be done without weight when necessary.

Bar Dips (See Chapter 19). For rehabilitative purposes these can be done between two benches or chairs, with the legs supported on the floor.

Bench Press (See Chapter 19)

Lateral Raises. These are done in the standing position by elevating (abducting) the shoulders. The arms which are held straight out to the sides are moved to a position directly overhead (fig. 6.6).

Shoulder Exercises

Bar Dips (See Chapter 19). For rehabilitative purposes these can be done between two benches or chairs, with the legs supported.

Bent-Arm Laterals (See Chapter 19)

Incline Flys. These are simply Bent-Arm Laterals done on an inclined bench. The upper chest and shoulders are strengthened (fig. 6.7).

Figure 6.6 Lateral Raises

Bent-Arm Pullovers (See Chapter 19)
Military Press (See Chapter 19)
Lat Pulls (See Chapter 19)
Bench Press (See Chapter 19)

Straight Arm Hanging. This is done by simply hanging from a chinning bar. It can be done for from one to sixty seconds.

Neck

Neck Extension (See Chapter 19)
Neck Flexion (See Chapter 19)
Neck Rotation (See Chapter 19)
Shoulder Shrug (See Chapter 19)

Isometric and Isotonic Neck Exercises. Resistance is applied smoothly by a partner. This is a quick and fairly effective way to warm up or strengthen the neck.

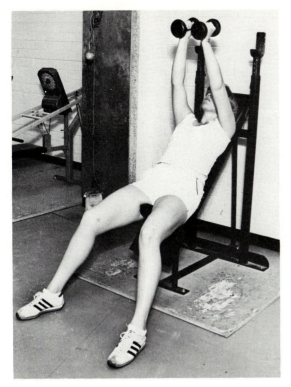 

Figure 6.7 Incline Flys

SUMMARY

In this chapter we have discussed the need for preventive conditioning exercises to reduce the potential for injury. Such exercises include aerobic and anaerobic conditioning, flexibility, agility, and strength. The nature of minor sports conditioning injuries is discussed along with information on treatment. Basic guidelines for rehabilitation are listed and the role of the physician in rehabilitation is stressed. Preventive and rehabilitative exercises are listed, some of which also appear in Chapters 5 and 19.

REFERENCES

1. Abbot, H. G., and J. B. Kress. 1979. "Preconditioning in the Prevention of Knee Injuries," *Arch. Med. Rehabil.* 50:326–333.

2. Arnheim, Daniel D. 1989. *Modern Principles of Athletic Training,* 7th ed. St. Louis: Times, Mirror, Mosby.

3. Burkett, Lee N. 1970. "Causative Factors in Hamstring Strains," *Medicine and Science in Sports and Exercise* 2:39–42.

4. Cahill, B. R., and E. H. Griffith. 1978. "Effect of Preseason Conditioning Program on the Incidence and Severity of High School Football Knee Injuries." *American Journal of Sports Medicine* 6:180–184.

5. Clements, D. B., et al. 1981. "A Survey of Overuse Running Injuries," *Physician and Sportsmedicine* 9:47–58.

6. Dominquez, M. D. 1980. "Shoulder Pain in Swimmers," *Physician and Sportsmedicine* 8:37–48.

7. Griffith, E. Winter. 1986. *Complete Guide to Sports Injuries.* Tucson, AZ: The Body Press.

8. Morris, Alfred F. 1984. *Sportsmedicine: Prevention of Athletic Injuries.* Dubuque, IA: Wm. C. Brown Publishers.

9. Olson, C. C. 1979. "The Spokane Study of High School Football Injuries," *Physician and Sportsmedicine* 7:75–80.

10. Sellock, F., and W. Prentice. 1985. "Warming Up and Stretching for Improved Physical Performance and Prevention of Sports-Related Injuries," *Journal of Sports Medicine* 2:267–278.

11. Wolpa, Mark A. 1982. *The Sports Medicine Guide: Treating and Preventing Common Athletic Injuries.* Champaign, IL: Human Kinetics.

CHAPTER
SEVEN

SPORTS NUTRITION

Efforts to improve athletic performance through manipulation of the diet date back to antiquity. The practice of having athletes consume large amounts of meat (protein) to build muscle tissue probably originated with the Greeks. Unfortunately, many myths and misconceptions have haunted nutritional practices over the years. Although nutrition has grown in stature as a science in this country, nutritionists must constantly remind the public as well as athletes and coaches of the basic principles of nutrition. Coaches and athletes often lose sight of the basic function of foods in an effort to uncover exotic diets or combinations of foods that are reputed to improve athletic performance. The first portion of this chapter will serve as a reminder of the basic function of nutrition.

Throughout the world nutrition plays a major role in the maintenance of health. The relationship between malnutrition and the various deficiency diseases is most evident in developing countries or in areas of the world that lack sufficient food.[2] An abundance of food, rather than a shortage, is generally characteristic of the United States. Some nutritionists and medical scientists claim that the major nutrition-related health problems in this country involve overconsumption of calories and poor food selection despite the general abundance. Public knowledge about good nutrition is growing significantly, but many myths and misconceptions about proper nutrition still persist.

GOOD NUTRITION

Nutrition can be defined as the "science of food and its relation to optimal health and performance."[2] It involves nourishing the body properly. This means providing adequate fuel for energy, material for building and maintenance, and nutrients for regulating the bodily processes. One of the major functions of nutrition is to keep calorie input and output in balance (energy balance). This concept is particularly important for athletes in training, which involves major increases in energy output. A major chore for most athletes is consuming sufficient calories to maintain energy balance and to *not* lose weight. Details of energy balance for athletes will be discussed later in the chapter. Energy balance assumes not only sufficient fuel for sports activities, but also sufficient maintenance materials for bodily tissues.

The digestive system is physiologically responsible for breaking down foods into usable nutrients, leading to good nutrition. The process involves enzymes which are secreted in the small intestine and "break down" food mechanically and chemically. From the small intestine, the broken-down foodstuffs are absorbed into the blood to enter into the metabolic cycle. A detailed description of digestion or the biochemistry of muscular energy is beyond the intended scope of this chapter. Both processes involve a complex series of biochemical steps that are linked together. A simplified description of muscle-energy metabolism can be found in figure 7.1.

Figure 7.1 illustrates the importance of both carbohydrates (CHO) and fats in supplying energy for sports activities. Protein is *not* a significant energy supply in physical activity. As described in Chapter 3 (Conditioning/AER-AN), the real "fuel" for sports activities at the muscle tissue level is ATP (adenosine triphosphate). ATP is a high-energy phosphate found in the muscle fiber. The foods that we consume are directly involved in the metabolic processes which ultimately enable ATP to "explode" in the muscle tissue and produce contraction. Thus the cookie that the athlete consumes days before the athletic contest eventually is involved in contributing energy for the resupply of ATP to fuel muscle contraction during the sports event.

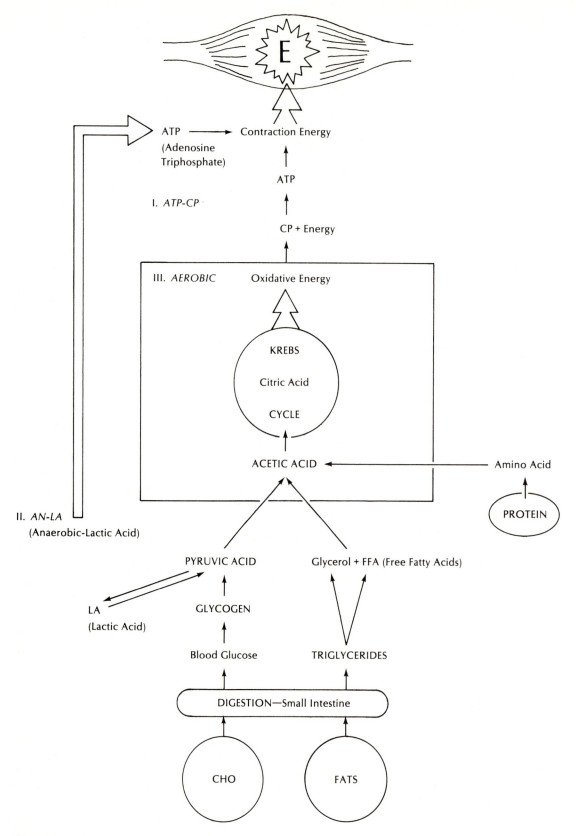

Figure 7.1 Muscle-Energy Metabolism

BASIC NUTRIENTS

There are six classes of basic nutrients: protein, carbohydrates, fat, vitamins, minerals, and water. Carbohydrates, protein, and fat are the most abundant nutrients in our diet and the only ones that supply energy (calories) during sports or work activities. Nutrients are the important chemical substances responsible for nourishing the body properly, i.e., supplying energy, providing building and maintenance materials, and regulating bodily processes.

It is estimated that there are about fifty basic nutrients needed by the human body.[11] Ten of those nutrients are considered to be "leader" nutrients and are described in figure 7.2. A balanced diet which supplies sufficient amounts of the ten leader nutrients will probably supply enough of the other forty basic nutrients.

Each nutrient has a specific effect that can be fulfilled only by that nutrient. In some instances nutrients must work together as a team in order to produce a desired effect. Nutrients are found in food, but in varying amounts in different foods. All of the nutrition needed for good nutrition for anyone, including athletes, can be obtained by eating a *variety* of different foods. Therefore, it is particularly important to consume a variety of different foods. It is also the reason why nutritionists educate us to consume the "balanced diet."

Carbohydrates

CHO is the most abundant nutrient and is the major source of energy in our diet. The range of calories supplied by the CHO in most diets is from 45 to 60 percent. Nutritionists and sports scientists generally agree that athletes as well as nonathletes can benefit from a complex CHO intake on the high end of that range. There is no minimum requirement for CHO, which is primarily an energy nutrient in anaerobic activities. It should be noted, however, that excess intake of CHO is converted to fat and stored in the body. CHO loading is one of the few successful manipulations of diet to influence athletic performance. See Carbohydrate Loading later in this chapter.

The principal kinds of CHO are sugars and starches. Starches are complex forms of sugar which are broken down by digestion into simple sugar such as glucose. It should be noted that both starches and sugars can be broken down into glucose but at a different rate. Complex CHO breaks down more slowly than do simple sugars. In addition, starches usually contain more nutrients and dietary fiber than do simple sugars. The energy yield of CHO is 4.3 calories per gram, which is similar to that of protein. Since three-fourths of the stored glycogen in the body is found in the muscles, it is obviously important for athletes to maintain sufficient muscle glycogen levels.

Protein

Protein must be resupplied daily via essential amino acids (EAA). This range of calories supplied by protein in most diets is from 12 to 20 percent. Because protein is involved in building body tissue, including muscle, it has often been assumed that a high protein intake is necessary for athletes. Most Americans on an adequately balanced diet are consuming twice as much protein (100 gm/day) as necessary (46 gm/day). Although it is an extremely important nutrient, protein is frequently overconsumed.

Animal protein is of high quality and a complete source of EAA. Vegetable protein, on the other hand, is incomplete unless combined with some animal protein. This is a very important concept for athletes. A vegetarian diet is usually *not* compatible with intense athletic conditioning and competition unless it is very carefully and scientifically designed.

Fat

Fat is an essential component of the balanced diet; it represents a concentrated form of energy. Fat supplies twice as many calories (9.5/gm) as CHO or protein (4.3/gm). The range of calories supplied by fat in most diets is 25 to 45 percent. For good health fat consumption should be on the lower end of that range, for both athletes and nonathletes.

Because excess fat consumption is often associated with overweight and heart disease, fat is frequently overlooked as a basic and necessary nutrient. Fat is a major fuel in aerobic exercise and has other essential functions in the body, as shown in figure 7.2. A major function is its role in carrying the fat-soluble vitamins. It is also true that many nutritionists and medical scientists recommend a low to moderate intake of unsaturated fats to reduce the potential of coronary artery disease.

Vitamins

Vitamins do not supply calories (energy); rather, they function as catalysts or action regulators in body metabolism. In that way, their function is not unlike the inorganic elements and hormones that are involved in human metabolism.

There are Recommended Dietary Allowances (RDA) of the various vitamins to prevent vitamin deficiency diseases. Many athletes and nonathletes have

Nutrients for health

Nutrients are chemical substances obtained from foods during digestion. They are needed to regulate body processes and to supply energy.

About 50 nutrients, including water, are needed daily for optimum health. If one obtains the proper amount of the 10 "leader" nutrients in the daily diet, the other 40 or so will likely be consumed in sufficient amounts.

One's diet should include a variety of foods. No single food supplies all the 50 nutrients, and many nutrients must work together.

When a nutrient is added or a nutritional claim is made, nutrition-labeling regulations require listing the 10 leader nutrients on food packages.

Protein

Supplies four calories of energy per gram

Sources: Meat, fish, poultry, dried beans and peas, egg, cheese, milk

Functions: Constitutes part of the structure of every cell. Supports growth and maintains healthy body cells. Constitutes part of enzymes, some hormones and body fluids, and antibodies that increase resistance to infection.

Carbohydrate

Major souce of energy for central nervous system—four calories per gram

Sources: Cereal, corn, potatoes, dried beans, bread, sugar

Functions: Supplies energy so protein can be used for growth and maintenance of body cells. Unrefined products—complex carbohydrates in fruits, vegetables and whole grains—supply fiber for regular elimination. Assists in body's use of fat.

Fat

Supplies nine calories of energy per gram

Sources: Shortening, oil, butter, margarine, salad dressing, sausages

Functions: Constitutes part of the structure of every cell. Supplies essential fatty acids. Provides and carries fat-soluble vitamins (A, D, E and K).

Vitamin A (Retinol)

Sources: Carrots, liver, greens, sweet potatoes, butter, margarine

Functions: Assists formation and maintenance of skin and mucous membranes (such as nasal passages and intestinal tract), increasing resistance to infection. Functions to promote healthy eye tissues and eye adaptation in dim light.

Vitamin C (Ascorbic acid)

Sources: Broccoli, grapefruit, orange, strawberries, papaya, mango

Functions: Forms cementing substances, such as collagen, that hold body together. Strengthens body, hastens healing, increases resistance to infection. Aids body's use of iron.

Calcium

Sources: Milk, yogurt, cheese, sardines and salmon with bones, kale, mustard, collard and turnip greens

Functions: Combines with other minerals to give structure and strength to bones and teeth. Assists in blood clotting. Functions in normal muscle contraction and relaxation and normal nerve transmission.

Niacin

Aids in utilization of energy

Sources: Liver, meat, poultry, fish, peanuts, fortified cereal products

Functions: Functions as part of a coenzyme in fat synthesis, tissue respiration and body's use of carbohydrate. Aids digestion and fosters normal appetite.

Figure 7.2 Nutrients for Health

Thiamin (B$_1$)

Aids in utilization of energy

Sources: Lean pork, nuts, fortified cereal products

Functions: Functions as part of a coenzyme to promote body's use of carbohydrate. Promotes normal appetite. Contributes to normal functioning of nervous system.

Riboflavin (B$_2$)

Aids in utilization of energy

Sources: Liver, milk, yogurt, cottage cheese

Functions: Functions as part of a coenzyme in production of energy within body cells. Promotes healthy skin and eyes.

Iron

Aids in utilization of energy

Sources: Enriched farina, prune juice, liver, dried beans and peas, red meat

Functions: Combines with protein to form hemoglobin which carries oxygen to cells. Prevents nutritional anemia. Increases resistance to infection. Functions as part of enzymes involved in tissue respiration.

Figure 7.2 (Continued)

consumed excessive amounts (megadoses) of vitamins. This has not proved beneficial to athletic performance or to health in general. Moreover, some excess consumption can be toxic. It is the fat-soluble vitamins which are stored in the tissues of the body that have the potential for excessive buildup and toxicity. The fat-soluble vitamins include vitamins A, D, E, and K. Their sources and functions can be seen in figure 7.2.

The water-soluble vitamins must be replenished daily. They are not stored in the tissues, and excess consumption is not toxic (but does produce the world's most expensive urine!). The water-soluble vitamins include Vitamin C and the B complex (Thiamin, Riboflavin, and Niacin). The function of those vitamins and good sources of them are seen in figure 7.2.

Minerals

Small amounts of essential minerals must be ingested or deficiency diseases can occur. The classic example is iron deficiency, which, it is estimated, affects 15 percent of the population of the United States. Among the most essential mineral nutrients can be found iron, iodine, calcium, phosphorus, sodium, and potassium. Calcium and phosphorus help build strong bones and body structure. Some of the essential minerals are involved in the energy metabolism of sports activities, while others are important in maintaining water balance for the athlete. See figure 7.2.

Water

Water is frequently overlooked as a basic nutrient. It is, however, the second most important element for sustaining life, overshadowed only by oxygen. The main-

tenance of water balance is a crucial function of the body and is extremely important for the athlete. Water is responsible for regulating body temperature and dissolving and transporting nutrients and other essentials.

BASIC FOOD GROUPS

In order to ensure that sufficient amounts of the basic nutrients are consumed, the Recommended Dietary Allowances (RDA) were developed and are constantly being restudied and revised.[15] Most of the nutrients and amounts listed on the RDA are not meaningful except to nutritionists and scientists. A simplified guide for athletes and nonathletes is the United States daily food guide, which identifies the four Basic Food Groups (figure 7.3).

Figure 7.3 lists the number of servings recommended in each of the four Basic Food Groups and what constitutes a serving. By consuming the recommended number of servings daily, the athlete or nonathlete is assured of meeting the RDA, with few exceptions. Each food group makes specific nutrient contributions. Foods from all of the groups work together to supply energy and nutrients for good health and growth. The intake can be easily adjusted to meet the needs of special groups such as growing children or teenagers. It is important to note that persons of all ages and both sexes require food selections from each of the four groups daily.

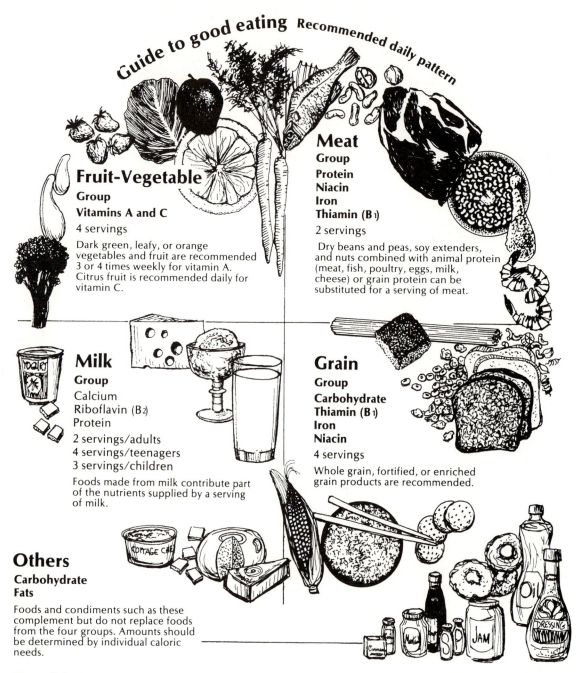

Figure 7.3 contains the following text:

Guide to good eating Recommended daily pattern

Fruit-Vegetable
Group
Vitamins A and C

4 servings

Dark green, leafy, or orange vegetables and fruit are recommended 3 or 4 times weekly for vitamin A. Citrus fruit is recommended daily for vitamin C.

Meat
Group
Protein
Niacin
Iron
Thiamin (B₁)

2 servings

Dry beans and peas, soy extenders, and nuts combined with animal protein (meat, fish, poultry, eggs, milk, cheese) or grain protein can be substituted for a serving of meat.

Milk
Group
Calcium
Riboflavin (B₂)
Protein

2 servings/adults
4 servings/teenagers
3 servings/children

Foods made from milk contribute part of the nutrients supplied by a serving of milk.

Grain
Group
Carbohydrate
Thiamin (B₁)
Iron
Niacin

4 servings

Whole grain, fortified, or enriched grain products are recommended.

Others
Carbohydrate
Fats

Foods and condiments such as these complement but do not replace foods from the four groups. Amounts should be determined by individual caloric needs.

Figure 7.3 Basic Food Groups

NUTRITION AND THE ATHLETE

It is often difficult for coaches and athletes to believe that some magic manipulation of the diet will not produce better physical performance. Studies of dietary supplements have repeatedly confirmed that improved performance will not occur as a result of extra intake of vitamins, proteins, or other supplements. Rogozkin states that the major concerns for sports nutrition include (1) providing adequate energy supplies (calories), (2) maintaining a balanced diet, (3) choosing adequate forms of nutrition, and (4) dealing with individual needs (weight gain or loss) and likes and dislikes.[13]

The authors do not imply that good nutrition is a simple process. Detailed study of the nutrition of athletes reveals a very complex process influenced by many variables. Muscle glycogen levels are important in many sports performances and there are ways of increasing the resting levels. Many females, including female athletes in heavy training, are susceptible to iron deficiencies. As a result of medical screening, iron supplements are recommended for many female athletes in heavy training. An important aspect of sports nutrition is an understanding of the basic information that has preceded this section. In the next section the special aspects of nutrition for athletes will be discussed.

Energy Balance

The relationship between caloric expenditure (output) and caloric consumption (intake) represents energy balance. If intake and output are balanced, body weight will remain constant. If caloric consumption *exceeds* physical activity, the excess intake is stored as fat and the individual gains weight. This is a major cause of obesity in our society. If the physical activity *exceeds* the caloric intake, the individual loses weight by diminishing fat storage.

The amount of calories required per day for a "moderately active" college student is estimated to be 15 calories times the body in pounds. Thus a 125-pound female would require 1,875 calories per day to maintain energy balance ($15 \times 125 = 1,875$), while a 175-pound male would require 2,625 calories. A wide range of daily caloric consumption can exist for individuals of similar "moderately active" levels. The range might extend from 1,500 calories for a 100-pound person to 3,375 calories for a 225-pound individual.

The athlete in training and competition is more than "moderately active." An athlete can easily burn 1,000 to 1,500 additional calories in a lengthy vigorous workout. A more realistic caloric intake consumption per pound for athletes could be 20, resulting in a daily consumption of 2,500 calories for the 125-pound female athlete and 3,500 calories for the 175-pound male. The caloric consumption for many large, highly trained athletes has been found to be in the range of 4,000 to 6,000 calories per day. This is not an astounding intake when one considers the size of the athletes and the number of workouts per day. Football players who undergo two- or three-a-day workouts consume 4,000 to 6,000 calories daily without gaining weight because of the tremendous energy expenditure. Many may actually lose weight under such regimens despite a generous training table. Vigorous activity raises metabolism for many hours after the exercise is over. This additional burning of calories is *in addition to* the calories burned during the exercise.

Besides the body weight of the athlete, the duration and intensity of the sports activity should be considered in estimating the caloric consumption for maintaining energy balance. The caloric cost of several sports activities is listed in table 7.1.

Age will also have a bearing on the caloric consumption of young athletes. Boys and girls aged 10 to 12 years will require approximately 30 calories per pound daily, while junior high and high school athletes (aged 14 to 18) will require approximately 23 calories

Table 7.1 Caloric Cost of Sports Activities (Calorie Per Hour)

125 lbs.	Activity	178 lbs.
700–1000	Running (7–12 mph)	1000–1400
—	Wrestling	900
550	Swimming (Crawl)	600–750
550	Jogging	750
500	Racquetball	750
450	Soccer	650
350–500	Basketball	500–700
350–500	Tennis	500–700
—	Football	600
300–500	Volleyball	400–700
250–300	Softball/Baseball	325–425
200–275	Golf	300–400

per pound of body weight daily.[10] As the authors have previously stated, college athletes, usually between the ages of 18 and 22, will require approximately 20 calories per pound daily. As a result, an athletic 12-year-old boy may consume as many calories daily as a college-age female athlete (75 lbs. $\times$ 30 = 2,250 calories *versus* 110 lbs. $\times$ 20 = 2,200 calories).

If the athlete must lose weight, it is recommended for good nutrition that caloric intake not fall below certain base levels. Those levels are 1,600 calories per day for female athletes and 2,000 for male athletes.[7] Sufficient base levels are necessary to maintain adequate nutrient intake for good nutrition. It is unlikely that many athletes would need to lose weight, as we shall see here.

Body Composition

The need to lose weight is not usually a problem for athletes since being over-fat is usually associated with below-normal activity levels. Excess fat stored in the body is also detrimental to physical performance, and it is unlikely that an athlete could achieve successful performance in an over-fat state.

At this point it is appropriate to distinguish between overweight and obesity. *Overweight* refers to body weight exceeding the standard height/weight charts. *Obesity* refers to excess body fat above the recommended levels. It is not uncommon for athletes, both male and female, to be overweight according to the height/weight charts, but not be obese. As a matter of fact, many such athletes are actually less fat than average individuals.

Body composition is made up of (1) Lean Body Weight (LBW), which is composed of muscles, bones, and connective tissue, and (2) fat weight. The percentage of body weight in fat is a far more accurate

Table 7.2 Standard for % Body Fat
College-Age Males, Females, and Athletes

Females		Males
<17%	Lean—"Athletic"	<9%
18–19%	Below Average	10–11%
20–23%	Good—Average	12–15%
24–30%	Above Average	16–20%
>31%	Obese	>21%
ATHLETES		
Females		**Males**
12–14%	Runners	4–6%
	Gymnasts	6–8%
16–20%	Basketball	
	Football—Backs	6–9%
	Football—Linemen	12–14%
23%	"Nonathletes"	15%

determinant of the athlete's fatness than is the weight alone when compared to the height/weight charts. If we consider two athletes of the same height and weight (150 pounds), one may be considerably fatter than the other. At 150 pounds, one athlete may have 15 pounds of fat, or 10 percent of body weight in fat. The other athlete may have 30 pounds of fat, or 20 percent of fat weight. From an athletic performance standpoint, the second athlete is over-fat but not, perhaps, overweight according to the height/weight charts.

Occasionally both male and female athletes are overweight according to the height/weight charts. For example, a 225-pound football player may exceed the weight chart by 25 or 30 pounds according to height. If he is heavily boned and muscled, which is very likely, he may be only 10 to 12 percent fat, which is below average for his age and sex. Coaches and athletes need to be aware that the percentage of body fat is far more important in determining an ideal weight than height/weight charts and the scale. Sometimes coaches and athletes expect additional weight loss when the athlete is already extremely lean. This may result in weight loss from the muscle tissue (LBW) and may have a negative effect on performance. Some standards for percentage of body fat are listed in table 7.2. Athletes are generally very lean, compared to the college-age populations.

Measurement of body fat. How is body fat measured? The most accurate (but time-consuming) technique is underwater weighing. The technique is designed to measure body density and is usually done in medical clinics or university laboratories. To simplify the concept, the reader should recall that the body composition includes LBW and fat. Since muscle and bone are heavier by volume than fat, the individual with *less* fat will have a higher body density. Fat does not "weigh" in water; rather, it floats. Let us consider again an individual who weighs 150 pounds (dry) on the scale. When weighed underwater, the individual may "lose" 15 pounds of body weight which can be assumed to be fat. That 15 pounds represents 10 percent of the total body weight when dry—hence, 10 percent body fat. The technique is actually more complex than described here because we must also consider the air trapped in the lungs, which makes the individual more buoyant and less dense (fig. 7.4).

A simple and less time-consuming technique for estimating body fat involves the use of skinfold calipers. The skinfold technique involves measuring a "pinch" of subcutaneous fat at several anatomical sites. While the skinfold is not as accurate for estimating body fat as is underwater weighing, it is reasonably accurate to use in clinical and athletic settings. Correlations between skinfold techniques are high enough for predictions ($r = .90$) if the skinfolds are taken accurately by an experienced individual. Formulas have been devised to estimate percentage of body fat from several (one to six) skinfold site measurements. The formulas for skinfold estimates of body fat are very age- and sex-specific, i.e., they are designed to be used *only* on persons of the same sex and in a narrow age range. Specific formulas have been devised for athletes in training, and they can be very accurate if proper techniques are employed. Figure 7.5 illustrates the skinfold technique.

Lean body weight (LBW). Among the many beneficial effects of exercise training on the body is a decrease in stored body fat and an increase in LBW, primarily muscle tissue. This effect is added to the self-selection process which discourages over-fat individuals from remaining in sport while encouraging those with a higher muscle mass and less body fat. Some athletes may actually desire to gain weight for added body mass. From the previous discussion it is evident that it is most desirable for weight gain in athletes to be primarily in LBW or muscle tissue. It can be accomplished by increasing caloric intake while concentrating on muscle tissue building exercise (weight training). Aerobic exercise will tend to counter these efforts since it consumes calories (primarily fat) over long periods of time.

Carbohydrate Loading

It was previously recommended that the ideal distribution of nutrients in a balanced diet for athletes, as well as others, be comprised of total calories: 55 to 60 percent carbohydrates, 25 to 30 percent fat, and 10 to 15 percent protein. Carbohydrate represents the most important fuel source during exercise. It is the sole energy source during anaerobic activity and is also a

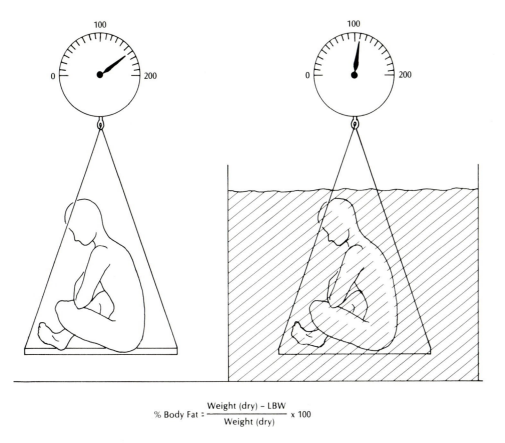

$$\% \text{ Body Fat} = \frac{\text{Weight (dry)} - \text{LBW}}{\text{Weight (dry)}} \times 100$$

Figure 7.4 Measurement of Body Fat (Underwater Weighing)

Figure 7.5 Measurement of Body Fat (Skinfold Technique)

significant source, along with fat, during aerobic activity. Fat cannot be adequately utilized during aerobic activity without sufficient stored glycogen.

Glycogen is an extremely important fuel source during sports performance. About three-fourths of the glycogen in the body is stored in the muscles; one-fourth is stored in the liver. For most sports activities, stored glycogen is far more than sufficient to maintain the ATP cycle. This is especially true of anaerobic performances which last for only brief moments and are not carried on long enough to seriously deplete muscle glycogen. Many vigorous team sports which combine both aerobic and anaerobic metabolism, however, will gradually reduce muscle glycogen. This is particularly true over a period of time when several games are played in a few days. Generally it takes 24 to 48 hours to replace muscle glycogen, even on a 60 percent CHO diet.[3]

The main exception to the concept that dietary manipulation cannot significantly alter performance is the employment of CHO loading. CHO loading is effective *only* in athletic situations that call for sustained high energy expenditure over a long period of time, e.g., the marathon. While team sports may gradually erode some muscle glycogen over several days, the endurance athlete (such as the marathoner) can face rapid depletion of muscle glycogen in just a few hours. The CHO loading technique has proved to be an effective way to increase stored muscle glycogen and thus to enhance performance.[4]

There are several techniques that have proved to increase stored muscle glycogen. The most simple method involves increasing carbohydrate intake for several days prior to an endurance event while simultaneously reducing physical training. The most effective technique, however, involves a week-long plan of diet and exercise. As the competitor approaches the final week before the endurance event, the process is begun. About seven days before the event, the athlete engages in a final exhausting and glycogen-depleting workout. This results in a muscle glycogen level that falls below normal. For several days the athlete continues to work out (not as vigorously) and consumes a *low* carbohydrate diet. This results in additional lowering of muscle glycogen levels. In the last several days prior to the event the athlete consumes a very high CHO diet and ceases work, or reduces it to a minimum. A significant rebound effect occurs, and muscle glycogen may exceed the normal resting level by nearly three times, just prior to the event. This effect can mean a significant difference in the athlete's performance.

A few words of *caution* are in order about CHO loading. First, it has a very limited use in sports, namely, for intense endurance events such as the marathon. Even when used by endurance athletes, it should be employed infrequently. It is not a nutritionally sound diet to be used weekly because it becomes very unbalanced with high fat and protein consumption followed by high CHO intake. In addition, some athletes do not tolerate high carbohydrate diets well. Elevated blood glucose from the high carbohydrate intake may result in excessive insulin secretion, which results in abnormally lowered blood glucose. This overreaction by insulin is also known as hypoglycemia. It is generally recommended that the athlete experiment with CHO loading long before a major event, to determine if the brief unbalanced dietary routine is well tolerated.

It has been noted earlier that athletes consume many more calories daily than do normally active individuals. Much of the additional intake of calories is in the form of carbohydrate. This is beneficial for two reasons: (1) less fat is consumed proportionally, which is beneficial from the health standpoint; and (2) CHO is the major source of energy fuel for the body.

Protein Intake

Much of the mystique associated with diet and sport involves protein. Since muscle tissue is largely protein, athletes from antiquity to today have assumed that muscle tissue must constantly be replenished. Protein is not a source of muscle energy, as was thought in the past, and it should constitute only 10 to 15 percent of caloric intake. Protein is used as tissue-building material, and some athletic diets have been as high as 20 percent of calories in protein. It is often a surprise to most individuals, especially to coaches and athletes, that protein can constitute such a small proportion of the diet. Significant increases in the protein component of the diet do not enhance physical performance, nor do they increase muscle tissue.

Most Americans consume far more protein than is necessary for good health or optimum performance. The recommended protein intake for moderately active individuals is approximately one gram per kilogram of body weight (1 gm/kg).[11] A 165-pound (75 kg) athlete on a 3,000-calorie-per-day diet would receive 75 to 112 grams of protein if the diet were 10 to 15 percent protein. The requirement for that athlete would be 75 grams of protein per day. First, the recommended allowances are set high; then most individuals overconsume protein, so the error is usually on the plus side. As the activity level of the athlete increases, the caloric intake increases and keeps pace with any additional demand. The 253-pound (115 kg) football player on a 5,000-calorie-per-day intake will receive 138 to 187 grams of protein if the diet is only 10 to 15 percent protein.

When excessive amounts of protein are taken in, since they are not required for food, they are excreted by the body. Some excess protein can also be converted to fat, but the major portion of it will be excreted by the kidneys. It joins overdoses of water-soluble vitamins to produce that expensive urine mentioned earlier. Even if the protein requirements of athletes were doubled, the demand could still easily be met by most American diets.

Water Balance

As mentioned earlier, water is rarely recognized as an essential nutrient by most persons. Adequate water intake is very critical for athletes. Perhaps nothing produces so detrimental an effect on performance as rapidly as does dehydration. Most of the life-threatening situations associated with physical activity and sport involve dehydration. Exercise in high heat and humidity conditions can lead to rapid water loss and can require special attention. Studies of exercise and water intake in hot environments have repeatedly demonstrated that voluntary intake of water *does not* keep up with water loss. Athletes replenished only about two-thirds of the loss. Even forced water intake during exercise in heat fails to balance water loss completely. Water balance means that water in all forms of liquid or foods must constantly balance water lost from the body by urination, perspiration, and other sources. Since it appears difficult for the body to maintain water balance during and immediately after exercise, additional water is taken in for many hours after exercise. In some cases, water balance may not be re-established for 24 hours.

Under moderately active conditions, approximately one liter of water is required for each 1,000 calories of food consumed daily.[7] Thus athletes on 3,000–5,000-calorie-a-day intake should consume at least 3 to 5 liters of water. When high heat or humidity adds to the metabolic heat of exercise, *additional* amounts of water are required. Fortunately coaches have abandoned withholding of water during practice and performance. That practice only hastens fatigue. Most coaches and athletes now recognize the need to maintain water intake during prolonged periods of heavy exercise. Perhaps the major question remaining involves how to schedule water intake to best bring about water balance. A few principles of sound water intake are as follows:

1. Ensure that the athlete is well hydrated during the weeks and days prior to the event. In the hours before activity the athlete should take in additional fluid, especially in hot weather.
2. During practice or an event it is best to schedule water intake in small amounts every 15 minutes or so. Since water is continually being lost during exercise, this procedure is preferable to attempting to "load up" before and after practice or a game.
3. Athletic drinks can be important in replenishing glucose and potassium. It should be noted, however, that water intake should be the first priority, and that water loss will begin to affect performance before electrolyte loss. In addition, the high concentration of glucose in athletic drinks will pull additional water from the tissues to balance higher concentrations of blood glucose. The solution to this problem for many endurance athletes is to dilute the athletic drink with water, or merely restrict fluid intake to water only.

Dehydration is a serious problem and it can proceed rapidly under certain conditions (high heat and humidity, heavy exercise, and insufficient water intake). The combination of those conditions can be deadly. Nearly every year dehydration problems cause one or more deaths in sports, usually in late summer as high school and college football players practice under the conditions listed above. Another group of athletes who habitually flirt with serious dehydration problems are wrestlers. Medical and sports medicine groups have consistently warned the wrestling community about the dangers of "making weight" through voluntary dehydration.[16] They have suggested that a standard weight be established on the athlete during the off- or pre-season, and that weight loss be controlled and limited on the basis of that weight.

Dehydration can become a serious problem for wrestlers. As a group, wrestlers, like many other athletes, are very lean with the exception of those in the upper weight categories. There are limits to the amount of fat weight loss that can occur to athletes who are already below 10 percent body fat, or in some cases at or below 5 percent fat. No one knows the minimum limit to body fat before additional loss becomes detrimental to health. It is known, however, that as fat stores are seriously diminished, the body resists additional loss of fat. Some observers have identified 5 percent as "essential" fat. This means that at very low body fat levels, additional weight loss is accomplished primarily by water (possible dehydration) and LBW (muscle tissue) loss. Both of these losses are detrimental to physical performance. A rapid loss of only one percent of body weight begins to affect performance, and at 3 to 5 percent, the performance will be seriously affected.

Perhaps the most reasonable approach for wrestlers is to establish the standard weight during the off-season, as was earlier suggested, and to monitor body composition carefully. As the wrestler reaches 5 percent body fat, no additional weight loss should be permitted, since it is likely to be at the cost of body water and muscle tissue. Remember that a 10- or 20-pound weight loss has a much greater effect on a 120-pound wrestler than on a 200-pound wrestler. A higher percentage of body water and muscle tissue will be lost by the smaller wrestler.

The Pre-Game Meal

Much of the mysticism associated with the pre-game meal is also diminishing. The old habit of high protein (steak and eggs) intake before the contest has proved not beneficial for two reasons: (1) protein is not a major source of energy fuel, and (2) high protein intake may cause additional water loss during digestion and metabolism. The preferred, and recommended, pre-game meal should be relatively high in carbohydrate. This will require additional water intake to assist in glycogen storage. Meals high in complex carbohydrate will usually be easy to digest, and CHO will be reduced to simple sugars more slowly. Since glycogen utilization comes from muscle stores during most sports events, it does little good to load the body with simple sugars just prior to activity. This procedure results primarily in elevating blood glucose. Such a practice may be beneficial, however—even necessary—during prolonged activities, since muscle glycogen and blood glucose can both be depleted. The marathoner, again, is the best example.

A few simple principles are suggested for the pregame meal.

1. Have the athlete eat at least two to three hours before activity. Although complete digestion will not occur during that time, most food will have left the stomach.
2. A meal high in complex carbohydrates (starches) such as spaghetti or pancakes is preferred. The likes and dislikes of the athlete should be considered also, and a choice of several dishes high in CHO is suggested.
3. The "liquid meal" is preferred by many coaches and athletes because of its nutritional balance and ease of digestion. Many athletes, including professionals, are too anxious before a contest to eat normally. The liquid meal has the additional advantage of adding fluid at a time when it is very much needed. If a liquid meal is not selected, it is imperative to remind the athlete of the importance of consuming water with the pregame meal.

SUMMARY

It is hoped that this discussion of sports nutrition has illustrated the importance of consuming a well-balanced diet of sufficient calories to maintain good health as well as sports performance. Perhaps the greatest concern for coaches and athletic trainers is that teen-age athletes may be prone to poor nutritional habits regardless of family income. Both boys and girls are likely to resort to "junk food" during a busy schedule period. Although coaches frequently voice a need to be more knowledgeable about nutrition in general, they usually do not establish diet as high priority in the preparation of the athlete. It is strongly recommended that they, as well as athletic trainers, take an active part in disseminating accurate nutrition information to athletes. Where appropriate and feasible, they should also assist in the selection of food for the athlete.

REFERENCES

1. Astrand, Per-Olaf, and Kaare Rodahl. 1986. *Textbook of Work Physiology,* 3d ed. New York: McGraw-Hill.

2. Briggs, George M., and Doris H. Calloway. 1979. *Bogert's Nutrition and Physical Fitness,* 10th ed. Philadelphia: W. B. Saunders Co.

3. Costill, David L. 1978. "Sports Nutrition: The Role of Carbohydrates," *Nutrition News* 41:1–4.

4. Fox, Edward L. 1984. *Sports Physiology,* 2d ed. Philadelphia: W. B. Saunders Co.

5. Fox, Edward L., et al. 1988. *The Physiological Basis of Physical Education and Athletics,* 4th ed. Philadelphia: W. B. Saunders Co.

6. Katch, Frank I., and William D. McArdle. 1977. *Nutrition, Weight Control and Exercise.* Boston: Houghton-Mifflin Co.

7. Lapidus, Jayne. 1979. "Basic Nutrition for Sports Participants," *Osteopathic Annals* 7:18–21.

8. McArdle, William D., et al. 1988. *Exercise Physiology: Energy, Nutrition, and Human Performance.* Philadelphia: Lea & Febiger.

9. "Nutrition and Physical Fitness." 1980. *Journal of the American Dietetic Association* 76:437–443.

10. *Nutrition for Sports Success.* 1984. Reston, VA: AAHPERD.

11. *Nutrition Source Book.* 1978. Rosemont, IL: National Dairy Council.

12. Palumbo, John D., and George L. Blackburn. 1980. "Human Protein Requirements," *Contemporary Nutrition* 5:1–2.

13. Parizkova, Jana, and V. A. Rogozkin, eds. 1978. *Nutrition, Physical Fitness, and Health.* Baltimore: University Park Press.

14. Peterson, Marilyn S., and Keith Peterson. 1988. *Eat to Compete: A Guide to Sports Nutrition.* Chicago: Year Book Medical Publishers, Inc.

15. Serfuss, Robert C. 1982. "Nutrition for the Athlete Update, 1982," *Contemporary Nutrition* 7:1–2.

16. *Sports Nutrition.* 1982. Department of Nutrition and Food Service. Tucson, AZ: University of Arizona.

17. "Toward a National Nutrition Policy." 1980. *Nutrition News* 9:1–2.

18. "Weight Loss in Wrestlers." 1976. ACSM Position Stand. *Medicine and Science in Sports and Exercise* 8:xi–xii.

19. Williams, Melvin H. 1988. *Nutrition for Fitness and Sport,* 2d ed. Dubuque, IA: Wm. C. Brown Publishers.

20. Young, D. R. 1977. *Physical Performance, Fitness and Diet.* Springfield, IL: Charles C. Thomas.

CHAPTER
EIGHT

THE CONDITIONING PROGRAM: PUTTING IT ALL TOGETHER

Guidelines and principles for using conditioning programs in the off-season, pre-season, and in-season are discussed in this chapter. Ways of implementing a year-round conditioning program are developed for the coach and athlete. In Chapter 3 we discussed specific techniques for developing aerobic and anaerobic conditioning, in Chapter 4 we discussed specific techniques for developing strength for sports, and in Chapter 5 we discussed techniques for increasing flexibility in sports. Armed with the basic information developed in those chapters, and with the principles suggested for putting the program all together, the coach or athlete should be better able to use the programs designed for specific sports in subsequent chapters.

YEAR-ROUND CONDITIONING

The concept of year-round conditioning may appear alarming to some coaches and athletes. Younger athletes especially should be given an opportunity to develop skills and playing ability in a variety of sports before concentrating on one sport or one position. In youth sports leagues the major objective is fun, and conditioning should not become a year-round chore. Many experienced athletes and even professionals object to the concept of conditioning year round. For the athlete who has reached the level of specialization, however, year-round conditioning is essential in order to remain competitive.

Year-round conditioning is a logical step aimed at improving performance, maintaining sports conditioning, and preventing injuries. The authors have already discussed at length the contributions conditioning can make to improving performance and preventing injuries. All of the training effects described so far are reversible, thus training at various levels must be maintained year round.[8,17]

DE-CONDITIONING

While most research conducted in the conditioning area looks at training effects, there is some information on de-training or de-conditioning. Most athletes and coaches are familiar with the de-conditioning effect that takes place during periods of no training. It is most evident after the off-season when an athlete has not maintained sports conditioning. The professional football player often waits until pre-season camp before announcing a retirement. That announcement frequently comes after several days of trying to get an "out-of-shape" body back into playing condition. In most instances it cannot be done, and probably the difficulty could have been avoided with some low-intensity off-season work.

Sports conditioning, which is often achieved after many weeks and months of concentrated effort and hard work, can be lost very rapidly. Every training effect previously discussed can be rapidly lost. Aerobic power is lost rapidly while strength decreases more slowly. Even within two weeks there can be a significant reduction in work capacity. Depending upon the initial level of condition, the loss of work capacity can drop from 50 to 100 percent in three to eight months.[13]

Total rest is not essential for the de-conditioning effect to take place. Since training effects and sports conditioning are specific, discontinuance of one aspect of training can result in a loss of power in that system. Kroll found a loss in throwing power in a collegiate baseball team that discontinued weight training *during* the season.[10] Of greater interest is that a second baseball team *maintained* a reduced-strength training program in season and lost no throwing power. Clarke reports that once strength has been built to a plateau, it can be maintained with as few as one training session per week.[4] Coleman found that major league baseball players actually increased strength and reduced body fat with approximately two strength training sessions per week.[5] Also of importance, the degree of muscular symmetry was greater than that of teammates who did not maintain a strength program in-season. All of these changes occurred without a loss of flexibility.

Athletes in a predominantly anaerobic sport can also lose AER power if AER training is not maintained in-season. Hickson and Rosenkoetter found that AER power could be maintained with as little as two conditioning sessions per week.[9] This format followed a strenuous six-day-a-week training routine for ten weeks. The two-day-a-week maintenance program held AER power at a constant level for fifteen weeks. This is a very important concept for coaches and athletes—namely, that maintenance programs either off-season, and especially in-season, do not require as much time as does the developmental phase of training.

OFF-SEASON CONDITIONING

Many professional athletes and high-level performers recognize the necessity to maintain physical condition during the off-season. Maintenance of aerobic and anaerobic condition and strength for sports reduces the chore of pre-season conditioning for both the coach and the athlete. For professional athletes, maintaining sports conditioning can oftentimes mean a prolonged athletic career. For the young and developing athlete, the off-season conditioning program may be a particularly important time for developing strength and sports fitness.

During the off-season coaches and athletes will usually reduce the concentration of time spent on developing sports skills and strategy. This enables the athlete to place greater concentration on physical conditioning in terms of time and effort. In the school setting the coach will often recommend an extensive physical conditioning program for athletes during the summer months. Varying concentrations should be made on aerobic, anaerobic, strength conditioning, and flexibility during the off-season.

Aerobic Conditioning

In Chapters 2 and 3 we outline the basic reasons for the development of good aerobic conditioning for most team sports. The off-season period is an ideal time to concentrate on aerobic conditioning for athletes. Time is available for the continuous type of training described in Chapter 3. Continuous aerobic conditioning, such as running two to three miles at least three times a week, is an effective means of developing a good aerobic conditioning base for the athlete. A GOAL can be established during the off-season conditioning pro-gram, such as being able to run 2.0 miles in fifteen minutes or less as a minimum requirement for entering pre-season conditioning for all athletes. The intensity of off-season AER conditioning should be low (65–75 percent) with emphasis on continuous work (LSD).

Anaerobic Conditioning

Anaerobic conditioning does not receive as much emphasis during the off-season as does aerobic conditioning. There are several reasons for this situation. For sports that rely heavily on aerobic and anaerobic conditioning, such as track and field and swimming, the intensity of training gradually increases from the off-season to the pre-season to the in-season period. Athletes and coaches in these sports prefer to have a peaking of athletic performance toward the latter stages of the sport season.

Anaerobic conditioning is very intense, both physiologically and psychologically. Anaerobic interval training produces a great deal of work during the training session, as described in Chapter 3, but it also leaves the athlete with a high level of fatigue. During in-season training coaches and athletes will avoid repeated days of intense anaerobic interval training because of the accumulated fatigue.

Real problems of psychological fatigue occur when intense anaerobic training is carried on for months on end. This form of training requires a great deal of persistence and motivation on the part of the athlete. Inhibition can be built up in the athlete if it is carried on year round. Therefore, anaerobic training receives little attention during the off-season.

Strength Training

Since the athlete is not engaged in regular athletic competition during the off-season, he or she can afford to undertake a more intensive strength program. The intensity of the force of contraction of the muscle determines the amount of strength the muscle can develop. Heavier weights are thus used during the off-season, resulting in a reduction in the speed of contraction. The athlete should nevertheless concentrate on making the contraction as explosive as possible. Although the slower speed is not immediately advantageous to performing high-speed athletic movements, the overall increase in strength is desirable at this time and serves as a basis for strength development similar to the "basis" role of aerobic training prior to anaerobic training. Later (pre-season and in-season), speed of muscle contraction will be increased to match more specifically the speed of the sports skill. Strength training in the off-season thus focuses on slower speed movements and fewer repetitions than most sports usually require.

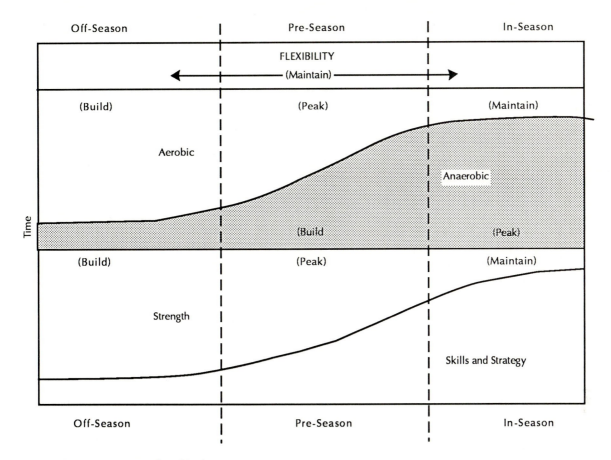

Figure 8.1   Year-Round Conditioning

The number of repetitions of each exercise to be done in the off-season will be less than the number done in-season. Even for high endurance sports, this number will be below ten.

The year-round strength program should entail a cohesive plan aimed at (1) developing maximum strength off-season; (2) adjusting the strength levels to match the muscular endurance, range of motion, and speed of the sport pre-season; and (3) maintaining the strength with those specific characteristics in the off-season. The general rule is that fewer repetitions will be used in the off-season. It should also be emphasized that many different systems of training containing a wide variation of sets and reps have been shown to be effective.

Flexibility

Flexibility training "knows" no season. Flexibility must be maintained year round and does not require, at any time, intense effort from the athlete. Special remedial exercises are sometimes used during the off-season, but the basic aims and programs of flexibility should be consistent throughout the year. The athlete should continue to work on either the development or the maintenance of flexibility throughout the year.

PRE-SEASON CONDITIONING

The objectives of a year-round conditioning program are to develop and maintain aerobic conditioning and strength during the off-season, increase the intensity of aerobic conditioning during the pre-season, and peak and maintain aerobic, anaerobic, and strength conditioning during the in-season period (fig. 8.1). If off-season programs are used properly, pre-season conditioning can be designed to bring the athlete to a peak of condition in the briefest possible time. Coaches and athletes are well aware of the time pressures during the pre-season period to develop physical skills and strategy, and also physical conditioning. During the pre-season coaches often must resort to prolonged practice sessions or multiple sessions during the practice days.

Table 8.1 The Conditioning Session

Warm-Up and Stretching	5–10 mins.
Aerobic Conditioning	15–20 mins.
Strength Training	15–45 mins.
Anaerobic Conditioning	15 mins.
Stretching	5 mins.
	30–90 mins.

Aerobic Conditioning

Aerobic intervals can be used during the pre-season conditioning period to develop peak aerobic condition. An example of aerobic intervals would be:

RUN	Distance	% Max	Rest
	½ mi.	80% +	3–5 min.

Reps	Times per Week
4–6 times	3

Aerobic intervals as compared with continuous aerobic work, will increase the intensity of the aerobic conditioning and also begin to incorporate some anaerobic conditioning. Since the aerobic work is not as intense as anaerobic conditioning, it is recommended that the aerobic portion of the pre-season practice session be done at the beginning of the session and be incorporated as part of the warm-up. If all four conditioning systems will be involved in a single training session or circuit, it is generally recommended that flexibility and aerobic training precede strength training, with anaerobic training concluding the session (table 8.1).

Anaerobic Conditioning

Interval training will be utilized to develop anaerobic capacity, as described in Chapter 3. An example would be sprinting fifty to one hundred yards, all-out–rest period, five to fifteen seconds–five to twenty reps, five times per week. Anaerobic conditioning should come at the latter portion of the practice session during the pre-season program because of the fatigue built up during intense interval training.

Strength Training

The main goal of the pre-season strength program is to prepare the athlete to meet the strength demands of the sport. Strength must be adjusted to be usable at the specific speed, muscular endurance, and through the exact range of motion of the sport. Special concentration is also given at this time to the areas of the body most vulnerable to injury.

Special high-speed equipment can be used at this time, if it is available. The circuit training technique is recommended by the authors because of the potential time savings and combining of aerobic, anaerobic, and strength conditioning. For more specific information about the adjustments in the strength program pre-season, see Chapter 4.

IN-SEASON CONDITIONING

It is the authors' contention that far too many coaches and athletes abandon serious physical conditioning during the in-season period. The reasons voiced are usually lack of time, the claim that conditioning is unnecessary during the season, and the difficulties of arranging a conditioning program in terms of facilities and equipment. The authors maintain that the rationale for year-round conditioning including in-season work, is well established in Part I of this book. Physical condition and strength increases are *reversible*. The athlete who trains seriously and diligently during the pre-season period faces the prospect that a certain amount of de-conditioning may take place during the season. This is particularly true for sports that are not physically demanding, and for athletes who do not receive a great deal of playing time during the season.

The problems of time and equipment are real and are not minimized by the authors. We contend, however, that it is both necessary and possible to maintain aerobic conditioning and strength during the in-season period. Coaches and athletes probably find more time for anaerobic conditioning during the in-season period than the other two conditioning systems, perhaps because it generally requires less time.

Aerobic Conditioning

Aerobic conditioning can be maintained for most sports with as little as two or three training sessions per week of from five to fifteen minutes. Obviously, this minimum time period will not suffice for highly aerobic sports, but should maintain base aerobic conditioning for most team sports. A combination warm-up run and aerobic conditioning period prior to practice will meet the requirements set forth for maintaining aerobic conditioning. During the season AER conditioning generally should be of higher intensity (75–85 percent) and less time (intervals) than the off-season period.

Anaerobic Conditioning

Anaerobic conditioning can be maintained by essentially the same interval training techniques used in the preconditioning period. The intensity and duration of the interval training should be determined by the anaerobic demands of the sport; i.e., the more anaerobic sports will require anaerobic training of greater intensity during the in-season period.

Strength Training

The main goals of in-season strength training are to maintain the strength level demanded of the sport and to help prevent injuries. Like aerobic conditioning, strength and power can be maintained by far less work than is required to attain peak levels of strength and power. For most team sports, one or two strength training sessions per week will be sufficient to maintain strength.

The same number of repetitions are usually followed during the in-season program as in the pre-season period, although the amount of resistance may be reduced slightly. Concentration is still focused on speed of movement, maintenance of muscular endurance, and exact range of motion. Short sessions will produce sufficient work to maintain usable strength. Athletes who are capable of increasing resistance during this period should do so gradually, taking care not to sacrifice speed or endurance.

To aid in injury prevention, the areas of the body most subject to injury should be given special attention. (See Chapter 6.) Maintaining strength in those muscle groups will reduce the risk of muscle injury.

Within-Practice Conditioning

One technique of aerobic and anaerobic conditioning often overlooked by coaches and athletes is within-practice conditioning. This term simply suggests that aerobic and anaerobic overload can occur during skills practice or in actual game practice in several ways. Coaches and athletes should be alert to take advantage of conditioning opportunities within the skills practice session. In football, for example, when plays are run continuously without a huddle, as is done in the two-minute drills, there is overload on the anaerobic system. In basketball, repeated fast break drills also produce an overload on the anaerobic system. In both examples the athlete is practicing the skills involved in the sport, but he is also producing higher levels of conditioning in the anaerobic system.

Scrimmage sessions in basketball may be held continuously without break for substitutions, free throws, or other time-out. This is an excellent example of aerobic conditioning taking place within the practice session. Continuous play in volleyball can produce similar aerobic conditioning results.

Opportunities for aerobic and anaerobic conditioning in less physically demanding sports will obviously be limited. This is the major rationale for supplementary conditioning, as outlined in Part I of this book. The coach or athlete, however, who does not take advantage of opportunities to condition during the practice session is not really making the best use of the time available for full development of the athlete.

Sometimes the coach must make decisions as to when certain conditioning areas should be stressed during the practice session. As mentioned earlier, there is a recommended sequence to follow for conditioning activities whether they stand alone in the off-season or are incorporated within the practice. It is not recommended that strength training be conducted on the same day as intense anaerobic work. The general sequence of activities is illustrated in table 8.1. Flexibility exercises will always precede and conclude practice or conditioning sessions. Aerobic work should come early in the session since it is low in intensity and can also serve to prepare the athlete for more intense conditioning. Skills practice or strategy work should follow (if appropriate). Either strength training or anaerobic conditioning should occur in the latter part of the session because of the intensity and residual fatigue.

Circuit Training

Circuit training has many advantages for total conditioning, and they are outlined in detail in Chapter 3. Because of these advantages (leading to aerobic, anaerobic, and strength conditioning) the authors recommend circuit training as an ideal way of putting all conditioning together during the in-season program. A circuit specific to the individual sport involved can be easily utilized by the athlete or coach. Such a circuit can include muscular endurance, flexibility, and agility exercises as needed by the specific sport. Circuits designed for a number of specific sports are outlined in subsequent chapters.

OVERTRAINING

It has been proposed that more athletic events have been lost because of overtraining than from undertraining. The authors share the concerns of coaches and athletes about the problems of staleness and overtraining. In the case of overtraining, there is a physiological basis for declining performance, injury, or illness. When skilled performance declines, there is a psychophysiological basis for staleness and a reduced interest in the sport. The two types of problems can be interdependent.

Overtraining is a form of stress. Selye has presented the General Adaptation Syndrome (GAS) to explain the body's response to stress.[15] The initial response to a higher level of stress (or training) is the alarm reaction. When the athlete must suddenly encounter two- or three-a-day practices, the body is highly

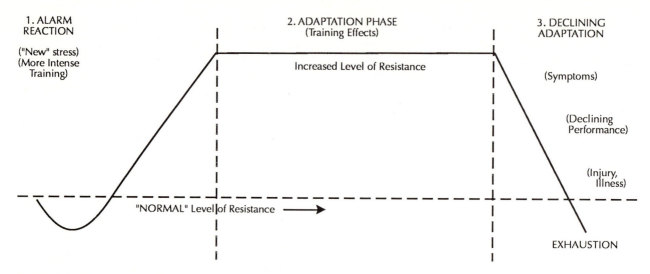

Figure 8.2 The General Adaptation Syndrome (GAS): Implications for Overtraining

stressed. During the first several days, the body's resistance is lowered, and the athlete is at higher risk of injury or illness. During the second phase of the GAS, an adaptation takes place, and the resistance to stress, or training, is increased. That phase is similar to the training effects that occur with sports conditioning. If, however, the stress level is too high, or continued too long, the organism begins to enter a stage of declining adaptation. Under intense stress for prolonged periods, individuals will have symptoms, become ill, and can ultimately die. For the athlete, symptoms, declining performance, and even injury may halt the downslide. Figure 8.2 illustrates the GAS (overtraining) cycle.

There is increasing evidence that overtraining stress can also result in a suppression of the immune system.[7] That can lead to an increased susceptibility to disease and a worsening of existing diseases. While moderate exercise has been touted as a way of boosting the immune system, most athletes, especially elite athletes, do not train "moderately." Elite athletes and Olympians have been found to suffer more illnesses as their training periods get longer or reach peak intensity. The intense training is superimposed on the athlete during a period of intense psychological stress, and possible muscle damage. The combination may add to immune system suppression.

The deterioration of skilled performance can follow a pattern similar to that described by Selye. Psychologists employ a term that describes the kind of staleness affecting the athlete from overpractice of skills. *Reactive inhibition* means that excessive amounts of practice which have already occurred are affecting the performance at the present time. By repeating a skill over and over, the athlete builds up an inhibition toward repeating the skill again. If we were to observe an athlete practicing under forced conditions over a long

period, performance would ultimately begin to deteriorate. The combination of both fatigue and the inhibition toward repeating the performance would result in decreased performance. It is not inferred that fatigue alone is the cause of inhibition. When staleness builds up to this point, the only means of reducing it is to rest or discontinue practice for a time. A few classic examples of athletes who became victims of the Staleness Syndrome in the 1970s and 1980s include Dave Cowens of the NBA, and both Chris Evert and Bjorn Borg in professional tennis.

The more effective means of dealing with the problem is to prevent it, by not making practice so continuous and so repetitious that it results in staleness. Rest periods or a change of activity are the best means the coach can use to avoid staleness. Most coaches are well aware of this concept and organize practice with frequent changes of activity.

There can be a physiological staleness resulting from excess conditioning in the practice of highly physical sports. Astrand reminds us that high-level competition requires overload to increase physiological capacities, which means an almost endless cycle of increasing training intensity.[2] This is a good argument to vary sports conditioning and especially to alternate days or periods of high-intensity training with days or periods of low-intensity training. Prokop long ago proposed that there may be a limit to the body's capacity to sustain and adapt to high-intensity training periods.[14] After the initial stress of increased intensity, the body will adapt to conditioning, but if overstressed continually, a declining adaptation will occur within a period ranging from five weeks to three months. Most athletes will show symptoms of overtraining (when it occurs) at approximately six to eight weeks. The symptoms of overstress or overtraining are more than subjective, and the coach and athlete should be alert to their appearance.

The physical symptoms of overstress on the body may be very similar regardless of the nature of the stress. Selye reminds us that overstress results in non-specific responses, i.e., the same stress symptom may result from very different stressors.[15] Physical manifestations of stress may be a problem for most individuals but they can be insurmountable for the athlete. The athlete relies on, and comes to expect, a good physical response from a well-conditioned body. When overtraining symptoms occur, the results can be devastating for the athlete, both physically and mentally.

With overtraining, some or all of the overstress symptoms may be felt.[12] The muscles may feel stiff and sore, with discomfort in the muscle, joints, or tendons. The athlete sometimes complains of "heavy legs." A frequent symptom involves loss of appetite and body weight. There may be headache, fatigue, and sluggishness; sometimes lymph node swelling and gastrointestinal or stomach disorders. The athlete's physical performance typically declines and he or she may appear nervous, depressed, or unable to relax. The athlete may exhibit loss of interest not only in sports performance, but also a decline in school or other work.

There may be a fine line between optimum or "peak" training and overtraining. No certain method of measuring or anticipating overtraining exists, but some efforts have been made to identify physiological correlates. Many athletes record their resting heart rate (HR) before getting out of bed in the morning. If the HR is eight to ten beats above average, the athlete either lowers the training intensity that day or rests entirely if other symptoms are present (cold or flu). Some swimming coaches have used the same sub-max effort to begin each workout and have recorded HR after the standard work load. If it is above normal, the athlete is instructed to train less intensely that day. The East Germans have even used LA levels as well as HR response to determine the individual variance in response to a standard work load each day. If the LA (lactic acid) level is up, the work intensity is reduced. Blood counts have also been used in elite athletes as a measurement of training stress.

Brown has reported the results of efforts to avoid overtraining with a group of elite athletes.[3] Four easily monitored measurements were able to warn the group that they were stressed from training. They included 1) getting 10 percent less sleep than normal, 2) morning pulse 10 percent greater than normal, 3) skinfolds (use weight) 3 percent less than normal, and 4) failure to complete the last workout. It is necessary to keep accurate records prior to the training and monitoring period. If the answer to two of the stress indicators is positive, the next workout should be scaled back. If three or four indicators are positive, the recommendation is to take the day off.

In addition to avoiding the results of overtraining (declining performance), efforts to identify overstress are also designed to avoid injury. The rate of injury can be expected to increase with overtraining and indeed some sports injuries are called "overuse" syndromes. Some long-time coaches, especially in track and swimming, maintain that more athletes fail to perform to expectation because of overtraining than from undertraining.

Since there is a lack of clearly effective, yet simple tests to measure potential overtraining, the coach or athlete can best prevent overstress by following several principles.

1. The year-round training routine is designed to prevent a loss of sports conditioning and also to alternate periods of low intensity (off-season), high intensity (pre-season), and maintenance (in-season).
2. High-intensity training should not be continued for long periods. Within two or three months most athletes will encounter a period of declining adaptation and declining performance.
3. An ideal schedule involves alternating days of high or low intensity. If this is not possible, then two or three days of high intensity should be followed by a similar period of low intensity work.

MEASUREMENT OF SPORTS CONDITIONING

A logical question for coaches and athletes is how to measure sports conditioning for aerobic, anaerobic, flexibility, strength development, and body composition. If conditioning is to become a year-round process, then the coach or athlete must have some means of evaluating the progress of the conditioning program. Elsewhere the authors have referred to the establishment of goals to be met at the beginning of the preseason conditioning period. Any time an athlete begins a conditioning program, it is essential to establish the existing aerobic, anaerobic, flexibility, strength, and body composition status. Periodic testing then enables the coach or athlete to determine the effectiveness of the conditioning program.

There is no widely used or widely accepted test battery of athletic power for all sports. Much of the testing of aerobic power or muscular strength has been restricted to performance laboratories. Sophisticated tests requiring extensive equipment have been conducted on athletes in many laboratories, but only a small portion of coaches and athletes have access to such facilities.

Some techniques and field tests could be used effectively to estimate aerobic power, anaerobic power, flexibility, strength, and body composition. The authors have included tests or techniques for each of those areas in this chapter. Perhaps one of the simplest ways of measuring progress in sports conditioning is to record daily or weekly performance in each of the areas on recording charts, such as the ones listed in the Appendix.

Aerobic Power

Because it represents the base of sports conditioning, aerobic power is probably the most widely tested area of sports conditioning. The most accurate test of aerobic power is a maximum treadmill, bicycle ergometer, or bench-step test during which oxygen consumption is monitored (fig. 8.3). Such tests are far too time-consuming and costly for most sports teams. A variety of tests that involve running, either for time or distance, can very easily be used by the coach or athlete.[1,6] Such field tests usually estimate aerobic power from distance run in a given time, or from the time it takes to run a specified distance. The authors recommend the use of field running tests to measure aerobic power, as such tests do not require unusual equipment or facilities. One of the most widely used running tests of aerobic power is the 1.5–mile run. With a motivated effort, the test can predict maximum oxygen uptake ($\dot{V}O_2$ max) with a high degree of accuracy. A simple conversion chart can be used to estimate aerobic power from time on the 1.5-mile run (table 8.2).

The two standard tests are the 12-Minute Run for distance and the 1.5-Mile Run for time. Either of these tests can be administered easily with an entire team in less than thirty minutes. They can require only a track and a stopwatch, but the 1.5-Mile Run is easier to score and maintain records of progress. The procedures are as follows.

1. Each player selects a partner. One-half of the team takes the test at one time while the other half records distance (12-Minute Run) or time (1.5-Mile Run).
2. The coach "starts" the run and athletes continue for 12 minutes or 1.5 miles, depending upon the test selected.
3. The object of the test is to run as far as possible in 12 minutes or to run 1.5 miles as fast as possible.
4. At the conclusion of the test, the partner records the distance or time and the athletes trade places. Consult table 8.3.

Table 8.2 Conversion Table: 1.5-Mi. Run Time to $\dot{V}O_2$ max (estimated)

Time for 1.5 Mi.	Est. $\dot{V}O_2$ max (ml/kg/min)	Time for 1.5 Mi.	Est. $\dot{V}O_2$ max (ml/kg/min)
8:00	66.2	12:00	42.6
8:10	65.2	12:10	42.0
8:20	64.2	12:20	41.4
8:30	63.2	12:30	40.8
8:40	62.2	12:40	40.2
8:50	61.2	12:50	39.6
9:00	60.2	13:00	39.0
9:10	59.2	13:10	38.4
9:20	58.2	13:20	37.9
9:30	57.3	13:30	37.3
9:40	56.3	13:40	36.8
9:50	55.4	13:50	36.2
10:00	54.5	14:00	35.6
10:10	53.5	14:10	35.0
10:20	52.5	14:20	34.4
10:30	51.6	14:30	33.8
10:40	50.6	14:40	33.2
10:50	49.6	14:50	32.6
11:00	48.6	15:00	32.0
11:10	47.6	15:10	31.4
11:20	46.6	15:20	30.8
11:30	45.6	15:30	30.2
11:40	44.6	15:40	29.6
11:50	43.6	15:50	29.0

The scoring tables for aerobic power are only suggested. Your athletes, because of sport or age, may have noticeably greater or less aerobic power. The scoring table should serve as a guideline, and with repeated testing of your athletes you can develop your own scale for aerobic power.

Anaerobic Power

Anaerobic power has been the least tested element of sports conditioning. Tests of Stage II anaerobic power have been developed, but they require a 30- to 60-second all-out effort either on a bicycle ergometer or on a treadmill. They also require laboratory equipment, which makes them impractical for most sports settings. Margaria, et al., have devised a simple test of anaerobic power that requires only steps and a stopwatch.[11] The test evaluates the Stage I anaerobic power system and yields a score for anaerobic speed and power. The procedures are as follows.

1. Use stairs (12–16) with a 6–8″ rise, and weigh the subject before the test.
2. Position the subject six feet in front of the first step and require a maximal effort from the start to beyond the twelfth step.

a. Treadmill Test of Maximal Aerobic Power (VO$_2$max)

b. Bicycle Ergometer Test of VO$_2$max

Figure 8.3 Lab Tests of Aerobic Power

Table 8.3 Aerobic Scoring Table for Running Test

Aerobic Power Scores: Junior High School and High School (13–18 Yrs.)

Score	Males	Test	Females
Excellent	1.73 Mi.↑ 9:40 Mins.↓	12-Min. Run 1.5-Mi. Run	1.27 Mi.↑ 14:00 Mins.↓
Good	1.60–1.72 9:41–10:35	12-Min. Run 1.5-Mi. Run	1.16–1.26 14:01–15:25
Fair	1.47–1.59 10:36–11:30	12-Min. Run 1.5-Mi. Run	1.06–1.16 15:25–17:00

Aerobic Power Scores: College Age and Above (19–29 Yrs.)

Score	Males	Test	Females
Excellent	2.0 Mi.↑ 9:00 Mins.↓	12-Min. Run 1.5-Mi. Run	1.65 Mi.↑ 11:00 Mins.↓
Good	1.75–2.0 9:01–10:29	12-Min. Run 1.5-Mi. Run	1.35–1.64 11:00–11:59
Fair	1.50–1.75 10:30–12:00	12-Min. Run 1.5-Mi. Run	1.15–1.34 12:00–15:59

3. The subject takes *two steps at a time,* and the stopwatch is started as the foot hits the *fourth step.* The stopwatch is stopped as the same foot hits the *twelfth step.* (The subject is assumed to have reached peak acceleration at the fourth step.)

4. Allow the subject *three* trials, with two to three minutes rest between trials. Record each trial and average the three, or take the best effort.

Power and vertical speed can be calculated from the recording formula. They are the most significant factors in measuring anaerobic power with the step test. Calculate anaerobic power and vertical speed as follows.

Wt. (lbs.) _____ Vertical rise: 8 steps × ( ) = _____ feet.

Test trials 1. _____ 2. _____ 3. _____
(T) AVG. _____

Work (ft.-lbs.) = F × D
  W = Wt. (_____) × Vertical Rise (_____)
  W = _____ ft.-lbs.

Power (Work per unit time) =
$$\frac{W(_____)}{\text{Time Avg. }(_____)} = \text{ft.-lbs./sec.}$$

Power (hp) = $\dfrac{P\ (_____)}{550\ \text{ft.-lbs./sec.}}$ = _____ hp.

Vertical speed = $\dfrac{D}{T}$ = _____
  = _____ ft./sec.

Note: There are no age and sex standards for athletes. Compare scores within your own team.

Strength

Sophisticated tests of strength can use dynamometers, tensiometers, or isokinetic recording devices. Perhaps the most universally used technique for measuring strength in specific muscle groups is an all-out effort (1RM). That technique can be incorporated periodically on the strength recording sheet that appears in the Appendix. Perhaps the two most widely used tests of maximum strength (1RM) are the bench press for upper body, and the squat for lower body. They are described in detail in Chapter 19, Strength Exercises. There are no age- or sex-related standards for athletes; hence individual improvement should be used for comparison.

Flexibility

As with most of the conditioning components, there is no widely accepted battery of tests for evaluating the flexibility of athletes. In the laboratory, flexibility has been measured by a variety of scientific devices including goniometers, flexometers, and elgons. Just as strength can be evaluated by measuring the capacity

Sit and Reach Scoring

(15" @ edge of box) →

Excellent	22" <
Good	19-21"
Average	14-18"
Fair	12-13"
Poor	11" >

Figure 8.4 Sit and Reach Test of Flexibility

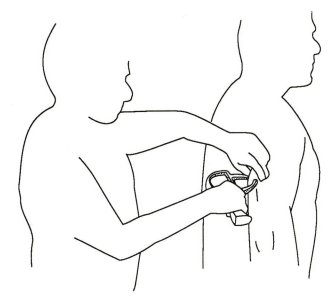

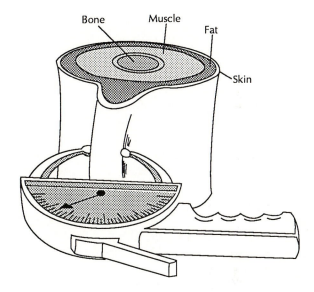

Figure 8.5 The Skinfold Technique

of many muscles, flexibility evaluation could involve the assessment of range of motion in many joints. Perhaps the single most widely used field test of flexibility is the sit and reach test. The test does require a sit and reach box, which can either be purchased commercially, or easily constructed in preparation for testing. A yardstick (3′) should be placed on the box so that the 15″ mark is placed at the edge of the box, where the feet make contact. Figure 8.4 illustrates the sit and reach test, and the scoring system. The procedures are as follows.

1. Sit with legs (knees) straight, shoes off, and feet against box.
2. Slowly and deliberately reach forward, keeping knees straight and hands even. Partner holds the knees down.
3. Hold the position for 2 to 3 seconds, record, and repeat twice more, using the best effort for score. Count only those efforts done with correct form.

Body Composition

The measurement of body composition was described in some detail in Chapter 7, Sports Nutrition. Although it is not generally identified as one of the components of sports conditioning, body composition is an important aspect of sports performance. As indicated in Chapter 7, laboratory tests of percent body fat usually involve underwater weighing. Recent developments in the field also offer the choice of bioinstrumentation, such as bioelectrical impedence. The most widely used field test of percent body fat is the skinfold technique, which does require some expertise and a skinfold caliper. The specific techniques of using skinfolds to estimate body fat are described, and a formula that is specific to athletes, both male and female, is also included.[20]

The use of the skinfold calipers is both an art and a science, and practice is needed to become an accurate technician.

These are the procedures (fig. 8.5).

1. Firmly grasp the skinfold between the left thumb and forefinger about 1″ above the site, and do not release during measurement.

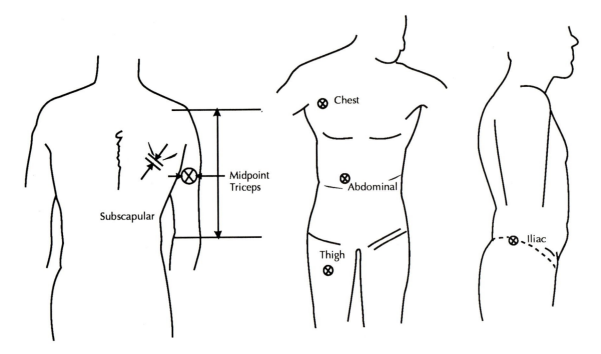

Figure 8.6   Skinfold Sites: 6-Site Athlete's Formula

2. Place caliper directly over the site, lightly touching the fingers holding the skinfold, and well onto the fold.
3. Slowly release the right thumb from the caliper trigger, allowing the caliper jaws to exert their full pressure on the skinfold.
4. After the needle stops (1 to 3 seconds after releasing the trigger), read skinfold to the nearest millimeter, and record. The skinfold measurement should be repeated once or twice more in the interest of accuracy. Relax the fingers holding the skinfold between trials.

The site descriptions are illustrated in figure 8.6. The six sites are 1) the triceps, 2) the subscapular, 3) abdominal, 4) iliac crest, 5) anterior thigh, and 6) posterior thigh for *women* or chest (pectoral) for *men*. The formula for estimating the percent body fat for athletes is

% Body Fat = 3.64 + (.097 × _____ sum of 6 sites)

SUMMARY

In this chapter we have offered suggestions for developing a year-round conditioning program, including off-season, pre-season, and in-season programs. The emphasis on aerobic, anaerobic, or strength conditioning will vary from one part of the season to another. Flexibility training remains constant throughout the year. The authors particularly underscore the need for coaches and athletes to take advantage of conditioning opportunities during the in-season period. A circuit training program is recommended as an excellent technique for developing total conditioning year round and especially during the in-season program. All of the training effects from sports conditioning are reversible and underscore the need to maintain some training out of season. Overtraining is also a potential that should not be ignored by coach or athlete. Techniques and tests are also offered to evaluate sports conditioning for aerobic, anaerobic, flexibility, and strength, as well as body composition.

REFERENCES

1. *AAHPER Youth Test Manual.* 1976. Rev. ed. Washington, D.C.: AAHPER.

2. Astrand, Per Olaf & Kaare, Rodahl. 1986. *Textbook of Work Physiology,* 3d ed. New York: McGraw-Hill.

3. Brown, Dick. 1986. "Stop Signs," *Runners World* 21:72–73.

4. Clarke, David H. 1973. "Adaptations in Strength and Muscular Endurance Resulting from Exercise," *Exercise & Sports Sciences Reviews* (Vol 1). New York: Academic Press.

5. Colemen, Eugene A. 1982. "In-season Strength Training in Major League Baseball Players," *The Physician & Sportsmedicine* 10:125–132.

6. Cooper, Kenneth H. 1983. *The Aerobic Program for Total Well-Being.* New York: Bantam Books.

7. Fitzgerald, Lynn. 1988. "Exercise and the Immune System," *Immunology Today* 9:337–339.

8. Fox, Edward L. 1984. *Sports Physiology.* 2d ed. Philadelphia: W. B. Saunders.

9. Hickson, Robert C. & Maureen A. Rosenkoetter. 1981. "Reduced Training Frequencies and Maintainence of Increased Aerobic Power," *Medicine & Science of Sport & Exercise* 13:13–16.

10. Kroll, William A. 1973. "The Effects of an In-Season Training Program on the Throwing Power of Junior College Baseball Players," Masters thesis. Arizona State University.

11. Margaria, Rudolf et al. 1966. "Measurement of Muscular Power (Anaerobic) in Man," *J. of Applied Physiology* 21:1662–1664.

12. Mirkin, Gabe & Marshall Hoffman. 1978. *The Sportsmedicine Book.* Boston: Little & Brown.

13. Pollack, Michael L. 1978. *Health and Fitness Through Physical Activity.* New York: John Wiley & Sons.

14. Prokop, L. 1963. "Adrenals and Sport," *J. of Sports Medicine and Physical Fitness* 3:115–121.

15. Selye, Hans. 1974. *Stress Without Distress.* New York: Signet.

16. Stone, William J. 1974. "A Pre-Conditioning Program for Team Sports," *Arizona Prep* 4:18–20.

17. Stone, William J. 1981. "Sports Conditioning," *Osteopathic Annals* 9:12–15.

18. Wells, Christine L. 1979. "Physiological Principles of Training for Maximal Performance," *Arizona JOHPERD* 23:2–7.

19. Wilmore, Jack H. & David L. Costill. 1988. *Training for Sport and Activity* 3d ed. Dubuque, IA: Wm. C. Brown.

20. Yuhasz, Michael S. 1962. "The Effects of Sports Training on Body in Man with Predictions of Optimal Body Weight," Doctoral dissertation, University of Illinois.

PART
TWO

CONDITIONING PROGRAMS FOR SPORTS

This section of the book deals with the application of conditioning programs to specific sports. These chapters offer specialized programs in football, soccer, basketball, hockey, volleyball, wrestling, baseball, softball, swimming, track and field, and individual sports (archery, golf, gymnastics, tennis, and triathlon).

General conditioning, stretching, and strengthening of basic muscle groups may be beneficial to nearly any sports performer. There are distinct differences, however, in the way various factors such as strength, speed, or endurance contribute to the performance of different sports skills. The objective of the conditioning programs for the various sports covered in this volume is to match the training techniques as specifically as possible to the demands of the sports.

CHAPTER
NINE

FOOTBALL

In this chapter we include aerobic and anaerobic conditioning programs and strength building programs for football. In order to make the most effective use of the programs offered here, the reader is referred to Chapter 3 for the basis of aerobic and anaerobic training programs, to Chapter 4 for the basis of strength programs, to Chapter 5 for the basis of warm-up and stretching programs, and to Chapter 8 for the most efficient means of incorporating those objectives into a single workout. The programs are offered as off-season, pre-season, and in-season programs at three levels. The three levels include junior high school, senior high school, and college level training programs. The reader is also referred to sample recording charts offered in the Appendix. These charts will facilitate the measurement of progress that the athlete makes on the training program and will also indicate the athlete's standing in regard to training goals.

Football could be described as the "perfect" *anaerobic* game. It requires a maximum of *anaerobic power*. Speed, strength, acceleration, and agility are the basic elements of the game and thus requirements of the athletes who play the game.[3,7] There is significant evidence that faster, stronger, and more powerful athletes are at a real advantage in football and that those factors can best be developed by specific conditioning.[5] The typical play in football may last three, five, or eight seconds. Occasionally a longer play may last up to fifteen seconds, but this is rare. Football is the epitome of Stage I (ATP–CP) energy metabolism. If all of the time involved in such action is added together, it has been determined that the ball is in play only eight to twelve minutes in the typical sixty-minute game. The remainder of the time is taken up with picking oneself off the turf, walking back to the huddle, listening to the play, and returning to the line of scrimmage in preparation for the next burst of energy. A recent Super Bowl was analyzed for "action" and it tallied only twelve minutes. In the NFL most pass plays allow only 3.0 seconds for blocking.

Recovery from all-out bursts of activity requires good *aerobic* capacity. Increasing the general endurance will enable the football player to perform longer with less fatigue. Repeated bouts of maximum effort, such as occur in football, require general endurance as well as local muscular endurance. Football players often fail to see the need for aerobic capacity in a highly anaerobic sport. Repeated bouts of anaerobic effort result in an accumulation of lactic acid. During the approximately 20- to 25-second rest interval between plays, the player shifts to aerobic metabolism and recovery begins. Full recovery is not possible in that time frame, but greater aerobic capacity results in a higher percentage of recovery. While the conditioning to improve football *performance* is primarily short-burst, maximum sprinting, aerobic work is also included although its contribution is primarily for *recovery*.

Football is ideally suited to *strength* programs designed to enhance speed, power, acceleration, and agility. The action is "explosive" and the strength training should match the explosive characteristic of the game. Similar to the aerobic basis prior to intense anaerobic training, slower speed, heavy strength training will precede the pre-season and in-season emphasis on high-speed "explosive" training. The concepts reviewed here are discussed in more detail in Chapters 3, 4, 5, and 8.

Football is one of the most complex of team games. Not only is there a variety of positions to be played, but players reflect a number of different body types fulfilling very different roles.[2] Because of the complexity of the game and the team, the conditioning program needs to be well organized in order to meet the demands placed on various players. At the professional level, the Dallas Cowboys of the NFL have solved the problem by computerizing their conditioning program.[8] This solves not only various role differences in conditioning, but also allows an individualized approach. Most football programs do not have a conditioning coach and a computer available to them. Some conditioning programs divide the football team into four or five groups, while others maintain that all players should follow the same basic program.[3] The authors were successful in developing a year-round conditioning program at Arizona State University by dividing the team into two primary groups, linemen and backs.[6] Significant improvement was found in strength, power, percent body fat, and endurance in a four-month period. More important, the gains were maintained during the season without interruption of the practice sessions.

JUNIOR HIGH, HIGH SCHOOL, AND COLLEGE FOOTBALL

Junior High School

Athletes in junior high school usually fall in a range of physical development from prepubescent to postpubescent. No other competitive sports age group offers such a wide range of physical development and potential for athletic injury. This presents an unusual challenge to the athlete or coach to select a training regimen that will match the needs of the individual and reduce the potential for injury. Conditioning needs may be met through after-school programs or within the physical education class. A few guidelines are offered for the training of junior high footballers.

Training sessions should be limited to two or three per week for junior high athletes. Intense anaerobic training should not become such a heavy burden that young athletes become mentally and physically "turned off." Since football requires a high level of tolerance to pain and discomfort, the young athlete should be *gradually* conditioned to undergo vigorous training and play.

Weight training at this level will not be as highly specialized as later, when it becomes directed toward improving performance at a single position. It should be directed primarily toward developing total body strength and enhancing fundamental athletic skills such as running, jumping, and throwing. Combination programs that include aerobic, anaerobic, and strength training are recommended.

High School

Most high school athletes have completed the adolescent growth spurt and have gravitated toward a particular sport and position. A few youngsters will be multisport athletes. In the day of age-group (Pop Warner, Little League) programs, specialization can occur earlier and certainly the high school athlete will be more specialized than the junior high athlete. He is also prepared to undergo more intensive supplementary training.

The athlete and coach should develop conditioning programs that can be conducted in the off-season (summer). For the novice strength trainer, the coach should include instructions with conditioning programs or refer the athlete to an experienced strength coach. High school is a good time for football players with serious ambitions about athletic careers to become familiar with year-round conditioning.

Young athletes must be cautious in the early stages of weight training and avoid the temptation to lift as much weight as possible (1RM). Heavy squats, to the parallel position (upper leg) or lower, *should not* be attempted until the youngster is 16 years old. Until then squats should be performed only to the ½ squat position. (See p. 250.) The long-term goals of strength training for athletics should be emphasized rather than short-term efforts at maximum strength. Progress can be very motivational for the high school or junior high athlete if records are maintained as suggested by examples in the Appendix. Six to eight weeks of conditioning can produce gains significant enough to impress the most eager young athlete.

Collegiate Football

Like his professional counterparts, the collegiate football player is usually the epitome of specialization. Special-position strength programs are offered later in this chapter to accommodate the special positions. The principles involved in training are essentially the same, however, as for younger athletes. Collegiate football programs pioneered the conditioning approaches that are commonly used at the high school and junior high school level.

There is likely to be a great diversity of equipment available at the collegiate level. High-powered athletic programs at major universities may have a wide range of strength building equipment at hand. Some collegiate football players have limited experience with weight training or off-season conditioning. Most institutions have "strength coaches" whose major responsibility will be to develop conditioning programs for athletes. The conditioning of the collegiate player is essentially the same as for the professional.

OFF-SEASON

The major objectives of the off-season program are the development of maximum *strength* and *aerobic power*.[1] Both of these objectives require time and, as mentioned earlier, time is available during the off-season to concentrate on these two objectives. Greater aerobic capacity will enable the football player to recover from the repeated anaerobic bursts of activity that characterize football. Greater general endurance means the ability to practice or play longer and harder without becoming fatigued as readily as those who do not train aerobically!

Table 9.1 Off-Season Circuit for Junior High Football

Warm-Up and Stretching
Arm circles—Squat with hands on hips—Sit-ups—Trunk rotations

Aerobic Conditioning

	Distance	% Max.	Time
Run: Minimum	0.5 mi.	75%	3–5 mins. (approx.)
Goal	2.0 mi.	75%	15–16 mins. (approx.)

Strength Training
To be used on a standard multi-exercise selectorized machine. The exercises can vary according to the stations offered on the particular machine. These exercises were selected to conform with a common commercially available machine. Strength Circuit 1: Train with designated repetition intervals or timed intervals (25-second stations, 5-second rotations); rotate through circuit 3 to 5 times.

Circuit: 60-second station, rotate through circuit two times

Station #1—Bench Press, 6–10 reps
    2—Pull-Ups, max 15 reps and Sit-Ups
    3—Military Press, 6–10 reps
    4—Back Hyperextension, 10–15 reps
    5—Chin-Ups on Y bar, 15 reps max
    6—Upright Rowing, 10–15 reps

7—Lat Pulls, 10–15 reps
    8—Leg Press, 10 reps
    Toe Raises, 30 reps
    9—Bar Dips, 15 reps max
   10—Leg Extension, 10–15 reps
   11—Neck Extension, 10–15 reps
   12—Grip Exercise series

Stretching Exercises

The strength conditioning during the off-season will focus on high resistance, low repetition work. The speed of contraction will be slower than pre-season and in-season training because of the greater resistance. The off-season is the ideal time for the football player to concentrate on the two objectives (strength and aerobic power) that are less specific to the game than the pre-season and in-season objectives (anaerobic and explosive power).

Strength training circuits can be designed for off-season conditioning. However, the large muscle groups developed by major and assistant strength can best be developed utilizing a "set system." This allows a longer rest period between sets. In the off-season programs included in this chapter which recommend a "set system," 3- to 4-station walking circuits (Strength Circuit 1) can be used for the supplemental and specialty exercises. These "mini-circuits" are performed with designated repetition intervals.

If full strength circuits are to be utilized during the off-season, the limitation in the maximum development of the major muscle groups should be understood. They can be used effectively to supplement the developmental period of another type of physical conditioning. This would normally be aerobic and anaerobic (sprint training). This is not to mean that strength will not be developed by this circuit, but only that a *maximal* amount of strength in major muscle groups will be limited. A strength circuit can be excellent strength training for junior high football players as the heaviest part of their off-season program. A heavy set system strength program at least 6 to 8 weeks in length should be a requirement for high school and college football players.

An unlimited variety of strength circuits can be designed for off-season strength training. An entire program can be completed in approximately one hour, if a standard multi-exercise machine is available (table 9.1). Other types of strength equipment, including free weights and a multitude of commercially available equipment, can be utilized in creative ways to keep off-season strength training circuits interesting. Be sure to follow the Essentials of Strength Training for Athletes (Chapter 4).

In designing a circuit, it is desirable that the muscle groups being used be varied so that two consecutive stations do not use the same muscle group as the main movers. If barbells are available, the Clean and Squat movements should be included. The Clean is imitative of the fundamental explosive football movement necessary to deliver a rising blow.

Additional exercises can be done to improve throwing power if a wall pulley is available. When training with wall pulleys to improve throwing, the exact range of movement should be followed. A common mistake is to get out of the range of movement by bringing the upper arm too close to the body, or failing

Table 9.2 Off-Season Conditioning Program for Junior High Football

Warm-Up and Stretching

Aerobic Conditioning

		Distance	% Max.	Time
Run:	Minimum	0.5 mi.	75%	4–5 min. (approx.)
	Goal	2.0 mi	75%	15–16 min. (approx.)

Strength Training

3 days per week; major and assistant exercises: apply set system; supplemental and specialty exercises: apply set system or circuit system 1.

Monday	Wednesday	Friday
Bench Press	**Military Press**	**Bench Press**
10-10-8-6-4-2-2-2	10-10-8-8-6-6-4-4	10-10-8-8-5-5-5-5
(Start with more reps if you're not already lifting. Heavy max. reps are not necessary. Do only once a week if at all.)	**High Pulls or Cleans (Similar to Upright Rows)**	(Start with more reps if you're not already lifting. Heavy max. reps are not necessary. Do only once a week if at all.)
Squats	5-4-3-3-3-2	**Squats**
10-10-8-6-4-2-2-2	(Great for interior linemen.)	10-10-8-8-5-5-5-5
(Unnecessary to go down to parallel.)	**Tricep Extension**	(Unnecessary to do down to parallel.)
Toe Raises	8-5-5-5-5	**Toe Raises**
8 sets, 30 reps	**Curls**	8 sets, 30 reps
Tricep Extension	5 sets, 10 reps	**Tricep Extension**
8-5-5-5-5	**Sit-Ups**	8-5-5-5-5
Curls	5 sets, 10–20 reps	**Curls**
5 sets, 10 reps	**Neck Extension**	5 sets, 10 reps
Sit-Ups	4–6 sets, 10 reps	**Sit-Ups**
5 sets, 10–20 reps	**Bent-Arm Pullover**	5 sets, 10–20 reps
Neck Extension	5 sets, 10 reps	**Bent-Arm Pullover**
4–6 sets, 10 reps	**Inclines or Dips**	5 sets, 10 reps
Bent-Arm Pullover	(Could be substituted for Military Press)	**Shoulder Shrugs**
5 sets, 10 reps	**Shoulder Shrugs**	5 sets, 8 reps
Shoulder Shrugs	5 sets, 6 reps	
5 sets, 10 reps		

Stretching Exercises

---

to "lead with the elbow." These types of throwing exercises can be followed with the regular weight training program, 10–15 repetitions, 5–6 sets.

For the more highly competitive programs, strength training programs are offered with consecutive sets of each exercise, e.g., see the set system in Chapter 4. Fewer reps (1–8) will be used with the noncircuit programs. Special programs that can be used in the off-season are also included. Such programs include training regimens of more than the traditional every-other-day approach. For brief periods (4–8 weeks) some athletes will be able to condition for five or more days per week. The authors identify this as "high-intensity" training and certainly *do not recommend* such a regimen for most athletes.

A series of off-season conditioning programs follows. They are appropriate for junior high, high school, or college level conditioning. The collegiate programs could indeed be used by professionals. Some of the programs are specified according to position.

Table 9.3   Off-Season Conditioning Program for Offensive and Defensive Backs (*H.S.-College*)

Warm-Up and Stretching

Aerobic Conditioning

	Distance	% Max.	Time
Run: Minimum	1.0 mi.	75%	7–8 min. (approx.)
Goal	2.0 mi.	75%	14–15 min. (approx.)

Strength Training

3 days per week; major and assistant exercises: apply set system; supplemental and specialty exercises: apply set system or circuit system 1.

Monday	**Wednesday**	**Friday**
Bench Press	Incline	Bench Press
10–10–8–8–6–6–4–4	10–10–8–8–6–6	10–10–8–5–3–3–3–3
Half Squat	High Pulls or Cleans	Half Squat
8–8–6–6–4–4–3–3	5–4–3–3–3–2	8–8–8–6–6–4–4–4
Toe Raises	Speed Exercise	Toe Raises
8 sets, 30 reps	6 sets, 10–15 reps	8 sets, 30 reps
Speed Exercise	Sit-Ups	Speed Exercise
(30 lbs. max.)	5 sets, 14 reps	6 sets, 10–15 reps
6 sets, 10–15 reps	Grip Exercises	Sit-Ups
Sit-Ups	305 sets	5 sets, 18 reps
5 sets, 10 reps		Neck Extension
Neck Extension		4–6 sets, 10 reps
4–6 sets, 10 reps		Grip Exercises
Grip Exercises		3–5 sets
3–5 sets		

Optional

Split Squats, Jumping Squats, Wrist Curls, Good Mornings, Tricep Extensions, Shoulder Shrugs

Stretching Exercises

Table 9.4   Off-Season Conditioning Program for Linemen and Linebackers (*H.S.–College*)

Warm-Up and Stretching

Aerobic Conditioning

	Distance	% Max.	Time
Run: Minimum	0.5 mi.	75%	4–5 mins. (approx.)
Goal	2.0 mi.	75%	15–16 mins. (approx.)

Strength Training

3 days per week; major and assistant exercises: apply set system; supplemental and specialty exercises: apply set system or circuit system 1.

Monday	**Wednesday**	**Friday**
Bench Press	Incline Press	Bench Press
8–8–3–2–1–1–4–4	10–10–8–8–6–6	10–10–8–8–5–5–5–5
Half Squat	Dips	Half Squat
8–8–6–3–2–1–1–4–4	10–10–8–8–6–6	10–10–8–8–5–5–5–5
Toe Raises	(Military Press can be substituted	Toe Raises
8 sets, 30 reps	for Dips and trained as Incline	8 sets, 30 reps
Tricep Extension	Press.)	Tricep Extension
8–5–5–5–5	High Pulls or Cleans	8–5–5–5–5
	8–6–5–5–5	

Table 9.4—*Continued*

Monday	Wednesday	Friday
Sit-Ups 5 sets, 10 reps	Tricep Extension 8–5–5–5–5	Sit-Ups 5 sets, 18 reps
Neck Extension 4–6 sets, 10 reps	Sit-Ups 5 sets, 14 reps	Neck Extension 4–6 sets, 10 reps
Grip Exercises 3–5 sets	Grip Exercises 3–5 sets	Grip Exercises 3–5 sets

Optional

Lat Pulls, Upright Rowing, Presses Behind Neck, Leg Presses, Wrist Curls, Good Mornings, Curls, Shoulder Shrugs
Linebackers and Defensive Ends—Frontal Delts, Wrist Curls

Stretching Exercises

Table 9.5   Off-Season Conditioning Program for Quarterbacks (*H.S.-College*)

Warm-Up and Stretching

Aerobic Conditioning

		Distance	% Max.	Time
Run:	Minimum	1.0 mi.	75%	7–8 min. (approx.)
	Goal	2.0 mi.	75%	14–15 min. (approx.)

Strength Training

3 days per week; major and assistant exercises: apply set system; supplemental and specialty exercises: apply set system or circuit system 1.

Monday and Friday	Wednesday
Bench Press 10–10–8–8–6–6–4–4	Dips 6 sets, 10 reps
Half Squat 8–8–6–6–4–4–3–3	Incline Press 8–8–8–6–6–6–4–4
Throwing Pullover 5 sets, 10 reps	High Pulls or Cleans 8–6–5–5–5
Toe Raises 8 sets, 30 reps	Toe Raises 8 sets, 30 reps
Sit-Ups, Twisting 5 sets, 10 reps (18 on Friday)	Sit-Ups Twisting 5 sets, 14 reps
Throwing Motion (wall pulley) 5 sets, 10 reps	Throwing Motion (wall pulley) 5 sets, 10 reps
Wrist Roller or Wrist Curl 5 sets	Wrist Roller or Wrist Curl 5 sets
Neck Extension 5 sets, 10–15 reps	Neck Extension 5 sets, 10–15 reps

Optional

Upright Rowing, Bent-Over Rowing, Lat Pull, Curls, Tricep Extension, Incline Press.

Throwing

Stretching

Table 9.6 Off-Season Conditioning Program for Kickers (*H.S.-College*)

Warm-Up and Stretching

Strength Training 3 days per week; major and assistant exercises: apply set system; supplemental and specialty exercises: apply set system or circuit system 1.

Monday and Friday	Wednesday
Half Squat	Leg Extension
6 sets, 8 reps	5 sets, 10 to 15 reps
Leg Extension (from flexed position)	High Pulls or Cleans
5–6 sets, 10 to 15 reps	8-6-5-5-5
Toe Raises	Toe Raises
8 sets, 30 reps	8 sets, 30 reps
Wall Pulley (kicking motion)	Wall Pulley (kicking motion)
5 sets, 10 to 15 reps	5 sets, 10 to 15 reps
Sit-Ups	Sit-Ups
5 sets, 10 reps (18 on Friday)	5 sets, 14 reps
Leg Lifts	Leg Lifts
5 sets, 10 reps	5 sets, 10 reps
Bench Press	Military Press
5 sets, 8 reps	5 sets, 8 reps

Optional

Lat Pull, Bench Press, Incline Press, Bent-Over Rowing

Kicking

Anaerobic Exercise

	Distance	% Max.	Rest	Reps
Run:	100 yds.	100%	30 secs.	5–10

Stretching Exercises

Table 9.7 High-Intensity Off-Season Conditioning Programs for College Football Player "A"

Aerobic Conditioning (3/Week)
Warm-Up and Stretching

	Distance	% Max.
Run:	1.5–2.0 mi.	75%

Strength Training 3 days per week; major and assistant exercises: apply set system; supplemental and specialty exercises: apply set system or circuit system 1.

Monday		Tuesday	
Bench	Upright Rowing	Incline	Good Morning
8–10 sets	5 sets, 10 reps	8–10 sets	5 sets, 8 reps
10-10-8-8-6-6-6-6-4-4		10-10-8-8-6-6-4-4	
Squat	Sit-Ups	High Pulls or Cleans	Sit-Ups
8–10 sets	5 sets, 10 reps	5–6 sets	5 sets, 12 reps
8-8-8-8-6-6-6-6		8-6-5-5-5	
Toe Raises	**Specialty Exercise**	Toe Raises	Neck Extension
8–10 sets, 30 reps		8–10 sets, 30 reps	5 sets, 10–15 reps
Tricep Extension			
8-5-5-5-5			

Table 9.7—*Continued*

Thursday

Military Press
8–10 sets
10–10–8–8–6–6–6–6

Bar Dips
8–10 sets
10–10–8–8–8–8

Tricep Extension
8–5–5–5–5

Friday

Press Behind Neck
8–10 sets

High Pulls or Cleans
5 sets 8–6–5–5–5

Deadlift
5–4–3–2–1

Good Morning
5 sets, 10 reps

Specialty Exercise

Stretching Exercises

Leg Press or Rack Squat
6–10 sets

Sit-Ups
5 sets, 14 reps

Specialty Exercise

Toe Raises
8–10 sets

Bent-Over Rowing
5 sets, 10 reps

Sit-Ups
5 sets, 16 reps

Neck Extension
5 sets, 10–15 reps

Saturday

Bench
8–10 sets
10–10–8–6–4–2–1–1–4–4

Dumbbell Bench
5 sets
8–8–8–6–6

Squat
8–10 sets
8–8–8–6–4–2–1–1–4–4

Toe Raises
8–10 sets, 30 reps

Tricep Extension
8–5–5–5–5

Sit-Ups
5 sets, 16 reps

Table 9.8   High-Intensity Off-Season Conditioning Programs for College Football Player ''B''

Warm-Up and Stretching

Aerobic Conditioning (3/Week)

	Distance	% Max.
Run:	1.5–2.0 mi.	75%

Strength Training 3 days per week; major and assistant exercises: apply set system; supplemental and specialty exercises: apply set system or circuit system 1.

Monday

Behind Neck Press
10 sets
10–10–10–8–8–6–6–4–4–2

Dips
10–10–8–8–8–8–6–6–6–6

Bent-Over Rowing
5 sets, 10 reps

Tuesday

Bench
12–12–10–10–6–6–4–4–2–2

Squat
8–8–8–8–6–6–4–4–2–2

Calves
10 sets, 30 reps

Sit-Ups
5 sets, 12 reps

High Pulls or Cleans
8–6–5–5–5

Neck Extension
5 sets, 10–15 reps

Curls
5 sets, 14 reps

Sit-Ups
5 sets, 14 reps

Tricep Extension
8–5–5–5–5

Table 9.8—*Continued*

Thursday

Dips	Sit-Ups
10–10–8–8–6–6–6–6–4–4	5 sets, 16 reps
Incline	**Specialty Exercise**
10–10–10–10–8–8–6–6–6–6	
Curls	Neck Extension
5 sets	5 sets, 10–15 reps

Friday

Military Press	Curls
10–10–8–8–6–6–4–4–4–4–2–2	5 sets, 10 reps
Squat	Sit-Ups
8–8–8–8–6–6–4–4–4–4–2–2	5 sets, 18 reps
Calves	Tricep Extension
10 sets, 30 reps	8,5,5,5,5

Stretching Exercises

PRE-SEASON

As the pre-season approaches there will be a dramatic shift in the conditioning approach. The shift will be from aerobic to anaerobic conditioning and from slow-speed, heavy-resistance strength conditioning to fast-speed, high-repetition strength training.

The major objectives of pre-season conditioning are the development of *anaerobic power, explosive strength,* and *injury prevention.* For those athletes who have been on an off-season program, the shift is to more intensive anaerobic training and high-speed strength training. The resistance must be reduced to produce the latter objective. Agility drills and quick reaction training increase.

For athletes who have not engaged in an off-season program, rapid strength and anaerobic development can be hastened by the use of a special circuit. High-repetition, high-speed strength training should be emphasized. Anaerobic training can be very unpleasant and fatiguing for the athlete who has not developed good aerobic power to aid recovery from sprints. The authors recommend a *test* at the beginning of the pre-season period to determine if the athlete can meet the aerobic GOAL listed in the off-season programs (2.0 mi. in 14–16 mins.). This will quickly determine which players have not followed the aerobic portion of the off-season conditioning program.

Specificity of conditioning becomes the major consideration as the football player approaches the playing season. If some kind of "training camp" is held pre-season, coaches and athletes may desire to shift to a pre-season regimen before going to the training camp. This is also the time to employ *football specific* (anaerobic) conditioning. Football specific conditioning involves a series of explosive efforts in the range of 3 to 12 seconds. The bouts of exercise may involve sprints or other specific movements in a *random pattern* similar to the order of plays in a single quarter of football. Fifteen to twenty plays should be run with a brief rest period between. Sprints are done at maximum effort.

A variety of pre-season programs are offered from junior high through college level. Tables 9.9 through 9.13 are to be performed employing a set system. They are offered for individuals who are training the final two to three weeks in preparation for football camp, or in circumstances more conducive to the utilization of the set system.

Table 9.14 is a pre-season strength circuit. It can be utilized by either junior high, high school, or college football players. It is suggested that junior high players go through the circuit only one time. High school and college football players can perform the circuit twice. To administer this circuit, systems 3, 4, 5, or 6 can be used. (Chapter 4). After the circuit is performed, players can work on specialty exercises using a set system.

Table 9.9   Pre-season Conditioning Program for Junior High Football

Warm-Up and Stretching

Strength Training—Train Explosively!

Monday–Friday	Wednesday
Bench Press 10,10,8,8,8,8	Military Press 10,10,8,8,8,8
Squats 8,8,8,8,8,8	High Pulls or Cleans 8,5,5,4,3
Toe Raises 8 sets, 30 reps	Curls 5 sets, 10 reps
Tricep Extension 5 sets 8,5,5,5,5	Tricep Extension 5 sets 8,5,5,5,5
Sit-Ups 5 sets, 10–20 reps	Sit-Ups 5 sets, 10–20 reps
Neck Extension 4–6 sets, 10 reps	Neck Extension 4–6 sets, 10 reps

Anaerobic Conditioning

	Distance	% Max.	Rest	Reps	Times/Week
Run:	100 yds.	100%	30 secs.	5–10	3–5

Run: FB (Football) specific sprints (plays), random order, max effort, 15–20 reps.

Stretching Exercises

Table 9.10   Pre-season Conditioning Program for Offensive and Defensive Backs (*H.S.-College*)

Warm-Up and Stretching

Strength Training—Train Explosively!

Monday	Wednesday	Friday
Bench Press 2 weeks 10–10–10–10–8–8	Incline 2–4 weeks 10–10–8–8–8–8	Bench Press 2 weeks 10–10–10–10–10–10–8–8
Half Squats 2 weeks 6 sets, 8 reps	Alternate, Single Set and Double Sit-Ups	Half Squats 2–4 weeks 6 sets, 8 reps
Toe Raises 8 sets, 30 reps	High Pulls or Cleans 8–6–5–5–5	Toe Raises 8 sets, 30 reps
Speed Exercise (30 lbs. max.) 6 sets, 10–15 reps	Speed Exercise 6 sets, 10–15 reps	Speed Exercise 6 sets, 10–15 reps
Sit-Ups 5 sets, 10 reps	Sit-Ups 5 sets, 14 reps	Sit-Ups 5 sets, 18 reps
Neck Extension 4–6 sets, 10 reps	Grip Exercise 3–5 sets	Neck Extension 4–6 sets, 10 reps
Grip Exercise 3–5 sets		Grip Exercise 3–5 sets

Optional

Split Squats, Jumping Squats, Wrist Curls, Good Mornings

Anaerobic Conditioning (daily)

	Distance	% Max.	Rest	Reps
Run:	100 yds.	100%	30 secs.	10–15

Run: FB (Football) specific sprints (plays), random order, max effort, 15–20 reps

Stretching Exercises

Table 9.11   Pre-season Conditioning Program for Linemen and Linebackers (*H.S.-College*)

Warm-Up and Stretching

Strength Training—Train Explosively!

Monday	Wednesday	Friday
Bench Press	Incline Press	Bench Press
10-10-8-8-8-8	2 weeks 10-10-8-8-8-8	2 weeks 10-10-8-8-8-8
Half Squat	Dips	Half Squat
10-10-8-8-8-8	2 weeks 10-10-8-8-8-8	10-10-8-8-8-8
Toe Raises	(Military Press can be substituted	Toe Raises
8 sets, 30 reps	for Dips and trained as Incline	8 sets, 30 reps
Tricep Extension	Press.)	Tricep Extension
8-5-5-5-5	High Pulls or Cleans	8-5-5-5-5
Sit-Ups	8-6-5-5-5-5	Sit-Ups
5 sets, 10 reps	Tricep Extension	5 sets, 18 reps
Neck Extension	8-6-5-5-5	Neck Extension
4-6 sets, 10 reps	Sit-Ups	4-6 sets, 10 reps
Grip Exercise	5 sets, 14 reps	Grip Exercise
3-5 sets	Grip Exercise	3-5 sets
	3-5 sets	

Optional

Lat Pulls, Upright Rowing, Presses Behind Neck, Leg Presses, Wrist Curls, Good Mornings, Curls

Linebackers and Defensive Ends. Frontal Delts, Wrist Curls

Anaerobic Conditioning (daily)

	Distance	% Max.	Rest	Reps
Run:	100 yds.	100%	30 secs.	10

Run: FB (Football) specific sprints (plays), random order, max effort, 15-20 reps.

Stretching Exercises

Table 9.12   Pre-season Conditioning Program for Quarterbacks (*H.S.-College*)

Warm-Up and Stretching

Strength Training—Train Explosively!

Monday & Friday	Wednesday
Bench Press	Dips
2 weeks 10-10-10-10-8-8	6 sets, 10 reps
Half Squat	Incline Press
2-4 weeks 8-8-8-8-8-8	8-6-5-5-5
Throwing Pullover	High Pulls or Cleans
5 sets, 10 reps	8-6-5-5-5
Toe Raises	Toe Raises
8 sets, 30 reps	8 sets, 30 reps
Sit-Ups, Twisting	Sit-Ups, Twisting
5 sets, 10 reps (18 on Friday)	5 sets, 14 reps
Throwing Motion (wall pulley)	Throwing Motion (wall pulley)
5 sets, 10 reps	5 sets, 10 reps
Wrist Roller or Wrist Curl	Wrist Roller or Wrist Curl
5 sets	5 sets
Neck Extension	Neck Extension
5 sets, 10 to 15 reps	5 sets, 10 to 15 reps

Table 9.12—*Continued*

Optional

Upright Rowing, Bent-Over Rowing, Lat Pull, Curls, Triceps Extension, Incline Press

Anaerobic Conditioning (daily)

	Distance	% Max.	Rest	Reps
Run:	100 yds.	100%	30 secs.	10–15

Run: FB (Football) specific sprints (plays), random order, max effort, 15–20 reps

Throwing

Stretching Exercises

Table 9.13   Pre-season Conditioning Program for Kickers (*H.S.-College*)

Warm-Up and Stretching

Strength Training—Train Explosively!

Monday & Friday	Wednesday
Half Squat	Leg Extension
6 sets, 8 reps	5 sets, 10 to 15 reps
Leg Extension (from flexed position)	High Pulls or Cleans
5–6 sets, 10 to 15 reps	8-6-5-5-5
Toe Raises	Toe Raises
8 sets, 30 reps	8 sets, 30 reps
Kicking Motion (wall pulley)	Kicking Motion (wall pulley)
5 sets, 10 to 15 reps	5 sets, 10 to 15 reps
Sit-Ups	Sit-Ups
5 sets, 10 reps (18 on Friday)	5 sets, 14 reps
Leg Lifts	Leg Lifts
5 sets, 10 reps	5 sets, 10 reps
Bench Press	Military Press
5 sets, 8 reps	5 sets, 8 reps

Optional

Lat Pull, Bench Press, Incline Press, Bent-Over Rowing

Running, Kicking: Stretching should follow each weight training session.

Anaerobic Conditioning (daily)

	Distance	% Max.	Rest	Reps
Run:	100 yds.	100%	30 secs.	10–15

Kicking

Stretching Exercises

Table 9.14　Pre-season Strength Circuit for Junior High, High School, or College Football Players

Warm-up and Stretching

Strength Training Apply circuit systems 1, 2, 3, or 4.

Leg Extension	Leg Extension
Lat Pull	Upright Row or Clean
Toe Raises	Squat or Fast-Speed Squat Machine
Bar Dips	Bench Press
Neck Extension (front and back)	Wrist Curl
Shoulder Shrugs	Military Press
Neck Extension (side to side)	Wrist Curl
Leg Curls	Upright Row
Curls	Sit-Ups
Squat or Fast-Speed Squat Machine	Pull-Ups
Cable Row	Leg Lifts
Abduction–Adduction Machine	Incline Press
Bench Press	

Specialty exercises to follow circuit:

Linemen and Linebackers:	Bench Press, Military Press, or Incline Press, 4–6 sets　8,8,6,6,4,4 and/or specialty exercises 5 sets, 10 reps
Backs and Receivers:	Speed Exercises and/or Bench Press 5 sets, 12 reps　5 sets, 8,8,6,6,4
Quarterbacks:	Throwing Motion and/or Bar Dips 5 sets, 12 reps　5 sets, 10 reps
Kickers:	Kicking Motion and/or Leg Lifts 5 sets, 12 reps　5 sets, 20 reps

---

Table 9.15　Pre-season Strength Circuit for College Football Players

Warm-up and Stretching

Strength Training Apply circuit systems "H" or "E."

Bench Press	Leg Curl	
Leg Lifts	Lat Pull	
Leg Extension	Shoulder Shrug	
Lat Pull	Leg Extension	
Toe Raises	Neck Extension (front and back)	
Neck Extension (front and back)	Cable Row	
Shoulder Shrug	Wrist Curl	
Neck Extension (side to side)	Sit-Ups	
Military Press	Power Clean	
Squat or Fast-Speed Squat Machine	Sit-Ups	
Cable Row	Power Clean	
Leg Curl	Wrist Curls	
Tricep Extension	Bench Press	
Curl	Incline Press	
Leg Extension	Bench Press	. . . Murderers'
Upright Row	Squat	Row
Leg Press	Incline Press	
Bent-Arm Pullover	Bench Press	
Squat or Fast-Speed Squat Machine	Seated Military Press	
Neck Extension (side to side)	Sit-Ups	

This circuit was created for a particular weight room. Unlimited variations of the exercise order and placements of super sets are possible.

Table 9.16 In-season Conditioning and Strength Circuit for Junior High Football Players

Warm-Up and Stretching

Aerobic Conditioning

	Distance	% Max.	Times/Week
Run:	1.0–1.5 mi.	75%	2

Strength Training (2 per week) Apply circuit systems 1, 2, 3, or 4. Rotate through the circuit twice.

Half Squat, Leg Press, or Fast-Speed Squat Machine	10–12 reps
Bench Press	10 reps
Leg Extension	10 reps
Seated Military Press	10 reps
Leg Curl	10 reps
Upright Rowing	10 reps
Neck Extension (front and back)	10 reps
Lat Pulls	10 reps
Neck Extension (side to side)	10 reps
Sit-Ups	10 reps
Toe Raises	10 reps

Anaerobic Conditioning (daily)

	Distance	% Max.	Rest	Reps
Run:	50 yds.	100%	30 secs.	10–20

Run: FB (Football) specific sprints (plays), random order, max effort, 15–20 reps.

Stretching Exercises

Table 9.17 In-season Strength Circuit for High School or College Football Players

Warm-Up and Stretching

Strength Training (1 day per week) Apply circuit system 10.

Neck Extension (front and back)	3 sets, 10 reps
Shoulder Shrug	3 sets, 12–15 reps
Neck Extension (side to side)	3 sets, 10 reps
Leg Extension	3 sets, 10 reps
Leg Curl	3 sets, 10 reps
Abduction-Adduction	3 sets, 10 reps
Toe Raises	3 sets. 10 reps
Bench Press	3 sets, 10 reps
Power Clean	3 sets, 10 reps
Incline Press	3 sets, 8 reps
Squat	3 sets, 8 reps
Wrist Curl	6 sets, 25 reps

Stretching Exercises

This program is normally the first of two in-season workouts to be done each week.

IN-SEASON

As detailed in Chapter 8, aerobic condition and strength can be maintained with a minimum time expenditure during the in-season period. Anaerobic conditioning should be continued *daily,* either at the conclusion of practice or within practice. During the brief and intense pre-season period aerobic conditioning has been minimized.

The major objectives of in-season conditioning are the continuation of *aerobic* conditioning (daily), maintenance of *aerobic power* and *strength,* and *prevention* of injuries.[3, 4] Aerobic and strength conditioning can be reduced to two sessions weekly. Strength training will emphasize fast-speed, high-repetition work as was used in the pre-season period. The specialty exercises can be added if not already used. The reader is referred to Chapter 6 for preventive exercises designed to reduce injury.

Table 9.18 In-Season Strength Circuit for High School and College Football Players

Warm-Up and Stretching

Aerobic Conditioning

	Distance	% Max.	Times/Week
Run:	1.5 mi.	75%	2

Strength Training (1 or 2 days per week) Apply circuit systems 2, 3, 4, or 6.

Leg Extension, 10 reps	Leg Curl, 10 reps
Lat Pull, 10 reps	Lat Pull, 10 reps
Toe Raises, 30 reps	Leg Extension, 10 reps
Bar Dips, 10 reps	Wrist Curl, 25 reps
Abduction-Adduction Machine, 10 reps	Cable Row, 10 reps
Neck Extension (front and back), 10 reps	Bench Press, 10 reps
Shoulder Shrug, 15 reps	Leg Press, 10 reps
Neck Extension (side to side), 10 reps	Bench Press, 10 reps
Leg Curl, 12 reps	Leg Extension, 10 reps
Tricep Machine, 10 reps	Cable Row, 10 reps
Curl Machine, 10 reps	Fast-Speed Squat Machine
Fast-Speed Squat Machine, 12 reps	Wrist Curl, 25 reps
Pullover Machine, 10 reps	Seated Military Press, 10 reps
Neck Extension, 10 reps	Shoulder Shrug, 15 reps

Specialty exercises to follow circuits:

Linemen and Linebackers:	Bench Press, Military Press, or Incline Press 4–6 sets 8,8,6,6,4,4 and/or specialty exercises 5 sets, 10 reps
Backs and Receivers:	Speed Exercises and/or Bench Press 5 sets, 12 reps 5 sets, 8,8,6,6,4
Quarterbacks:	Throwing Motion and/or Bar Dips 5 sets, 12 reps 5 sets, 10 reps
Kickers:	Kicking Motion and/or Leg Lifts 5 sets, 12 reps 5 sets, 20 reps

Anaerobic Conditioning (daily)

	Distance	% Max.	Rest	Reps
Run:	50 yds.	100%	30 secs.	10–20

Run: FB (Football) specific sprints (plays), random order, max effort, 15–20 reps.

Stretching Exercises

The coach should look for ways to condition the team within the regular practice session. The two-minute drill, for example, is an excellent overload for the anaerobic system. Many agility or other football drills can serve the purpose of developing skills and conditioning at the same time. There are many ways to save that ever-precious time that must be spent on skills development and strategy and still condition a football team. The sport-specific conditioning described and used in pre-season programs is an excellent example of in-season conditioning specifically designed for football. The *random order* sprints or plays are designed to match the way plays actually are run in the game, e.g., 3 seconds, 8 seconds, 5 seconds, etc.

A variety of brief in-season conditioning programs are offered from junior high to college level.

SPECIALTY EXERCISES AND PROGRAMS

Specialty exercises for football can serve two purposes: 1) they may be designed to strengthen the muscles involved in a specific football skill, or 2) they may be designed to aid in the rehabilitation of injury. An example of the latter is diagonal movements of the legs done with pulleys following knee surgery. Such action is designed to strengthen the lateral movements of players after surgery or injury.

Among the football specialty exercises that have been used in programs in this chapter are:

Kicking Motion (with wall pulley)

The kicking motion is produced with the pulley attached to the ankle. An upright support is recommended so that the kicker can hold himself in the upright position during the exercise. The athlete should do this exercise with each leg to maintain muscular balance and to prevent a possible injury.

Throwing Motion

The throwing motion is done with a football or a handle attached to the high wall pulley. Quarterbacks training with this exercise should be certain that the stance and throwing motion are imitated exactly. The wrist turns *out* when releasing a football, and this motion should be emphasized.

Bent-Arm Deltoid Raises

This exercise is done with a dumbbell, and the range of motion should imitate the "forearm rip." The exercise is used by linemen and running backs.

Centering Motion

The movement is done with a pulley at ground level or as close to ground level as possible. The exercise is designed to aid in developing power for the longer snaps at center, and for speed in making the short snap. The motion desired should be imitated as exactly as possible. For the long snap, the arms are extended and greater resistance can be used. The short snap should be practiced at higher speed and less resistance.

Close Grip Incline Press

Incline presses done with dumbbells or the hands 4 to 6 inches apart on the bar are excellent for offensive linemen.

SUMMARY

Football is a predominately anaerobic game. The action involves Stage I (ATP-CP) almost entirely. Occasionally the demands of the game require Stage II (AN-LA) during the "two-minute offense" periods at the end of the first half and the game. Stage III (AER) comes into play primarily during the recovery phase or rest interval between plays.

Strength, explosive power, speed, agility, and flexibility are all important in good performance. In this chapter the authors have offered programs to develop all of the essential factors in football. The programs are designed for three levels (junior high school, high school, and college) during the off-season, pre-season, and in-season.

REFERENCES

1. "Coaches Roundtable—Winter Conditioning: Off-Season Training for Football." 1983. *NSCA Journal* 4(6):14–31.

2. Fracas, G. 1975. "Football," *The Scientific Aspects of Sports Conditioning*. Springfield, IL: Charles C Thomas.

3. Kroll, William A. 1983. *Physical Conditioning for Winning Football*. Boston: Allyn & Bacon.

4. Mangold, Jeff. 1983. "Philosophies of In-Season Strength and Conditioning for Football," *NSCA Journal* 5(2):27–28.

5. Paige, Roderick R. 1973. *What Research Tells the Coach about Football*. Washington, DC: AAHPERD.

6. Stone, William J., and William A. Kroll. 1977. Unpublished research data. Arizona State University.

7. Thiry, Peter K. 1982. "The Physiological Basis of Conditioning for Football," *NSCA Journal* 3(6):42–43.

8. Ward, Bob, et al. 1982. "Optimizing Human Performance Through Computerization of the Conditioning Program Design," *NSCA Journal* 4(3):6–9.

Figure 9.1 Kicking Motion

Figure 9.2 Throwing Motion

Chapter 9

Figure 9.3 Centering Motion

CHAPTER

TEN

SOCCER

This chapter includes aerobic and anaerobic conditioning programs and strength building programs for soccer. In order to make the most effective use of the programs offered here, the reader is referred to Chapter 3 for the basis of aerobic and anaerobic training programs, Chapter 4 for the basis of strength programs, and Chapter 5 for the details of stretching programs. It is also recommended that the reader refer to Chapter 8 for the most efficient means of incorporating those objectives into a single workout. The programs are offered for off-season, pre-season, and in-season. The reader is also referred to the sample recording charts in the Appendix. These charts facilitate the measurement of the athlete's progress in the training program, and will also indicate the athlete's standing in regard to training goals.

Soccer is clearly the most popular sport in the world. It has also elicited more emotion from spectators than any other game. Deaths associated with soccer games are not uncommon, and in 1969 a full-scale war erupted over a playoff series between Honduras and El Salvador. The Salvadoran army invaded Honduras and over 2,000 lives were lost. Since the publication of the first edition of this book, soccer has grown tremendously in popularity in this country. This is especially true of youth sports leagues, which in turn has led to the development of high school teams and leagues. The North American Soccer League (NASL) and the Major Indoor Soccer League (MISL) also reflect the growing interest in soccer at the professional level. There is every indication that soccer will continue to grow in popularity as a spectator sport and in number of participants in the future. Soccer is also one of the most thoroughly researched sports in terms of energy demands of the activity, physiological characteristics of players, and training routines.[8]

One of the most obvious characteristics of soccer is that it is very aerobic in nature. In international rules the game is played in two 45-minute halves of nearly continuous play. Ninety minutes of action was not sufficient to determine a winner in the 1978 World Cup final between Argentina and Holland. A 30-minute overtime was played resulting in a total of 120 minutes of continuous action, halted only by the halftime and a rest period after the regulation time had expired. Extensive studies indicate that nearly 90 percent of the movement is aerobic and that forwards, who range over the most territory, will cover five to nine miles per game.[8] The aerobic power of soccer players is very high among team sports athletes, averaging from 56–66 ml/kg/min. for VO_2 max (maximal oxygen uptake).[3]

Explosive power and speed are also important factors in soccer performance. About 10 percent of the time in the game the soccer player is involved in anaerobic bursts which include sprinting over short distances, jumping explosively, and making movements that require much agility and flexibility.[8] Strength development in the legs is obviously important because of the requirements for jumping, turning, kicking, and quick starts. A strong neck and upper body should also be developed, not only to improve the performance of some soccer skills (heading), but also to prevent injuries.

Soccer is certainly one of the most physically demanding of team sports with players averaging heart rates of 155–165 during play. This converts to approximately 75 percent of maximal aerobic power for the more active positions. Although highly skilled players can reduce the energy expenditure by accurate passing and good position play, soccer obviously is a game that requires a significant conditioning effort in addition to the skills and strategies that must be developed. Conditioning efforts should be directed toward developing aerobic power, agility and flexibility, anaerobic power (sprinting), and strength.

YOUTH SPORTS LEAGUES

Most soccer participants in the United States are concentrated in youth sports leagues. Because of the late arrival of soccer as a popular sport, most of the current players are in the six- to sixteen-year-old range. The greatest concentration of youth sports performers is usually in the seven- to twelve-year-old bracket. The programs offered in this chapter are not designed or intended to be used by very young athletes. Most youth sports leagues are philosophically committed to fun, widespread participation, and low-key competition. Intense training is usually not recommended for most athletes prior to the junior high school level.

Table 10.1   Off-Season Conditioning Program for Soccer

Warm-Up and Stretching

Aerobic Conditioning

	Distance	% Max.	Time (approx.)
Run: *Goal*	3–5 mi.	75%	21:00–35:00

Strength Training—Train Explosively!

Monday and Friday	Wednesday
Bench Press	Military Press
10, 10, 8, 8, 6, 6, 4, 4	10, 10, 8, 8, 6, 6, 6, 6
Half Squat	Leg Press
8, 8, 8, 6, 6, 6, 4, 4	8, 8, 8, 6, 6, 6, 4, 4
Leg Extension	Leg Extension
10, 10, 8, 8, 8, 8	10, 10, 8, 8, 8, 8
Leg Curl	Leg Curl
5 Sets, 10 Reps	5 Sets, 10 Reps
Leg Lifts	Leg Lifts
5 Sets, 10–15 Reps	5 Sets, 10–15 Reps
Sit-Ups	Sit-Ups
5 Sets, 10–15 Reps	5 Sets, 10–15 Reps
Toe Raises	Toe Raises
6 Sets, 30 Reps	6 Sets, 30 Reps
Throw-In Motion	Throw-In Motion
5 Sets, 10 Reps	5 Sets, 10 Reps
Kicking Motion	Kicking Motion
5 Sets, 10 Reps	5 Sets, 10 Reps
Upright Rowing	Upright Rowing
5 Sets, 10 Reps	5 Sets, 10 Reps
High Knee Lift	High Knee Lift
5 Sets, 10 Reps	5 Sets, 10 Reps

Stretching Exercises

Youth sports performers in soccer can benefit, however, from low-key conditioning programs, which are usually dominated by running activities. Aerobic power can and should be developed in young soccer players by "warm-up" runs, continuous practice sessions, and lead-up games which also include a great deal of aerobic movement. Sprint races and relays can become a fun part of practice to aid in the development of speed and anaerobic power. Calisthenics and flexibility exercises can precede practice or game so that the young athlete begins to learn the importance of a good warm-up and stretching routine. Such efforts are restricted to the pre-season and in-season periods. They should not become a burden for the youthful competitor and the coach needs to keep in mind that the goals of youth sports are fun, participation, and low-key competition.

OFF-SEASON

The off-season conditioning program should concentrate on developing aerobic power and strength. Both of these capacities require significant amounts of time for training, which should be available during the off-season. Off-season conditioning should consist of running for aerobic development. Strength training will be aimed primarily at developing leg power and upper body power, particularly arm, shoulder, and neck strength. Greater resistance and fewer repetitions will be characteristic of the strength training in the off-season. Table 10.1 offers an off-season conditioning program for soccer. Flexibility training continues year round. The major and assistant exercises in table 10.1 are to be performed employing a "set system" (Chapter 4). The supplemental and specialty exercises can be done using 3- or 4-station mini-circuits with circuit system 1 (walking circuit).

Table 10.2 Pre-Season Conditioning Program for Soccer

Warm-Up and Stretching

Aerobic Conditioning (3/Week)

		Distance	% Max.	Rest	Reps
Run:		2.0 mi.	75%	—	—
	or	0.5 mi.	90%	3 mins.	3–5

Strength Training (3 days per week)
Use circuit systems 1, 3, 4, 5, 6, or 9. For larger groups, this circuit can be expanded into as many stations as necessary, keeping the same exercises. The number of sets, and therefore the number of times to rotate through the circuit, will depend on the circuit system utilized. Train Explosively!

Bench Press or Military Press
2–6 sets, 8–15 reps

Half Squat, Jumping Squat or Leaper
2–6 sets, 8–15 reps

Leg Extension
2–6 sets, 10–15 reps

Leg Curl
2–6 sets, 10–15 reps

Leg Lifts
2–6 sets, 10–15 reps

Sit-Ups
2–6 sets, 10–25 reps

Upright Rowing
2–6 sets, 10 reps

Throw-In Motion
2–6 sets, 10 reps

Kicking Motion
2–6 sets, 10 reps

High Knee Lift
2–6 sets, 10 reps

Toe Raises
2–6 sets, 30 reps

Anaerobic Conditioning

	Distance	% Max.	Rest	Reps	Times/Week
Run:	50–100 yds.	100%	30–60 secs.	5–10	2–3

Stretching Exercises

PRE-SEASON

The object of the pre-season program is to bring the soccer player to peak playing condition in as brief a time as possible. Training becomes more intense during the pre-season period. There is a shift to more intense aerobic intervals and to anaerobic conditioning. The shift in strength training is toward higher speed, greater repetition, low-resistance training. A pre-season conditioning program for soccer is offered in table 10.2.

IN-SEASON

The objectives of the in-season conditioning program are to maintain strength and aerobic conditioning, continue anaerobic conditioning, and prevent injuries. Strength and aerobic conditioning sessions are reduced to one or two per week, while anaerobic conditioning is maintained daily. A relatively short expenditure of time is sufficient to maintain strength and aerobic conditioning.

The coach should be alert for opportunities to condition within the regular practice session. Aerobic conditioning can be maintained or improved with continuous play such as scrimmages with no time-outs. Various high-speed passing and/or ball handling drills, as well as supplemental sprints, can be used to develop anaerobic conditioning.

An in-season conditioning program for soccer is offered in table 10.3.

SUMMARY

Approximately ninety percent of the game of soccer is played aerobically. Despite that fact, the game also calls for occasional bursts of speed and high levels of agility. Leg strength and power are very important for the soccer player.

In this chapter the authors have developed off-season, pre-season, and in-season conditioning programs. The programs are aimed at the development of the major factors contributing to soccer performance.

Table 10.3 In-Season Conditioning Program for Soccer

Warm-Up and Stretching

Aerobic Conditioning (2/Week)

	Distance	% Max.	Rest	Reps
Run:	2–3 mi.	75%	—	—
or	0.5 mi.	90%	3 mins.	3

Strength Training (1 or 2 days per week)
Use circuit systems 2, 3, 4, 5, or 6. For larger groups, this circuit can be expanded into as many stations as necessary keeping the same exercises. The number of sets, and therefore the number of times to rotate through the circuit, will depend upon the circuit system utilized. Train Explosively!

Bench Press or Military Press
2–5 sets, 8–15 reps

Half Squat, Jumping Squat or Leaper
2–5 sets, 8–15 reps

Leg Extension
2–5 sets, 8–15 reps

Leg Curls
2–5 sets, 8–15 reps

Sit-Ups and/or Leg Lifts
2–5 sets, 10–15 reps

Throw-In Motion and/or Kicking Motion
2–5 sets, 10–15 reps

High Knee Lift
5 sets, 10–15 reps

Anaerobic Conditioning

	Distance	% Max.	Rest	Reps	Times/Week
Run:	75 yds.	100%	45 secs.	5–10	4–5

Stretching Exercises

REFERENCES

1. Beim, George. 1977. *Principles of Modern Soccer.* Boston: Houghton Mifflin Co.

2. Clues, Andrew, and David Jack. 1980. *Soccer for Players and Coaches.* Englewood Cliffs, NJ: Prentice-Hall.

3. Ekblom, Bjorn. 1986. "Applied Physiology of Soccer," *Sports Medicine* 3:50–60.

4. Fardy, Paul S. 1980. "Scientific Basis of Training for Soccer," *Toward an Understanding of Human Performance.* Ithaca, NY: Mouvement Publications.

5. Micheli, Lyle, and John Leard. 1981. "Conditioning for Soccer," *Coach & Athlete* 43:32–36.

6. Mosher, R. E., et al. 1985. "Interval Training: The Effects of a 12-Week Program on Elite, Pre-Pubertal Male Soccer Players," *Journal of Sports Medicine* 25:5–9.

7. Ratliff, John. 1982. "Strength and Conditioning for Soccer at Wake Forest University," *NSCA Journal* 4(4):10–23.

8. Reilly, Thomas. 1979. *What Research Tells the Coach about Soccer.* Washington, DC: AAHPERD.

9. Sarianides, Gus. 1985. "Pre-Season Conditioning and Season Maintenance for the Professional Soccer Player," *NSCA Journal* 7(4):46–49.

Chapter 10

CHAPTER

ELEVEN

BASKETBALL

In this chapter the authors include aerobic and anaerobic conditioning programs and strength building programs for basketball. In order to make the most effective use of the programs offered here, the reader is referred to Chapter 3 for the basis of aerobic and anaerobic training programs, to Chapter 4 for the basis of strength programs, to Chapter 5 for the basis of warm-up and stretching programs, and to Chapter 8 for the most efficient means of incorporating those objectives into a single workout. The training is offered as off-season, pre-season, and in-season programs at three levels. The three levels include junior high school, senior high school, and college training programs. The reader is also referred to the sample recording charts shown in the Appendix. These charts will facilitate the measurement of the athlete's progress on the training program and will also indicate the athlete's standing in regard to training goals.

Unlike football, basketball involves all three energy Stages (I–III) during the active portion of the game. Basketball can be a very *aerobic* game although it also includes many *anaerobic power* (Stage I) skills in jumping, shooting, and rebounding.[3] The continuous nature of the game and the constant movement required of high-caliber play contribute toward making basketball a game of high endurance. Occasional bursts of fast-break basketball rely on *anaerobic* capacity and this, too, must be considered in the conditioning program. No other sport described in this book, with the possible exception of hockey, requires as many energy capacities *during play* as does basketball. The athlete or coach must be prepared to condition for the specific requirements of the game.

The level and style of play can greatly influence the pace of the game and thus the energy expenditure. Obviously, a "run-and-gun" fast-break offense involves higher levels of both aerobic and anaerobic power. The slow-paced, deliberate style of play places less demand on physical conditioning, but it is still necessary.

The authors have found that the 24-second clock in the NBA generally ensures that the action will be fast paced, but "breaks" in the action will be more frequent. Timing studies indicate that the ball tends to stay in play an average of 30 seconds before the clock stops for an out-of-bounds or foul.[8] Closer examination of the data, however, indicated the play or action did not stop when the clock was

off for five seconds or less.[8] Players would continue down court on a turnover or go into the transition with a non-shooting foul. As a result, it was determined that the ball remained in play an average of 65 seconds before there was as long as a ten-second rest interval. In recent years play in the NBA has speeded up considerably. The style of play in the league tends to very trendy, and the current style puts great emphasis on players who can "run the floor," fast-break basketball, and on scoring many points. Current players are significantly bigger, but also faster and fitter than players of twenty years ago. In high school and college basketball the ball can generally remain in play longer before a shot will be made, thus decreasing the chance of a break in action for a free throw or out-of-bounds.

Strength training is an important part of basketball conditioning because of the need for leg strength and total body power for jumping, rebounding, and playing defense. Movements on the floor must be quick, explosive, and agile. Upper body and grip strength are necessary in rebounding. Increased leg power may add inches to the player's jump, and greater strength will aid in controlling the ball—neither of these, of course, can replace proper positioning, timing, or shooting skill. Many young basketball players are in need of greater strength and power to go with their natural height. It has been found that teams that discontinue weight training during the season lose vertical jumping ability,[9] also that a variety of strengthening regimens will increase vertical jumping power, including jumping practice alone.

Strength training for basketball players carries one note of caution from the authors. *Everyone, but especially very tall players (6' 8'' and above) should be very careful to keep the back straight when doing Squats.* Because of the long upper body, it is possible to get the bar too far from the base of support (feet) by leaning forward, thus putting undue pressure on the lower back. The Squat should not be omitted from basketball programs, however, because of its value in building leg strength and power.

Improving the aerobic capacity of basketball players will mean that they can play longer and more vigorously. Teams that rely on a "running" game should benefit greatly from increased aerobic capacity. Studies with the Phoenix Suns of the NBA indicate that a year-round program of aerobic training can pay dividends not only in higher aerobic capacity, but also in improved performance. The Suns as a

Table 11.1   Off-Season Conditioning Program for Junior High Basketball Players

Warm-Up and Stretching

Aerobic Conditioning

	Distance	% Max.	Time (approx.)
Run: Minimum	1.0 mi.	75%	7–8:00 mins.
Goal	2.5 mi.	75%↑	18–20:00 mins.

Strength Training (3 days per week)

Major and assistant exercises: apply set system; supplemental and specialty exercises: apply set system or circuit system 1.

Monday–Friday	Wednesday
Half Squat	Leg Press
10, 10, 8, 8, 8, 8, 6, 6	10, 10, 10, 10, 8, 8, 8, 8
Bench Press	Incline or Military Press
10, 10, 8, 8, 6, 6, 4, 4	10, 10, 8, 8, 6, 6, 6, 6
Upright Row	Upright Row
3–5 sets, 10 reps	3–5 sets, 10 reps
Leg Extension	Leg Extension
3–5 sets, 10 reps	3–5 sets, 10 reps
Lower Back Machine	Lower Back Machine
*Good Morning or *Stiff-Legged Deadlift	*Good Morning or *Stiff-Legged Deadlift
3–5 sets, 10 reps	3–5 sets, 10 reps
Leg Curl	Leg Curl
3–5 sets, 10 reps	3–5 sets, 10 reps
Toe Raises	Toe Raises
3–5 sets, 30 reps	3–5 sets, 30 reps
Wrist Roller or Wrist Curls	Wrist Roller or Wrist Curls
3–5 sets, 25 reps	3–5 sets, 25 reps
Pulldown Close Grip	Pulldown Close Grip
3–5 sets, 10 reps	3–5 sets, 10 reps
Sit-Ups	Sit-Ups
3–5 sets, 20 reps	3–5 sets, 20 reps

*Use a very light weight for this exercise (approximately 50 percent of 10–15 RM).

team consistently test higher in aerobic capacity than the results reported for many other NBA teams. With the inception of a "running" program at the conclusion of the 1977 season, they appeared in the playoffs every year for the next nine seasons. By training for anaerobic power, the basketball player should also be better able to tolerate all-out effort.

OFF-SEASON

During the off-season period a great deal more time can be spent in conditioning for both aerobic capacity and strength. Both of these capacities require time for conditioning and that time is available during the off-season. The aerobic conditioning should proceed until the athlete meets the listed GOAL. The young athlete with expectations of a college or professional career should learn to condition year round.

Strength training for basketball should always be explosive but the off-season exercises are done with greater resistance which slows the movement slightly. For most exercises, maximum repetitions will be done in the range of 1–10 RM, usually on the upper end of that range for greater muscular endurance. Strength exercises that are done primarily for muscular endurance (Good Mornings or Toe Raises) are done with low resistance and high repetition during the off-season.

The authors recommend that off-season programs be done in circuit training style. This enables conditioning for all aspects of basketball to be included in a

Table 11.2 Off-Season Strength Circuit for Junior High, High School, or College Basketball Players

Warm-Up and Stretching

Strength Training
Apply circuit systems 1, 3, 4, 6, or 9. Rotate through the circuit two or more times.

Jumping Squat or High-Speed Squat Machine	12 reps
Bench Press	10 reps
Lower Back Machine, *Good Morning, or *Stiff-Legged	10 reps
Deadlift	30 reps
Toe Raises	25 reps
Wrist Roller or Wrist Curl	10–25 reps
Throwing Pullover	10 reps
Ankle Exercise	10 reps
Pulldown Close Grip	20 reps
Sit-Ups	10 reps
Military Press	10 reps
Leg Extension	10 reps
Cable Rowing	10 reps
Incline Press	10 reps
Leg Curl	10 reps
Upright Rowing	

*Use a very light weight for this exercise (approximately 50 percent of 10–15 RM).

single training session. It also concentrates the conditioning and reduces the amount of time spent in each session.

A heavy 6- to 8-week strength program should be performed during the off-season. For the maximum amount of development in the large muscle groups, it is necessary to utilize the set system for the major and assistant exercises during this program. The heavier amounts of resistance require the longer rest periods between sets that the set system allows. The supplemental and specialty exercises can be trained in 3- or 4-station mini-circuits with circuit system 1 (walking circuit, Chapter 4). Various circuit systems can be used for basketball players at other times during the off-season. This may supplement the development of the aerobic base, or other activities such as a summer league, informal "pick-up type" practices, or other organized sports activity.

PRE-SEASON

During the pre-season period there is a shift to more intense (anaerobic) conditioning and strength training more specific to the nature of basketball. Both the speed of contraction and the number of repetitions should be increased for the strength training. The objective is to increase the local muscular endurance by high-speed, high-repetition training.

The anaerobic conditioning at this point in the season will be more intense than during the in-season period. The objective is to train the anaerobic (lactic acid) system, and this is the most rigorous of all training techniques. This kind of training prepares the player to tolerate high-level bursts (fast breaks) in a continuous sequence.

Pre-season conditioning should be designed to bring the basketball player to playing condition in the shortest possible time. The player should be expected to meet the goals set down in tables 11.3 and 11.4 for aerobic power. The more intense conditioning occurs just prior to the season so that the player will be at top condition for the first time just as the season opens. This is designed to reduce the potential for fatigue or staleness in the latter part of the season. The coach who is particularly pressed for time can use the circuit training technique both pre-season and in-season.

Pre-season programs are offered at the junior high, high school, and college levels.

Table 11.3   Off-Season Conditioning Program for High School and College Basketball Players

Warm-Up and Stretching

Aerobic Conditioning

	Distance	% Max.	Time (approx.)
Run: Minimum	1.0 mi.	75%	6:30–7:00 mins.
Goal	3.0 mi.	75%↑	20:00–24:00 mins.

Strength Training (3 days per week)
Major and assistant exercises: apply set system; supplemental and specialty exercises: apply set system or circuit system 1. Train Explosively!

Monday and Friday

Squat
10, 10, 8, 8, 8, 8, 6, 6
10, 10, 8, 8, 6, 6, 6, 6

Bench Press
10, 10, 8, 8, 6, 6, 4, 4
Mon.: 10, 8, 5, 3, 3, 3, 3, 3
Fri.: 10, 8, 6, 5, 5, 5, 5, 5

Clean or High Pull
5, 4, 3, 3, 3, 2 or 5, 4, 3, 2, 1, 1

Leg Extension
5 sets, 10 reps

Lat Pull
5 sets, 10 reps

Lower Back Machine, *Good Morning, or *Stiff-legged Deadlift
5 sets, 10 reps

Wrist Curl or Wrist Roller
3–5 sets, 25 reps

Stretching and Ankle Exercise
(Dorsiflexion of the foot, p. 89)
3–5 sets, 10–50 reps

Leg Curl
5 sets, 10 reps

Upright Rowing
5 sets, 10 reps

Sit-Ups
5 sets, 20 reps

Toe Raises
5 sets, 30 reps

Abduction-Adduction Machine
5 sets, 12 reps

Wednesday

Leg Press
10, 10, 10, 10, 8, 8, 8, 8

Incline or Military Press
10, 10, 8, 8, 6, 6, 4, 4

Leg Extension
5 sets, 10 reps

Lat Pull
5 sets, 10 reps

Lower Back Machine, *Good Morning, or *Stiff-legged Deadlift
5 sets, 10 reps

Wrist Curl or Wrist Roller
3–5 sets, 25 reps

Stretching and Ankle Exercise
(Dorsiflexion of the foot, p. 89)
3–5 sets, 10–50 reps

Leg Curl
5 sets, 10 reps

Upright Rowing
5 sets, 10 reps

Sit-Ups
5 sets, 20 reps

Toe Raises
5 sets, 30 reps

*Use a very light weight for this exercise (approximately 50 percent of 10–15 RM).

Table 11.4 Pre-Season and In-Season Conditioning for Junior High Basketball Players

Warm-Up and Stretching

Aerobic Conditioning

	Distance	% Max.
Run:	1.5 mi.	75%

Strength Training
Pre-Season:
Apply circuit systems 1, 3, 4, 5, 6 or 9. Rotate through circuit twice.

In-Season:
Apply circuit systems 1, 3, 4 or 6. Perform circuit once. Train Explosively!

Shooting Exercise, 10 reps
Leg Extension, 10 reps
Lat Pull, 10 reps
Upright Rowing, 10 reps
Abduction-Adduction machine, 12 reps
Upright Rowing, 10 reps
Leg Curl, 10 reps
Military Press, 10 reps
Toe Raises, 30 reps
Fast-Speed Squat Machine or Jumping Squats, 12 reps
Bench Press, 10 reps
Leg Extension, 10 reps

Cable Rowing or Bent-Over Rowing, 10 reps
Fast-Speed Squat Machine or Jumping Squats, 12 reps
Press, 10 reps
Wrist Curl, 25 reps
Bench Press, 10 reps
Wrist Curl, 25 reps
Bench Press, 10 reps
Sit-ups, 20 reps
Wrist Curl, 25 reps
Ankle Exercise, 10–50 reps
(Dorsiflexion of the foot, p. 89)

Pre-Season Anaerobic Conditioning

	Distance	% Max.	Rest	Reps
Run: Minimum	220 yds.	90%↑	2 mins.	5
Maximum	440 yds.	90%↑	3 mins.	5

or: (Anaerobic Conditioning—*Indoor*)

	Time	Rest	Reps
Run: Continuous sprints	30 secs.	2 mins.	5
(floor length)	45 secs.	3 mins.	5

In-Season Anaerobic Conditioning (Daily)

	Time	Rest	Reps
Run: Continuous sprints	20–30 secs.	1 min.	5–8
(floor length)			

Stretching Exercises

Table 11.5　Pre-Season and In-Season Conditioning Programs for High School and College Basketball Players

Warm-Up and Stretching

Aerobic Conditioning

	Distance	% Max.
Run:	2.0 mi.	75%

Strength Training

Pre-Season (3 days per week):
Apply circuit systems 1, 3, 4, 7, or 9. Rotate through circuit 2 to 3½ times depending on system used. Circuit systems 5 and 6 can also be used, pre-season, for a light workout.

In-Season (2 days per week):
Apply circuit systems 3, 4, 5, 6, or 7. System 3 may be used as the first of two in-season workouts per week. Train Explosively!

Sit-Ups	Upright Rowing
Wrist Curls	Fast-Speed Squat Machine or Jumping Squat
Shooting Exercise	Bench Press
Leg Extension	Leg Extension
Lat Pull	Cable Rowing or Bent-Over Rowing
Upright Rowing	Fast-Speed Squat Machine or Jumping Squat
Abduction-Adduction Machine	Upright Rowing
Toe Raises	Wrist Curl
Leg Curl	Bench Press
Cable Rowing or Bent-Over Rowing	Wrist Curl
	*Bench Press

Pre-Season Anaerobic Conditioning:

	Distance	% Max.	Rest	Reps
Run: Minimum	220 yds.	90%↑	2 mins.	5–10
Maximum	440 yds.	90%↑	3 mins.	5–10

In-Season Anaerobic Conditioning (Daily)

	Time	Rest	Reps
Run: Continuous sprints (floor length)	20–30 secs.	1 min.	5–10

Stretching Exercises

*Indicates the designated competition station for circuit system 7.

IN-SEASON

The purpose of in-season conditioning for basketball is to maintain a high level of aerobic and anaerobic condition, and strength and muscular endurance. With the exception of anaerobic conditioning, two sessions per week will maintain aerobic capacity and strength. Anaerobic conditioning should be continued *daily* during the season either during or after practice.

The strength training program is abbreviated by use of only two or three sets of each exercise at high repetition. High-speed training is emphasized, as it is more specific to the explosive nature of basketball skills (jumping, rebounding, and quick movements). Injury prevention is the major reason for ankle exercises in the strength program during the in-season period.

Basketball offers many opportunities for conditioning during the in-season period and within the regular practice. Continuous scrimmage with no time-outs is an excellent way of maintaining aerobic power. Repeated fast break drills or other high-speed drills such as passing or dribbling can be used for anaerobic conditioning. Rebound drills can develop leg power as well as rebounding skills if they are done in continuous fashion. One-on-one or two-on-one drills are also good conditioners as well as skill drills if the players are involved in continuous play. Most coaches employ a wide range of skill drills that can double as conditioning exercises by making them continuous or high speed.

Figure 11.1 Jumping Squats

SPECIALTY EXERCISES

Dorsiflexion of the Foot

(See Chapter 6.)

Jumping Squats

These may be done using a light barbell or dumbbells. The weight is usually held at the shoulders in front of the body, but may be held behind the head. The athlete then takes the normal position for jumping and leaps vertically with a maximum effort. This may be done with the legs split slightly (or one foot in front of the other).

SUMMARY

Basketball is generally an aerobic game that is punctuated with short bursts (Stage I, ATP-CP) of action and occasionally intense Stage II involvement (AN-LA). It is one of the more demanding sports since it involves all three of the energy mechanisms during play. In addition, it also requires explosive power, strength, flexibility, and agility at high levels.

In this chapter the authors have offered programs to develop all of the essential factors in basketball. The programs are designed for off-season, pre-season, and in-season at three levels (junior high school, high school, and college).

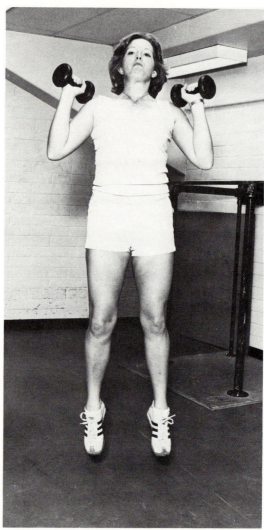

Figure 11.2   Jumping Squats (Dumbbell)

REFERENCES

1. Anderson, Bob. 1980. "Stretching for Basketball," *NSCA Journal* 2(5):22–25.

2. Elam, Reid. 1983. "Basketball Conditioning," *NSCA Journal* 5(4):50–52.

3. Gillam, G. McKenzie. 1985. "Basketball Bioenergetics—Physiological Basis," *NSCA Journal* 6:59–61.

4. Hoolahan, Paul. 1980. "Strength and Conditioning for Basketball: The University of North Carolina Program," *NSCA Journal* 2(4):20–21.

5. Kroll, William A. 1983. "Conditioning for Basketball," *NSCA Journal* 5(2):24–26.

6. Semenick, Doug. 1985. "Basketball Energetics—Practical Applications," *NSCA Journal* 6(6):45–73.

7. Simmons, Jerry, and Tom Hille. 1985. "Year-Round Basketball Strength and Conditioning," *NSCA Journal* 7(4):54–56.

8. Stone, William J. 1978. Unpublished research data. Arizona State University.

9. Yarr, A. D. 1975. "Basketball," *Scientific Aspects of Sports Training.* Springfield, IL: Charles C Thomas.

TWELVE

HOCKEY

This chapter contains year-round conditioning programs for hockey. The programs are designed for the off-season, pre-season, and in-season periods. In order to make the most effective use of these programs the reader is referred to Chapter 3 for the basis of aerobic and anaerobic training programs, to Chapter 4 for the basis of strength programs, to Chapter 5 for the basis of warm-up and stretching exercises, and to Chapter 8 for the most efficient means of incorporating those objectives into a single workout. The reader is also referred to the sample recording charts offered in the Appendix. These charts will facilitate the measurement of progress of the athlete in the training program, and will indicate the athlete's standing in regard to the training goal.

In the opening chapter of this book, ice hockey was used to illustrate the importance that superior conditioning can mean in a team game. The example, the reader may recall, involved the USSR versus "Team Canada" in a series begun during the 1970s. Although the Soviets had been successful against U.S. collegiate teams in the past, no one seriously expected the Soviet national team to be a difficult opponent for the NHL All-Star group making up Team Canada. The pattern of the games was set early in the series with the Canadians dominating play early, the Soviets shifting the momentum in the second period, and then typically out-skating the NHL players in the third period.

The superior conditioning of the USSR team was no accident. Koloskov, a Russian sports scientist, has outlined the premise behind the Soviet hockey conditioning.[4] He maintains that the most important trend in modern international hockey is an increase in the number of plays which puts a premium on speed, endurance, strength, and agility. If a team can generate more plays and more shots on goal, and the goalie's stop percentage remains constant, the team will score more goals!

Hockey is one of the most vigorous of team sports and requires a great deal of physical conditioning. Like basketball, it requires a high level of *aerobic* and *anaerobic* conditioning. Like basketball, it also contains a great deal of continuous activity (aerobic) interrupted by anaerobic bursts of speed. Approximately two-thirds of the maximal aerobic

capacity is the average expenditure of energy for the hockey player, who skates an average of 2.5 miles per game.[6] At least 20 to 25 percent of the game is played in the *anaerobic* mode, which makes the game so intense.[3] One of the reasons for the Soviet success against the NHL players is that they had conditioned their team to go anaerobically for 65 to 75 percent of the time. Average heart rates range from 87 to 92 percent of max during game action.

Strength training is also a significant factor in the preparation for hockey. Leg power is necessary for quick acceleration, while upper body strength and arm and wrist strength are important in controlling the puck, shooting, and checking opponents.

There are two unique aspects to hockey from a training standpoint. Since lines can be changed on the fly, action can be more continuous and at a higher aerobic level than in many other sports. Fatigued players do not have to wait for time-out to be relieved, thus a high level of aerobic play can be maintained almost constantly. Players may remain on the ice in the range of one to four minutes, depending upon position. The forward line does more high-speed skating and covers more distance, while the defensemen can pace their energy expenditure and remain on the ice longer.

Another unique aspect of hockey is the movement on ice. This raises the question of specificity in training. In most sports, movement on the court or on the field is by foot, thus running is an excellent and specific training mode. The inevitable question is, should hockey players condition aerobically and anaerobically on ice? The answer obviously is yes, if it is available. If ice is not available to the hockey player in the off-season, running is a good substitute training mode. Many hockey players may prefer to train aerobically by running during the off-season.

Since hockey requires a high aerobic and anaerobic power and a great deal of arm strength and leg power, the training regimen must be very rigorous, and year-round conditioning is almost essential to develop the kinds of capacities needed to play the game. Young athletes with career aspirations in hockey should become accustomed to year-round training by the time they reach the high school level.

Table 12.1   Off-Season Conditioning Program for Hockey

Warm-Up and Stretching

Aerobic Conditioning

	Distance	% Max.	Time (approx.)
Run: *Goal*	3 mi.	75%↑	20–24:000 mins.

Strength Training (3 days per week)

Major and assistant exercises: apply set system; supplemental and specialty exercises: apply set system or circuit system 1. Train Explosively!

Monday and Friday	**Wednesday**
Bench Press	Incline or Military Press
6–10 sets, 10, 10, 8, 8, 6, 6, 4, 4, 2, 2	6–8 sets, 10, 8, 8, 6, 6, 4, 4
Half Squat	Bar Dips
6–10 sets, 8, 8, 8, 6, 6, 4, 4, 4, 2, 2	6–8 sets, 10, 10, 8, 8, 6, 6
Toe Raises	Toe Raises
6–8 sets, 30 reps	6–8 sets, 30 reps
Good Morning or Stiff-legged Deadlift	Good Morning or Stiff-legged Deadlift
5 sets, 10 reps	5 sets, 10 reps
Upright Rowing	Clean
5 sets, 10 reps	5 sets, 8, 5, 5, 3, 3
Slap Shot Motion	Slap Shot Motion
5 sets, 10 reps	5 sets, 10 reps
Backhand or Reserve Slap Shot Motion	Backhand or Reverse Slap Shot Motion
5 sets, 10 reps	5 sets, 10 reps
Sit-Ups (twisting)	Sit-Ups (twisting)
5 sets, 10–20 reps	5 sets, 10–20 reps
Ankle Exercise	Ankle Exercise
3–5 sets	3–5 sets
Wrist Roller and/or Wrist Curl	Wrist Roller and/or Wrist Curl
3–5 sets	3–5 sets
Neck Extension	Neck Extension
3–5 sets, 10 reps	3–5 sets, 10 reps

Optional Exercises

Bent-Arm Pullover, Bent-Over Rowing, Leg Extension, Tricep Extension, Lat Pull, Curl, Leg Curl, High Knee Lift, Leg Thrust.

Stretching Exercises

OFF-SEASON

The off-season conditioning program should concentrate on developing aerobic power and strength. Both of these capacities require large amounts of time for training and that time should be available during the off-season. Off-season conditioning should consist of running (skating preferred) for aerobic development. Strength training will be aimed primarily at developing leg power and upper body power, particularly arm, shoulder, and wrist strength. Greater resistance and fewer repetitions will be characteristic of the strength training in the off-season. Table 12.1 offers an off-season conditioning program for hockey.

PRE-SEASON

The objective of the pre-season program is to bring the hockey player to peak playing condition in as brief a period of time as possible. Training becomes more intense during the pre-season period. There is a shift from aerobic to anaerobic conditioning, which must be done on the ice. The shift in strength training is toward higher speed, greater repetition, low-resistance training. A pre-season conditioning program for hockey is offered in table 12.2.

Table 12.2   Pre-Season and In-Season Conditioning Program for Hockey Players

Warm-Up and Stretching

Aerobic Conditioning
In-Season (2 per week)

	Time	% Max.	Rest	Reps
Skate:	10–15 mins.	75%↑	—	1

Strength Training
Pre-Season (3 days per week):
Apply circuit systems 1, 3, 4, 5, 6, or 9; rotate through circuit twice (junior high or high school) or up to 3½ times (for college players).

In-Season (2 days per week):
Apply circuits 2, 3, 4, and 6; ALL levels perform circuit one time through.

Bench Press, 10 reps
Fast-Speed Squat Machine or Jumping Squat, 12 reps
Upright Rowing, 10 reps
Leg Extension, 10 reps
Lower Back Machine, Good Mornings, or Stiff-legged Deadlifts, 10 reps
Bench Press, 10 reps
Leg Curl, 10 reps
Slap Shot Motion, 10 reps
Sit-Ups, 20 reps
Fast-Speed Squat Machine or Jumping Squats, 12 reps
Upright Row, 10 reps
Ankle Exercise (Dorsiflexion of the foot, p. 89), 10–50 reps
Reverse Slap Shot Motion, 10–15 reps
Leg Extension, 10 reps
Wrist Curl or Wrist Roller, 25 reps
Military Press, 10 reps
Wrist Curl or Wrist Roller, 25 reps
Toe Raises, 30 reps
Military Press, 10 reps
Cable Rowing or Bent-Over Rowing, 10 reps

Optional Exercises:
Bent-Arm Pullover, Incline Press, Bar Dips, Tricep Extension, Leg Lifts

Anaerobic Conditioning:
Pre-season, daily

	Distance	% Max.	Rest	Reps
Skate:	Rink length	95%↑	15 secs.	8–12

In-Season, daily

	Distance	% Max.	Rest	Reps
Skate:	Rink length	100%	15 secs.	10–15

Stretching Exercises

IN-SEASON

The objectives of the in-season conditioning program are to maintain strength and aerobic condition, continue anaerobic conditioning, and prevent injuries. Strength and aerobic conditioning sessions are reduced to one or two per week, while anaerobic conditioning is maintained daily. A relatively short expenditure of time is sufficient to maintain strength and aerobic condition.

The coach should be alert for opportunities to condition within the regular practice session. High-speed stick handling or skating drills can be used repeatedly to develop anaerobic condition. Aerobic condition can be maintained or improved with continuous play such as scrimmages with no time-outs.

An in-season conditioning program for hockey is offered in table 12.2.

SUMMARY

Hockey is a high-intensity game played in the upper one-third of the aerobic mode or fully anaerobic (Stages II and III). Like basketball, it requires all three energy mechanisms during play as well as explosive power and strength. A unique aspect of the game is the ability to change lines during play, thus keeping the intensity of the game high.

In this chapter the authors have offered programs to develop all of the essential conditioning factors in hockey. The programs are designed for off-season, pre-season, and in-season.

REFERENCES

1. Bjornarnea, Bud. 1981. "Power Training for Hockey," *NSCA Journal* 3(1):24–27.

2. Croce, Pat, and Bruce C. Cooper 1983. *Conditioning for Ice Hockey: Year Round.* Champaign, IL: Human Kinetics.

3. Jette, Maurice. 1980. "The Physiological Basis of Conditioning for Ice Hockey Players," *Toward an Understanding of Human Performance,* 2d ed. Ithaca, NY: Mouvement Publications.

4. Koloskov, V. 1978. "Conditioning the Hockey Player," *Ice Hockey: Research Developments and New Concepts.* Miami, FL: Symposia Specialists.

5. Landy, Fernand, and William A. R. Orban, eds. 1978. *Ice Hockey: Research Developments and New Concepts.*

6. Marcotte, Gaston, and Ray Hermison. 1975. "Ice Hockey," *The Scientific Aspects of Sports Training.* Springfield, IL: Charles C Thomas.

CHAPTER
THIRTEEN

VOLLEYBALL

This chapter contains year-round conditioning programs for volleyball. The programs are designed for the off-season, pre-season, and in-season periods. The reader is referred to four previous chapters for the basis of the programs. Chapter 3 deals with aerobic and anaerobic conditioning, Chapter 4 with strength training, Chapter 5 with warm-up and stretching programs, and Chapter 8 with year-round conditioning. The latter chapter describes ways of most efficiently putting training objectives together into a single program. The reader is also referred to sample recording charts offered in the Appendix. These charts will facilitate the measurement of the athlete's progress on the training program and will indicate the athlete's standing in regard to training goals.

The movements required to play volleyball are very *anaerobic,* with the average play lasting 7 to 9 seconds. Setting, spiking, jumping, and blocking are all anaerobic power actions. The players are also in continuous movement throughout an entire game. An average rest (ball out-of-play) is less than twenty seconds, and the ball is in play an average of seven minutes during a game. The ball is out-of-play an average of seventeen minutes during the average game (24 minutes). Because a match consists of three wins, out of five games, it can become rather lengthy. This requires endurance of an *aerobic* nature and is particularly important in skilled play when a match may run into several hours. Conlee, et al.[2], found that volleyball players had a slight predominance (56 percent) of fast twitch fibers (FT) but also had a reasonably high aerobic capacity (56 ml/kg) compared to most team sports athletes. This means that the volleyball player is one who is capable of explosive leg power for the jump, and is also able to maintain high-level play over several hours. The most active players must vertical jump an average of once every 43 seconds, sometimes jumping two or three times successively. This requires a high level of *local muscular endurance* as well as a good aerobic training base. Volleys last an average of 8 to 10 seconds, with the ball

staying in play a maximum of 20 seconds. There are approximately 10 to 12 seconds between serves. Depending upon the level of play, the contest may last an hour (junior high school) to two and one-half hours in high-level collegiate play.[3]

Strength training is extremely important in preparation for volleyball because of the explosive nature of the skills.[3] Power volleyball requires leg power for jumping, and arm and shoulder strength for spiking. The requirement for local muscular endurance in the legs is extreme. The repeated jumping that occurs in the game taxes not only the leg power of the player, but also leg endurance.

The Japanese led the way with scientific studies of training, especially those designed to improve the vertical jump.[7] More recently, the Soviets and Cubans have emphasized endurance jumping and have also used depth jumping. Nearly a half century of research on vertical jump training suggests that there are many effective techniques to improve the vertical jumping ability of players in volleyball and basketball.[4] In addition to modern strength machines, free weights, rope skipping, depth jumping, and jump training have also proved to be effective.

Jump training and plyometrics are a very important part of the conditioning program for volleyball. Plyometrics should be done only by athletes 16 years of age or older because of the possibility of serious damage to the joints (in particular the epiphyseal plate) in younger athletes. Some volleyball programs employ jump training three times per week in the off-season. The authors recommend twice per week off-season and pre-season, and once a week in-season. Volleyball players can incorporate various types of jump training into their programs. In addition to power bounding and the various hops described in Chapter 4, "L"-shaped bounding jumps can be done in any combination of forward, backward, to the right, and to the left. These can be done one-legged, two-legged, or in combinations of alternating legs. In addition to depth jumps, obstacle

Table 13.1 Off-Season Conditioning Program for Volleyball

Warm-Up and Stretching

Aerobic Conditioning

	Distance	% Max.	Time (approx.)
Run:	1:5–3.0 mi.	75%	12:00–24:00 mins.

Plyometric Training (2 days per week)

Strength Training (3 days per week)
Major and assistant exercises: apply set system; supplemental and specialty exercises: apply set system or circuit system
1. Train Explosively!

Monday and Friday	Wednesday
Bench	Military or Incline Press
5–8 sets, 10, 10, 8, 8, 6, 6, 4, 4	5–8 sets, 10, 10, 8, 8, 6, 6
Squat	Leg Press
5–8 sets, 8, 8, 8, 8, 6, 6, 6, 6	10, 10, 10, 10, 8, 8, 8, 8
Toe Raises	Toe Raises
5–8 sets, 30 reps	5–8 sets, 30 reps
Throwing Pullover	Throwing Pullover
5 sets, 10 reps	5 sets, 10 reps
Wrist Curl	Wrist Curl
3–5 sets (25 front, 15 reverse)	3–5 sets (25 front, 15 reverse)
Serving Motion (with pulley)	Serving Motion (with pulley)
3–5 sets, 10–15 reps	3–5 sets, 10–15 reps
Spiking Motion (with pulley)	Spiking Motion (with pulley)
3–5 sets, 10–15 reps	3–5 sets, 10–15 reps
Reverse Curl	Reverse Curl
5 sets, 10 reps	5 sets, 10 reps
Sit-Ups and/or Leg Lifts	Sit-Ups and/or Leg Lifts
5 sets, 10–20 reps	5 sets, 10–20 reps
Set Shot Motion (with dumbbells)	Set Shot Motion (with dumbbells)
5 sets, 10–15 reps	5 sets, 10–15 reps

Optional Exercises
Tricep Extension, Leg Extension, Bent-Over Rowing, Bent-Arm Pullover, Ankle Exercise, Bar Dips.

Stretching Exercises

---

jumping over hurdles, chairs, or boxes can be created, approximately 8 to 10 jumps in length. Various specialized devices such as adjustable *jump boxes* and *jumping boards* which use surgical tubing, jump belts, and foam landing material, have also been created for volleyball players.

Flexibility and agility are also very important for the volleyball player, since many of the "saves" come on dives or other out-of-position plays.

Highly skilled "power volleyball" can be deceptive to the casual observer. At first glance the game may not appear to be very physically demanding. Volleyball players and coaches, however, will quickly recognize the physical requirements just described. Year-round conditioning programs that meet those requirements are described in the next section.

YEAR-ROUND CONDITIONING

The objectives of the off-season program for volleyball are to develop the aerobic condition, and leg and arm power necessary to play the game properly. Considerably more time is available to the player to condition for those two objectives during the off-season than later in the year-round conditioning regimen. Considerable amounts of whole-body aerobic conditioning are combined with strength training for leg and arm power. There will be greater emphasis on the muscular endurance end of the strength-endurance continuum.

As the pre-season conditioning program develops the emphasis is on more intense aerobic conditioning. Aerobic intervals are recommended during this period in order to attain peak aerobic power at the beginning

Table 13.2 Pre-Season and In-Season Conditioning Program for Volleyball Players

Warm-Up and Stretching

Aerobic Conditioning
Pre-Season:

(Daily) Run:	Distance	% Max.	Rest	Reps
	880 yds.	85%↑	3 mins.	4–6

In-Season:
(2 sessions/week)

	Distance	% Max.	Time (approx.)	Reps
Run:	2.0 mi.	75%↑	14–16:00 mins.	1

Anaerobic Conditioning

(In-Season)	or			
Run:	Floor length	100%	—	10–20

Plyometric Training (1 or 2 days per week)

Strength Training
Pre-Season
(3 days per week): Apply circuit systems 3, 4, 5, 6, and 9. Rotate through circuit twice (junior high or high school players) or up to 3½ times (college players).

In-Season (2 days per week): Apply circuit systems 2, 3, 4, or 6. All levels perform circuit one time through.

Leg Extension, 10 reps	High-Speed Squat Machine or Jumping Squats
Cable Rowing or Bent-Over Rowing, 10 reps	Bench Press
Leg Curl, 10 reps	Toe Raises
Military Press, 10 reps	Sit-Ups or Leg Lifts
High-Speed Squat Machine or Jumping Squats, 12 reps	Throwing Pullover
Upright Rowing, 10 reps	Wrist Roller or Wrist Curl
Toe Raises, 30 reps	Throwing Pullover
Bench Press, 10 reps	Wrist Roller or Wrist Curl
Abduction-Adduction machine	Abduction-Adduction Machine
Throwing Pullover	Sit-Ups or Leg Lifts
Leg Extension	Ankle Exercise (Dorsiflexion of the foot, p. 89)
Military Press	
Leg Curl	
Upright Row	

Specialty Exercises to be performed following the circuit:
Serving Motion with pulley
Spiking Motion with pulley
Set Shot Motion with dumbbells

Optional Exercises
Tricep Extension, Arm Curl, Bent-Arm Pullover, Ankle Exercise, Bar Dips, Incline Press

of the season. The major goal of pre-season conditioning should be to bring the athlete to top playing condition as rapidly as possible with a minimum expenditure of time. Strength training should continue to emphasize fast-speed, high-repetition work, with low resistance. The emphasis is on the development of local muscular endurance, particularly in the legs.

Since flexibility training has no seasonal emphasis, it will continue year round on a maintenance level.

During the in-season period, strength and aerobic condition can be maintained with a minimum expenditure of time. A two-day-a-week program will be suf-ficient to maintain strength and aerobic condition. Anaerobic conditioning for the legs must be continued daily during this period. During the in-season training program the coach can use skill drills or jumping drills as conditioners. Repeated spiking drills, for example, will serve not only for practicing the skill of spiking but also for developing leg power and endurance.

Year-round conditioning programs for volleyball are offered in tables 13.1 and 13.2.

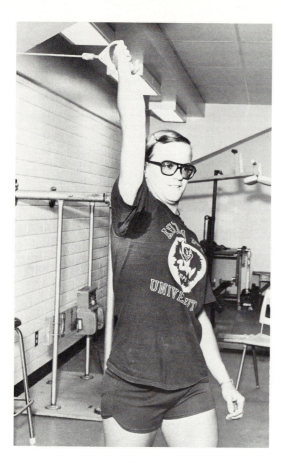

Figure 13.1 Serving Motion

SPECIALTY EXERCISES

Serving Motion (with wall pulley)

This motion in volleyball is identical to the Throwing Motion (with wall pulley) described in Chapter 19.

Spiking Motion (with wall pulley)

This movement is done with a slightly higher pulley than the serving motion so that the angular downward motion of the spike can be strengthened.

Set Shot Motion (with dumbbells)

This is done by crouching in the normal SET position with dumbbells held in each hand. The athlete then extends the arms and body upward in the exact Set Shot motion.

SUMMARY

Volleyball involves many anaerobic power movements using Stage I (ATP-CP). Since the movements are repeated, sometimes over a period of several hours, aerobic capacity is also highly important. Much attention is paid to strength development in the legs and upper body. The volleyball player must also develop a high level of flexibility and agility in order to keep the ball in play.

The authors have offered off-season, pre-season, and in-season conditioning programs for volleyball. Those programs are aimed at developing the major performance factors associated with volleyball.

REFERENCES

1. Andersen, Rolf. 1981. "Consideration of a Volleyball Team," *NSCA Journal* 2(1):19.

2. Conlee, Robert K., et al. 1982. "Physiological Effects on Power Volleyball," *Physician and Sportsmedicine* 10:93–97.

3. Disch, James G. 1981. "Theories of High-Level Performance Applied to Volleyball: Performance Analysis and Conditioning," *Volleyball Technical Journal* 6:69–74.

4. Lacy, Alan. 1982. "A Half-Century of Research on Vertical Jump Training." Unpublished research paper. Arizona State University.

5. McClellan, Tim. 1989. *Strength Training and Conditioning for Volleyball at Arizona State University: The Yearly Systematic Design.* Department of ICA, A.S.U.

6. Semenick, Douglas, and Kela Adams. 1987. "The Vertical Jump: A Kinesiological Analysis with Recommendations for Strength and Conditioning Programming," *NSCA Journal* 9(3):5–9.

7. Toyoda, H. 1971. *Training for Volleyball in Japan.* Ontario, Canada: Canadian Volleyball Association Publication.

Figure 13.2 Set Shot Motion

FOURTEEN

WRESTLING

This chapter contains year-round conditioning programs for wrestling. The programs are designed for the off-season, preseason, and in-season periods. The reader is referred to four previous chapters for the basis of the programs. Chapter 3 deals with aerobic and anaerobic conditioning, Chapter 4 with strength training, Chapter 5 with warm-up and stretching programs, and Chapter 8 with year-round conditioning. The latter chapter describes ways of most efficiently putting training objectives together into a single program. The reader is also referred to sample recording charts offered in the Appendix. These charts will facilitate the measurement of the athlete's progress on the training program and will indicate the athlete's standing in regard to training goals.

Wrestling is unique in at least two respects: 1) competition is divided into ten weight categories, and 2) the action is divided into specific intervals of time.[7] The former results in a major concern for selecting the ideal weight, and the latter in a range of wrestling time from three or five minutes at junior high school level to seven minutes at the collegiate level. High school competition usually involves three two-minute intervals for a total wrestling time of six minutes. Collegiate wrestling has a three-two-two (minutes) sequence, while freestyle amateur wrestling uses two three-minute intervals. It is not unusual to wrestle seven matches in two days at a tournament. At least 45 minutes must be allowed between matches at national tournaments. Kraemer has found extremely high levels of blood lactate after a single match.[6] Since there is very little rest between wrestling intervals (one minute), a three- to seven-minute period of action falls well within the *aerobic* Stage III energy mechanism. Numerous studies have confirmed the high aerobic capacity of wrestlers and the need to make endurance training a major portion of conditioning for wrestling.[8,10]

Wrestling is a sport that requires a great deal of both *aerobic* endurance and *strength*. Upper-body strength, agility, and rapid acceleration are specific needs of the wrestler. The total block of time for a wrestling match must be considered an aerobic energy period, but within any one- to three-minute sequence *anaerobic* output could be involved. The result is that the wrestler must be prepared for an aerobic work period with anaerobic bursts of activity coming at any time during the match. Year-round conditioning for wrestling should focus on those requirements of the sport. A year-round conditioning regimen is offered in the next section of this chapter.

Maintaining minimum body weight for classification is a major concern for the wrestler. Strength training must be done very selectively to avoid adding to body weight. The practice of dehydration, which is used by some wrestlers, is not recommended by the authors and is discussed in more detail in Chapter 7. Wrestlers as a group are very lean athletes. Research indicates that many of the most successful wrestlers are five percent body fat or less.[10] Since wrestlers spend so much time and effort reducing body weight to a minimum effective category, one should not attach a cause and effect to the success of very lean wrestlers. Among a group of very lean athletes (many begin the season at eight percent fat), successful wrestlers may be those who can tolerate body weight loss and continue to train and perform. Recent evidence supports the supposition that rapid weight loss and rehydration have a detrimental effect on muscle glycogen levels and strength.[3]

YEAR-ROUND CONDITIONING

During the off-season there should be concentration on the development of aerobic power and the development of strength in the upper body. More time can be expended on these two training objectives during the off-season when the time spent on skills development is reduced. The wrestler should be careful not to allow his body weight to increase significantly during the off-season. If it becomes necessary to combat weight problems, increased aerobic conditioning will help to con-

Table 14.1 Off-Season Conditioning Program for Wrestling

Warm-Up and Stretching

Aerobic Conditioning (3 days per week)

	Distance	% Max.	Time (approx.)
Run	3–5 mi.	75%	21–40:00 mins.

Strength Training (3 days per week)
Major and assistant exercises: apply set system; supplemental and specialty exercises: apply set system or circuit system 1. Train Explosively!

Monday and Friday

Bench Press
8–10 sets, 10, 10, 8, 8, 6, 6, 4, 4

Squat
8–10 sets, 10, 10, 8, 8, 8, 8, 6, 6

Toe Raises
8–10 sets, 30–50 reps

Good Morning, Stiff-legged Deadlift, or Hyperextension
5 sets, 10 reps

Curls
5 sets, 10–15 reps

Sit-Ups
5 sets, 10–50 reps

Bent-Over Rowing or Cable Curl
5 sets, 10–15 reps

Neck Extension
5 sets, 10 reps

Support Curl
5 sets, 10–15 reps

Wrist Roller and/or Wrist Curls
3–5 sets

Reverse Curl
5 sets, 10–15 reps

Wednesday

Incline Press
6–10 sets, 10, 10, 8, 8, 8, 8

Leg Press
10, 10, 10, 10, 8, 8, 8, 8

Bar Dips
6–8 sets, 10, 10, 8, 8, 8, 8

Toe Raises
8–10 sets, 30–50 reps

Good Morning, Stiff-legged Deadlift, or Hyperextension
5 sets, 10–15 reps

Curls
5 sets, 10–15 reps

Sit-Ups
5 sets, 10–50 reps

Bent-Over Rowing or Cable Curl
5 sets, 10–15 reps

Neck Extension
5 sets, 10 reps

Support Curl
5 sets, 10–15 reps

Wrist Roller and/or Wrist Curls
3–5 sets

Reverse Curl
5 sets, 10–15 reps

Optional Exercises
Military Press, Lat Pull, Bent-Arm Pullover, Clean, Deadlift, Tricep Extension, Leg Extension, Ankle Exercise

Stretching Exercises

trol body weight. A combination of diet and exercise is the most effective means of reducing or maintaining body weight.

During the pre-season period aerobic training becomes more intense and strength training becomes increasingly geared to the development of muscular endurance. The major goal of the pre-season conditioning program is to bring the wrestler to peak physical condition in the briefest possible time. During this period the coach or athlete may desire to add specific anaerobic conditioning related to wrestling.

During the in-season period the major objective is to maintain high aerobic capacity with a minimum time expenditure. Strength training can be drastically re-

duced during the in-season period because strength is also developed by wrestling practice. There are many opportunities for the coach to include either aerobic or anaerobic conditioning in the wrestling practice session. Extending the duration of the practice wrestling bout produces an aerobic training effect. Short maximum bouts with brief rest intervals will increase the anaerobic training effect. Wrestlers are fortunate in that the activity itself produces a training effect for aerobic and anaerobic capacity as well as strength.

Year-round conditioning programs are offered for off-season, pre-season, and in-season in tables 14.1, 14.2, and 14.3. Flexibility training follows a year-round program that is consistently aimed at maintenance.

Table 14.2   Pre-Season and In-Season Conditioning Program for Wrestling

Warm-Up and Stretching

Aerobic Conditioning
Pre-season (3 to 5 days per week):   Run: 2–3 miles at 75% Max↑
In-Season (1 to 2 days per week):

Strength Training
Pre-Season (3 days per week):
Apply circuit systems 1, 2, 3, 4, 5, 6 and 9.

In-Season (2 days per week):
Apply circuit systems 1, 2, 3, 4, 6, and 7.

Leg Extension	10–15 reps
Neck Extension (front and back)	10–15 reps
Reverse Curls	10–15 reps
Back Hyperextension	10–15 reps
Support Curls	10–15 reps
Sit-Ups	20–30 reps
Curls	10–20 reps
Leg Curl	10–15 reps
Bent-Over Rowing or Cable Rowing	10–20 reps
High-Speed Squat Machine or Squat	10–15 reps
Bench Press	10–15 reps
Abduction-Adduction Machine	10–20 reps
Bar Dips	10–20 reps
High-Speed Squat Machine or Squat	10–15 reps
Military Press	10–15 reps
Leg Curl	10–15 reps
Bench Press	25–35 reps
Toe Raises	20–30 reps
Sit-Ups	20–30 reps
Leg Extension	10–15 reps
Neck Extension (side to side)	10–15 reps
*Pull-Ups	MAX

Optional Exercises: Tricep Extension, Bent-Arm Pullover, Clean, Ankle Exercise

Anaerobic Conditioning: In-Season, daily
(Specific anaerobic wrestling intervals should be selected by coach and athlete.), e.g.,

	Time	% Max.	Rest	Reps
Wrestle:	1 min.	90%	2 mins.	6–10
	3 mins.	85%	3 mins.	5–8

Stretching Exercises

*Indicates designated competition station for circuit system 7, *Muscular Endurance Circuit.*

SUMMARY

Wrestling is almost the perfect "interval" sport, with total wrestling time ranging between three and nine minutes. Wrestling is highly aerobic *(Stage III) but is punctuated with* anaerobic *bursts of effort. Strength (whole body) is also important in wrestling, as are* agility *and* speed.

The programs offered in this chapter are aimed at improving the major factors involved in wrestling. Programs are designed to be used in the off-season, pre-season, and in-season.

REFERENCES

1. Anderson, Bob. 1980. "Stretching for Wrestling," *NSCA Journal* 2(6):18–22.

2. Cipriano, Nick. 1987. "Wrestling: Physical Conditioning Principles and Protocols for Amateur Wrestling," *NSCA Journal* 9:44–49.

3. Houston, Michael E., et al. 1981. "The Effects of Rapid Weight Loss on Physiological Functions in Wrestlers," *Physician and Sportsmedicine* 9:73–78.

Table 14.3   Pre-Season Strength Circuit for Wrestling (the *Survival Super-Set Circuit*)

Warm-up and Stretching

Aerobic Conditioning:
See table 14.2

Strength Training
Survival Super-Set Circuit, circuit system 8. This circuit can be administered from one to three days per week. Pre-season only, or allow 10 to 13 days for recovery before competition.

Leg Extension	10–15 reps
Military Press	10–15 reps
Leg Curl	10–15 reps
Neck Extension, front and back	10–15 reps
Shoulder Shrug	10–20 reps
Neck Extension, side to side	10–15 reps
Abduction-Adduction Machine	10–20 reps
Bench Press	10–15 reps
Toe Raises	30–40 reps
Bench Press	10–15 reps
Leg Extension	10–15 reps
Bench Press	10–15 reps
Leg Curl	10–15 reps
Sit-Ups	20–30 reps
Back Hyperextension	10–15 reps
Upright Rowing or Clean	10–20 reps
Wrist Curl or Wrist Roller	25–35 reps
Toe Raises	30–40 reps
Upright Rowing or Clean	10–15 reps
Bar Dips	10–20 reps
Sit-Ups	20–30 reps
Back Hyperextension	10–15 reps
Bar Dips	10–20 reps
Wrist Curl	25–35 reps
Abduction-Adduction Machine	10–20 reps

Bent-Over Rowing or Cable Rowing	10–20 reps	S
Curl	10–20 reps	U S
Reverse Curl	10–15 reps	P E
Wrist Curl	25–35 reps	E T
		R S
Fast-Speed Squat Machine or Squat	10–15 reps	
Support Curl	10–15 reps	S
Bent-Over Rowing or Cable Rowing	10–20 reps	U S
Reverse Curl	10–15 reps	P E
Wrist Curl	25–35 reps	E T
		R S
High-Speed Squat Machine or Squat	10–15 reps	
Lat Pull	10–15 reps	S
Military Press	10–15 reps	U S
Incline Dumbbell Curls	10–20 reps	P E
Bent-Over Rowing or Cable Rowing	10–20 reps	E T
Sit-Ups	20–30 reps	R S
*Pull-Ups —THE CHAMPS' SET—	MAX	

MURDERER'S ROW

Stretching Exercises

*To Hold the CHAMPS' SET RECORD, the wrestler must go through every station of Murderers' Row first.

4. Johnson, Mark, and Charles Yesalis. 1986. "Wrestling: Strength Training and Conditioning for Wrestling: The Iowa Approach," *NSCA Journal* 8:56–59.

5. Klinzging, James. 1986. "Wrestling: Guidelines for Conditioning in Wrestling," *NSCA Journal* 8(2):58–60.

6. Kraemer, William J. 1984. "Wrestling: Physiological Aspects for Conditioning," *NSCA Journal* 6(1):40–67.

7. Leyshon, G. 1975. "Wrestling," *The Scientific Aspects of Sports Training.* Springfield, IL: Charles C Thomas.

8. Rasch, Phillip, and Walter Kroll. 1974. *What Research Tells the Coach about Wrestling.* Washington, DC: AAHPERD.

9. Stuckey, John, and Gerard Palmieri. 1985. "Wrestling: Strength and Conditioning for Wrestling," *NSCA Journal* 7(5):40–42.

10. Zambeski, Edward J. 1980. "Wrestling and Research," *Toward an Understanding of Human Performance,* 2d ed. Ithaca, NY: Mouvement Publications.

CHAPTER
FIFTEEN

BASEBALL AND SOFTBALL

This chapter contains year-round conditioning programs for junior high, high school, and college baseball and softball. The programs are designed for the off-season, pre-season, and in-season periods. The reader is referred to four previous chapters for the basis of the programs. Chapter 3 deals with aerobic and anaerobic conditioning; Chapter 4 with strength training; Chapter 5 with warm-up, stretching, and flexibility; and Chapter 8 with year-round conditioning. The latter chapter also includes ways of most efficiently putting training objectives together in a single program.

Baseball and softball are very *anaerobic* games. With the exception of the pitcher and catcher, players engage in brief bursts of effort requiring primarily acceleration, power, and speed. On defense, the actions of the pitcher and catcher are more frequent but still anaerobic.

Most of the conditioning efforts and much of past research in baseball has focused on the pitcher.[8] In a series of recent studies on major leaguers, Coleman[2,3] found pitchers to be taller, heavier, and fatter on the average than players at other positions. They also tended to have less upper body strength but greater leg strength than other players. Since the pitcher must deliver 100 to 150 pitches per game at a rate of about two per minute, it is evident why the pitcher also desires local muscular endurance in the legs. Pitchers engage in considerably more aerobic conditioning than players at other positions. *Aerobic* training for baseball and softball players serves primarily to assist in recovery from anaerobic performance and is more essential for pitchers and catchers. Coleman's studies also revealed that baseball players in the major leagues have aerobic capacities only slightly lower than those of volleyball players or soccer professionals.[3] It has also been found that baseball players as a group are very flexible, but are just slightly below the average college male in fatness.

Arm *strength* and leg *power* are very important, so strength training is directed primarily at those two areas. Baseball and softball players can benefit a great deal from strength training.

In order to gain maximum performance benefit from strength training, the authors recommend several principles for baseball and softball players: 1) Strength exercises should be done as close as possible to performance, speed, and range of motion. This is particularly important during the pre-season and in-season periods. 2) Practice of the skill (throwing, batting, or running) is recommended after the strength building exercise. Only one set of ten reps is sufficient. 3) Strength *must* be maintained *during* the season to be effective. Unpublished research by Kroll indicates that throwing power actually *decreases* during a season of baseball without supplementary strength training.[6] Kroll's study was conducted with junior college athletes and Coleman[4] has recently confirmed those results with major league players. Not only was the strength training group stronger at the conclusion of the season, but they also had reduced body fat and increased muscle tissue. There was no loss in the range of motion for the stronger players.

Many athletes and coaches are adamant in their attitude that in-season strength training is not feasible, but it can be accomplished with an expenditure of very little time. The programs that follow are designed for year-round conditioning.

OFF-SEASON

The off-season program in most sports is directed toward developing aerobic power and strength. Baseball and softball players should also be concerned with strength and power development but less concerned with aerobic development. Aerobic conditioning should be practiced by pitchers and catchers, while players at other positions ought to concentrate on anaerobic conditioning.

Off-season strength training should utilize greater resistance and fewer reps than pre- or in-season training. Major muscle groups should receive the greatest concentration at this time as well as injury preventive exercises (see Chapter 6). Incline Flys, Arm Circles, and Lateral Raises are recommended to strengthen the shoulder joint, thus reducing the potential for soreness or injury as a result of throwing. Specialty exercises are provided within the programs (tables 15.1 and 15.2).

Flexibility programs for baseball and softball can be initiated in the off-season, and then followed year round on a maintenance regimen.

Table 15.1 Off-Season Conditioning Program for Junior High Baseball and Softball

Warm-Up and Stretching

Strength Training (3 days per week)
Major and assistant exercises: apply set system; supplemental and specialty exercises; apply set system or circuit system 1.

Strength Training—Train Explosively!

Bench Press
5–8 sets, 10, 10, 8, 6, 4, 2, 1

Half Squat
5–8 sets, 10, 8, 6, 4, 2, 1

Military Press
5–8 sets, 10, 10, 8, 8, 6, 4

Lat Pulls
5 sets, 10 reps

Sit-Ups
5 sets, 10–25 reps

Lower Back Machine or Hyperextensions
5 sets, 10 reps

Throwing Pullover and/or Throwing Motion (wall pulley)
5 sets, 10 reps

Toe Raises
5 sets, 30 reps

Hitting Motion
5 sets, 8–10 reps

Wrist Roller and/or Wrist Curl
3–5 sets

Lower Back Machine or Hyperextensions
5 sets, 10 reps

Aerobic Conditioning (pitchers and catchers)

	Distance	% Max.	Time (approx.)
Run:	2.0 mi.	75%↑	15–17 mins.

Optional Exercises

Arm Circles, Lateral Raises, Incline Flys, Leg Extension, Neck Extension, Bar Dips, Pitcher's specialty exercises.

Stretching Exercises

Table 15.2 Off-Season Conditioning Program for High School and College Baseball and Softball

Warm-Up and Stretching

Strength Training (3 days per week)
Major and assistant exercises: apply set system; supplemental and specialty exercises: apply set system or circuit system 1.

Monday and Friday
Bench Press
Mon.: 6–10 sets, 10, 10, 8, 8, 6, 6, 6, 6
Fri.: 6–10 sets, 10, 10, 8, 6, 3, 3, 3, 3, 3

Squat
Mon.: 6–8 sets, 8, 8, 8, 6, 6, 6, 6, 6
Fri.: 6–10 sets, 8, 8, 8, 6, 4, 4, 4, 4

Toe Raises
6–8 sets, 30 reps

Throwing Motion (wall pulley) or Throwing Pullover
5 sets, 6–10 reps each

Wrist Roller
3–5 sets

Sit-Ups, Twisting
5 sets, 10–20 reps

Wednesday
Military Press
6 sets, 10, 10, 8, 8, 6, 6

Dips
10, 10, 8, 8, 6, 6

Jumping Squat (with light weight)
6 sets, 10–12 reps

Toe Raises
6–8 sets, 30 reps

Throwing Motion (wall pulley) or Throwing Pullover
5 sets, 6–10 reps each

Wrist Roller
3–5 sets

Sit-Ups, Twisting
5 sets, 10–20 reps

Table 15.2—*Continued*

Monday and Friday

Wrist Curls
Palms up	25 reps
Palms down	15 reps
3–5 sets,	40 reps

Incline Flys, Arm Circles, and/or Lateral Raises
3–5 sets, 10 reps (These exercises are highly
recommended for preventing arm and shoulder soreness.)

Hitting Motion (with pulley or weighted bat)
3–5 sets, 10 reps

Wednesday

Wrist Curls
Palms up	25 reps
Palms down	15 reps
3–5 sets	40 reps

Incline Flys, Arm Circles, and/or Lateral Raises
3–5 sets, 10 reps

Hitting Motion (with pulley or weighted bat)
3–5 sets, 10 reps

Pitchers

Speed Exercise
5 sets, 8–15 reps

Hip and Leg Motion
5 sets, 10 reps

Hip Extension or Hyperextension
5 sets, 10 reps

Optional Exercises

Leg Extension, Incline Press, Bent-Arm Pullover, Neck Extension, Upright Rowing.

Aerobic Conditioning (pitchers and catchers)

	Distance	% Max	Time (approx.)
Run:	3.0 mi.	75%	20–24:00 mins.

Stretching Exercises

PRE-SEASON

The objective of the pre-season program is to bring the player to peak condition in the briefest possible time. Training thus becomes more intense than at any other period in the year-round plan. Strength exercises are done at high speed with slightly less resistance than previously. Specificity should be stressed, and specificity exercises should be performed as closely as possible to the skills they mimic.

Pre-season programs are offered at the junior high, high school, and college levels (see table 15.3).

IN-SEASON

The objectives of in-season conditioning are to maintain anaerobic power and strength, and to prevent injuries. A minimum amount of time will enable athletes to meet all those objectives. For example, two or three sets of exercises at high speed and less resistance will maintain strength. Training, as such, once or twice a week, will enable one to maintain strength for an entire season. Aerobic (for pitchers and catchers) and anaerobic conditioning must also be maintained in-season (table 15.3).

SPECIALTY EXERCISES

Arm Circles

These are done with the arms extended straight out to the sides, making small circles in alternating directions. They may be done with no weight or with a light (5 to 15 pound) dumbbell. This exercise will help prevent shoulder soreness and will aid throwing power (Chapter 6).

Lateral Raises

These are done in the standing position by elevating (abducting) the extended arms straight out to the sides and directly overhead (Chapter 6).

Incline Flys

These are performed on an inclined bench with dumbbells. The dumbbells are held with the arms extended directly overhead. They are then lowered until the arms are parallel to the ground. Sometimes a slight bend in the elbows is necessary in the lowered position (Chapter 6).

Warm-Up and Stretching

Strength Training

Pre-Season (3 days per week):
Apply circuit systems 1–6 and 9. All levels rotate through circuit once or twice.

In-Season (1 or 2 days per week):
Apply circuit systems 1–4 and 6. All levels rotate through circuit one time. Pitchers perform strength workouts a maximum of once per week in-season.

Leg Extension	10 reps
Lateral Raises	10–20 reps
Leg Curl	10 reps
Bench Press	10 reps
Toe Raises	30 reps
Bar Dips	10 reps
High-Speed Squat Machine or Half Squat	12–15 reps
Incline Flys	10–15 reps
Abduction-Adduction Machine	10–20 reps
Military Press	10 reps
Sit-Ups, Twisting	20–30 reps
Lateral Raises	10–20 reps
Leg Lifts or Hip Flexion Machine	10–20 reps
Bar Dips	10 reps
Leg Extension	10 reps
Bench Press	10 reps
High-Speed Squat Machine or Half Squat	12–15 reps
Incline Flys	10 reps
Wrist Curl or Wrist Roller	25 reps
Leg Curl	10 reps
Sit-Ups, Twisting	20–30 reps
Abduction-Adduction Machine	10–20 reps
Toe Raises	30 reps
Leg Lifts or Hip Flexion Machine	10–20 reps
Military Press	10 reps

Aerobic Conditioning

Junior High:

Pre-Season (pitchers and catchers)

	Distance	% Max.	Time (approx.)
Run:	1.5 mi.	75%↑	10–12 mins.

In-Season (pitchers and catchers)

	Distance	% Max.	Time (approx.)
Run:	1.5 mi.	75%↑	10–12 mins.

High School and College:

Pre-Season (pitchers and catchers)

	Distance	% Max.	Time (approx.)
Run:	2.0 mi.	75%↑	14–16:00 mins.

In-Season (pitchers and catchers)

	Distance	% Max.	Time (approx.)
Run:	2.0 mi.	75%↑	14–16:00 mins.

Table 15.3—*Continued*

Anaerobic Conditioning

Junior High:

Pre-Season

	Distance	% Max.	Rest	Reps
Run:	100 yds.	100%	30 secs.	8–10

In-Season

	Distance	% Max.	Rest	Reps
Run:	50 yds.	100%	15 secs.	8–10

High School and College:

Pre-Season

	Distance	% Max.	Rest	Reps
Run:	100 yds.	100%	30 secs.	10–12

In-Season

	Distance	% Max.	Rest	Reps
Run:	50 yds.	100%	15 secs	10–15

Stretching Exercises

Pitcher's Hip Motion

This exercise is done by attaching a wall pulley to the thigh just above the knee. The hip motion is then imitated exactly.

Throwing Motion

(See Chapter 19.)

SUMMARY

Both baseball and softball are highly anaerobic *games involving a series of highly skilled movements performed primarily in Stage I (ATP-CP). Aerobic power serves primarily to aid recovery from the anaerobic effort. Pitchers require the highest aerobic capacity among players. Strength and explosive power are very important to the baseball player, as are agility and flexibility.*

This chapter contains programs designed to improve the major factors contributing to baseball and softball. The programs are designed for off-season, pre-season, and in-season periods.

REFERENCES

1. "Coaches Roundtable: Strength and Conditioning for Baseball." 1983. *NSCA Journal* 5(3):11–73.

2. Coleman, A. Eugene. 1981. "Skinfold Estimates of Body Fat in Major League Baseball Players," *Physician and Sportsmedicine* 9:77–82.

3. Coleman, A. Eugene. 1982. "Physiological Characteristics of Major League Baseball Players," *Physician and Sportsmedicine* 10:51–57.

4. Coleman, A. Eugene. 1982. "In-Season Strength Training in Major League Baseball Players," *Physician and Sportsmedicine* 19:125–132.

5. Kephart, Keith. 1984. "Strength Training for Baseball," *NSCA Journal* 6(2):34–37.

6. Kroll, William A. 1974. "The Effects of an In-Season Weight Training Program on the Throwing Power of Junior College Baseball Players." Masters thesis. Arizona State University.

7. Moore, Mike. 1983. "You Can't Play Yourself into Shape for Baseball These Days," *Physician and Sportsmedicine* 11:162–174.

8. Reiff, Guy G. 1971. *What Research Tells the Coach about Baseball.* Washington DC: AAHPERD.

Figure 15.1 Pitcher's Hip Motion

Chapter 15

CHAPTER

SIXTEEN

SWIMMING

This chapter contains year-round conditioning programs for swimming. The programs are designed for the off-season, pre-season, and in-season periods. The reader is referred to four previous chapters for the basis of the programs. Chapter 3 deals with aerobic and anaerobic conditioning, Chapter 4 with strength training, Chapter 5 with stretching, and Chapter 8 with year-round conditioning. The latter chapter also describes ways of most efficiently putting training objectives together into a single program. The reader is also referred to the sample recording charts offered in the Appendix. These charts will facilitate the measurement of the athlete's progress in the training program and will indicate the athlete's standing in regard to the training goal.

Swimming and track and field are unique compared to other team sports listed in Part Two. The two areas represent the epitome of aerobic, anaerobic, and, in some cases, strength and power performances. Conditioning is a major aspect in preparation for both swimming and track and field. Entire books have been written on training and conditioning for both sports. The authors could not, within the limitations of a single chapter, expect to lay out a day-by-day, week-by-week conditioning program for swimming or track. They have, however, attempted to develop a basic and cohesive year-round conditioning program for both sports.

The authors have found swimming and track coaches to be the most scientific practitioners among coaching professionals. The United States has a long history of excellent swimming performance in international and Olympic competition. Swimming especially has been the subject of considerable research, much of it focused on conditioning.[6] In the United States much of the technique and training programs have stemmed from the work of J. E. "Doc" Counsilman, the legendary swimming coach of Indiana University.[4] Some observers believe that swimming records may be approaching a "stall" point since so much efficiency and power have been attained through stroke mechanics and training. Another significant factor in U.S. success in swimming is its age-group programs.[10] No other group of young sports athletes undergo training of the intensity and magnitude of age-group swimmers. A carefully controlled program early may enhance ultimate performance, but it would be extremely difficult to study such a proposal.

The terms *off-season, pre-season,* and *in-season* may sound foreign to some swimmers and swimming coaches. For many swimmers, conditioning goes on literally year round, but there is usually a shift in the emphasis and intensity of conditioning from one portion of the year to another. Conditioning intensity increases from off-season, to pre-season, to in-season, reaching its peak in the latter stages of the in-season. Swim coaches and swimmers also use the "taper" just prior to the major event. The taper, or reduction in training intensity or distance, is used because of the extreme overdistance practiced by many swimmers. Swimming has the added unique factor that the conditioning mode must be specific to swimming. This requires year-round access to a swimming pool. Conditioning in water enables the swimmer to spend many more hours in training. (Many elite swimmers cover more than 20,000m daily.) The swimmer does not have to contend with the trauma to the joints experienced by the runner. The cool medium of the pool also enables the swimmer to work at higher percentages of max capacity with less body heat buildup compared to runners.[6] Basically, swimming performances can be clustered into three groups: 1) sprint, 2) intermediate, and 3) long-distance swimming.

SPRINT, INTERMEDIATE, AND DISTANCE SWIMMING

Sprint Swimming

The sprint events consist of 50m and 100m races. Elite times range from 20 to 50 seconds, and the events involve Stages I (ATP-CP) and II (Anaerobic-Lactate). Major performance factors in sprint swimming are speed, acceleration, and arm power. These performances rely entirely upon *anaerobic* (Stage I, ATP-CP) energy sources. A maximum burst of effort is needed to begin the event and it can be performed with a minimum of breathing because of its brevity. Stored ATP is sufficient to fuel the energy requirements of very short sprints (50 meters, 20–30 seconds). In the 100m sprint swim, the athlete is also making use of *anaerobic* (Stage II, AN–LA) energy sources. That effort, similar to the 440-yard run in track, produces the maximum oxygen debt. The details of that mechanism are described in Chapter 2.

Strength and power are major factors in sprint swimming. Arm power is a crucial factor in sprints, just as is leg power. Strength requirements are greater in swimming than in running because of the need to move the limbs rapidly and forcefully through the resistance of the water. Sharp and Costill[9] have found that increases in sprint speed were associated with increases in power regardless of the strength training device used. This suggests that power, which is best developed through high speed and repetitions at reduced resistance, may be the major focus of future training in swimming as well as in other sports.[7]

Intermediate Distance

The intermediate distance events include the 200m and 500m races. Elite times range from 1:30 to over four minutes, and the events involve Stages II (AN–LA) and III (Aerobic). The 200m swim engages both Stage II and Stage III and is approximately 60 percent anaerobic and 40 percent aerobic. Bonner[2] has carefully analyzed the energy systems used in swimming. The 500m swim times will vary from just over four minutes to just under five minutes. It is almost the reverse of the 200m race in energy system contribution, and is approximately 70 percent aerobic and 30 percent anaerobic.

Intermediate events also put a premium on strength and power despite the increasing aerobic involvement. The constant battle to overcome the resistance of the water requires strength and power in both the arms and legs. These swimming events are excellent examples of the need to train slow-twitch (red) aerobic fibers as well as fast-twitch (white) anaerobic fibers. Only a few other sporting events require the intense training of both types of fibers that intermediate distance swimming requires. Running in the range of one-half mile to two miles is similar.

Long-Distance Swimming

Long-distance swimming is a maximum challenge of *aerobic* power. Swimming in the range of 800m to 1650m requires a mixture of *aerobic* and *anaerobic* performance. The amount of energy drawn from aerobic sources increases from 800m to 1650m, while the amount of energy supplied by anaerobic resources during those distances decreases.

Strength training for both distance and intermediate swimmers is predominately high-repetition, fast-speed, low-resistance training. The objective is to increase primarily local muscular endurance and, to a lesser degree, muscular strength. Resistance of the water, even at slower swimming speeds, does require development of muscular strength.

Every effort should be made to train aerobically and anaerobically if both energy systems are required by a particular event. If an activity requires 50 percent aerobic energy and 50 percent anaerobic energy, then the training regimen should match the energy requirements of the task. It has been found that strength can be developed in a wide range of sets and repetitions. Like strength, aerobic or anaerobic power can also be developed through a wide range of sets and repetitions of either aerobic or anaerobic conditioning. This suggests that there is no one best combination of sets and repetitions for producing maximum aerobic or anaerobic power. The guideline intervals listed in table 3.5 are intended to be just that—guidelines. Precise intensity and duration of aerobic or anaerobic training must be determined by the capacity of the individual athlete. Eynon and Thoden[5] have completed a lengthy review of the science and art of training for competitive swimming. They concur with the view of the authors that the application of more specificity in training would significantly increase the efficiency of conditioning programs. The "season training plan" is similar in objectives to the year-round conditioning approach proposed by the authors.

OFF-SEASON

The major objectives of the off-season conditioning program for sprint swimmers are to increase strength and arm power, and to maintain anaerobic swimming power. Strength training is designed to meet the first objectives, and anaerobic conditioning of a reduced intensity is designed to meet the latter. Since anaerobic performance in the lactic acid energy range is so intense and fatiguing, the swimmer must be cautioned not to overtrain during the off-season.

Off-season conditioning for intermediate and long-distance swimming is designed primarily to help the athlete maintain aerobic power and strength. Aerobic conditioning will not be as intense as it will be later in the pre-season and in-season periods. Strength training is designed primarily to increase local muscular endurance and, to a lesser degree, strength. The endurance swimmer should always do many repetitions with less resistance in strength training in order to develop muscular endurance. Like the sprint swimmer, the distance swimmer piles up many thousands of yards in training and must be cautious not to train too intensely during off-season. Probably no other athletes train as long and consistently during the off-season as endurance swimmers and runners.

An off-season conditioning program for swimming is offered in table 16.1.

The flexibility and stretching program for swimmers, like other athletes, should follow a consistent, year-round maintenance approach.[1]

PRE-SEASON AND IN-SEASON

In the pre-season period, training for anaerobic development intensifies for sprint swimmers. At this point in the training season, programs must be individualized by coaches and athletes. The programs offered here can serve only as a general guide because some athletes may be capable of much greater amounts of work, while others may struggle to maintain the recommended programs. Strength training for the sprint swimmer will taper off during the pre-season and in-season periods. At the same time, anaerobic conditioning will increase in both amount and intensity. Strength training should be done at high speed with low resistance during these periods. Since some athletes will be capable of tolerating tremendous amounts of anaerobic interval work,

both coaches and athletes must use care to avoid staleness in the latter stages of the competitive season. (See Chapter 8.)

For the long-distance swimmer, the pre-season and in-season training periods will show a gradual increase in the amount and intensity of aerobic training. Middle-distance swimmers will increase both anaerobic and aerobic conditioning. More emphasis will be placed on the anaerobic portion of the middle-distance swimmer's training regimen toward the latter stages of the in-season. As with sprint swimmers, the training program becomes increasingly individualized in the pre-season and in-season periods. The basic objectives of training during these periods will be the same, regardless of the capabilities of the individual swimmer. Through the use of interval training techniques, or continuous training, some swimmers will be capable of covering between fifteen and forty miles of training distance per week as they begin to peak.

In-season strength training for swimmers is minimal. It is designed primarily to maintain strength and should be done not more than once or twice per week. The emphasis is always on high-repetition, fast-speed, and low-resistance exercise. Pre-season and in-season conditioning programs for swimmers are offered in tables 16.2 and 16.3.

Table 16.1 Off-Season Conditioning Program for Swimming

Warm-Up and Stretching

Anaerobic Conditioning (Sprint Swimmers)

	Distance	% Max.	Rest	Reps
Swim: (alternate sessions)	50m	75–85%	1 min.	10
	100m	75–85%	2 mins.	10

Aerobic Conditioning (Intermediate and Long-Distance Swimmers)

Intermediate Distance

	Distance	% Max	Rest	Reps
Swim: (alternate sessions)	200m	75%↑	3 mins.	4–6
	800m	75%	—	1

Long Distance

	Distance	% Max.	Rest	Reps
Swim: (alternate sessions)	1500–3000m	75%	—	
	200m	75%↑	3 mins.	4–16

Strength Training (3 days per week)
Major and assistant exercises: apply set system; supplemental and specialty exercises: apply set system or circuit system 1.

Table 16.1—*Continued*

Monday & Friday

Bench Press
6–10 sets, 10, 10, 8, 8, 6, 6, 4, 4

Half Squat
6–10 sets, 8, 8, 8, 8, 6, 6, 4, 4

Lateral Raises
5 sets, 10–15 reps

Sit-Ups and/or Leg Lifts
5 sets, 10–25 reps

Tricep Pushdown
5 sets, 8–10 reps

Hyperextension
5 sets, 10 reps

Leg Curl
5 sets, 10–15 reps

Upright Rowing
5 sets, 10 reps

Bent-Arm Pullover
5 sets, 10 reps

Bent-Over Rowing (with dumbbells)
5 sets, 10 reps

Specialty Exercises

Backstroke

Backstroke Motion (with pulley)
5 sets, 10 reps

Kicking Motion (with ankle weights)
5 sets, 10–50 reps

Breaststroke Motion (prone, with pulley)
5 sets, 10 reps

Kicking Motion
5 sets, 10–25 reps

Arm Rotators

Wednesday

Military Press
6–8 sets, 10, 10, 8, 8, 6, 6

Jumping Squat
5 sets, 8–15 reps

Clean
5 sets, 8, 6, 5, 4, 3

Sit-Ups and/or Leg Lifts
5 sets, 10–25 reps

Tricep Pushdown
5 sets, 8–10 reps

Hyperextension
5 sets, 10 reps

Leg Curl
5 sets, 10–15 reps

Upright Rowing
5 sets, 10 reps

Bent-Arm Pullover
5 sets, 10 reps

Bent-Over Rowing (with dumbbells)
5 sets, 10 reps

Butterfly

Butterfly Power Movement (prone with pulley)
5 sets, 10 reps

Arm Rotators (with dumbbells or pulleys)
5 sets, 8–15 reps

Crawl Stroke Arm Motion (prone with pulley)
5 sets, 10 reps

Kicking Motion (with ankle weights)
5 sets, 10–50 reps

Arm Rotators (with dumbbells or pulleys)
5 sets, 8–15 reps

Optional Exercises

Hyperextension, Behind Neck Press, Bar Dips, Incline Press, Frontal Deltoid Raises, Toe Raises.

Stretching Exercises

Table 16.2 Pre-Season Conditioning Program for Swimming

Warm-Up and Stretching

Anaerobic Conditioning (daily)—Sprint Swimmers

	Distance	% Max.	Rest	Reps
Swim: (alternate sessions)	100m	85–95%	2 mins.	10
	50m	85–95%	1 min.	10

Aerobic Conditioning (daily)—Intermediate- and Long-Distance Swimmers

Intermediate Distance

	Distance	% Max.	Rest	Reps
Swim: (alternate sessions)	100m	85–95%	3 mins.	8–12
	200m	85–95%	3 mins.	4–6

Long Distance

	Distance	% Max.	Rest	Reps
Swim: (alternate sessions)	1500–3000m	85–95%	—	1
	200m	85–95%	3 mins.	4–6

Strength Training (3 days per week)
Apply circuit systems 1–7 and 9. The number of rotations through the circuit, the circuit chosen, and the specialty exercises to be included depend upon the level and age of the athletes and the event ROM and ME specificity.

Bent-Arm Pullover
Hyperextension, 10–20 reps
Bent-Over Rowing or Cable Rowing, 10–20 reps
Abduction-Adduction Machine, 10–20 reps
Bent-Arm Pullover, 10–15 reps
Leg Curl, 10–15 reps
Bent-Over Rowing or Cable Rowing, 10–20 reps
High-Speed Squat Machine or Jumping Squat, 12–15 reps
Specialty Exercise, 10–20 reps
Hyperextension, 10–20 reps
Military Press, 10–15 reps

Leg Extensions, 10–20 reps
Bar Dips, 10–20 reps
Sit-Ups or Leg Lifts, 20–30 reps
Specialty Exercise, 10–20 reps
High-Speed Squat Machine or Jumping Squat, 12–15 reps
Upright Rowing, 10–15 reps
Toe Raises, 30–40 reps
Bench Press, 10–15 reps
Abduction-Adduction Machine, 10–20 reps
Lateral Raises, 10–20 reps
Leg Curl, 10–15 reps
Hyperextension, 10–20 reps
Leg Extension, 10–20 reps
*Lat Pull or Pull-Ups, Power/MAX

Specialty Exercises

A. Imitative stroke motion (with pulley) for backstroke, breaststroke, butterfly, or freestyle
B. Imitative kicking motion for various kicks
C. Arm rotators (with dumbbells or pulleys)

Optional Exercises

Hyperextension, Behind Neck Press, Bar Dips, Incline Press, Frontal Deltoid Raises, Toe Raises.

Stretching Exercises

*Indicates designated competition station for circuit system 7, Muscular Endurance Circuit.
Swimmers can employ a timed competition "power" station, recording the number of complete repetitions that can be done in a given time as the athlete's PR.

Table 16.3 In-Season Conditioning Program for Swimming

Warm-Up and Stretching

Anaerobic Conditioning (daily)—Sprint Swimmers

	Distance	% Max.	Rest	Reps	Sets
Swim: (alternate sessions)	50 yds.	95%↑	1 min.	10	1
	25 yds.	100%	30 secs.	10–15	1–2

Aerobic Conditioning (daily)—Intermediate- and Long-Distance Swimmers

Intermediate Distance

	Distance	% Max.	Rest	Reps
Swim: (alternate sessions)	50 yds.	100%	1 min.	12–16
	100 yds.	95%↑	3 mins.	8–12
	200 yds.	95%	3 mins.	4–6

Long Distance

	Distance	% Max.	Rest	Reps
Swim: (alternate sessions)	3000–6000 yds.	LSD	—	1
	1500–3000 yds.	95%	—	1
	200 yds.	95%↑	3 mins.	4–6

Strength Training

In-Season (2 days per week)
Apply circuit systems 1–4, 6–7, and 9. The number of rotations through the circuit, the circuit chosen, and the specialty exercises to be included depend on the level and age of the athletes and the event ROM and ME specificity.

Bent-Arm Pullover
Hyperextension, 10–20 reps
Bent-Over Rowing or Cable Rowing, 10–20 reps
Abduction-Adduction Machine, 10–20 reps
Bent-Arm Pullover, 10–15 reps
Leg Curl, 10–15 reps
Bent-Over Rowing or Cable Rowing, 10–20 reps
High-Speed Squat Machine or Jumping Squat, 12–15 reps
Specialty Exercise, 10–20 reps
Hyperextension, 10–20 reps
Military Press, 10–15 reps
Leg Extensions, 10–20 reps
Bar Dips, 10–20 reps

Sit-Ups or Leg Lifts, 20–30 reps
Specialty Exercise, 10–20 reps
High-Speed Squat Machine or Jumping Squat, 12–15 reps
Upright Rowing, 10–15 reps
Toe Raises, 30–40 reps
Bench Press, 10–15 reps
Abduction-Adduction Machine, 10–20 reps
Lateral Raises, 10–20 reps
Leg Curl, 10–15 reps
Hyperextension, 10–20 reps
Leg Extension, 10–20 reps
*Lat Pull or Pull-Ups, Power/Max

Specialty Exercises

A. Imitative stroke motion (with pulley) for backstroke, breaststroke, butterfly, or freestyle
B. Imitative kicking motion for various kicks
C. Arm rotators (with dumbbells or pulleys)

Optional Exercises

Hyperextension, Behind Neck Press, Bar Dips, Incline Press, Frontal Deltoid Raises, Toe Raises.

Stretching Exercises

*Indicates designated competition station for circuit system 7, Muscular Endurance Circuit.
Swimmers can employ a timed competition "power" station, recording the number of complete repetitions that can be done in a given time as the athlete's PR.

SPECIALTY EXERCISES FOR SWIMMERS

Butterfly, Backstroke, Freestyle, and Breaststroke Motion (with pulley)

These exercises are done by lying on a bench and performing the exact range of motion of the stroke with two wall pulleys. A "Y" attachment may be used if only one pulley is available.

Kicks

The various kicking motions can be performed by supporting the upper body and hips on a bench and imitating the particular kicking motion. Ankle weights, weighted boots, or no weight at all usually work better than a pulley.

Arm Rotators

This exercise is done by rotating the forearm around the elbow, which is used as a pivotal point. Both dumbbells and wall pulleys are effective.

SUMMARY

Swimming involves all three stages of metabolism, individually or in varying combinations according to the event. The sprint events are anaerobic, involving both Stage I or II, while the middle-distance and long-distance events are predominately aerobic. Some intermediate events may mix Stage II (AN-LA) and Stage III (AER). Strength and flexibility are also required for swim events, and power is needed to overcome the resistance of the water.

This chapter contains year-round conditioning programs aimed at developing the appropriate performance factors for the event. The off-season, pre-season, and in-season programs are intended to be event-specific.

REFERENCES

1. Anderson, Bob. 1981. "Stretching for Swimming," *NSCA Journal* 3(1):20–23.

2. Bonner, Hugh W. 1980. "Energy Systems Used During Swimming," *Swimming Technique* 17:10–13.

3. Costill, David L., et al. 1980. "Muscle Strength: Contributions to Sprint Swimming," *Swimming World* 21:29–34.

4. Counsilman, James E. 1977. *The Complete Book of Swimming.* NY: Atheneum.

5. Eynon, Robert, and James Thoden. 1975. "Competitive Swimming," *The Scientific Aspects of Sports Training.* Springfield, IL: Charles C Thomas.

6. Faulkner, John A. 1976. *What Research Tells the Coach about Swimming.* Washington, DC: AAHPERD.

7. Jopke, Terry. 1982. "Training Swimmers: How Coaches Get Results," *Physician and Sportsmedicine* 10:161–165.

8. Maglischo, Edward W. 1982. *Swimming Faster: A Comprehensive Guide to the Science of Swimming.* Palo Alto, CA: Mayfield Publishing Company.

9. Sharp, R. L., and David L. Costill. 1982. "Force, Work, and Power: What They Mean to the Competitive Swimmer," *Swimming World* 23:41–43.

10. Zauner, Christian W. 1980. "Training the Child Swimmer," *Toward an Understanding of Human Performance,* 2d ed. Ithaca, NY: Mouvement Publications.

CHAPTER
SEVENTEEN

TRACK AND FIELD

This chapter contains year-round conditioning programs for track and field. The programs are designed for the off-season, pre-season, and in-season periods. In order to make the most effective use of the programs offered here, the reader is referred to Chapter 3 for the basis of aerobic and anaerobic training programs, to Chapter 4 for the basis of strength programs, to Chapter 5 for the basis of warm-up, stretching, and flexibility programs, and to Chapter 8 for the most efficient means of incorporating those objectives into a single workout. The reader is also referred to the sample recording charts offered in the Appendix. These charts will facilitate the measurement of the athlete's progress in the training program and will indicate the athlete's standing in regard to training goals.

Track and field, as well as swimming, are unique compared to the other team sports listed in Part Two. The two areas represent the epitome of aerobic, anaerobic, and in some cases strength and power performances. Conditioning is a major aspect of preparation for both track and field and swimming. Entire books have been written on training and conditioning for both sports. Track events are probably the most thoroughly researched sports activities discussed in this book.[4,8] The authors could not, within limitations of a single chapter, expect to lay out a day-by-day, week-by-week conditioning program for either track or swimming. They have, however, attempted to develop a basic and cohesive year-round conditioning program.

The terms *off-season, pre-season,* and *in-season* may sound foreign to some track athletes and coaches. In some events, conditioning literally goes on year round, but there is usually a shift in the emphasis and intensity of conditioning from one portion of the year to another. Conditioning intensity increases from off-season, to pre-season, to in-season, reaching its peak in the latter stages of the in-season. Because of the distinct differences in the various track and field events, the authors have clustered track and field performances into four basic groups: 1) sprints and hurdles, 2) long- and intermediate-distance running, 3) jumping events, and 4) throwing events.

SPRINTS AND HURDLES

The major performance factors in short (50m–100m) sprint races and hurdles are speed, acceleration, and leg power. These performances rely entirely on *anaerobic* (ATP-CP) energy sources. There is a maximum burst of effort and the event can literally be performed without breathing because it is so brief. Stored ATP is sufficient to fuel the energy requirements of short sprints and hurdles. In sprint races between 200m and 400m, the athlete is also making use of *anaerobic* Stage II (AN-LA) energy sources. The 400m event produces the maximum oxygen debt, the details of which are described in Chapter 2. While acceleration and leg power as well as speed are the major factors in the short sprints, anaerobic capacity becomes increasingly important beyond 80m, as readily available ATP is exhausted.[8]

Dintiman[8] has made a major review of sprinting research. He has made several important generalizations: 1) increased strength leads to an increase in the speed of muscle contraction; 2) more recent work has found a significant correlation between lower body strength and speed in sprinting; and 3) a program of flexibility training, strength training, and sprinting resulted in the best 40-yd. speed and was significantly better than sprinting only. Supplemental training must be conducted *in addition* to sprinting practice to be effective.

CONDITIONING INSTRUCTIONS

The sprint speed conditioning program is specifically designed to develop sprint speed by "improving (1) stride length, (2) starting ability and acceleration to maximum speed, (3) the rate and efficiency of leg movements per second, (4) form and technique, and

Table 17.1   Off-Season Conditioning Program for Sprints and Hurdles

Warm-Up: 1-mile easy jog

Stretching: 15 minutes. Hurdlers do additional groin stretches.

Anaerobic Conditioning:

Monday
2 × 600 (75% max), rest 15 minutes
2 × 300 (85% max), rest 2 minutes
1 × 300 (100% max), rest 5 minutes

Tuesday
3 × 110s build-ups, good form 50% max
Resistive sled runs, good arm and leg action
3 × 50, 3 × 70, 3 × 110, 75% max
3 × 200 (75% max), rest 3 minutes
Strength Training (table 17.2)

Wednesday
4 × 300 (85% max), rest 7 minutes
3 × 200, 80%, 80%—1 sec, 80%—2 secs, rest 3 minutes

Thursday
3 × 110s build-ups, good form
Bounding Drills (R) leg 3 × 30 yards, (L) leg 3 × 30 yards; both legs 3 × 30 yards, alternate legs 3 × 30 yards (first 3 weeks, 30 yards; second 3 weeks, 40 yards; third 3 weeks, 50 yards)
6 × 110s, ½ speed, rest one minute
Strength Training (table 17.2)

Friday
6 × 200, 85–90% max, rest 2 minutes

Saturday
30-minute run
Resistive sled run, good arm and leg action
3 × 50, 3 × 70, 3 × 110
Strength Training (table 17.2)

Sunday
Jogging suggested (20 minutes)
Hurdlers: Monday, Wednesday and Friday: perform technique work, 45 minutes: trail leg, lead leg, 9-yard drill, technique work over 9 hurdles; technique work over 3 hurdles
This is performed in addition to the regular sprint workout.

Stretching Exercises: performed after each workout

(5) conditioning levels."[12] Each workout must be performed in the precise way that it is written. This includes doing the workouts on the proper days, in the right sequence, and at the proper speed and intensity level, with concentration on form and technique. Every workout is also preceded by a warm-up of a one-mile easy jog, and then 15 minutes of flexibility exercises. After each workout, 3 laps (3/4 mile) cool-down is always performed. The cool-down precedes strength training on the days when a strength workout is prescribed. In most cases the athlete may also choose to do post-exercise stretching and cool-down following the strength program. Hurdlers emphasize groin stretches by performing 2 or 3 times the repetitions for sprinters.[12] Hurdlers also include twice as many abduction-adduction sets in their strength program.

Off-Season

The major objectives of the off-season conditioning program for sprinters and hurdlers are to increase strength and leg power, and to maintain anaerobic running speed. Strength training is designed to meet the first objectives, and anaerobic conditioning of reduced intensity is designed to meet the latter. Since anaerobic performance in the lactic acid energy range is so tense and fatiguing, the athlete must be cautioned not to overtrain during the off-season. Off-season programs for sprinters and hurdlers are offered in tables 17.1 and 17.2.

Pre-Season and In-Season

In the pre-season period, training for anaerobic development intensifies for sprinters and hurdlers. At this point in the training season programs must be individ-

Table 17.2 Off-Season Strength Program for Sprinters and Hurdlers

Warm-Up and Stretching

Strength Training (3 days per week)

Major and assistant exercises: apply set system; supplemental and specialty exercises, apply set system or circuit system 1.

Tuesday and Saturday

Squat
2–4 weeks, 10, 10, 8, 8, 8, 8, 8, 8
4–8 weeks, 10, 10, 8, 8, 8, 8, 6, 6

Bench
10, 10, 8, 8, 6, 6, 4, 4

Toe Raises
3–8 sets, 30 reps

Sit-Ups
3–5 sets, 20 reps

Pull-Ups
2–5 sets, max reps

Leg Curl
3–5 sets, 10–15 reps

Leg Extension
3–5 sets, 8–12 reps

Leg Lifts or Hip Flexion Machine
3–5 sets, 10–20 reps

Arm Action Exercises
3–5 sets, 10–20 reps

Bent-Over Row or Cable Row
3–5 sets, 10 reps

Abduction-Adduction Machine
3–5 sets, 10–20 reps

Hurdlers: Abduction-Adduction Machine, 5–6 sets, 10–20 reps

Thursday

Leg Press
10, 10, 10, 10, 8, 8, 8, 8

Incline or Military Press
10, 10, 8, 8, 6, 6, 4, 4

Toe Raises
3–8 sets, 30 reps

Sit-Ups
3–5 sets, 20 reps

Pull-Ups
2–5 sets, max reps

Leg Curl
3–5 sets, 10–15 reps

Leg Extension
3–5 sets, 8–12 reps

Leg Lifts or Hip Flexion Machine
3–5 sets, 10–20 reps

Arm Action Exercises
3–5 sets, 10–20 reps

Bent-Over Row or Cable Row
3–5 sets, 10 reps

Abduction-Adduction Machine
3–5 sets, 10–20 reps

Stretching Exercises

---

ualized by coaches or athletes. The programs offered here can serve only as a general guide because some athletes will be capable of much greater amounts of work, while others may struggle to maintain the recommended programs. Strength training will taper off during the pre-season and into the in-season period, while anaerobic conditioning will increase both in amount and intensity. Strength training should be done at high speed with low resistance during these periods. Since some athletes will be capable of tolerating tremendous amounts of (anaerobic) interval work, both coaches and athletes must use care to avoid staleness in the latter stages of the competitive season (Chapter 8).

Pre-season and in-season conditioning programs for sprinting and hurdling are offered in tables 17.3, 17.4, and 17.5.

LONG- AND INTERMEDIATE-DISTANCE RUNNING

Much of the basis for both anaerobic and aerobic running has been discussed in Chapter 3, Aerobic and Anaerobic Conditioning. It is no surprise that elite distance runners are among the greatest aerobic athletes with maximal oxygen uptakes in the range of 70–80 ml/kg of body weight.[4] This exceeds the range for elite endurance swimmers.

Long-distance running has also been the subject of a tremendous amount of research. There are several excellent scientific reviews of the topic of distance running.[4,5,6,16] Much of the research on distance running has focused on the need to accomplish long-slow-distance training versus the need to develop speed

Table 17.3 Pre-Season Conditioning Program for Sprints and Hurdles

Warm-up: 1-mile easy jog

Stretching: 15 minutes; hurdlers do additional groin stretches

Anaerobic Conditioning

Monday
2 × 500, 75–80% max, rest 12 minutes
3 × 200, 80%, 80%–1 sec, 80%–2 secs, rest 3–4 minutes
Rope Jumping, 10 minutes

Tuesday
Resistive runs
3 × 60—3 × 110 (fast)
5 × 200, 80% max, rest 2 minutes
Stride easy, 400
Strength Training (table 17.4)

Wednesday
500–300–200–300–500 (50% max), rest 3–5 minutes

Thursday
Bounding Drills—(L) leg, 3 × 30, (R) leg, 3 ×30, both legs, 3 × 30, alternate legs, 3 × 30, good explosion
Strength Training (table 17.4), or sled run, alternate with Saturday

Friday
3 × 200, 80%–1, 80%–2, 80%–3, rest 3 minutes
2 × easy 300, 70% max

Saturday
30-minute run
Strength Training (table 17.4) or sled run, alternate with Thursday

Sunday
Jogging suggested (20 minutes)

Hurdlers: Monday and Wednesday, perform technique work 45 minutes (trial leg, lead leg, 9-yard drill; technique work over 9 hurdles; technique work over 3 hurdles)

Stretching Exercises Performed after each workout

through shorter and more intense intervals. Costill[4] has concluded that both speed (interval) and overdistance work are necessary for maximum training effect and performance. Daniels, et al.[6] maintain that there is no all-encompassing training routine for distance runners and that programs must be individualized to meet specific strengths and weaknesses.

Long-distance running is the ultimate challenge of *aerobic* power. The marathon run is the greatest competitive endurance feat. Running in the range of one-half mile to two miles requires a mixture of anaerobic and aerobic performance. The amount of energy drawn from aerobic sources increases during the distance from one-half mile to two miles, while the amount of energy supplied by anaerobic resources during that distance decreases. These events provide an excellent example of the need to train slow-twitch (red) aerobic fibers as well as fast-twitch (white) anaerobic fibers. Only a few other sporting events require the kind of intense training of both types of fibers that intermediate-distance running requires. Strength training for long- and intermediate-distance runners is predominately high-repetition, low-resistance training. The objective is to increase primarily local muscular endurance and, to a lesser degree, muscular strength.

Every effort should be made to train aerobically and anaerobically if both energy systems are required by a particular event. If an activity requires 50 percent aerobic energy and 50 percent anaerobic energy, then the training regimen should match the energy requirements of the task. Strength can be developed in a wide range of sets and repetitions of either aerobic or anaerobic conditioning. This suggests that there is no one best combination of sets and repetitions for producing maximum aerobic or anaerobic power. The guideline intervals listed in table 3.5 are intended to be just that—guidelines. The precise intensity and duration of aerobic or anaerobic training must be determined by the capacity of the athlete.

Distance running is particularly conducive to the tightening of muscles and a loss of flexibility. A year-round stretching and flexibility program should be part of the preparation for intermediate- and long-distance runners.[1] Once a program has been established, it should be followed year round on a maintenance schedule.

Table 17.4 Pre-Season or In-Season Strength Program for Sprinters and Hurdlers

Warm-Up and Stretching

Strength Training (2 or 3 days per week)
Apply circuit systems 1–6 and 9. All levels perform circuit once or twice.

Leg Extension	10–15 reps
Lat Pulls	10–12 reps
Upright Row	10–12 reps
Abduction-Adduction Machine	10–20 reps
Toe Raises	30–40 reps
Leg Curl	10–12 reps
Arm Action Exercise (with dumbbells)	20–40 reps
Hip Flexion Machine or Leg Lifts	10–20 reps
Bent-Over Rowing or Cable Rowing	10–15 reps
High-Speed Squat Machine or Jumping Squats	10–15 reps
Bench Press	10–12 reps
Leg Extension	10–15 reps
Bent-Over Rowing or Cable Rowing	10–15 reps
High-Speed Squat Machine or Jumping Squats	10–15 reps
Arm Action Exercise (with dumbbells)	20–40 reps
Sit-Ups	20–30 reps
Military Press or Incline Press	10–15 reps
Hip Flexion Machine or Leg Lifts	10–20 reps
Bench Press	10–12 reps
Leg Curls	10–12 reps
Pull-Ups	MAX

Hurdlers: 2 or 3 sets extra, Abduction-Adduction Machine

Stretching Exercises

Table 17.5 In-Season Conditioning Program for Sprints and Hurdles

Warm-Up: 1-mile easy jog

Stretching: 15 minutes; hurdlers do additional groin stretches

Anaerobic Training

Monday
6 × 200 (95% max), rest 3 minutes
2 × 450 (80% max), rest 15 minutes

Tuesday
2 × 110 resistive sled run (75% max)
8 × 110 (75% max), rest 2 minutes
Stride 2 × 450 (easy), good arm and leg action
Strength Training (table 17.4)

Wednesday
4 × 300 (95% max), rest 5 minutes
5 × 110 (build up to 75% effort), rest 2 minutes

Thursday
3 × 200 (90%, 90%–1 sec, 90%–2 secs), rest 3 minutes
3 × 150-yard build-ups; slow to 75% effort
Strength Training (table 17.4)

Friday
2 × 300, 90–95% max, rest 5 minutes

Saturday
Build-Up 40–50–100, 50–75% effort
Time Trials: 60–100–200–400; complete recovery
Strength Training after workout (table 17.4)

Sunday
30-minute run

Hurdlers: Monday and Wednesday, perform technique work 45 minutes, trail leg, lead leg, 9-yard drill; technique work over 9 hurdles; technique work over 3 hurdles

Stretching Exercises: performed after each workout

Off-Season

Off-season conditioning for long- and intermediate-distance running is designed primarily to maintain aerobic power. Aerobic training will not be as intense as it will be later in the pre-season and in-season periods.

Strength training is designed primarily to increase local muscular endurance and, to a lesser degree, increase strength. This means that the endurance athlete will emphasize many repetitions with lesser resistance in strength training. Like the sprinter, the distance runner

Table 17.6 Off-season Conditioning Program for Long- and Intermediate-Distance Running

Warm-Up and Stretching

Aerobic Conditioning

Intermediate-Distance Runners

	Distance	% Max.	Rest	Reps
Run: (alternate days)	880 yds.	75%↑	3 mins.	4–6
	2 mi.	75%↑	—	1

Long-Distance Runners

	Distance	% Max.	Rest	Reps
Run: (alternate days)	3–5 mi.	75%	—	1
	880 yds.	75%↑	3 mins.	4–6

Strength Training (3 days per week)
Apply set system or circuit system 1, 3, or 9. If performed as a circuit, rotate through 2 to 4 times.

Monday and Friday	**Wednesday**
Bench Press 6–8 sets, 3–15 reps	Incline, Military Press or Bar Dips 5–8 sets, 3–15 reps
Squat or Half Squat 6–8 sets, 6–15 reps	Leg Press 6–8 sets, 8–15 reps
Upright Rowing 2–5 sets	Upright Rowing 2–5 sets
Leg Extension 2–5 sets, 10–20 reps	Leg Extension 2–5 sets, 10–20 reps
Arm Action Exercise 2–5 sets, 10–30 reps	Arm Action Exercise 2–5 sets, 10–30 reps
Leg Curl 2–5 sets, 10–15 reps	Leg Curl 2–5 sets, 10–15 reps
Lat Pull 2–5 sets, 10–15 reps	Lat Pull 2–5 sets, 10–15 reps
Toe Raises 2–5 sets, 30–40 reps	Toe Raises 2–5 sets, 30–40 reps
Sit-Ups 2–5 sets, 20–40 reps	Sit-Ups 2–5 sets, 20–40 reps
Lower Back Machine or Good Morning Exercise 2–5 sets, 10–15 reps	Lower Back Machine or Good Morning Exercise 2–5 sets, 10–15 reps
Curls (with dumbbells) 2–5 sets, 10–30 reps	Curls (with dumbbells) 2–5 sets, 10–30 reps
Abduction-Adduction Machine 2–5 sets, 10–20 reps	Abduction-Adduction Machine 2–5 sets, 10–20 reps
Bent-Over Rowing or Cable Rowing 2–5 sets, 10–20 reps	Bent-Over Rowing or Cable Rowing 2–5 sets, 10–20 reps
High Knee Lift, Hip Flexion Machine, or Leg Lifts 2–5 sets, 10–20 reps	High Knee Lift, Hip Flexion Machine, or Leg Lifts 2–5 sets, 10–20 reps

Stretching Exercises

Note: If the program is to be performed in a set system, 5 to 8 exercises in addition to the major and assistant exercises can be chosen. These exercises should involve the total body and can be employed for 3 to 6 weeks, then varied.

piles up many miles in training and must be cautious not to train too intensely during the off-season. Perhaps no other athletes train as long and consistently during the off-season as endurance runners and swimmers.

An off-season conditioning program for long- and intermediate-distance runners is offered in table 17.6.

Pre-Season and In-Season

In the pre-season and in-season training periods there is a gradual increase in the amount and intensity of aerobic training for distance runners. Middle-distance runners should increase the amounts of both anaerobic and aerobic conditioning. More emphasis should be placed on the anaerobic portion of the middle-distance runner's training regimen toward the latter stages of the in-season. As with sprinters, the training program becomes increasingly individualized during the pre-season and in-season periods. The basic objectives of training during these periods will be the same, regardless of the capabilities of the individual runner. Through the use of continuous training or aerobic intervals, some distance runners will be capable of covering between 100 and 200 miles of training distance per week as they begin to peak.

In-season strength training for intermediate- and long-distance runners is very minimal. It is designed primarily to maintain strength and should not be done more than once or twice per week. Strength training for these athletes is always high-repetition, fast-speed, and low-resistance exercise.

Pre-season and in-season conditioning programs are offered in table 17.7.

JUMPING EVENTS

Jumping events rely primarily upon leg power, acceleration, and, in three of the four jumping events, running speed. Strength training is a very significant factor in year-round conditioning for jumping events. Strength training is used to increase leg power for the high jumper, arm and upper body strength for the pole vaulter, and acceleration for the long jumper. The Soviets have evolved extensive progressive resistance programs for developing strength and explosive power.[13] They utilize a variety of weights and techniques from heavy resistance squats to high speed jumps with light weights. They also use depth jumps and as many as 1,200–1,300 practice jumps per year.

Anaerobic sprints should comprise a major portion of the conditioning for long jumpers and triple jumpers. Speed development as indicated is extremely important for jumpers. *Flexibility* is also especially important to the pole vaulter and high jumper. Year-round conditioning programs for high jumpers and long jumpers are offered in tables 17.8, 17.9, and 17.10.

THROWING EVENTS

Throwing in field events relies primarily upon *power* and *strength,* and thus strength training is the essential supplementary conditioning technique. Athletes in the throwing events were among the first to make significant use of weight training to improve their athletic performance. Parry O'Brien was a pioneer in the use of weight training as a supplement to his shot-putting preparation in the 1950s. He reported a corresponding increase in putting the shot with systematic increases in strength. Just as the endurance athlete focuses almost entirely upon aerobic conditioning, the throwing event athlete focuses almost entirely upon strength training. The general principles of strength training recommended for all athletes should be followed, and the intensity of training should peak during the in-season period.

The note to train explosively, which appears in almost every training program in this book, is particularly pertinent to throwing event athletes. These performers are involved in the development of anaerobic, fast-twitch fibers. The ability to make use of the strength developed in training will be determined by the specificity of training. High-speed, explosive movements in strength training are essential for throwing events. Strength training should always be accompanied with event (skill) practice.[10] Although strength is a major factor in throwing events, skill is also an important factor, especially with the hammer throw and the javelin. The discus and shot are more influenced by power, but also utilize skilled movements.

Flexibility is also important in throwing events, since a full range-of-motion is needed to achieve maximum throwing performance.[10] A flexibility program should be followed year round for maximum effectiveness.

For the heavy year-round strength program necessary for the weight events, it is best to utilize a cycle system (Chapter 4). The following cycle system has been designed especially for the weight events. This program can also be utilized as the base program for a heptathlon or decathlon athlete. The major and assistant exercises that involved the cycle system are trained with the addition of the specialty exercises for each event. To execute the system, follow these guidelines.

1. Find the athlete's 1RM for each major and assistant exercise to be trained.
2. Find the athlete's projected 1RM for the 16-week cycle. Use a 7½ percent increase for athletes in the first or second of heavy strength training, or a 5 percent increase for athletes with more advanced strength training experience.
3. The amount of weight (or the resistance level) to use in the numerous repetition series offered can be determined from table 17.1 and the individual's projected maximum.
4. The resistance levels are applied directly to the final two sets of each repetition series for the "heavy" weeks of the cycle.

Table 17.7 Pre-Season or In-Season Conditioning Program for Long and Intermediate Distances

Warm-Up and Stretching

Aerobic-Anaerobic Conditioning

Pre-Season (daily)

Intermediate-Distance Runners

	Distance	% Max.	Rest	Reps
Run: (alternate days)	440 yds.	85–95%	3 mins.	8–12
	880 yds.	85–95%	3 mins.	4–6

Long-Distance Runners

	Distance	% Max.	Rest	Reps
Run: (alternate days)	3–5 mi.	85–95%	—	1
	880 yds.	85–95%	3 mins.	4–6

In-Season (daily)

Intermediate-Distance Runners

	Distance	% Max.	Rest	Reps
Run: (alternate days)	220 yds.	100%	1 min.	12–16
	440 yds.	95%	3 mins.	8–12
	880 yds.	95%	3 mins.	4–6

Long-Distance Runners

	Distance	% Max.	Rest	Reps
Run: (alternate days)	5–10 mi.	LSD	—	1
	3–5 mi.	95%↑	—	1
	880 yds.	95%↑	3 mins.	4–6

Strength Training (2 or 3 days per week)
Apply circuit systems 1, 3, 4, 5, 6, or 9. Rotate through circuit 1 to 3 times, according to the intensity and duration needed to supplement the aerobic and anaerobic output.

Leg Extension	10–20 reps
Lat Pull	10–20 reps
Toe Raises	30–40 reps
Upright Row	10–15 reps
Abduction-Adduction Machine	10–20 reps
Curl (with dumbbells)	10–20 reps
Hip Flexion Machine, High Knee Lift, or Leg Lifts	10–20 reps
Arm Action Exercise	20–40 reps
High-Speed Squat Machine or Jumping Squat	12–20 reps
Bench Press	10–15 reps
Leg Curl	10–20 reps
Bent-Over Rowing or Cable Rowing	10–20 reps
Leg Extension	10–20 reps
Sit-Ups	20–40 reps
High-Speed Squat Machine or Jumping Squat	10–20 reps
Arm Action Exercise	20–40 reps
Toe Raises	30–40 reps
Lower Back Machine or Good Morning Exercise	10–15 reps
Bench Press	10–15 reps
Leg Curl	10–20 reps
Military or Incline Press	10–15 reps
Sit-Ups	20–40 reps
Curl (with dumbbells)	10–20 reps
Leg Lifts, High Knee Lifts, or Hip Flexion Machine	10–20 reps
Lower Back Machine or Good Morning Exercise	10–15 reps

Stretching Exercises

Warm-Up and Stretching

Strength Training (3 days per week)

Major and assistant exercises, apply set system; supplemental and specialty exercises, apply set system or circuit system 1.

Monday & Friday	**Wednesday**
Bench Press	Military Press or Incline Press
6–8 sets, 10, 10, 8, 8, 6, 6, 4, 4	6–8 sets, 10, 10, 8, 8, 6, 6, 4, 4
Half Squat	Jumping Squats
6–8 sets, 8, 8, 8, 8, 6, 6, 4, 4	6–8 sets, 10 reps
Toe Raises	Toe Raises
6–8 sets, 30–75 reps	6–8 sets, 30–75 reps
Cleans	Cleans
5 sets, 8, 5, 5, 3, 3	5 sets, 8, 5, 5, 3, 3
High Knee Lift	High Knee Lift
5 sets, 10 reps	5 sets, 10 reps
Leg Curl (toes in)	Leg Curl (toes in)
5 sets, 10 reps	5 sets, 10 reps
Sit-Ups and/or Leg Lifts	Sit-Ups and/or Leg Lifts
5 sets, 10-20 reps	5 sets, 10–20 reps

Optional Exercises

Running Arm Motion (with dumbbells), Bar Dips, Lat Pulls, Bent-Over Rowing, Rack Squat, Leg Extension, Curls, Upright Rowing, Good Morning, Frontal Deltoid Raises

Specialty Exercises

High Jump	**Pole Vault**	**Triple Jump**	**Long Jump**
High Jump Leg Motion	Bent-Arm Pullover	High Rack Squat	Ankle Exercise
5 sets, 10 reps	5 sets, 10 reps	5 sets, 5, 5, 3, 3, 1	3–5 sets, 15 reps
	Pull-Ups	Step-Ups	
	3–5 sets	3–5 sets, 5–10 reps	
	Grip Exercises		
	3–5 sets		

Anaerobic Conditioning

	Distance	% Max.	Rest	Reps
Run:	100 yds.	85–95%	1 min.	8–10

Plyometric Training (2 or 3 days per week)

Stretching Exercises

---

5. The next table shows the resistance levels to be employed for the final two sets of each repetition series. This is based on the previously indicated "percent of projected max" for that particular number of repetitions.

6. The warm-up and adjustment sets of each repetition series are found in the standard way described in Chapter 4. Figure 4.1 is used to determine the starting weights. The resistance levels of the adjustment sets are determined by spacing the increases shown by the "step-like" indicators, equidistant apart. When the exact resistance levels are not possible or preferable for the adjustment sets, remember the rule of thumb (Chapter 4). "Always make larger or equal increases first."

7. In peaking for important track meets, strict adherence to percentages is waived in favor of a drop in poundages. However, as the emphasis is on speed, the intensity level still remains high as the effective load on the muscles is increased by exploding, or accelerating the resistance.

Year-round programs for conditioning throwing events athletes can be found in tables 17.11 and 17.12.

Table 17.9   Pre-Season Conditioning Program for High Jump, Pole Vault, Triple Jump, and Long Jump

Warm-Up and Stretching

Strength Training (3 days per week)
Major and assistant exercises, apply set system; supplemental and specialty exercises, apply set system or circuit system 1.

Monday-Wednesday-Friday

Bench Press	High Knee Lift
3–6 sets, 10–20 reps	5 sets, 10–15 reps
Half Squat	Leg Curls (toes in)
3–6 sets, 10–20 reps	5 sets, 10–15 reps
Toe Raises	Sit-Ups and/or Leg Lifts
3–6 sets	5 sets, 10–25 reps
Cleans	
5 sets, 8, 5, 5, 3, 3	

Optional Exercises

Running Arm Motion (with dumbbells), Bar Dips, Lat Pulls, Bent-Over Rowing, Rack Squat, Leg Extension, Curls, Upright Rowing, Good Morning, Frontal Deltoid Raises

Specialty Exercises

High Jump	**Pole Vault**	**Triple Jump**	**Long Jump**
High Jump Leg Motion	Bent-Arm Pullover	High Rack Squat	Ankle Exercise
5 sets, 10 reps	5 sets, 10 reps	5 sets, 5, 5, 3, 3, 1	3–5 sets, 15 reps
	Pull-Ups	Step-Ups	
	3–5 sets	3–5 sets, 5–10 reps	
	Grip Exercises		
	3–5 sets		

Anaerobic Conditioning

	Distance	% Max.	Rest	Reps
Run:	100 yds.	95%↑	1 min.	10–12

Plyometric Training (2 or 3 days per week)

Stretching Exercises

Table 17.10   In-Season Conditioning Program for High Jump, Pole Vault, Triple Jump, and Long Jump

Warm-Up and Stretching

Strength Training (2 days per week)
Major and assistant exercises, apply set system or circuit system 1; supplemental and specialty exercises, apply circuit system 1.

Monday	**Wednesday**
Bench Press	Military Press
2–3 sets, 10–15 reps	2–3 sets, 10–15 reps
High Knee Lift	High Knee Lift
2–3 sets, 10–15 reps	2–3 sets, 10–15 reps
Jumping Squat	Jumping Squat
2–3 sets, 12–20 reps	2–3 sets, 12–20 reps
Toe Raises	Toe Raises
2–3 sets, 30 reps	2–3 sets, 30 reps

Specialty Exercises

Table 17.10—*Continued*

High Jump	Pole Vault	Triple Jump	Long Jump
High Jump Leg Motion 5 sets, 10 reps	Bent-Arm Pullover 5 sets, 10 reps	High Rack Squat 5 sets, 5, 5, 3, 3, 1	Ankle Exercise 3–5 sets, 15 reps
	Pull-Ups 3–5 sets	Step-Ups 3–5 sets, 5–10 reps	
	Grip Exercises 3–5 sets		

Anaerobic Conditioning (daily)

	Distance	% Max.	Rest	Reps
Run:	50 yds.	100%	30 secs.	10–15

Plyometric Training (2 or 3 days per week)

Stretching Exercises

Table 17.11 Off-Season Conditioning Program for Shot-Put, Discus, and Javelin

Monday-Wednesday-Friday

Squat and Bench Press

Preparation Period	Weeks	Rating	Weeks	Rating
	1) 15-15-15	L	5) 12-12-10-10	L
	2) 15-15-15	M	6) 10-10-10	M
	3) 15-15-15	MH	7) 10-10-10	MH
	4) 12-12-10-10	H	8) 10-10-10	H
Regular Off-Season	1) 10-10-8-8-6-6	L	9) 8-8-6-6-4-4	L
	2) 10-10-8-8-6-6	M	10) 8-8-6-6-4-4	M
	3) 10-10-8-8-6-6	MH	11) 8-8-6-6-4-4	MH
	4) 10-10-8-8-6-6	H	12) 8-8-6-6-4-4	H
	5) 8-8-6-6-5-5	L	13) 8-8-5-5-3-3	L
	6) 8-8-6-6-5-5	M	14) 8-8-5-5-3-3	M
	7) 8-8-6-6-5-5	MH	15) 8-8-5-5-3-3	MH
	8) 8-8-6-6-5-5	H	16) 8-8-5-5-3-3	H

Power Cleans or High Pulls

Preparation Period	Weeks	Rating	Weeks	Rating
	1) 5-5-5-5-5	L	5) 5-5-4-4-4	L
	2) 5-5-5-5-5	M	6) 5-5-4-4-4	M
	3) 5-5-5-5-5	MH	7) 5-4-4-4-3	MH
	4) 5-5-4-4-4	H	8) 5-4-4-3-3	H
Regular Off-Season	1) 5-4-4-4-4	L	9) 5-4-3-3-3	L
	2) 5-4-4-4-4	M	10) 5-4-3-3-3	M
	3) 5-4-4-4-4	MH	11) 5-4-3-3-3	MH
	4) 5-4-4-4-4	H	12) 5-4-3-3-3	H
	5) 5-4-4-3-3	L	13) 5-4-3-2-2	L
	6) 5-4-4-3-3	M	14) 5-4-3-2-2	M
	7) 5-4-4-3-3	MH	15) 5-4-3-2-2	MH
	8) 5-4-4-3-3	H	16) 5-4-3-2-2	H

Table 17.11—*Continued*

Supplemental and Speciality Exercises

Bent-Arm Laterals***
Preparatory, 5 sets, 8 reps
Regular, 4 sets, 8 reps

Incline Dumbbell Press**
Preparatory, 5 sets, 8 reps
Regular, 4 sets, 8 reps

Bent-Arm Pullover
Preparatory, 5 sets, 8 reps
Regular, 5 sets, 8 reps

Leg Extension
Preparatory, 4 sets, 12 reps
Regular, 4 sets, 10 reps

Leg Curl
Preparatory, 4 sets, 12 reps
Regular, 4 sets, 10 reps

Good Morning***, **
Preparatory, 4 sets, 8 reps
Regular, 4 sets, 8 reps

Hyperextension*
Preparatory, 5 sets, 12 reps
Regular, 4 sets, 10 reps

Tricep Pushdown
Preparatory, 4 sets, 10 reps
Regular, 4 sets, 8 reps

Toe Raises
Preparatory, 4 sets, 12 reps
Regular, 4 sets, 10 reps

Wrist Curl
Preparatory, 4 sets, 10 reps
Regular, 4 sets, 10 reps

Optional Exercises

Incline Press, Snatch Pull, Military Press

***Indicates specialty exercise for discus.
**Indicates specialty exercise for shot-put.
*Indicates specialty exercise for javelin.

Table 17.12 Pre-Season Conditioning Program for Shot-Put, Discus, and Javelin (with indoor peak)

Monday-Wednesday-Friday
Squat and Bench Press

Weeks	Rating	Weeks	Rating
1) 8-8-5-5-5-5	L	9) 8-8-8-8-8	MH
2) 8-8-5-5-5-5	M	10) 8-8-6-6-5-5	H
3) 8-8-5-5-5-5	MH	11) 8-8-6-6-5-5	L
4) 8-6-4-4-3-3	H	12) 8-8-6-6-5-5	M
5) 8-6-4-4-3-3	MH "Fast"	13) 8-8-5-4-4-4	H
6) 8-6-4-4-3-3	M "Fast"	14) 8-8-5-4-4-4	M
	Indoor Peak		
7) 8-8-8-8-8	L	15) 8-8-5-4-4-4	MH
8) 8-8-8-8-8	M	16) 8-8-5-4-4-4	H

Power Cleans or High Pulls

Weeks	Rating	Weeks	Rating
1) 5-4-4-3-3	L	9) 5-5-5-5-5	MH
2) 5-4-4-3-3	M	10) 5-4-3-3-3	H
3) 5-4-3-2-2	MH	11) 5-4-4-3-3	L
4) 5-4-3-2-1	H	12) 5-4-4-3-3	M
5) 5-4-3-2-1	MH "Fast"	13) 5-4-3-3-3	H
6) 5-4-3-2-1	M "Fast"	14) 5-4-3-3-3	M
7) 5-5-5-5	L	15) 5-4-3-3-2	MH
8) 5-5-5-5	M	16) 5-4-3-3-2	H

"Fast"—Indicates which weeks to increase the speed emphasis.

Table 17.12—*Continued*

Supplemental and Specialty Exercises

Bent-Arm Laterals***
3 sets, 8 reps

Incline Dumbbell Press**
3 sets, 6 reps

Bent-Arm Pullover*
4 sets, 6 reps

Leg Extension
4 sets, 10 reps

Leg Curl
4 sets, 10 reps

Good Morning***, **
Discus: 2 sets, 8 reps
Shot-Put: 2 sets, 6 reps

Hyperextension*
4 sets, 10 reps

Tricep Pushdown
4 sets, 8 reps

Toe Raises
4 sets, 10 reps

Jumping Squats (see Chapter 11, p. 155)
4 sets, 10 reps

Wrist Curls
4 sets, 10 reps

Optional Exercises

Incline Press, Snatch Pull, Military Press

***Indicates specialty exercises for discus.
**Indicates specialty exercise for shot-put.
*Indicates specialty exercise for javelin.

Table 17.13 In-Season Conditioning Program for Shot-Put, Discus, and Javelin

Monday-Wednesday-Friday

Squat and Bench Press

Weeks	Rating	Weeks	Rating
1) 5-3-3-3-2-2	L	5) 5-3-3-2-2-1	M "Fast"
2) 5-3-3-3-2-2	M "Fast"	6) 5-3-3-2-2-1	H
3) 5-3-3-2-2-2	H	7) 5-3-3-2-2-1	MH "Fast"
4) 5-3-3-3-2-2	L "Fast"	8) 5-3-3-2-2-1	M "Fast"

Power Cleans or High Pulls

Weeks	Rating	Weeks	Rating
1) 5-3-3-2-2-1-1	L	5) 5-3-2-2-1-1-1	M "Fast"
2) 5-3-3-2-2-1-1	M "Fast"	6) 5-3-2-2-1-1-1	H
3) 5-3-3-2-2-1-1	H	7) 5-3-2-2-1-1-1	MH "Fast"
4) 5-3-2-2-1-1-1	L "Fast"	8) 5-3-2-2-1-1-1	M "Fast"

"Fast"—Indicates which weeks to increase speed emphasis.

Supplemental and Specialty Exercises

Bent-Arm Laterals***
3 sets, 8 reps

Incline Dumbbell Press**
3 sets, 6 reps

Bent-Arm Pullover*
3 sets, 6 reps

Leg Extension
4 sets, 8 reps

Leg Curl
4 sets, 8 reps

Good Morning***, **
4 sets, 6 reps

Hyperextension*
4 sets, 10 reps

Triceps Pushdown
4 sets, 6–8 reps

Toe Raises
4 sets, 10 reps

Jumping Squats (p. 155)
4 sets, 8 reps

Wrist Curls
4 sets, 10 reps

***Indicates specialty exercises for discus.
**Indicates specialty exercises for shot-put.
*Indicates specialty exercises for javelin.

SPECIALTY EXERCISES FOR RUNNERS

ARM ACTION EXERCISES

The purpose of the arm action exercise is to help improve the athlete's arm action by strengthening the shoulder and back muscles involved in the forward and backward sprinter's arm action. The backward part of the arm action is developed by bent-over rowing and/or cable rowing. The forward part of the arm action is developed by the arm action exercise with dumbbells.

Arm Action Exercise for Sprinters and Intermediate-Distance Runners

This exercise is performed, using dumbbells, in the seated or standing position. The elbows are kept at a 90° angle, exactly as they are in the sprinting movement (fig. 17.1). It is best to pause at the bottom of the motion to prevent swinging the weight. This creates more forward thrust on the next forward arm movement, thereby strengthening the front deltoid and the biceps.

Arm Action Exercise for Long-Distance Runners

This exercise is performed in the standing position. The distance runner is not concerned about keeping the elbow angle at 90° or about driving the elbow back. He or she concentrates on the local muscular endurance involved in keeping the arms moving smoothly without tightening up. The exercise is performed using 5- to 15-pound dumbbells. The runner moves the arms through his or her normal running movement, keeping the hands high in the forward part of the motion in a relaxed, free-swinging movement at the shoulders.

Figure 17.1 Arm Action Exercise with Dumbbells for Sprinters and Intermediate-Distance Runners

Table 17.14 Number of Repetitions for Projected Strength Maximum

Number of Reps	Resistance Level
2	95% of projected max
3	90% of projected max
4	85–87% of projected max
5	80% of projected max
6	75% of projected max
7	72½% of projected max
8	70% of projected max
10	60% of projected max
15	50% of projected max

Table 17.15 Resistance Level for Cycle System

		Lower Body	Pulls and Upper Body
For athletes who squat over 225 pounds and bench press over 135 pounds			
Heavy week	indicated % of projected max		
Medium-heavy week	indicated % of projected max	−10	−5
Medium week	indicated % of projected max	−20	−10
Light week	indicated % of projected max	−30	−15
For athletes who squat less than 225 pounds and bench press less than 135 pounds			
Heavy week	indicated % of projected max		
Medium-heavy week	indicated % of projected max	−5	−5
Medium week	indicated % of projected max	−10	−5
Light week	indicated % of projected max	−15	−10

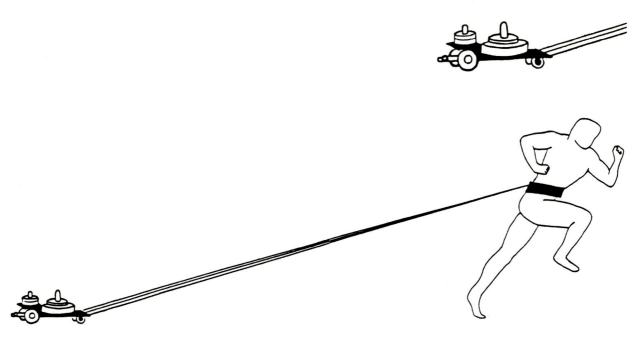

Figure 17.2   Resistive Sled Training

Sprint Resistive Sled

The sprint resistive sled helps develop sprint speed by enabling the athlete to train with resistance at high speed in the exact range of motion as sprinting itself. The resistive sled makes full use of the overload principle and the principle of specificity. The sled allows for specificity in terms of muscular endurance, range of motion, and speed. Since the resistance is attached to the athlete at a point very close to the center of gravity (fig. 17.2), the angle of body lean during the sled training varies little, if any, from the body lean when sprinting without the sled. The scientific principles indicate that this type of resistance training for sprinters is optimal. Before the development of this type of device, uphill running, weighted vests, and elastic bands were the only common methods of resistive sprinting.[7] Reduced stride length was a major problem, and the results in terms of increased speed were much more limited.

The resistive sled training develops the explosive foot-and-leg thrust off the ground on each stride (fig. 17.2). Sleds of various types are available (fig. 17.3). The more complex type (a) has wheels and a braking system so that the resistance stays the same at all speeds. When the athlete stops, the braking system also keeps the sled from rolling into him or her from behind. Other styles designed for the grass (b) or the astroturf (c) are also available.

The method of using the resistive sled: Secure the belt around the waist, removing the slack from the cable. Rise high on the balls of the feet, proceeding to pull the resistive sled with the specified weights for distance described in the program (tables 17.1, 17.3, 17.5). Three-week cycles with varying distances and weights are recommended.

1st week, 3 × 60 yards, repeat 3 times
2nd week, 3 × 80 yards, repeat 3 times
3rd week, 3 × 100 yards, repeat 3 times

Gradually increase weight, repetitions, and distance up to the recommended programs (tables 17.1, 17.3, 17.5). The weights and reps will naturally be increased according to individual strength and size. The distance can be varied to accommodate the "event distance" to be run in competition.

ACKNOWLEDGEMENT

The authors would like to thank coach Willie Williams for contributing the conditioning programs for sprinters and hurdlers presented in this chapter. Willie Williams is an assistant track coach at the University of Illinois. He has been the Big 10 sprint and hurdles champion nine times, the NCAA 100-yard-dash champion twice, a Gold Medalist at the Pan Am Games in 1955, and a former world record holder in the 100 meters. Willie

Figure 17.3 Types of Resistive Sleds

coached five Indiana high school state championship teams in seven years. Since returning to Illinois in 1982 as Illinois sprint coach, his sprinters have broken all University of Illinois sprint records. Coach Williams has also invented and developed the resistive sleds shown in figure 17.3, to enhance the development of sprint speed for athletes.

SUMMARY

Track and field events run the full range of energy mechanisms and skilled activities. Some of the most specific applications of energy mechanisms can be found in track and field events. Stage I anaerobic (ATP-CP) is epitomized by the sprinter at 50 meters, while the marathoner represents the ultimate aerobic (Stage III) athlete. Perhaps no other effort in sport stresses the anaerobic lactic-acid (Stage II) system like a 400-meter run. Strength, explosive power, and flexibility are also epitomized in field events such as shot-putting and high jumping.

Year-round programs for the various track and field events are offered in this chapter. Entire books have been written on a single track event. In the space of this chapter the authors have diligently attempted to outline the major principles involved in training for track and field events.

REFERENCES

1. Anderson, Bob. 1978. "The Perfect Pre-Run Stretching Routine," *Runners World* 78:56–61.

2. Black, Bill. 1987. "Scientific Basis of Training for the Shot Put," *Track & Field Quarterly Review* 87:14–17.

3. Costello, Frank. 1985. Training for Speed Using Resisted and Assisted Methods," *NSCA Journal* 7(1):74–76.

4. Costill, David L. 1978. *What Research Tells the Coach about Distance Running.* Washington, DC: AAHPERD.

5. Costill, David L. 1979. *A Scientific Approach to Distance Running.* Los Altos, CA: Tafnews Press.

6. Daniels, Jack, et al. 1978. *Conditioning for Distance Runners.* New York: John Wiley & Sons.

7. Dintiman, George B. 1971. "Techniques and Methods of Developing Speed in Athletic Performance," *Proceedings: International Symposium on the Art and Science of Coaching.* Ontario, Canada: F. I. Productions.

8. Dintiman, George B. 1974. *What Research Tells the Coach about Sprinting.* Washington, DC: AAHPERD.

9. Fox, Edward L., and David R. Mathews. 1974. *Interval Training: Conditioning for Sport and Physical Fitness.* Philadelphia: W. B. Saunders.

10. Gowan, G. 1975. "Field Events," *The Scientific Aspects of Sports Training.* Springfield, IL: Charles C Thomas.

11. Henderson, Joe. 1978. "Training to Run Marathons: A Schedule for Runners," *Runners World* 78:74–79.

12. Kroll, William A., and Willie Williams. 1987. *Strength Training Charts: Programs for Sprint Speed.* Urbana, IL: Strength Training, Inc.

13. Nedobivailo, V. 1984. "Weight Training for High Jumpers," *Track & Field Quarterly Review* 84:16–18.

14. Peronnet, Francois, and Ronald J. Ferguson. 1975. "Interval Training," *The Scientific Aspects of Sports Training.* Springfield, IL: Charles C Thomas.

15. Sparks, Ken, and Garry Bjorklund. 1984. *Long Distance Runners Guide to Training.* Englewood Cliffs, NJ: Prentice-Hall.

16. Wilt, Fred. 1977. *The Marathon: Physiological, Medical, Epidemiological, and Psychological Studies.* New York: New York Academy of Sciences.

EIGHTEEN

INDIVIDUAL SPORTS: ARCHERY, GOLF, GYMNASTICS, TENNIS, AND TRIATHLON

This chapter contains year-round conditioning programs for archery, golf, gymnastics, tennis, and triathlon. The programs are designed for the off-season, pre-season, and in-season periods. The reader is referred to four previous chapters for the basis of the programs. In Chapter 3 we discuss aerobic and anaerobic conditioning, in Chapter 4 we describe strength training, in Chapter 5 the authors discuss warm-up, stretching, and flexibility, and in Chapter 8 we outline year-round conditioning. The latter chapter also describes ways of most efficiently putting training objectives together into a single program. The reader is also referred to the sample recording charts offered in the Appendix. These charts will facilitate the measurement of the athlete's progress on the training program and will indicate the athlete's standing in regard to training goals.

ARCHERY

Major conditioning requirements for archery involve *strengthening* the muscles of the upper back, shoulders, and arms, and increasing grip strength. To draw the bow with comparative ease and hold it steady, the archer needs to strengthen the muscles involved. A specific overload exercise for archery would be the repeated drawing of a bow that is heavier than the one used in shooting. Very few sports offer as specific an example of strength overload as does the use of the heavier bow.

Strength training for archery emphasizes *muscular endurance* as well as muscular strength. Repeated drawing of the bow in a match taxes the local endurance of muscles in the arms and the upper back. Strength training aimed at increasing muscular endurance will involve lighter weight, fast speed, and high-

repetition work.[1,2] During the in-season period strength training should be conducted only twice a week, and not before shooting practice. A minor expenditure of time in the in-season program will maintain strength for the archer. Flexibility exercises can be practiced by the archer on a year-round or a maintenance schedule.

Off-season, pre-season, and in-season conditioning programs for archery are offered in tables 18.1, 18.2, and 18.3.

REFERENCES

1. Dunnock, Joanne. 1977. "Archery: From the Backwoods to the Weight Room," *Scholastic Coach* 47:64–65.

2. Stone, William J. 1970. "Some Scientific Aspects of Archery," *Target Archery*. Reading, MA: Addison-Wesley.

GOLF

The golf swing is strictly an *anaerobic* action. The primary conditioning would involve strengthening of the grip, arms, shoulders, and back. Since the game is played for a period of several hours and includes walking over sometimes hilly terrain, *aerobic* capacity is also involved in playing the game of golf. Tournaments are played over several consecutive days, and the cumulative effect challenges the local muscular endurance in the legs.

Table 18.1 Off-Season Conditioning Program for Archery

Warm-Up and Stretching

Strength Training (3 days per week)
Major and assistant exercises: apply set system; supplemental and specialty exercises: apply set system or circuit system 1.

Monday & Friday

Bench Press
5–8 sets, 10, 10, 8, 6, 4, 2

Half Squat or Leg Extension
5–8 sets, 8, 8, 6, 6, 4, 4

Bent-Over Rowing (with dumbbells; hold flexed position 1–5 secs.)
5 sets, 8–15 reps

Wrist Roller and/or Wrist Curl
3–5 sets

Archery Bow Drawing Motion (with pulley)
5 sets, 10 reps

Sit-Ups and/or Leg Lifts
5 sets, 10–25 reps

Good Morning or Hyperextension
5 sets, 10 reps

Upright Rowing
5 sets, 6–10 reps

*Lateral Raises
5 sets, 10–15 reps

*Side Bends (with dumbbells)
5 sets, 10–15 reps

Cable Curls
5 sets, 10–15 reps

Optional Exercises
Toe Raises, Arm Circles, Bent-Arm Pullover

Stretching Exercises

Wednesday

Military or Incline Press
5–8 sets, 10, 10, 8, 6, 4, 2

Half Squat or Leg Extension
5–8 sets, 8, 8, 6, 6, 4, 4

Wrist Roller and/or Wrist Curl
3–5 sets

Archery Bow Drawing Motion (with pulley)
5 sets, 10 reps

Sit-Ups and/or Leg Lifts
5 sets, 10–15 reps

Good Morning or Hyperextension
5 sets, 10 reps

Upright Rowing
5 sets, 6–10 reps

*Lateral Raises
5 sets, 10–15 reps

*Side Bends (with dumbbells)
5 sets, 10–15 reps

*Light weight, fast speed, high reps

Table 18.2 Pre-Season Conditioning Program for Archery

Warm-Up and Stretching

Strength Training—Train Explosively!

Monday & Friday
Bench Press
3–8 sets, 10, 10, 8, 6, 4, 2

Half Squat or Leg Extension
3–8 sets, 8, 8, 8, 8, 6, 6

Bent-Over Rowing (with dumbbells; hold flexed position 1–5 secs.)
3–5 sets, 10–20 reps

Wrist Roller and/or Wrist Curl
3–5 sets

Archery Bow Drawing Motion
3–5 sets, 10–20 reps

Sit-Ups and/or Leg Lifts
3–5 sets, 10–50 reps

Good Morning or Hyperextension
3–5 sets, 10–20 reps

Wednesday
Military or Incline Press
3–8 sets, 10, 10, 8, 6, 4, 2

Half Squat or Leg Extension
3–8 sets, 8, 8, 8, 8, 6, 6

Bent-Over Rowing (with dumbbells; hold flexed position 1–5 secs.)
3–5 sets, 10–20 reps

Wrist Roller and/or Wrist Curl
3–5 sets

Archery Bow Drawing Motion
3–5 sets, 10–20 reps

Sit-Ups and/or Leg Lifts
3–5 sets, 10–50 reps

Good Morning or Hyperextension
3–5 sets, 10–20 reps

Table 18.2—_Continued_

Monday & Friday	Wednesday
Upright Rowing 3–5 sets, 10–15 reps	Upright Rowing 3–5 sets, 10–15 reps
*Lateral Raises 3–5 sets, 10–25 reps	*Lateral Raises 3–5 sets, 10–25 reps
*Side Bends (with dumbbells) 3–5 sets, 10–25 reps	*Side Bends (with dumbbells) 3–5 sets, 10–25 reps
Cable Curls 3–5 sets, 10–15 reps	

Optional Exercises

Toe Raises, Arm Circles, Bent-Arm Pullover

Stretching Exercises

*Light weight, fast speed, high reps

Table 18.3 In-Season Conditioning Program for Archery

Warm-Up and Stretching

Strength Training—Train Explosively!

Monday & Wednesday	
Bench Press 2–5 sets, 10, 10, 8, 8, 6, 6	Wrist Roller and/or Wrist Curl 2–3 sets
Bent-Over Rowing (with dumbbells) and/or Archery Bow Drawing Motion 2–3 sets, 10–20 reps	*Side Bends 2–3 sets, 10–25 reps

Optional Exercises

Toe Raises, Sit-Ups, Leg Lifts, Good Morning, Hyperextension, Upright Rowing, Lateral Raises, Arm Circles, Bent-Arm Pullover, Cable Curls

Stretching Exercises

*Light weight, fast speed, high reps

Strength training for golf is aimed primarily at the upper body, particularly the shoulders, arms, and forearms, and grip strength. The legs are also involved in developing power in the swing. The emphasis is on lighter resistance, many repetitions, and high-speed strength training. Training of that nature develops muscular endurance as well as strength. A two-day-a-week in-season program will help a golfer maintain muscular strength and aerobic condition with a minimum expenditure of time.

Another important facet of the golf game is flexibility. The number of strokes both in practice and in tournament conditions place significant stress on the golfer's musculoskeletal system, especially the back. A year-round stretching program should be developed and maintained.

Off-season, pre-season, and in-season conditioning programs for golf are listed in tables 18.4 and 18.5.

GYMNASTICS

The events for men's gymnastics include pommel horse, rings, parallel bars, horizontal bar, vault, and floor exercise. The events for women's gymnastics include balance beam, uneven bars, vault, and floor exercise. Performance time for all events except the vault (5 seconds) and the floor exercise (1:30 to 2:00 minutes) ranges from 15 to 40 seconds. Most of gymnastics performances are in Stage I, with some AN-LA involvement in Stage II. Only in floor exercise and in event recovery does the aerobic system operate. Men's events involve upper body support 60 percent of the time vs. 30 percent for women's events.

The major conditioning requirements for gymnastics involves _upper body strength:_ shoulders, abdominals, arms, and grip strength. Many events also require

Table 18.4 Off-Season Conditioning Program for Golf

Warm-Up and Stretching

Aerobic Conditioning

	Distance	% Max.	Time (approx.)
Run:	2–3 mi.	75%	14–24:00 mins.

Strength Training (3 days per week)
Major and assistant exercises, apply set system or circuit system 1; supplemental and specialty exercises, apply circuit system 1.

Monday & Friday

Bench Press
5–10 sets (A) 10, 10, 8, 8, 8, 8, 6, 6
       (B) 20, 20, 8, 8, 6, 6, 4, 4

Half Squat
5–8 sets (A) 8, 8, 8, 8, 6, 6, 6, 6
      (B) 8, 8, 8, 6, 6, 6, 4, 4

Reverse Curl
5 sets, 10 reps

Side Bends
5 sets, 10 reps

Wrist Roller and/or Wrist Curls
3–5 sets

Wrist Extension
3–5 sets, 10–25 reps

Golf Swing
5 sets, 10 reps

Sit-Ups
5 sets, 10–50 reps

Wednesday

Incline or Military Press
5–8 sets, 10, 8, 8, 6, 6

Lat Pulls
5 sets, 10 reps

Jumping Squats
5 sets, 10–15 reps

Reverse Curl
5 sets, 10 reps

Side Bends
5 sets, 10 reps

Wrist Roller and/or Wrist Curls
3–5 sets

Wrist Extension
3–5 sets, 10–25 reps

Golf Swing
5 sets, 10 reps

Sit-Ups
5 sets, 10–50 reps

Stretching Exercises

Table 18.5 Pre-Season and In-Season Conditioning Program for Golf

Warm-Up and Stretching

Aerobic Conditioning

Pre-Season

	Distance	% Max.	Time (approx.)
Run:	2–3 mi.	85%	14–22:00 mins.

In-Season

	Distance	% Max.	Time (approx.)
Run:	2–3 mi.	85%	14–22:00 mins.

Strength Training
Pre-Season: 3 days per week; apply circuit system 1–5 or 6; rotate through circuit once or twice. In-Season: 1 or 2 days per week; apply circuit system 1–3 or 4. Perform circuit one time.

Leg Extension	10–15 reps
Lat Pull	10–15 reps
Toe Raises	30–40 reps
Upright Rowing	8–12 reps
Abduction-Adduction Machine	10–20 reps
Wrist Curl	25–35 reps
Side Bends	20–50 reps
Leg Curl	10–15 reps
Reverse Forearm Curl	15–25 reps
High-Speed Squat Machine or Jumping Squats	10–15 reps
Sit-Ups (twisting)	20–30 reps

Table 18.5—*Continued*

Strength Training

Bench Press	10 reps
Golf Swing with Wall Pulley or Weighted Club	10–12 reps
Leg Extension	10–15 reps
Lateral Raises	10–20 reps
Toe Raises	30–40 reps
Military Press	10–12 reps
Wrist Curl	25–35 reps
Sit-Ups (twisting)	20–30 reps
Leg Curl	10–15 reps
Reverse Forearm Curl	15–25 reps

Stretching Exercises

a great amount of explosive leg power. The practice of gymnastics routines produces some strength training. Gymnasts must maintain strength and performance condition practically year round, hence a year-round conditioning program is almost essential.

Until recently, most gymnasts used the resistance involved in their routines to develop specific strength. Boone,[1] however, has noted that most gymnastics skills require strength for proper execution, and that strength should be developed first, before muscular endurance. He suggests a combination of progressive resistance (weights or machines) and resistance while practicing gymnastics skills. It is important to remember that resistance to the skill before it can be executed properly violates the principle of motor skill specificity. Others have also acknowledged the need to use weight training or weight machines to develop sufficient strength.[5-8] They also utilize resistance while practicing specific routines through the use of a partner.

Some specific gymnastics routines (such as vaulting) require running speed and leg power. *Anaerobic* sprints should be used to condition the gymnast for such events. Sprints in the range of twenty-five to fifty yards are required to develop anaerobic leg power (speed and acceleration).

During the off-season the gymnast may concentrate on developing greater amounts of strength, thus the time spent in the conditioning program should be proportionately greater than that spent in skills practice. While the intensity may increase, the time spent on strength training during the pre-season period will diminish. During the in-season period a minimum of time (one to two sessions per week) will be sufficient to maintain strength. At any time during the year-round regimen the gymnast may desire to use strength training designed specifically for one event. The necessary strength to perform some gymnastic routines may not be developed until a specific strength training program is devised and followed.

Off-season, pre-season, and in-season conditioning programs for gymnastics are offered in tables 18.6, 18.7, and 18.8.

SUMMARY

The primary requirements for gymnasts are upper body strength *and explosive* leg power. *Gymnastics is a very anaerobic sport, and only during free exercise routines does the gymnast wander out of the anaerobic Stage I (ATP–CP). Flexibility is a major component also of gymnastics and should be maintained year round. Year-round programs aimed at improving the components of gymnastics are included in this chapter.*

REFERENCES

3. Boone, Tommy. 1980. "Muscle Strength and Gymnastics," *Toward an Understanding of Human Performance,* 2d ed. Ithaca, NY: Mouvement Publications.

4. Goranson, Gary. 1981. "Kip Strength: Explosive Power for Olympic Gymnasts," *NSCA Journal* 3(3):4–55.

5. Fukushimo, Sho. 1980. "Physical Conditioning: A Review," *International Gymnast* 23:12–16.

6. James, Steve. 1987. "Periodization of Weight Training for Women's Gymnastics," *NSCA Journal* 9:28–31.

7. Kirkendall, Donald. 1985. "Physiological Aspects of Gymnastics," *Clinics in Sports Medicine* 4:7–9.

8. O'Shea, Pat, and Katie O'Shea. 1986. "Power Endurance Training for the Female Gymnast," *NSCA Journal* 7:47–50.

Table 18.6   Off-Season Conditioning Program for Gymnastics

Warm-Up and Stretching

Strength Training (3 days per week)
Major and assistant exercises: apply set system; supplemental and specialty exercises: apply set system or circuit system 1.

Monday & Friday

Military or Incline Press
6–12 sets, 10, 10, 8, 6, 4, 2, 1, 1, 4, 4, 6, 6

Bench Press (with dumbbells)
3–5 sets, 6–10 reps

Half Squat
6–10 sets, 8, 8, 8, 6, 4, 2, 2, 2

Toe Raises
5–8 sets, 30 reps

Lat Pulls or Bent-Over Rowing
5 sets, 10, 10, 8, 8, 8

Wrist Roller and/or Wrist Curls
3–5 sets

Sit–Ups and/or Leg Lifts (upright position, with ankle weights)
3–5 sets, 10–50 reps

*Stiff-Legged Deadlift, Hyperextension, and/or Good Morning
3–5 sets, 10–15 reps

Upright Rowing
3–5 sets, 8–10 reps

Straight Arm Pulldown (with pulley, using handgrips or bar)
3–5 sets, 8–15 reps

Ankle Exercises
5 sets

Wednesday

Bench Press
6–12 sets, 10, 10, 8, 6, 4, 4, 4, 4, 4

Bar Dips
6–8 sets, 10, 10, 8, 8, 8, 8, 6, 6

Jumping Squat
5–8 sets, 10, 10, 8, 8, 8, 8

Toe Raises
5–8 sets, 30 reps

Lat Pulls or Bent-Over Rowing
5 sets, 10, 10, 8, 8, 8

Wrist Roller and/or Wrist Curls
3–5 sets

Specialty Exercises
Movements with resistance and range of motion imitative of the power phase of the particular gymnastic trick

Still Rings
  A. Iron Cross movement (with pulleys)
  B. Lateral Raises
  C. Straight Arm Pulldown (with handgrips or rings on pulleys)

Horizontal Bar and Uneven Bar
Straight Arm Pulldown (i.e., Kip movement, with bar on pulley)

Parallel Bars
Bar Dips (2–3 days per week)

Floor Exercise and Tumbling, Vaulting
  A. Jumping Squats (2–3 days per week)
  B. Hyperextension (2–3 days per week)

Side Horse
Lateral Leg Lifts (with ankle weights or pulley)

Balance Beam
Good Morning
Ankle Exercises

Optional Exercises
Lateral Raises, Bent-Arm Pullover, Triceps Extension, Leg Extension, Clean

Stretching Exercises

*Light weight, fast speed, high reps

Table 18.7 Pre-Season Conditioning Program for Gymnastics

Warm-Up and Stretching

Strength Exercises—Train Explosively!

Monday & Friday

Military or Incline Press
3–8 sets, 6–10 reps

Bench Press (with dumbbells)
3–5 sets, 6–10 reps

Jumping Squat
3–5 sets, 8–15 reps

Toe Raises
3–8 sets, 30 reps

Lat Pulls or Bent-Over Rowing
3–5 sets, 8–15 reps

Wrist Roller and/or Wrist Curls
3–5 sets

Sit-Ups and/or Leg Lifts (upright position, with ankle weights)
3–5 sets, 10–50 reps

Stiff-Legged Deadlift, Hyperextension, and/or Good Morning
3–5 sets, 10–20 reps

Upright Rowing
3–5 sets, 8–12 reps

Straight Arm Pulldown (with pulley)
3–5 sets, 10–15 reps

Ankle Exercises
3–5 sets

Wednesday

Bench Press
3–8 sets, 6–10 reps

Bar Dips
3–8 sets, 6–10 reps

Jumping Squat
3–5 sets, 8–15 reps

Toe Raises
3–8 sets, 30 reps

Specialty Exercises

Movements with resistance and range of motion imitative of the power phase of the particular gymnastic trick

Still Rings
  A. Iron Cross movement (with pulleys)
  B. Lateral Raises
  C. Straight Arm Pulldown (with handgrips or rings on pulleys)

Horizontal Bar and Uneven Bar
Straight Arm Pulldown (i.e., Kip movement, with bar on pulley)

Parallel Bars
Bar Dips (2–3 days per week)

Floor Exercise and Tumbling, Vaulting
  A. Jumping Squats (2–3 days per week)
  B. Hyperextension (2–3 days per week)

Side Horse
Lateral Leg Lifts (with ankle weights or pulley)

Balance Beam
Good Morning
Ankle Exercises

Optional Exercises
Lateral Raises, Bent-Arm Pullover, Triceps Extension, Leg Extension, Clean

Stretching Exercises

Table 18.8 In-Season Conditioning Program for Gymnastics

Warm-Up and Stretching

Strength Training—Train Explosively!

Monday & Wednesday

Military or Incline Press 2–3 sets, 8–10 reps	Lat Pulls or Bent-Over Rowing 2–3 sets, 8–12 reps
Jumping Squat 2–3 sets, 8–20 reps	Ankle Exercise 2–3 sets
Wrist Roller and/or Wrist Curl 2–3 sets	

Specialty Exercises

Movements with resistance and range of motion imitative of the power phase of the particular gymnastic trick

Still Rings
  A. Iron Cross movement (with pulleys)
  B. Lateral Raises
  C. Straight Arm Pulldown (with handgrips or rings on pulleys)

Horizontal Bar and Uneven Bar

Straight Arm Pulldown (i.e., Kip movement, with bar on pulley)

Parallel Bars

Bar Dips (2–3 days per week)

Floor Exercise and Tumbling, Vaulting
  A. Jumping Squats
  B. Hyperextension (2–3 days per week)

Side Horse

Lateral Leg Lifts (with ankle weights or pulley)

TENNIS

Tennis is played in very short bursts averaging under four seconds, and often only two or three seconds in men's play. The rest between serves averages 10 to 15 seconds, and can be as long as 30 seconds. Between games the rest period can extend to 1:30 (minutes). A match can last over two hours and the ball will stay in play an average of 12 to 18 minutes per match. As much as 70 percent of play may involve Stage I (ATP-CP).

Even the shortest tennis match will likely involve at least an hour of continuous movement and play. Matches can last much longer, and the major contributing factor to this requirement is *aerobic* power. Quick and explosive movements are also characteristic of tennis, and they involve *anaerobic* leg power. Local muscular endurance in both the legs and arms is also challenged by tennis. Properly played, tennis can be a very vigorous game requiring a high level of physical conditioning.

Because tennis is played in short anaerobic bursts averaging two to three seconds, with ten to fifteen seconds between serves, it resembles football. There is, however, a longer rest period between football plays. Stewart[11] has identified aerobic power, anaerobic leg power, strength, and agility as the major factors in play.

Although extraordinarily short matches have been known to last only fifteen to twenty minutes, most last over an hour, and the extremely lengthy matches can drag on for hours. The longer, hard-fought matches are a real test of endurance for the athlete. The repetitious use and force involved in hitting the ball results in the classic hypertrophy and strength increase in the dominant arm.[10] The need for *agility* and *flexibility* is also high in tennis, and a well-planned stretching program should be conducted year round.[9]

During the off-season a great deal of emphasis can be directed toward the development of aerobic leg power and muscular strength. In the pre-season period the aerobic conditioning becomes more intense through the use of aerobic intervals. They are designed to bring the tennis player to peak condition in a brief period of time. During the in-season period aerobic condition can be maintained, as can strength, with a two-day-a-week program. Strength training should emphasize fast-speed, low-resistance, high-repetition work designed to increase muscular endurance in the arms and legs. Local muscular endurance is an essential part of tennis, as the player may take hundreds of strokes in a single match. Each stroke requires that the player get into a good hitting position, make the stroke, and return to the READY position. Repeating this sequence hundreds of times can be done effectively only if the tennis player is well-conditioned.

Table 18.9 Off-Season Conditioning Program for Tennis

Warm-Up and Stretching

Aerobic Conditioning

	Distance	% Max.	Time (approx.)
Run:	2–3 mi.	75–85%	14–24:00 mins.

Strength Training (3 days per week)
Major and assistant exercises: apply set system; supplemental and specialty exercises: apply set system or circuit system 1.

Monday & Friday	Wednesday
Bench Press 6 sets, 10, 10, 8, 8, 8, 8	Incline Press 6 sets, 10, 10, 8, 8, 8, 8
Throwing Pullover 5 sets, 10 reps	Upright Rowing 5 sets, 10 reps
Half Squat 6 sets, 10, 10, 8, 8, 8, 8	Good Mornings 5 sets, 10 reps
Toe Raises 6 sets, 30 reps	Toe Raises 6 sets, 30 reps
Forehand Motion (with wall pulley) 5 sets, 10 reps	Forehand Motion (with wall pulley) 5 sets, 10 reps
Backhand Motion 5 sets, 10 reps	Backhand Motion 5 sets, 10 reps
Sit-Ups (twisting) 5 sets, 10–25 reps	Sit-Ups (twisting) 5 sets, 10–25 reps
Wrist Curl 3–5 sets	Wrist Curl 3–5 sets
Arm Circles 3–5 sets, 10–50 reps	Arm Circles 3–5 sets, 10–50 reps
Bent-Over Rowing or Cable Rowing 3–5 sets, 10–15 reps	Bent-Over Rowing or Cable Rowing 3–5 sets, 10–15 reps

Optional Exercises
Lateral Raises, Incline Flys, Leg Extension, Leg Curl (toes in), Throwing Pullover, Ankle Exercise

Stretching Exercises

During the season the coach or athlete can use the practice time for aerobic or anaerobic conditioning. Continuous play without interruption will aid in the development of aerobic power. Drills requiring quick action and acceleration, repeated over and over, will aid in the development of anaerobic power. Skill drills help to develop local muscular endurance for specific strokes.

Off-season, pre-season, and in-season conditioning programs for tennis are offered in tables 18.9 and 18.10.

REFERENCES

9. Anderson, Bob. 1981. "For Tennis: Stretching Works When Done Correctly," *NSCA Journal* 3(3):18–20.

10. Grey, Mervin R. 1974. *What Research Tells the Coach about Tennis.* Washington, DC: AAHPERD.

11. Stewart, Kerry J. 1980. "Conditioning for Tennis: Some Basic Considerations," *Toward an Understanding of Human Performance,* 2d ed. Ithaca, NY: Mouvement Publications.

12. Strome, Steve. 1982. "Conditioning and Training Program for the School Tennis Coach," *Athletic Journal* 6:50–55.

TRIATHLON

The triathlon has become a rapidly growing sport for athletes who have conquered the marathon, or are simply looking for the ultimate aerobic challenge. By the standards of most sports, it is in its infancy. The inaugural Hawaii "Ironman" triathlon was run in 1978. Contestants swim 2.4 miles, cycle 112 miles, and finish

Table 18.10 Pre-Season and In-Season Conditioning Program for Tennis

Warm-Up and Stretching

Aerobic Conditioning

Pre-Season

	Distance	% Max.	Rest	Reps
Run:	880 yds.	95% ↑	3 mins.	4–6

In-Season

	Distance	% Max.	Time (approx.)
Run:	2–3 mi.	95%↑	14–22:00 mins.

Strength Training:

Pre-Season: 3 days per week; apply circuit systems 1, 3, 4, 5, 6, and 9. In-season: 2 days per week; apply circuit systems 1, 3, 4, or 6.

Leg Extension	10–15 reps
Lat Pull	10–15 reps
Toe Raises	30–40 reps
Bent-Over Rowing or Cable Rowing	10–20 reps
Abduction-Adduction Machine	10–20 reps
Forehand Motion (with wall pulley)	10–15 reps
High-Speed Squat Machine or Jumping Squats	12–15 reps
Wrist Curl	25–35 reps
Leg Curl	10–15 reps
Upright Rowing	10–15 reps
Lower Back Machine, or Good Morning Exercise	10–15 reps
Bench Press	10 reps
Sit-Up (twisting)	20–40 reps
Throwing Pullover	10–15 reps
Reverse Forearm Curl	15–25 reps
Bench Press	10–12 reps
Leg Extension	10–15 reps
Lateral Raises	10–20 reps
Hip Flexion Machine or Leg Lifts	10–20 reps
Wrist Curls	25–35 reps
High-Speed Squat Machine or Jumping Squat	12–15 reps
Bent-Over Rowing or Cable Rowing	10–20 reps
Bench Press	10–15 reps
Reverse Forearm Curl	15–25 reps
Military Press	10–15 reps

Stretching Exercises

---

the day with the traditional 26.2-mile marathon. The order of events has been set for safety reasons, although performances could be better with the swimming event between the two leg exercises. Elite performers will complete the event between eight and nine hours. More often in competition the event is shortened to a "half Ironman," or 1.2 miles of swimming, 56 miles of cycling, and a 13.1-mile run. Even shorter events are held, and the USTS distances are a 1.5km swim, a 40km cycle, and a 10k run.

Needless to say, the event can run from several hours to nearly twelve hours, and involves primarily the aerobic energy system, Stage III. Strength and power are required for swimming and cycling, and anaerobic capacity can be a factor in high-level competition. Conditioning for the triathlon presents a number of problems for the athlete. A major problem for competitors is the need for lengthy endurance training in three sports: swimming, cycling, and running. Other problems include the time requirements for specific training for all three sports and the danger of overuse injury caused from high volume training. Fortunately triathletes are able to use the cross training effect. Some portion of the aerobic training effect will "cross over" to the other two events. Although specificity training is very important to the triathlete, he or she does not have to do as much volume training for each event as would be necessary if the athlete were training for only one aerobic sport.

Triathlon Training

In the early days of triathlon competition, there was little known about how to train for a triple aerobic event. Many athletes, no doubt, overtrained because they followed the training patterns set by the individual sports

Table 18.11   Weekly Triathlon Training Schedule

	Mon.	Tue.	Wed.	Thur.	Fri.	Sat.
Swim	Distance	Hard		Easy		Distance
Bike		Hard	Easy	Distance		Hard
Run	Easy		Hard		Distance	

of swimming, cycling, and running. In a very short time, however, considerable research has been done on the triathlete, and much has been learned about training for the triathlon.[13–18]

There is general consensus that athletes should train approximately four to five times the race distance in each sport weekly. In practice, most triathletes train six times the swimming distance, and two to three times the cycling or running distances. Swimming is more foreign to many athletes, and also requires a greater concentration in terms of skills. Depending upon the triathlon distances to be covered, weekly training would range as follows:[17]

Event	Distance	Frequency
Swimming	3,000–15,000m	2–5x/week
Cycling	15–300 miles	2–5x/week
Running	5–60 miles	3–5x/week

Triathlon training schedules can range from three to six days per week. A three-day-per week schedule requires the athlete to train each event every workout day. With a six-day-per week schedule, the athlete can choose to train only two events each day. When the triathlete is peaking for competition, he or she may return to three events per day in preparation for competition. An example of a six-day-per week schedule with two events trained per workout is given in table 18.11.

Because of the prolonged endurance training that the triathlete undergoes, there is need to maintain flexibility throughout the year. Year-round programs for the triathlon are listed in tables 18.12 and 18.13.

REFERENCES

13. Edwards, Sally. 1983. *Triathlon: A Triple Fitness Sport*. Chicago: Contemporary Books, Inc.

14. Holly, R. G., et al. 1986. "Triathlete Characterizations and Responses to Prolonged Strenuous Competition," *Medicine and Science in Sports and Exercise* 18:123–127.

Table 18.12   Off-Season Conditioning for Triathletes

Warm-Up and Stretching

Aerobic Conditioning (3 days/week)

	Distance	% Max
Swim	500–1,000m	60–80%
Cycle	15–45 mi.	60–80%
Run	5–10 mi.	60–80%

Strength Training (2 days/week)

Bench Press
5–10 sets, 10–20 reps

Half Squats
5–10 sets, 10–20 reps

Sit-Ups
5 sets, 10–25 reps

Triceps Pushdown
5 sets, 8–10 reps

Leg Curl
5 sets, 10–15 reps

Upright Rowing
5 sets, 10 reps

Lateral Raises
5 sets, 10–15 reps

Military Press
6–8 sets, 10–15 reps

Stretching Exercises

15. Kohrt, Wendy M., et al. 1987. "Physiological Responses of Triathletes to Maximal Swimming, Cycling, and Running," *Medicine and Science in Sports and Exercise* 19:51–55.

16. O'Toole, M. L., et al. 1987. "The Ultraendurance Triathlete: A Physiological Profile," *Medicine and Science in Sports and Exercise* 19:45–50.

17. Scott, Dave. 1986. *Dave Scott's Triathlon Training*. NY: Simon & Schuster.

18. Zinkgraf, S. A., et al. 1986. "An Empirical Investigation of Triathlon Performers," *Journal of Sports Medicine* 26:350–356.

Table 18.13 Pre- and In-Season Conditioning for Triathletes

Warm-Up and Stretching

Aerobic Conditioning (2–5 days/week)
(Alternating Hard, Easy, and Distance workouts, depending upon time of season)

	Distance	% Max
Swim	3000–15,000m	75–85%
Cycle	15–300 miles	75–85%
Run	5–60 miles	75–85%

Strength Training (1 day/week)
Bench Press
5–10 sets, 10–20 reps

Half Squats
5–10 sets, 10–20 reps

Sit-Ups
5 sets, 10–25 reps

Triceps Pushdown
5 sets, 8–10 reps

Leg Curl
5 sets, 10–15 reps

Upright Rowing
5 sets, 10 reps

Lateral Raises
5 sets, 10–15 reps

Military Press
6–8 sets, 10–15 reps

Anaerobic Conditioning (1–2 days/week)
Anaerobic (specific) and sprint intervals at 90–100% max

Stretching Exercises

SPECIALTY EXERCISES

Bow Drawing Motion (with wall pulley)

This exercise is done with a wall pulley at shoulder height. The exact motion used to draw the bow should be followed, with the bow arm extended against the wall or a stationary object.

Golf Swing

This exercise employs a high pulley attached to a wall pulley to imitate the range of motion against resistance.

Straight Arm Pulldown (with hand grips, bar, and rings)

This exercise imitates the Kip movement. In the standing position using a high pulley or pulleys, with the arms completely extended, pull the resistance down directly in front of the body.

Figure 18.1 Iron Cross

Iron Cross

This exercise is similar to the Straight Arm Pulldown, using high pulleys to pull downward, with extended arms. In the Iron Cross, of course, the arms are extended to the side instead of in front. See figure 18.1.

Dorsiflexion of the Foot

(See Chapter 6.)

BUILDING A BETTER STRENGTH PROGRAM

This section is designed to assist the coach or athlete in implementing and improving the strength program. Chapter 19 includes the strength exercises to be used with the various sport-specific program offered in Part II. Chapter 20 includes information on the design and development of strength training facilities, and on the evaluation and selection of strength training equipment.

NINETEEN

STRENGTH EXERCISES

In the earlier two editions of this text, strength exercises were included in Chapter 4 along with the background information about strength training. There has been a proliferation of information on strength training during the past decade. The authors have decided to separate the strength exercises from the conceptual material for ease of use. The reader is cautioned to carefully review the materials in Chapter 4 prior to applying the various strength exercises. The material discusses different types of strength training, strength training terminology, essential elements for athletes, and ways of devising programs.

It is also important to note that there are many ways of applying resistance to the muscle, leading to increases in strength. A variety of equipment can be used to apply resistance, including free weights, multi-station machines, single-muscle group machines, and the body itself. Application of the various principles outlined in Chapter 4 should result in increased strength for sport, regardless of the mode of strength training. In addition to following the principles of scientific strength training, it is also important to follow the safety precautions offered in this chapter.

SAFETY PROCEDURES

Weight training can be one of the safest of physical activities. The authors, however, must caution the novice to seek help from a coach or knowledgeable weight trainer *before attempting* unfamiliar lifts. It is wise even for athletes with some experience at weight training to have new exercises explained or demonstrated. Most of the injuries that occur are muscle and tendon strains.

It seems likely that weight-lifting strains might aggravate or even cause hernia injuries, but such injuries are rare among weight lifters. It is safe to assume that most injuries incurred in weight training could have been prevented by the application of common sense and a few safety techniques.

1. The *weight belt* should be used when doing any moderately heavy or heavy weight training. The belt helps to prevent back and abdominal injuries. A competition belt is a maximum of four inches wide. An athlete, however, can use an even wider belt while training for sports.

2. Check the equipment you are using *before performing each exercise.*
   a. Collars on the bar need to be tight. Sometimes the threads will become stripped and although the collar may appear to be tight, if the bar is tilted it will slip off.
   b. Check the condition of cables and pulleys on all equipment. Worn-out or partially worn-through cables and ropes should not be used.
   c. All bolts and screws on Olympic bars or other equipment and machines should be checked for tightness.

3. *Good lifting technique* is one of the most important ways of preventing back injuries. When lifting any weight and particularly a heavy weight from the ground, the knees should be bent and the back should be kept straight with the head up. There are some exercises, such as Toe Touches and the Good Morning exercise, which are done by bending at the waist with the knees straight. These exercises are the exception to the bent leg rule, but only light weights are used.

SPOTTING PROCEDURES

Spotters are necessary in the following situations.

1. Any exercise either seated or standing where a weight is to be extended above the head. Examples included in this text are the Military Press (seated or standing), Behind the Neck Press, the Incline Press, and the Standing Tricep Extension.
2. Any supine exercise where the weight is to be held above the body. Examples included in this text are the Bench Press, Bent-Arm Lateral, Bent-Arm Pullover, Dumbbell Incline, Dumbbell Bench Press, Throwing Pullover, and Tricep Supine.
3. Any other exercise where aid may be necessary, either to help the athlete return to the upright or starting position, to maintain balance or a stable position, or to return the weight to a safety rack. Examples included in this text are Bar Dips, Dumbbell Curl, Lat Pull, Pull Down, and Squat.

Before discussing the spotting procedure itself, there are two rules of weight room etiquette that should be stated. Until this point they have been considered "unwritten rules." First, when training in the weight room, in any informal situation no matter how many persons are present, it is each person's responsibility to be sure that every other person has proper spotters for each set of their workout. It is very frustrating and creates an awkward, uncomfortable feeling to have to ask someone for a *spot* prior to performing each and every set. A spot should be offered voluntarily. This can be done verbally or in some cases by simply moving into position to spot. Second, the spotters and the other persons in the area should remain silent and not cause any distraction to the exerciser. The exerciser is also depending upon the complete concentration of the spotter.

Each exercise has its own subtleties that relate to the entire spotting procedure. For this reason it is necessary to have a predetermined set of commands and any other signal or understanding, usually to be requested by the exerciser. The spotters have three main functions.

1. Spotters provide whatever help is necessary to bring the resistance and the exerciser safely and smoothly into the starting position. In most cases this means lifting or helping to lift the weight to the starting position. When the spotters lift or help lift a weight from a rack to the starting position, the action is understandably called a *lift-off.* Prior to the lift-off the exerciser should *ask* the spotter or spotters for the lift-off, if he wants one. At that time the exerciser should give them any other instruction he feels necessary.

He then tells the spotters what the preparatory count will be. He might simply say "on three." He then sets his grip on the weight and counts, "one, two, three." In this way, the exerciser and the spotters can coordinate the lift-off and the exercise can begin. There is a *groove* or movement pathway through which each exercise motion proceeds. It is necessary for the spotter to know where the groove is if he or she is to provide the best spot. If the weight is handed to the exerciser outside the groove, adjustor synergistic muscles and possibly main movers and antagonists will need to be used and perhaps strained unnecessarily to move the weight into the groove. This could even cause the weight to be dropped, creating further possibility of injury. If the spotters are inexperienced, the exerciser may need to show them exactly where the weight should be placed. Most exercises allow the exerciser to control, to some degree, the movement of the weight to the starting position with the aid of the spotters. This helps smooth out the movement. But good spotting is definitely an acquired skill.

In some exercises where a barbell is used, it is normally best to have a single middle spotter help the exerciser with the lift-off (fig. 19.3). If two spotters are involved in moving the bar, it is difficult for them to work in unity.

When dumbbells are used the two spotters should coordinate the handing of the dumbbells to the exerciser so that he can receive them simultaneously (unless otherwise requested) and in the proper position.

In some cases, such as the Squat, the spotters are not usually involved in the lift-off except to be ready to help as a precautionary measure. The position of the spotters during the lift-off phase of the squat is the same as shown in figure 19.2, Behind the Neck Press. They are standing on each side of the bar with their hands positioned beneath the ends of the bar so that they would be able to grasp it immediately if necessary.

2. Spotters provide whatever help is necessary to ensure that the movement phase of the exercise can be performed as safely as possible. To accomplish this, the spotters remain positioned, as in the lift-off phase, to each side of the bar with their hands positioned beneath the bar. The spotters must be alert to any loss of balance or inability of the exerciser to complete the

movement. Prior to the set, the exerciser may have instructed the spotters to take the weight on a particular cue. For instance the exerciser can simply say "OK" or "get it." The spotters can also determine when to give help or to take the weight by observing the movement of the weight. Before the exerciser reaches failure, the weight will usually *pause* and then *sag slightly* before collapsing or going slowly downward. The exerciser, in many cases, may not desire any help unless he fails to complete the movement. The weight may actually pause, in some cases, and again continue upward, so the spotters should not grasp the bar on the pause. However, if it *sags downward,* they should take it immediately. The *pause,* or cessation of movement, should serve as a cue for the spotters to get ready to grasp the bar. If the spotters properly perform their function, they should have the weight under control before it can sag one-fourth to one-half of an inch.

In some cases the weight may collapse quickly and immediately, proceeding to fall almost straight downward. This is not uncommon and is obviously the most dangerous possibility. However, there is very little danger even in this case if the spotter or spotters are alert and have themselves and their *hands* positioned properly.

In either case, when two or more spotters are involved, a cue should be given by either or both of them if they decide to grasp the weight. This is done so that the other spotter and the exerciser can act immediately, in coordination. A spotter might decide to do this for any number of reasons. Examples are: a weight or a collar coming loose, any noticed equipment damage, an obstruction or distraction in the area, or the exerciser getting into a harmful biomechanical position. In this case the spotter announces "get it" and both spotters grasp the weight simultaneously. Whenever possible the exerciser should continue to help in moving the weight back to the starting position and then to the rack. *In no case* when spotters are already involved should another person rush into the situation to give aid. This occurs sometimes when beginners are present and it can cause an injury. An uninvited "helper" often grasps one end of a bar or jerks a weight out of the groove. Fortunately, in most cases, the worst thing this causes is a strained muscle.

3. Spotters provide whatever help is necessary to ensure that the weight is returned safely to the rack or the floor, and the exercise is thus completed. Many times this amounts to merely guiding or closely watching the weight into the rack, under the control of the exerciser. In some cases, the spotters may need to help the exerciser with this, or they may need to perform this function completely on their own. It is important that the spotters stay involved in this final procedure until the exerciser has completely finished and is safely out from under the weight.

Finally, spotting is a serious matter, and each exercise that utilizes spotters requires a slightly different groove and spotting technique. Some of this is learned by experience, but communication prior to the set and alert concentration by the spotters will provide the safest possible situation. Overall, weight training is one of the safest of all physical activities. When injuries occur, they are usually the result of improper use or lack of spotters.

DESCRIPTIONS OF STRENGTH EXERCISES

The following are explanations of how to do the various exercises that will be used in the strength programs in this book. The exercises are provided in more or less alphabetical order so that you may refer to them easily. In order to understand the exercise descriptions and programs that follow, several terms that will be used to describe body movements need to be defined.

Flexion and *Extension.* When discussing joint flexion, the decreasing angle of the joint is used to indicate that the joint is being flexed. An increasing joint angle therefore indicates joint extension. A muscle is *flexed* when it is contracted, making it shorter. For example, in the Bench Press, contraction of the tricep muscles causes extension of the elbow joints. Therefore, unless otherwise designated, flexion and extension will refer to joint flexion and joint extension.

Prone and *Supine.* The supine position is lying on the back face up. Prone is the opposite—lying on the stomach, face down.

Bar Dips

This exercise is done on parallel bars. The player mounts the bar in a straight-arm support position with the elbows extended, then lowers position until the middle of the chest is even with the bars. Flexing the elbows, the athlete then drives explosively back to the starting position. Repeat this pattern. After working up to ten reps for five sets, the athlete is ready to use

Figure 19.1 Bar Dips

weights for the dip. Bar Dips develop the chest, shoulders, and arms. The bottom part of the pectoralis is affected more strongly. Training with this exercise may be helpful in preventing many shoulder injuries. This exercise may require a spotter.

Behind Neck Press

Just as the name describes, presses are done by lowering the bar behind the neck. The bar is either taken from a rack, at shoulder level, or handed to the athlete with the arms held straight upward and the elbows extended. The movement is then performed by lowering the bar behind the head to a level below the ears and driving it back overhead. For the full range of motion, the bar is brought down to touch the very base of the

neck. Some individuals, however, find this puts excess strain on the posterior head of the deltoids and/or the insertions of the trapezius muscles. It is acceptable to begin slowly in gaining the full range of motion in this exercise, or if necessary, only to lower the bar to a level that is even with the ears. This exercise requires spotters. See Spotting Procedures.

Bench Press

This exercise is done in the supine position. The athlete should grip the bar with the hands, approximately at shoulder width, evenly spaced from the middle of the bar. Spotters are recommended to aid in getting the bar off the rack and into position. The bar is then lowered straight to the chest. There is a range of several inches

Figure 19.2 Behind Neck Press

Figure 19.3 Bench Press

in the position of the bar on the chest. The best position is usually at the origin of the pectoralis major or about six to eight inches below the shoulder sockets. From there the bar is moved to a position directly above the shoulders. The bar should be driven to that position in a straight line.

This exercise is an excellent one to develop the large muscles of the chest, shoulders, and arms—pectoralis major and minor, deltoids, and triceps. The strength of these muscles will determine the individual's explosive power in the upper body. These muscles are the main movers for most athletic movements, so it is not difficult to realize why the Bench Press is used for strength development in nearly every sport. (The exclusion of any one of these three main muscle groups will limit the performance of most athletic movements.) This exercise requires one or two spotters. (See Spotting Procedures.)

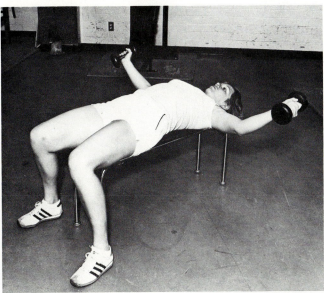

Figure 19.4 Bent-Arm Laterals

Bent-Arm Laterals (or Fly)

This exercise is done in the supine position (preferably on a bench), using a dumbbell in each hand. Begin with the dumbbells directly above the shoulder sockets, with the elbows slightly flexed and the hands held palms in. The elbows remain flexed throughout the movement. They are laterally lowered until the dumbbells are even with the sides—then back above the shoulders again. This exercise can require spotters.

Bent-Arm Pullovers

This exercise is also done in the supine position on a bench or with the head and upper shoulders supported on a bench. The exercise is usually done with a dumbbell but can be done by using an easy curl bar or a close grip on a barbell. The weight is held directly above the shoulders with the elbows slightly bent (flexed). It is then lowered behind the head toward the floor, with the

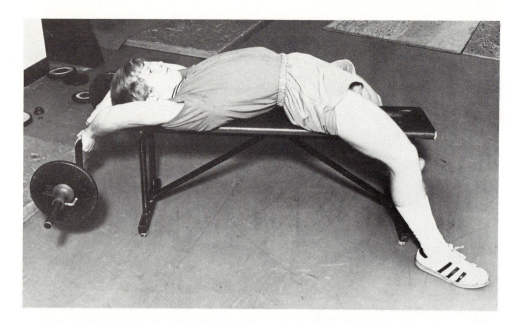

Figure 19.5 Bent-Arm Pullovers

elbows kept flexed in this position. The extreme position of the range of motion has the upper arms even with the ears. The muscles of the lower chest are completely extended in this position. The weight is then brought back to the starting position by contracting the muscles of the lower chest and abdomen. During the entire movement the elbows are kept in so that they pass close to the head. With a dumbbell (especially a large one) the elbows are not flexed as much in the starting position (picture A). With a barbell or curling bar, the flexing of the elbow is even greater, since the bar is held at the chest in the starting position (picture B). If the elbows are extended in the starting position, the triceps or elbow extensor muscles are exercised more. By bringing the bar directly to the chest, the lower chest and abdomen muscles are exercised more and the triceps less. If heavy weight is to be used, spotters may be necessary. The throwing pullover is another variation of the pullover—designed to help develop throwing velocity. (See *Throwing*.)

Figure 19.6 Bent-Over Rowing

Bent-Over Rowing

This is done by bending forward at the waist until the upper body is parallel to the floor. Either a barbell or two dumbbells are held in the hands. The arms are held downward directly toward the floor. If a padded, waist-high head support is available, it is advantageous to support the head to prevent movement of the trunk. The forehead, then, is placed on the head support. The movement is done by flexing the elbows and pulling the weight to the chest. The dumbbells may be pulled a little farther than the bar. Thus a fuller range of movement is one advantage of using dumbbells for this exercise.

Power Clean

In the Clean the barbell is brought from the floor to the chest in one continuous movement. The starting position is extremely important. The head is kept up, with the eyes focused at a point straight ahead. The bar is gripped at approximately shoulder width, with the elbows extended straight down to the bar. The feet are positioned with the heels from nine to fourteen inches apart, and the middle of the foot directly below the bar. The toes can be pointed straight ahead or slightly outward. The knees are kept inside the arms, and it is most important that the back be kept straight.

As the beginning or *drive* phase of the movement is started, the legs and hips are used to pull the bar from the floor. The athlete should concentrate on driving with the legs and thrusting the head straight toward the ceiling. In this way the back and arms are kept perfectly straight. The arms are not bent (or flexed) until the body is completely extended. The drive phase should be done explosively so that the bar is accelerating through this part of the movement. Then, as the elbows begin to flex, the body is beginning to move downward. Notice at this time that the knees are flexed as much as necessary to get the shoulders under the bar. The elbows are not passively flexing at this time, but are continuing to accelerate the bar straight up with a quick ripping movement. Throughout this movement the body is very close to the bar. As the athlete drops quickly under the bar, the elbows are thrust forward and the bar comes to rest high on the chest and shoulders. Notice at this point that the back is again straight, even though the knees are flexed. The Clean is completed when the athlete brings the bar from the squatting position and stands erect with it.

Squat Clean

This method of cleaning a barbell is used by most Olympic-style weight lifters. It is very similar to the Power Clean. In fact, the movement is identical for the lifter during the power phase, until he or she begins to drop under the weight. At that point, in the Squat Clean the lifter begins to move the body under the weight. As the weight contacts the shoulders, the momentum of the weight is allowed to drive the legs out of the Power Clean position into the squatting position. If this is to

Figure 19.7 Power Clean

Figure 19.8 Curl

be done successfully, the proper balance between the lifter and the weight must be maintained throughout the movement.

Split Clean

This is another effective and more traditional way of cleaning a weight to the shoulders in one movement. In this movement, after the power phase the athlete drops to a split position below the weight. This is done by thrusting one leg straight backward and the other leg slightly forward—dropping to a flexed position. The back leg is kept extended nearly completely through the knee joint. The same leg is usually used for each repetition, but alternating the legs can be done if desired.

Curl

The Curl can be done in many different ways. It is simply the flexing of the elbow against a resistance held in the hands or hand, with the palms facing forward (anatomical position).

The Curl is distinguished from other movements involving flexion of the elbows by the fact that "flexors of the elbow" are the only muscles involved in the movement. The regular standing Curl is done by first grasping the bar at approximately shoulder width grip and lifting the bar to the starting, standing position with the arms down at the sides. The elbows are flexed, bringing the weight as close to the shoulders as possible. The feet are also approximately shoulder width apart and the body is kept rigid throughout the movement. Complete flexion and extension are desirable in the Curl if flexibility for athletics is the desired result.

Cable Rowing

This can be done if wall pulleys are present. It can be done from a standing position or a sitting position. The cable row is similar to Bent-Over Rowing since the body position is the same and the muscles of the upper back and the elbow flexors (biceps and brachioradialis) are the main movers.

Strength Exercises

Figure 19.9 Cable Rowing

Close Grip Curls

These are simply regular standing Curls done with the hands held at close grip. The close grip causes greater isolation of the biceps, brachiolis, and brachioradialis, thus helping to strengthen this area.

Reverse Curl

This is done by reversing the grip on the bar so that the palms face downward instead of forward. This isolates the brachioradialis, which is one of the strongest mus-

cles of the forearm. The movement should be done with the elbows kept close to the body and the wrists as straight as possible.

Support Curl (or Scott Curl)

This curl is done by stabilizing the elbow on a pad or brace, so that the flexors of the elbows are isolated. Cable Curls or Reverse Curls may be done in this way as well when great isolation of the biceps is desired.

Figure 19.10 Reverse Curl

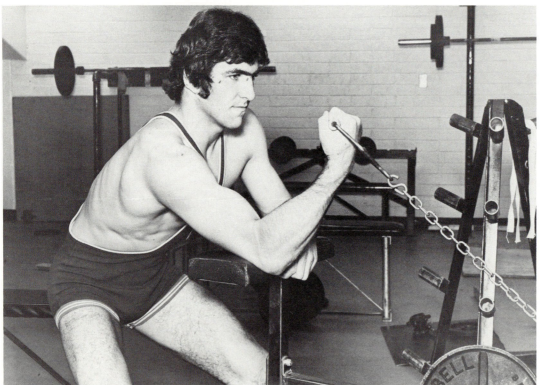

Figure 19.11   Support Curl

Dead Lift

The Dead Lift is an exercise designed to develop the powerful muscles of the thighs, hips, and lower back, which are critical in most athletic movements.

The athlete grasps a barbell and moves it from the floor to a position where he or she is standing upright, with the elbows extended straight downward supporting the weight. It is extremely important that this movement be done properly because of the hip and back stresses that can be experienced when handling a heavy weight.

The starting position is exactly the same as in the Clean, except in some cases one of the hands is reversed to provide a better grip for heavy weight. The head is kept up with the eyes focused at a point straight ahead. The bar is gripped at approximately shoulder width, with the elbows extended straight down to the bar. The feet are positioned with the heels from nine to fourteen inches apart and the middle of the foot is directly below the bar. The toes can be pointed straight ahead or slightly outward. The knees are kept inside the arms and *it is most important that the back be kept straight*.

As the movement is started, the legs and hips are used to pull the bar from the floor. The athlete should concentrate on driving with the legs and thrusting the head straight toward the ceiling. In this way the back and arms are kept perfectly straight throughout the movement. As the bar is raised the hips are moving forward until the body is straight and the Dead Lift is complete.

Dumbbell Exercises

Dumbbells are used for many movements in order to get greater isolation of a particular muscle or muscle group. They are also used to allow greater freedom of movement in many cases, for example, when rotation of the shoulder is desired and is not possible with a bar (picture A). Dumbbells also have the advantage of allowing a "true" full range of motion in some exercises such as the Bench Press (picture B) and the Incline Press (picture C). As shown in the photos, these exercises can require spotters (see Spotting Procedure).

"Good Mornings"

This exercise is begun by grasping a light barbell at slightly wider than shoulder width grip and placing it on the shoulders behind the head. It is best to have "squat racks" on which to set the weight. If they are not available, the bar must be cleaned and pressed overhead, then lowered to the shoulders. The bar will usually rest most comfortably just above the scapula bones. Keeping the head up and the back straight (picture A), the movement is then performed by bending

Figure 19.12 Dead Lift

Figure 19.13 Dumbbell Exercises. Dumbbell Incline Press

(a)   (b)

Figure 19.14 "Good Mornings"

forward at the waist, keeping the knees nearly extended, until the upper torso is parallel to the ground, and then going back to the starting position. As heavier weights are used, the knees must be flexed slightly to compensate the weight enough so that the center of gravity stays above the feet.

Grip Exercises

The development of the Grip requires the training of thumb and finger flexors as well as forearm flexors and extensors. Development of strength in this area many times requires extremely persistent efforts.

In training for the Grip, many different tools and methods are effective (for example, a rubber ball or hand gripper, spring devices, wrist roller, objects carried with the thumb and fingers extended downward).

Wrist Curl or Forearm Curl

This exercise is done by grasping a light barbell at shoulder width grip and supporting the forearms on a flat surface with the palms upward. The finger joints are flexed and extended throughout the full range of motion, allowing the bar to roll down the fingers as far as possible, then brought back into the fist again. This develops the flexors of the wrist.

Reverse Forearm Curl

This is done in a similar manner by simply changing the grip so that the palms face downward. The exercise is more difficult this way and a lighter weight may be needed. The extensors of the wrists are the benefited muscles.

High Pull

The starting position and power phase of the High Pull are identical to those of the Power Clean. (See Power Clean.)

It should be remembered that these are powerful athletic movements and require sophisticated muscular control to be done properly. For many people, time is required to learn the basic form. It can occur almost automatically or can take several weeks. For safe execution, this basic form must be learned with very light weights—before weights requiring forceful efforts are used.

As the movement is being learned the amount of weight can be increased after two or three sessions—as long as the correct form is being used.

Figure 19.15 Wrists Curls

Figure 19.16 High Pull

Snatch Pull

This exercise is another type of High Pull in which the bar is held with a very wide grip. The pull is slightly different and, consequently, the effect on the body is different. Greater development is offered in the shoulders and upper back. The timing of the explosive part of the movement is slightly quicker and lower than in the High Pull or the Clean Pull. The wider grip also creates greater stress on the hands. The increased difficulty in gripping the bar can be decreased, for training purposes, by using pull straps to help the grip so that the other muscles can be worked thoroughly.

Hyperextension

The Hyperextension gets its name from the hyperextension of the back that occurs at the top of the power phase of the movement. The hips and legs are supported so that the upper torso can bend forward to become perpendicular to the floor (picture A). The hands are held behind the head with the fingers interlocked. From here the movement is done by contracting the muscles of the hips and of the lower back, moving the upper body to a completely extended position—somewhat greater than 180 degrees.

In training for the Hyperextension, a weight may be held behind the head. In order to prevent possible injury, it is wise to do the exercise with no weight at all for at least one or two exercise sessions. This is especially true if this exercise is being done for the very first time.

Leg Curl

The Leg Curl is usually done in the prone position on a leg extension or leg curl machine (picture A, page 240). The knee or knees are taken from the fully extended position to a point where the knee joint is flexed ninety degrees or more. It can be done by using ankle weights or a weighted boot. Some training devices allow the Leg Curl to be done in the sitting position.

The affected area in the Leg Curl can be altered by changing the angle of the foot on the resistance arm of the machine.

Leg Press

In this exercise the knee goes from a flexed to an extended position, while the back remains somewhat stabilized. There are several types of leg presses, in nearly all directions.

The Leg Press is an assistant exercise to help develop hip and leg strength. Hamstrings and lower abdomen are also developed by some leg presses. The effects of different "leg press" equipment vary. The Leg Press is beneficial, however, in some situations because of its restrictive nature. An improper angle of body support and exceedingly high internal pressures can be experienced, causing damage to joints such as knees, hips, and the spinal column. *Proceed gradually and use care and common sense when attempting extremely heavy leg presses.*

Military Press

This exercise is done by simply standing straight with a barbell supported on the hands and shoulders and pressing it straight overhead. In this movement the body should be kept as straight as possible and the knees should not bend. The Military Press develops the upper arms (triceps), the shoulders (deltoids and trapezius), and the upper chest.

Figure 19.17 Snatch Pull

(a)

(b)

Figure 19.18 Hyperextension

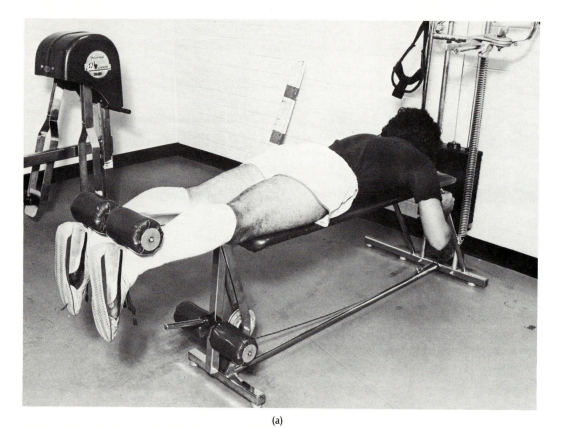

(a)

(b)

Figure 19.19 Leg Curl

Figure 19.20 Military Press

To execute the Military Press, the barbell may be cleaned to the shoulders or taken from a rack, then driven explosively upward until the elbows are extended. The press rack would be most preferable for someone who wanted to concentrate on pressing in particular. In many cases, the Clean is trained separately from the Press, since maximum strength in most cases is not necessary during any one workout. This exercise requires spotters.

Incline Press

The Incline Press is used to develop the upper part of the pectoralis muscles along with the anterior deltoids and triceps. The movement supplements both the Military Press and the Bench Press in providing even physical development and ultimately allowing greater strength gains in all three areas.

The Incline Press is done on an inclined bench. There are several types of these benches (see Equipment). Two spotters are usually necessary for inclines. The athlete may take the bar in either an "UP" position with arms extended, or in a "DOWN" position with the bar resting high on the chest, just below the collarbone. Either place may be considered the starting position.

When beginning, the unloaded bar can be taken in the "UP" position. It is lowered in a steady movement to the chest; then, as soon as it touches, it is driven straight upward to a point directly above the shoulder sockets. It is easier to start in the "UP" position, but the explosiveness developed from starting in the "DOWN" position is worth the effort in most cases.

Lat Pulls

These were so named because of the flexion of the latissimus dorsi muscle when performing them. A "lat machine" is necessary to perform the exercise, which is done in either the sitting or kneeling position (picture A). The bar is gripped with a wide grip and the kneeling position is taken. At this point the arms are extended overhead in the starting position. The movement is performed by flexing the arms and latissimus dorsi, pulling the bar down behind the head until it touches the shoulders, and then back up again. It sometimes becomes necessary to have a spotter or some other means of holding the body down as heavier weights are used.

Neck Exercises

The neck is capable of several types of movement, such as raising of the shoulders (shrugging—discussed under Shoulder Shrug); flexion (lowering the head toward the chest); extension (raising the head, or the opposite of flexion); lateral flexion (lowering the head toward the shoulder on either side), and rotation (moving the head on the vertical axis in both directions, as if shaking the head to say "No").

The flexion and extension movements can be done with a standard neck harness, a wrestler's bridge, or in other ways. The flexion movement is usually not as strong as extension with the standard neck harness. The weight is hung behind the head at about the middle of the back. The neck is extended as far as possible in the starting position, and then the movement is flexed as far as possible. With a neck device such as that employed on the Universal Gym or the Nautilus Neck Machine, greater resistance is provided throughout the full range of motion. (See Nautilus Four-way Direct Neck Machine in Appendix.)

Neck flexion is many times the only trained exercise using the neck harness. If the weight is to be hung from the harness, a stabilizing position of the upper body is important. This position can be done by placing the hands on the knees and keeping the back straight in either the sitting or standing position (pictures A and B).

Lateral flexion is done on either the Universal neck device or the Nautilus Neck Machine. (See Nautilus Four-way Direct Neck Machine in Appendix.)

Neck Rotation

At this time, neck rotation muscles must be developed by hand resistance or by a special machine such as the Nautilus Rotary Neck Machine. (See Appendix.)

Power Rack

This piece of equipment has removable pins so that the weight can be lifted off at many different heights. This allows several different exercises to be trained on it, with many different starting levels in any one movement. The Power Rack is many times called an Isometric-Isotonic Power Rack. When pins are placed above the bar and the athlete attempts to move the bar past the pins, isometric contractions are possible. By placing weight on the bar it is possible to create a minimum force level throughout an isometric contraction.

Figure 19.21 Incline Press

(a)   (b)

Figure 19.22   Lat Pulls

 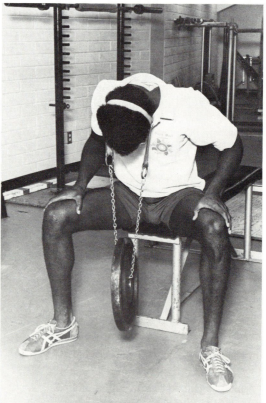

(a)   (b)

Figure 19.23   Neck Flexion

Rack Bench

The bench is set under the power rack. The pins are set at the desired height above the athlete's chest as he or she lies on the bench. Nine to twelve inches is usually a good height. The bar is placed on the pins, then the weight is loaded. The athlete is positioned on the bench beneath the weight in the Bench Press position. From here the bar is driven off the pins, extending the elbows through the partial Bench Press movement.

The Rack Bench is done to increase tricep and deltoid power. A greater pressure than a person might be accustomed to can be placed upon the deltoids.

Rack Press

The Rack Press can be done from shoulder height, but it is considered to be a partial press off a high rack. The deltoid, trapezoid, and tricep muscles are developed. A weight belt should be used for this exercise. After the desired height has been selected and the bar is in position and loaded, the movement is done by standing directly under the bar, gripping in at approximately shoulder width, and pressing it overhead.

Rack Squat

This exercise is done to develop the hips, thighs, and back above the level that is possible with the regular Squat. To execute the movement, the back should be kept straight and the head up. Although the movement encompasses almost the same distance as the one-quarter or one-half Squat, the Rack Squat is better for developing maximum strength for several reasons. The weight is stationary, and therefore inertia must be overcome to move the weight, making starting to move the weight difficult. This factor encourages the development of explosiveness. The bar is supported so that it can be attacked at the most difficult point—whenever the athlete is ready. From the safety standpoint, the weight cannot get outside the rack or go below the starting position. If the athlete cannot complete the movement, the bar is simply lowered to the pins, thereby relieving the athlete of the weight.

For most training purposes, the bar for the Rack Squat can be set at waist level.

Rack Dead Lift

This exercise is done to improve the Dead Lift power. Most athletes do not require heavy work on the Dead Lift or Rack Dead Lift, as it can be quite exhausting to the hips and lower back. The Rack Dead Lift has the same advantages over the regular Dead Lift as the Rack Squat has over the Squat. More weight can usually be handled through the movement than in the Dead Lift. The bar is confined within the rack, and the grip is also strengthened and confidence in handling heavy weight increased.

The Rack Dead Lift strengthens the same muscle groups as the Dead Lift. Like the Dead Lift, it can be trained for maximum efforts only over limited periods before rests are necessary.

Pulldowns

The Pulldown is done to strengthen the muscles of the lower chest and back. Using the "lat machine," the athlete either sits or kneels (just as in the Lat Pull) and the bar is pulled down in front of the body. Either a close grip or a shoulder width grip can be used. The close grip puts a greater stress on the wrists and forearms. The movement is similar to the Pullover, but the resistance is applied at a different angle. This exercise can require a spotter to hold the exerciser down. This is done by placing the hands on the shoulders and pushing down.

Pull straps

The use of pull straps will aid the grip when the bar or dumbbell is to be pulled up from the floor and/or held with the weight supported by the grip alone.

This technique should be used only to aid the grip so that other muscles can be worked thoroughly. Many times the grip fatigues before the "main mover." It is for this reason that pull straps are used. When the grip alone can do the job, it should be utilized.

When two pull straps are necessary, cotton, nylon, or leather straps are usually used. They should be from sixteen to twenty inches long and approximately one inch wide. The straps are held by wrapping them around the wrists and through the hands. It helps to keep the ends even.

If the athlete is right-handed, the left strap is wrapped first. The strap is then wrapped under the bar and the wrist is pulled down tight against the bar. The strap is then pulled around the bar next to the thumb, and is held in place by the thumb, palm, and fingers. The other hand is then wrapped; this is a little more difficult to do because the strap must be held by the fingers of the same hand to pull the wrist down to the bar and complete the wrap.

(a)

(b)

Figure 19.24 Shoulder Shrugs

Shoulder Shrugs

These are used to develop the trapezius muscles, which serve to elevate the shoulders.

In the standing position the bar is held in the hands, with the arms suspended straight down from the shoulders (picture A). The movement is performed by shrugging the shoulders, i.e., pulling them up toward the ears.

This may be done by pulling the shoulders straight up for a moment, then straight back down (picture A), or by rolling the shoulders in either direction. When the movement is developed, pull straps or straps with hooks may be used.

Sit-Ups

These are done to develop the abdominal muscles. Many variations of Sit-ups can be done. For regular Sit-Ups the knees should be kept flexed, relieving undesirable stress on the lower back. The hands may be held behind the head, down at the sides, crossed over the chest, or used to hold a weight on the chest (picture A). It is best for the feet to be held down by a partner if a Sit-up board is not available. As the movement is done, the trunk may be rotated or twisted to help maintain trunk flexibility and also to aid the development of the throwing movement, which utilizes the diagonal twisting movement of the trunk. Resistance is added by holding a weight flat on the chest.

Speed Exercises

A series of exercises used by sprinters to increase their running speed are discussed below. Athletes from many sports can benefit from the development of running speed, particularly in the use of the quick start.

Leg Curl for Speed

The Leg Curl is done in the prone position on the leg curl device. The toes are kept together, with the heels apart on the pads of the machine. This foot angle tends to isolate the long flexor muscle or semitendinosus. The hips should remain flat and against the bench so that the muscle gets complete extension. At the end of the movement the knee should be flexed well past ninety degrees for most individuals. The foot position causes knee flexion to be restricted slightly. Only light weights, generally from ten to thirty pounds, are used. Light stretching, in the sprinter's position, should follow this exercise.

High Knee Lift or Hip Flexion

This exercise is done by many sprinters in order to give them more power through the drive position (picture A)—or, as some would say, "I get better knee lift." The exercise can be done in several different ways. One way is to allow a weight to rest on the thigh near the knee, holding it there for a timed interval (picture A). A pulley can also be attached below (pictures B and C) or behind the runner. The best method to train this exercise is, of course, by utilizing a standing hip flexion machine. It should be worked explosively, if possible, and high speed equipment should be used if it is available.

(a)

(b)

Figure 19.25   Sit-Ups

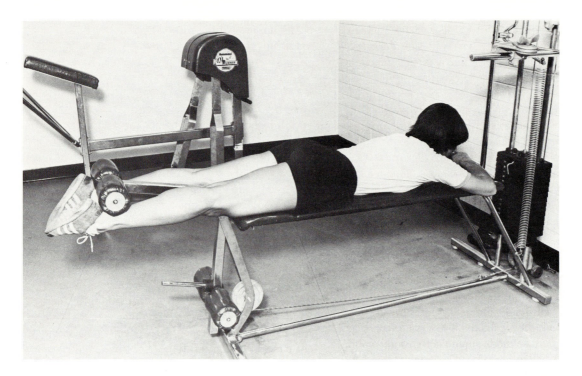

Figure 19.26 Leg Curl for Speed

(a)

(b)

(c)

Figure 19.27 High Knee Lift

Figure 19.28 Leg Drive

Leg Drive

This exercise helps the runner get a quicker start from the sprinter (picture A) or "DOWN" (picture B) position. There are several types of commercially available machines which include leg press stations that can be used. The exercise is done one leg at a time, with the same shoulder being supported as that which is driving. The athlete should keep his or her head up to imitate the running position. The foot is placed firmly upon the center of the pedal. It is best for the knee to be placed at an angle greater than ninety degrees at the start. The leg and hip drive backward explosively, obtaining complete extension of the hip and knee. The explosive movement cannot be done smoothly on some machines and must be done at a slower speed.

Squat

The Squat is the best exercise for the development of the legs and hips. The back erector muscles are also strengthened. A weight belt should be used when doing the Squat with weights. This exercise requires a spotter (see Spotting Procedure). The Squat can be done to various depths. To specify which of these movements is which, they are called Quarter Squat, Half Squat, Full Squat, and Deep Squat (pictures C–F).

When first starting to train with this exercise, light weights are used and Full Squats or Deep Squats are not done. *Persons under sixteen years of age should never do Full Squats with heavy weights.*

To perform the Squat, the bar is placed on a rack just below shoulder height. The athlete positions the bar on the back just above the scapula, on or against

(a)

(b)

(c)

Figure 19.29   Squat

the trapezius muscle (picture A) and takes it from the rack. *The back is kept straight in the Squat by keeping the chest out and the head up at all times* while handling the weight—both while removing it from the rack and while performing the movement. To help ensure that this position is maintained, a spot can be placed on the ceiling slightly in front of the point directly above the squatter's head. *The athlete should* then *keep the eyes focused on the spot throughout the entire movement.* The weight is removed from the rack by extending the knees and taking the weight onto the back. The athlete then takes one step backward to be in position to squat the weight. *The feet are placed at shoulder width or wider,* with the toes pointed slightly outward (picture B).

From there, the Squat is performed by flexing the knees and hips until the thighs, or at least the bottom of the thighs, are parallel to the floor. To get the maximum benefit from the Squat, *the athlete must be sure to squat low enough.* The major effort is made as the knees and hips are extended, raising the bar to the starting position. The athlete should begin the upward movement by concentrating first on extending the hips. When this is done correctly, *the hips seem to roll forward slightly under the bar* as it is raised, so that the back stays as erect as possible. This causes the final part of the upward movement to be, for the most part, knee extension.

Some athletes may prefer to use knee wraps when squatting—especially when Full Squats are to be done.

(d)

(e)

(f)

Figure 19.29   Squat (Continued)

Stiff-Legged Dead Lift (Caution: Use light weight.)

This exercise strengthens the lower back and hamstrings. The movement is similar to the "Good Mornings." The difference in the two exercises is that the weight is held in the hands instead of upon the back, and that more weight can be used for Stiff-Legged Dead Lifts than for "Good Mornings."

The movement is performed by grasping the bar with the overhand grip at approximately shoulder width. Keeping the elbows and knees completely extended, the back straight, and the head up, the barbell is pulled from the ground until the body is completely erect.

Throwing Exercises

Throwing Motion (Wall Pulley). A wall pulley is placed above the head or higher and can be used to increase throwing velocity. It is extremely important that the throwing motion be imitated exactly. Various types of pulleys can be used. Either isotonic or isokinetic ones are effective.

Throwing Pullover. To perform this exercise, a close grip is taken on the bar. The movement is similar to the Bent-Arm Pullover in that it is performed in the supine position on a bench, and the bar is brought down

Figure 19.30 Throwing Motion

to a bent arm position behind and below the head (picture A, page 254). After the bar is lowered to this position, the power phase of the movement begins. The bar is brought through the movement back to the starting position, with the elbows extended directly above the shoulders. The elbows are held in close to the body throughout the movement. The range of motion closely resembles the throwing motion (picture B, page 254). This exercise can require spotters (see Spotting Procedure).

Tricep Pushdown

The lat machine is used for this exercise, which is done to strengthen the triceps. The athlete stands erect, taking a close grip on the lat bar (picture A). He or she pulls the bar down to shoulder height (picture B) and then pushes it straight down as far as possible, using only the arms to move the weight. To keep the tricep isolated, the athlete must not lean or move the shoulders over the bar.

(a)

(b)

Figure 19.31 Throwing Pullover

(a)   (b)

Figure 19.32 Tricep Pushdown

Tricep Supine

This is another method of isolating the tricep. It is done in the supine position upon a bench, using a close grip upon the bar. In the starting position the weight is held directly over the shoulders with the elbows extended. The movement is performed by lowering the weight to the forehead and then back again, not allowing the elbows to slip outward (pictures A and B, page 256). This exercise requires spotters (see Spotting Procedure).

Upright Rowing

The shoulders (deltoids and trapezius) and the elbow flexors are strengthened by this exercise. It is done by standing erect, with the bar held down in front of the body at arm length (picture A). A close grip is used. The movement is performed by flexing the elbows, pulling the bar up to shoulder height and slightly back (picture B), then lowering it back to the starting position. The elbows are kept high throughout the movement and the body erect.

Toe Raises

Toe Raises are done to strengthen the calf muscle. The name of this exercise is sometimes misleading because the athlete stands on an elevated support and raises his heels, while the knees are kept straight.

For more complete calf development, the angle of the feet can be adjusted out, straight, or in. This exercise can be done on a calf machine, or upon other devices such as a leg press machine, a hip sled, or a bench press machine.

Standing Tricep Extension

This exercise is done to strengthen the triceps or elbow extensors. A barbell is used and a close overhand grip is taken. The weight is held directly overhead, with the elbows completely extended. The weight is then lowered behind the head, keeping the elbows close to the head, and then raised again to the starting position (pictures A and B). This is one of the best methods of isolating the tricep. This exercise can require spotters (see Spotting Procedure).

(a)

(b)

Figure 19.33 Tricep Supine

(a)   (b)

Figure 19.34 Upright Rowing

(a)   (b)

Figure 19.35 Standing Tricep Extension

Strength Exercises

CHAPTER
TWENTY

STRENGTH TRAINING FACILITIES AND EQUIPMENT

This chapter is being written for the benefit of the person responsible for designing and developing a strength training facility, and/or for evaluating and selecting the equipment for the facility. It could be a junior high, high school, or college coach, or a spa, club, or YMCA director. For the purposes of expediency, this person will be referred to as the *strength expert*.

If the person in this position has a limited background in the field of strength training, it is advisable to utilize a strength consultant. Since the utilization of expertise is necessary for the successful completion of the task, reference will be made to the strength consultant, strength coach, or strength expert throughout the chapter. It is recommended that an NSCA certified strength and conditioning specialist be utilized.

This chapter is divided into two parts: Part I, The Design and Development of the Strength Training Facility, and Part II, The Evaluation and Selection of Strength Training Equipment. The strength expert will need to conduct these processes simultaneously. Although they are separate processes, they are not totally independent of each other.

PART I THE DESIGN AND DEVELOPMENT OF THE STRENGTH TRAINING FACILITY

The design and development of a strength facility can be achieved by following an organized, step-by-step process.

1. Establish the major objective.
2. Establish minor objectives, the sum of which amounts to the achievement of the major objective.
3. Write detailed sub-objectives, the sum of which amount to the accomplishment of the minor objectives.

4. Review other comparable existing facilities and integrate the information gained into the objectives.
5. The architects develop a blueprint design (in some cases, this step may be bypassed).
6. The strength expert or consultant develops a strength facility floor plan.
7. The architects make final changes.
8. The construction of the facility takes place.
9. The equipment is ordered (evaluation and selection of strength equipment is discussed in Part II of this chapter).

Before discussing this procedure in detail, there are some *primary considerations* which may or *may not* need attention. In many cases, the facility may already be in place, thereby eliminating some basic concerns. Those basic problems involve matters such as 1) the selection of a site, 2) the architectural design of the building in which the strength facility is to be placed, 3) the cost of the building and the fund-raising sources for the facility, and 4) the plan for staffing and maintaining the facility, and for funding the plan.

The coach, physical educators, and/or administrative personnel who are responsible for planning and developing the details of the strength facility will probably *not* be responsible for the previously mentioned areas. It is recommended that involvement and input of the strength training expert be included early since there are specific problems inherent to a strength facility that will be best resolved in the initial stages. A considerable amount of time and detailed planning will need to be spent between the architects and the strength consultant.

ESTABLISH THE MAJOR OBJECTIVE

With the awareness of these major concerns, the planning of the strength facility can begin. The first step is to establish the *major objective*. The major objective obviously springs directly from the need for the facility. This could be a need within a school (elementary, junior high, high school, or college), a community, an existing spa or health club, a business or corporation, a professional athletic organization, a hospital or clinic, or even a home. It is also advantageous to look beyond the basic need to the possible expanded service that the facility might provide. That kind of foresight can be utilized to help with the funding of the facility. This is especially true when the facility is not being built within the school. Private or community agencies can sometimes develop contracts with other institutions within the community. Examples:

1. Hospitals and clinics often have need for weight training facilities for physical therapy and rehabilitation.
2. Spas and private clubs can use hospital or clinic medical personnel to conduct tests or can train employees to conduct screening tests for club members.
3. Schools without space for on-site strength facilities can contract to use private or community facilities.

This expanded recognition of the possible uses of a strength facility can also affect the selection of the site for the facility. Therefore, the writing of the major objective of the facility requires careful consideration. It needs to be stated in a detailed enough way that on the completion of the facility, it can be empirically shown that it has been achieved. In other words, the major objective should be objectively testable.

An example of a major objective used in the development of a university football strength complex:

"Major Objective: To develop, exclusively for the Illinois Football program, the most aesthetically modern, functional, state of the art, strength training facility in the most economical way possible." [25]

Analyzing this stated objective part by part:

1. The facility was to be developed "exclusively" for the Illinois Football program. It was, therefore, a priority that the facility be placed as close as possible to the football stadium and practice fields. In addition, every detail of the facility was to be designed with the football team—and no one else—in mind. This includes the structural design of the facility, the floor plan and equipment layout, the equipment itself (size, type, specific function, durability, etc.), the interior decorating, the flooring, the record-keeping system, the supervision pattern, traffic patterns, office space, storage spaces, repair shop and supplies, and temperature and humidity control. With all of the detailed planning to be done exclusively for football, the administrator needs to be certain that no one else besides the Illinois Football team will need to utilize the facility after its completion.

2. The next part of the major objective is that the facility be "the most aesthetically modern." This phrase was placed in the major objective to define the appearance of the facility and, thereby, satisfy the need to utilize it as a recruiting tool. Strength facilities at the major college level have become one of the major showplaces of the athletic program.

3. "Functional" refers to the necessity for the strength facility to be able to serve the large number of team members smoothly, quickly, and with an economy of space. Functionality also entails the idea that the space and equipment can be utilized for a large number of tasks to efficiently produce the specific results required.

4. "State of the art" makes reference to the fact that the facility, the interior environment, the programs and recording systems, and the equipment and supplies present will possess the most up-to-date scientific advancements available on the markets.

5. The phrase "in the most economical way possible" refers to the fact that the cost of the facility needs to be kept to an absolute minimum, without compromising the other requirements of the major objective.

ESTABLISH MINOR OBJECTIVES

After the major objective has been written, the *minor objectives* can be developed. As mentioned earlier, the accomplishment of all the minor objectives should amount to the achievement of the major objective. The minor objectives are, therefore, the exact descriptive statements of each of the elements contained within the major objective. To complete the Illinois example, the minor objectives used to support the major objective for the Illinois Football Strength Complex were as follows:

1. The facility must predominately emphasize the use of free weights.
2. The facility must be large enough to serve the strength training needs of the entire football team in the off-season, pre-season, and in-season periods, efficiently.

3. The facility must be arranged so that the off-season, pre-season, and in-season programs can be most effectively supervised.
4. The most important supplemental strength training machines, dumbbells, and other equipment must be easily accessible so that athletes can train with a maximum utilization of their time.
5. The facility must provide the most up-to-date specialized, variable resistance equipment to isolate and develop the entire range of muscle groups throughout the body. This is necessary to expedite the strengthening of any and all individual weaknesses. These include those originally or inherently present or those caused by an injury.
6. The facility should provide the best available equipment designed to strengthen the specific movements common to the game of football.
7. The facility should provide the most advanced, computerized, specialized recording and testing equipment available.
8. The facility should provide the best motivationally positive atmosphere for strength training possible.
9. There must be office space for the strength coach and the staff responsible for supervising and maintaining the facility. This should be positioned so that the working area can be seen from the offices.
10. There must be adequate storage area for supplies and equipment to be used in the strength complex, directly adjacent to the working area.
11. If possible, there should be a repair shop with the tools necessary for maintaining the strength equipment and repairing or replacing the most common types of breakage.

The ideas defined in the minor objectives are expressed in enough detail to ensure that the major objective will be achieved in the best way possible. This entails the utilization of the expertise of the strength consultant or strength coach in the area of strength training methods and strength program designs, supervision, methods, and strength work traffic patterns. That expertise will also be used for the strength training equipment specifications and designs to suit the specialized needs of the people who will be using the facility. The minor objectives also provide goals and express needs to be satisfied in detail through the expertise of the architects and interior designers. The architects deal with problems such as heating, humidity control, lighting, space utilization (i.e., traffic patterns, storage and office needs, etc.). Interior design experts help with developing the proper motivational and yet,

attractive, atmosphere. For this reason, communication among architect, interior designer, and strength training expert, concerning the psychological, as well as the physical needs involved, is recommended.

Writing Detailed Sub-Objectives

After the minor objectives have been established, the sub-objectives can be written. Just as the accomplishment of all the minor objectives amounts to the accomplishment of the major objective, the accomplishment of all of the sub-objectives amounts to the accomplishment of the minor objectives for which, and under which, they were created.

The strength expert who coordinates the overall development of the facility will write the sub-objectives to fulfill many of the minor objectives, but in some cases, the sub-objectives may be written largely by the architect or the interior designer.

An example of sub-objectives created by the strength expert may be shown by expanding upon the Illinois minor objective #5:

The facility must provide the most up-to-date, specialized, variable resistance equipment to isolate and develop the entire range of muscle groups throughout the body. This is necessary to expedite the strengthening of any and all individual weaknesses. These include those originally or inherently present or those caused by an injury.

Sub-objectives:
5–1. The facility must provide up-to-date specialized variable resistance equipment to isolate and develop the muscle groups of the neck and shoulders.

Tentative Recommendations:
list possible neck machines
list possible shrug machines

5–2. The facility must provide up-to-date specialized variable resistance equipment to isolate and develop the muscle groups of the shoulders (including chest and upper back) and arms.

Tentative Recommendations:
list possible chest press machines
list possible rowing machines
list possible overhead press machines
list possible lateral chest machines
list possible lateral shoulder machines
list possible pullover machines
list possible shoulder rotation machines
list possible Latisimuss dorsi (lat pull) machines

5–3. The facility must provide up-to-date specialized variable resistance equipment to isolate and develop the muscle groups of the arms.

Tentative Recommendations:
list possible bicep machines
list possible tricep machines

5–4. The facility must provide up-to-date specialized variable resistance equipment to isolate and develop the muscle groups of the forearms and hands.

Tentative Recommendations:
list possible grip machines

5–5. The facility must provide up-to-date specialized variable resistance equipment to isolate and develop the muscle groups of the torso, lower back, and abdomen.

Tentative Recommendations:
list possible lower back machines
list possible abdominal machines
list possible torso rotation machines
(also list possible squat machines which are best for lower back)

5–6. The facility must provide up-to-date specialized variable resistance equipment to isolate and develop the muscle groups of the hips and thighs.

Tentative Recommendations:
list possible hip flexion machines
list possible hip extension machines
list possible abduction/adduction machines
(combination and/or isolated movement)
(also list possible squat machines which are best for hips)

5–7. The facility must provide up-to-date specialized variable resistance equipment to isolate and develop the muscle groups of the legs.

Tentative Recommendations:
list possible leg extension machines
list possible leg curl (flexion) machines
list possible leg press machines
(also list possible squat machines which are best for legs)

5–8. The facility must provide up-to-date specialized variable resistance equipment to isolate and develop the muscle groups of the lower legs and feet.

Tentative Recommendations:
list possible calf machines

Note: The minor objective also states that the machines must be capable of strengthening individual weaknesses inherently present or caused by an injury. By this it is understood that it would be beneficial if machines were available to isolate all muscle groups without the aid of supporting muscle groups for stabilizers or fixators, or adjacent muscle groups for gripping or securing the mechanism itself, since these muscle groups could be incapacitated. Some machines which satisfy this need are now available, others are not; therefore, sub-objective 5–9 is stated in this way:

5–9. It is recommended that the facility provide up-to-date specialized variable resistance equipment, if possible. The equipment must be capable of

1. strengthening the muscles which flex and extend the elbow without involving the hand or the shoulder.
2. strengthening the muscles which flex, extend, abduct, adduct, circumduct, and rotate the shoulder without involving the elbow or the back.
3. strengthening the muscles which flex, extend, rotate, and laterally contract the neck and elevate the shoulders without involving the muscles of the middle and lower back and abdomen.
4. strengthening the muscles which rotate, hyperextend, or laterally flex the lower back, or flex or extend the hips, without involving the muscles which flex or extend the knee.
5. strengthening the muscles which flex and extend the knee without involving muscles which flex or extend the hip, or which move the ankle joint.
6. strengthening the muscles which dorsi or plantar flex or inwardly or outwardly rotate the ankle.

As this example illustrates, the sub-objective is defined in great detail in terms of the objectively observable performance that is expected. Sub-objectives are defined as being absolute necessities, or in some cases are offered as recommendations. In sub-objectives 5–1 through 5–8, the "Tentative recommendations" refer to possibilities to be investigated during the upcoming review of other facilities. They are offered as possible solutions to the sub-objective. Sub-objective 5–9, on the other hand, points out some beneficial features and recommends their inclusion be considered wherever possible.

An example of a minor objective to which the sub-objectives would be best completed by the architects and interior designers is Illinois minor objective #8. "The facility should provide the best motivationally positive atmosphere for strength training possible. The expertise to write the sub-objectives for this minor objective includes knowledge in the following areas: lighting, heating and cooling, humidity control, color coordination and its motivational effects, stereo systems, and graphical presentation of strength records highlighting individual achievements (figure 20.1).

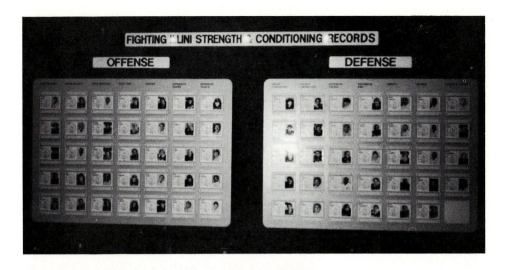

Figure 20.1 Motivational Technique

Reviewing Other Facilities

After the minor objectives are written, at least in a tentative form, the process of reviewing other facilities can begin. The detailed minor objectives serve as a guideline in this process. It would be a mistake to engage in the process of reviewing existing facilities without such a guideline upon which to reflect. The reviewer will gain a great deal more from the review if s/he knows what he or she is looking for and why. S/he can ask better questions about what s/he is seeing and will be likely to gain more information and creative ideas from the experience. Whenever possible, the architect and the interior designer should be involved with the strength expert in this process.

There are several steps which can be conducted as part of the review process.

1. Read and study and evaluate articles about other comparable facilities in the professional journals. (Suggested references are the *NSCA Journal* and *American Fitness Quarterly*.)

2. Review tapes and slide presentations related to facility development available through the National Strength and Conditioning Association.[25]

3. Personally visit as many facilities as possible. It may be beneficial to visit different types of facilities (high schools, junior colleges, colleges, universities, health spas, YMCAs, and private weight lifting clubs). The final part of the review process should concentrate on facilities comparable to the one that is to be created.

Information gathered in the reviewing process can be used to improve the overall plan for the facility to be developed. This information may prompt a major change or changes to the original plan, or may simply improve or clarify some of the details involved. Besides the new information which may precipitate major changes in the facility plan, the utilization of the detailed sub-objectives with their accompanying tentative recommendations will serve to ensure that the review is thorough. There should be no attempt to make final decisions while a particular review is being conducted; it is predominately an information-gathering effort. After each individual review, the new information can be synthesized into both the facility development and the equipment selection process. Decisions will be made later as to which new ideas are to be incorporated into the plan. When making these decisions, consider 1) the cost compared with the value to be received from the change; 2) any inhibitory effect that the change might have on any of the previously established objectives; and 3) the effect that the change might have on any other factors (such as structural design, staffing and supervision, or fund raising). Determining this may require discussions and analysis with administrators, architects, and others involved. For example, in some instances, a donation may be available in the form of a gift in kind. If it originates from a specialized source that is not the most preferred, an administrative decision will need to be made as to whether or not to utilize it in the facility. Situations such as this can require value judgments with positive and negative factors carefully considered on both sides of the problem.

After each change is considered and a decision is made, consider how the change will affect the objectives. First, make necessary adjustments to the sub-objectives. Next, consider how those adjustments might make necessary changes to minor objectives. Where necessary, rewrite or add to the minor objectives. Finally, if a change in a minor objective was necessary, evaluate whether or not that change caused a necessary change in the major objective. Since the review process produces new ideas, and inhibitory changes in the objectives were considered during their creation, changes to the objectives are usually positive. The positive changes normally cause additions to the objectives and, of course, to the facility. Negative changes are often made because of miscalculations or unexpected changes in the area cost or liability.

At some point during, or directly after, the completion of the facilities review, the strength expert should produce a sample floor plan representing the strength facility which would best satisfy the major objective. In other words, it should be as close as possible to the "ideal" solution to the major objective. To accomplish this, the strength expert needs to have independently carried out the process of evaluating and selecting strength training equipment described in Part II of this chapter.

The information relating to strength equipment gathered in the review process needs to have been incorporated into the plan. This means that decisions about the exact equipment to be purchased need to have been made, to some degree, prior to the creation of this first tentative floor plan. Figure 20.2 (A–F) represents a sample floor plan created for architects who had not at this point produced a building blueprint.

The Architects' Blueprint Design

Architects use the information they gather from reviewing other facilities, talking with other architects who have designed similar facilities, and discussing pertinent details of the facility with the strength expert. Some information unique about a strength facility needs to be considered. The recommended ceiling height is between 12 and 14 feet. There should be a method of humidity control, especially in humid climates, because of the tendency for expensive strength equipment to receive rust damage from high humidity. Double doors with outside access and a removable center post are advisable for the purpose of moving large pieces of equipment. There are many other details the architects must consider in developing the blueprint for the strength complex which will for the most part depend upon the particular facility to be built (see figure 20.3).

Strength Coach's Floor Plan

After the architects' blueprint is completed and is in the hands of the strength coach, and nearly all final decisions have been made about the strength training equipment to be purchased, the first "to scale" floor plan can be developed. To accomplish this, each of the sub-objectives must be taken into consideration. Again, using the Illinois example, the sub-objectives contained within minor objectives #1, #3, #4, #5, and #6, refer to the equipment to be placed in the floor plan and its positioning within the room. The strength experts' understanding of a multitude of factors and the complexity and interaction of these factors will determine how effective this floor plan will be. Several matters about which s/he must be knowledgeable are 1) the needs of the particular people who are to use the facility; 2) the

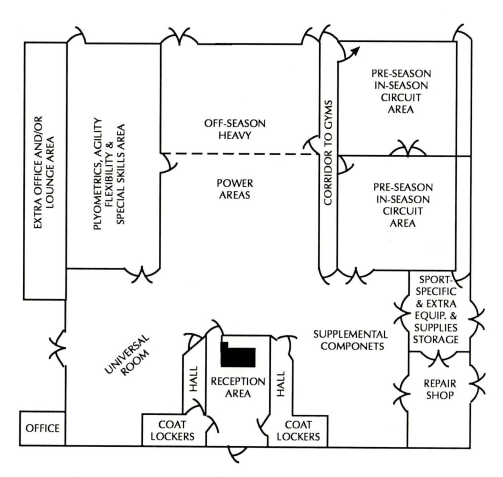

Figure 20.2A Strength Coach's Floor Plan

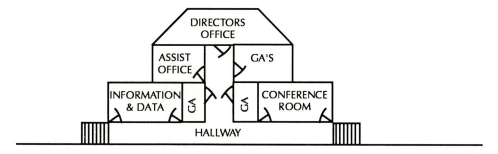

Figure 20.2B

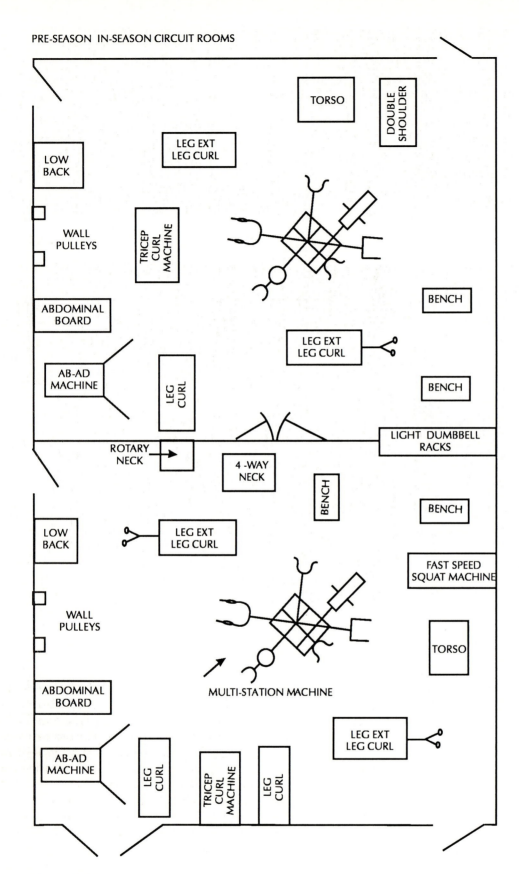

Figure 20.2C

Chapter 20

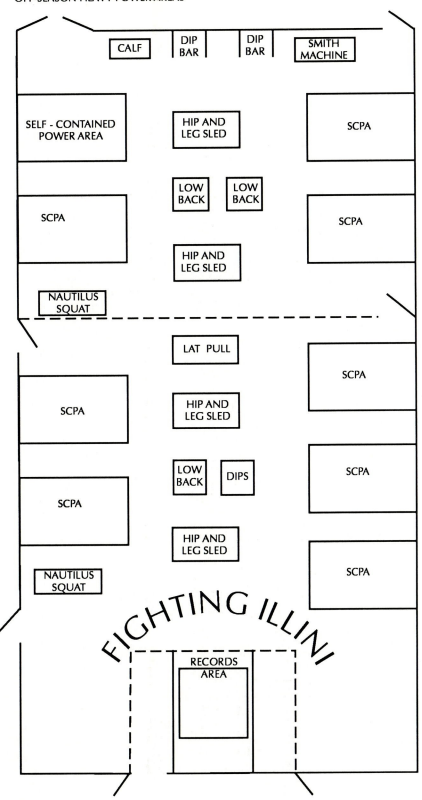

Figure 20.2D

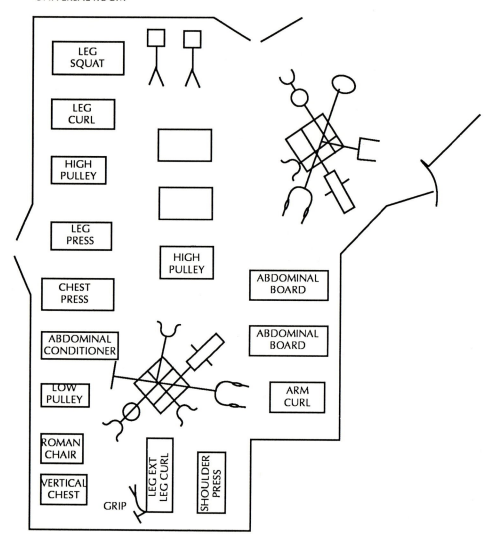

Figure 20.2E

strength training systems to be utilized, including the types of programs, circuits, etc., to be used; 3) the space needed for efficient access to various types of equipment; and 4) the teaching methods to be employed most often by the staff. Much of this knowledge is gained only through experience (fig. 20.3).

Minor objectives #4 and #8 also contain factors which must be considered by the strength expert in creating the floor plan. Recording and testing equipment mentioned in minor objective #7 needs to be placed within the offices and, in some cases, even its positioning within the room itself needs to be considered. The architects may be involved in this placement because of the advantageous placement of electrical outlets.

Note: Electrical outlets are also necessary to some types of strength equipment. Minor objective deals with the motivational atmosphere. If there are to be any decorative wall displays, records boards, or any areas or fixtures, they may require an easy-access viewing area; at least they should not be obstructed visually.

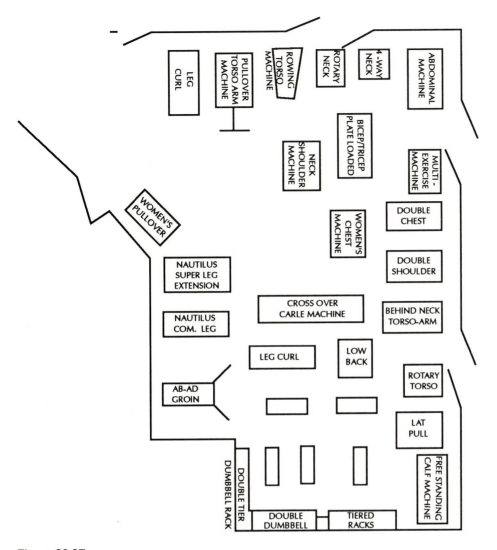

Figure 20.2F

These factors need to be coordinated with the interior designer and architects. At the university or college, the Graphics Department can sometimes be of assistance in this area. The high school or junior high may be able to make use of the Art Department for preparing decorative wall displays or graphical records boards, etc.

A copy of the strength expert's floor plan is sent to the administration, the architects, and the interior designers.

Architects' Final Changes and the Construction of the Facility

When the strength expert's floor plan is received by the architects, it will be incorporated into the master blue print (fig. 20.4). After this, but before the construction plans are set in motion—and even as the construction progresses—the architects may need to make further changes (fig. 20.5). In the Illinois example, the changes affected the floor plan layout and the equipment selection. If this is necessary, the strength expert must produce another floor plan, adjusting to the changes (fig. 20.6). This process of change and adjustment and redesign may continue throughout the construction period.

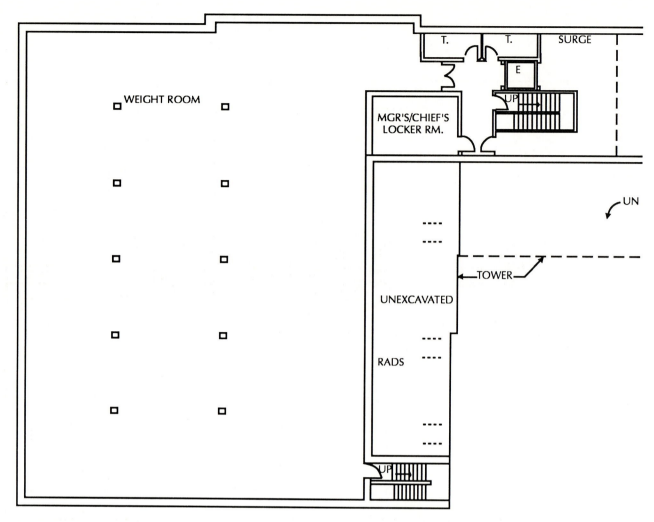

WEIGHT ROOM

MGR'S/CHIEF'S
LOCKER RM.

T. T. SURGE

E

UP

UN

TOWER

UNEXCAVATED

RADS

UP

Figure 20.3

PART II THE EVALUATION AND SELECTION OF STRENGTH TRAINING EQUIPMENT

The evaluation and selection of strength training equipment for any facility should be conducted carefully and systematically. This approach will help ensure that the best possible equipment to fulfill the objectives of the facility will be found. It will also help avoid the exploitation which can so easily occur by the large commercial equipment companies. It is the opinion of the authors that at this time there does not exist a single brand of commercially made strength training equipment which will best satisfy, completely, all the needs of the strength facility. Even the most skilled manufacturers appear to have their forte or specialty, yet other products they produce may be found to be unnecessary or unsatisfactory. This may be because of the wide variation in the needs of individual facilities or because of shortcomings within the manufacturers themselves. Whatever the reason, it is recommended that a thorough evaluation of each item be made before it is purchased.

Flooring

In addition to strength equipment, the strength expert may be required to make a decision about the type of flooring to be purchased. The flooring is usually the first thing to be purchased. In some cases it is even ordered by the construction company, since the funding for flooring and installation may be included in the cost of the building itself. In any case, the strength expert needs to be involved in the selection process.

The type of flooring generally determines if it will be fixed or movable. Factors which help determine whether fixed or movable flooring is to be purchased: 1) the percentage of free weights vs. machines, 2) the cost of the flooring, 3) the durability of the flooring, and 4) the level and importance of the appearance that needs to be maintained.

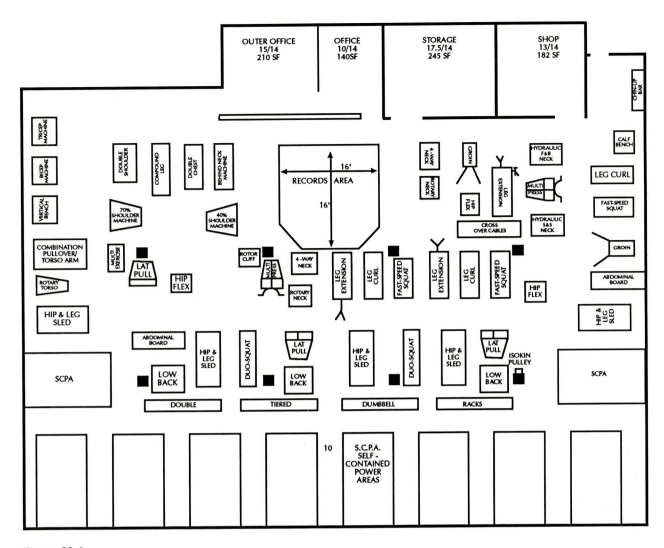

Figure 20.4

When free weights are to be used, it is best to have some type of rubberized floor surface. There are some surfaces which are "rubber-like" compositions that are not actually rubber. This does not mean that they may not be as durable as, or even more durable than, rubber. Many of the currently available weight room floor products have a "resealing" quality. This means that when they are cut by a falling weight or a sharp object, they tend to reseal themselves. This resealing ability has not been completely perfected, but it does help significantly to increase the durability of the floor. If this type of floor is cut with an extremely sharp object, such as a razor blade or a knife, the cut may not be visible at all. Weights, especially heavier weights, create a rougher cut, which may be visible after resealing. The self-sealing flooring is usually successful in keeping cuts from having loose or floppy edges, and from tearing further.

The negative factor of a permanent floor is that in order to repair it, a section of floor must be removed and replaced. Removal is sometimes a difficult process,

since the tiles are glued with epoxy adhesive. Each piece is removed with strenuous effort and the old piece is usually damaged. Because of this, a floor that is glued down cannot be removed and used in another location.

The advantage of removable floors, of course, is that damaged pieces can be replaced more easily, and the entire floor can be removed and relocated if desirable. There are several companies which produce interlocking rubber flooring for this purpose. The disadvantages of removable floors: 1) there is a tendency for the pieces to stretch or become misshapen with wear, causing new pieces not to fit properly; 2) they can move or creep, depending upon the underlying surface; and 3) dirt or mildew can collect under them, depending on the amount of dust, moisture, etc., in the environment.

In some cases where free weights are used, smaller sections of rubber flooring can be used. Sections can be purchased pre-cut in various sizes (4' × 6', 4' × 5', 3' × 4', 2' × 4', 2½' × 4'). These can be used in a

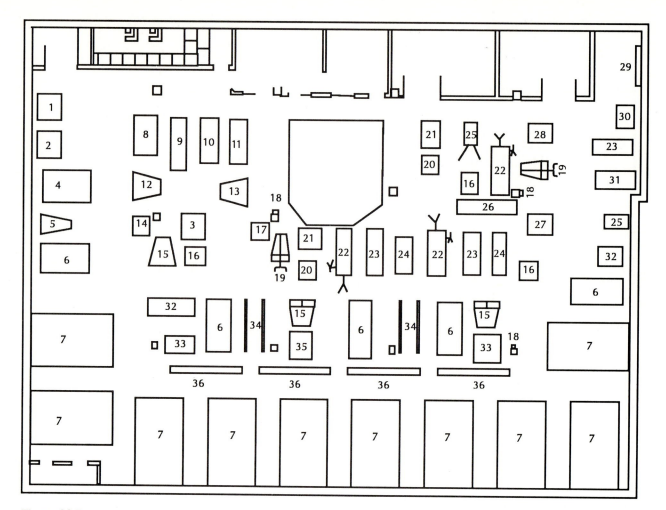

Figure 20.5

throw rug fashion in places where the most damage or heaviest traffic are likely to occur. They can be used on any surface or on top of permanent or removable rubber flooring to prevent damage.

In areas where strength training machines are utilized and no free weights or any hard metal objects will be striking the floor, carpeting can be installed. Heavy duty industrial carpet is recommended for this purpose. There are also some flooring materials which have a heavy duty carpet bonded to a vinyl or rubber backing. The backing is usually 3/16″ to 1/4″ thick. If this material is to be used in free weight areas, the previously described rubber "throw pads" are recommended.

The cost of most rubberized flooring is greater than that of industrial carpet (3 or 4 times as much per square foot). The carpet bonded to vinyl or rubber backing, or the rubber throw mats (1/2″ thick) should be approximately half the cost per square foot of the rubber flooring.

Information about the durability of the flooring can be gained 1) during the reviewing of other facilities, 2) by contacting other facilities who have previously installed the floor, 3) from analyzing the written materials, especially research tests conducted on the flooring, and 4) from the length of the warranty or guarantee offered.

Major universities and colleges who are involved in recruiting athletes, and health spas and clubs are usually extremely concerned about the appearance of the strength facility or weight room. Normally, carpeting is preferred as it presents the best appearance. Some facilities have used a combination of rubber flooring and carpet. In the Illinois example, the concept of the Self-Contained Power Area was utilized. This allowed for 8′ × 14′ areas where all free weight exercises can be performed. In other undesignated areas, 4′ × 6′ rubber throw mats were used.

High school and junior high facilities, although not as concerned with creating a luxurious atmosphere, will benefit from flooring which is installed neatly and can

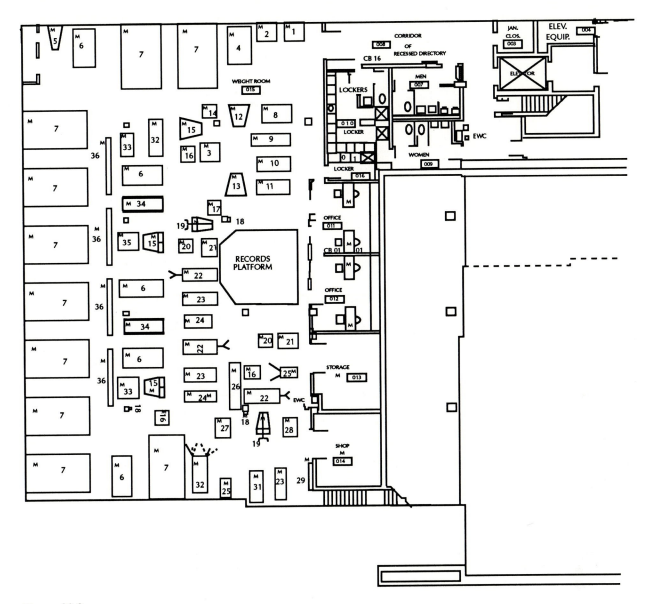

Figure 20.6

be kept clean. Both permanent and removable flooring can be purchased in black or in various colors. Black is usually less expensive than other colors. For this reason, many schools may wish to purchase flooring in black.

Strength Training Equipment

Strength Training Equipment categories:

1. Free Weight equipment
   a. Barbell equipment
   b. Dumbbell equipment

2. Strength Training machines
   a. Selectorized machines
      1. Standard isotonic
      2. Variable resistance
   b. Isokinetic equipment
      1. Mechanical
      2. Electromagnetic
   c. Others
      1. Air pump-type
      2. Compressed air resistance
      3. Water resistance
      4. Self-created resistance

Evaluation of Equipment

The evaluation of the various categories of strength training equipment is undertaken by subjecting each piece of equipment to the scrutiny of a stringent set of recommended specifications. Defining the specifications for the strength equipment can be viewed as a three-fold process:

1. Establishing the necessary functional criteria for the equipment. To achieve this, there seems to be little or no substitute for knowledge gained from personal experience. Those who have been personally involved in strength training, weight lifting, or body building over an extended period can immediately identify with this statement. There are many intricacies in the design of strength equipment that cannot be noted until the equipment is used in training. Slight differences or design changes can cause great problems in terms of the isolation of the proper muscle groups and the supporting muscles involved. Some examples where the smallest changes in equipment can be critical to the success of the exercise are 1) the height or width of a bench; 2) the proper handle or grip for the exerciser—or for the spotter, for that matter; 3) the stability of the equipment. (It needs to be heavy enough to be stable, yet some pieces that need to be maneuvered cannot be too heavy; 4) a comfortable place for the spotter to stand where his/her leverage is not impaired; 5) the moving parts must move smoothly and efficiently and must not come loose or need constant adjustment; 6) with machines, the exact range of motion to isolate the proper muscle group *must* be achieved, with the correct leverage (Achieving this is difficult enough, but is made even more complex when the differences in the size and the strength of individuals are taken into consideration.) Machines must be adjustable in exactly the right way, and in many cases in numerous ways, within a single exercise; 7) an exercise machine also must provide the proper resistance throughout the range of motion (this sometimes requires the use of a cam system); and 8) the equipment must be sufficiently durable.

2. Evaluating the specifications of the equipment already on the market. To evaluate the specifications of the equipment already on the market, a thorough step-by-step process must be undertaken. To accomplish this, the strength expert will compare the available equipment to the previously established functional criteria.

   The first step is to review the commercially available strength equipment. This process can, in most cases, be shortened greatly by the utilization of a strength consultant who is familiar with the currently available equipment. This is advisable even for junior high and high schools, since strength consultation is available for little or no expense and will in fact almost always save money. The facility review should not be the only review of the equipment. Perhaps the best way to become familiar with the market is to attend strength conventions, health clubs, or fitness industry shows. This procedure is somewhat expensive, and therefore, it may be advisable to attend one large national convention or show. Prior to attending, a short investigation can determine if a large number of strength equipment companies are to be displaying their products. Advertising brochures provide visual information and are of some value. Special concentration should be given to the equipment specifications usually provided in the brochures. These can be obtained by mail or at the convention or equipment show.

   A careful analysis of each piece of equipment can be conducted, utilizing the general equipment specifications provided in this chapter. A checklist can be used to point out the specification deficits of each piece of equipment. This will help to reveal how well the equipment compares with its competitors. There are many strength training products on the market which are not structurally sound. In addition, many—perhaps most—do not even closely approach the suggested specifications. This is usually because the equipment is created with inferior materials or parts that will wear out quickly or break easily. In fact, it may be difficult to find equipment that adheres to the suggested specifications in all areas. During the review process, when possible functional improvements for currently available equipment can be established, they should be noted. Negative factors that inhibit equipment from achieving the functional criteria should also be recorded.

3. Deciding upon the relative cost of the equipment to be made based on the funds available. This area requires judgmental decisions concerning a multitude of materials and workmanship to be used. Factors to consider in likely order of importance are:
   a. the heavy structural materials to be used (i.e., the size and gauge of the steel)
   b. the connecting materials (welds, bolts, nuts, sleeves, collars, gaskets, washers, clamps, etc.)
   c. the materials that affect the function of the equipment (i.e., bearings, bushings, rails, pulleys, cables, handles, springs, insulators, lubricators, etc.)

d. the materials and workmanship that affect the aesthetic quality of the equipment (i.e., paint, upholstery, plating, grinding and filling, etc.)

The following list of general specifications for strength training equipment was developed as a result of the application of the preceding three-step process.

RECOMMENDED SPECIFICATIONS FOR STRENGTH TRAINING EQUIPMENT[24]

Structural Materials

1. Equipment frames must be made of heavy wall 7 to 11 gauge steel tubing (7 gauge or 120 wall is preferred).

   Comments: The size of the steel is somewhat dependent upon the amount of usage and the individuals using the equipment. The appearance and sturdiness of the equipment also affects the training atmosphere, as well as the durability of the equipment. 3″ × 3″ or 2½″ × 2½″ steel tubing, for use in collegiate or professional athletics. Either 2½″ × 2½″ or 2″ × 2″ steel tubing for use in commercial establishments. 2″ × 2″ steel tubing for use in high school or junior high school weight rooms.

2. Round stock in pivot joints should be ¾″ to 1″.

   Comments: The size within this range varies according to the stress at the specific pivot joint.

3. Pad boards should be made of ¾″ plywood or 2″ lumber.

Connecting Materials

4. All frames should be electro-welded either by arc or MIG welder.

   Comments: Because of the sensitivity of the temperature control and the experience and skill involved, an expert welder is required. The best advice for the prospective purchaser here is that, when there is any doubt, check the past history of the company. Recommendations by others currently using the equipment should not be difficult for the company to provide.

5. For safety reasons, all welds must be ground to a smooth finish on the tops and sides of the steel. All sharp edges must be de-burred. All corners must be rounded. All slag or weld splatter must be removed. For elite equipment, all welds must be finish ground, filled, and polished to provide a clean aesthetic look to the frame design.

6. All exposed saw cut areas must be filed down and smoothed.

7. Bolts and nuts must be within the following limits: #3 to #5 hardness for ½ to ⁷⁄₁₆″ bolts and nuts; #5 to #8 hardness for ⅜″ bolts and nuts (never use less than ⅜″);[23] #3 hardness minimum for ⁵⁄₁₆″ bolts and nuts for upholstery pads (never less than ⁵⁄₁₆″ for upholstery pad boards). *Note:* Galvanized coating is preferred on all bolts and nuts to prevent rusting.

8. Cable must be nylon coated aircraft cable ³⁄₁₆″ or larger, coated to ¼″.[34,35]

9. If chain is to be used it must be #40 or higher.[10]

   Comment: The authors prefer nylon-coated cable rather than chain, since it will last longer, if properly installed, and is much easier to keep clean.

10. Crimp collar cable clamps rather than bolt-type cable clamps should be used. Also, for a safe, snug fit, it is important to be sure that the size of the clamp used matches the size of the cable. Cables should have sufficient stops so that clamps or cable fasteners do not enter the pulley area.

11. There should be no extensive cable overlap. (This also could cause an injury.) Approximately ½″ overlap is proper and should be further secured with nylon or plastic tape, or with specially made teflon sleeves.

Functional Materials

12. All guide bars must be secured into place by a steel collar with an allen set screw under the frame, or with a set screw through the frame, or by some other device which prohibits the undesirable vertical movement of the guide bars and is aesthetically acceptable.

13. All guide bars should be made of case-hardened shafting of polished steel. Guide bars with a chrome finish are available, and are acceptable, but are not preferred because of the possibility of chipping. The authors also prefer that the guide bars be not less than 1″ in diameter to insure the stability of the weight stack and to prevent sticking, although ¾″ guide bars are available.

14. Weight stacks should have springs on each guide bar supporting the stack. The springs should be made of ³⁄₁₆″ to ¼″ wire minimum and should match each other.[9] Rubber bumpers are acceptable but not preferred.

15. All seats and movable adjustment arms must have spring-loaded plungers, or other automatically adjustable devices. All spring-loaded plungers must have removable pins.

16. All pivot points must have oil-impregnated bronze bushings or precision sealed radial bearings (which are preferred). The bearings must be removable and replaceable and must allow a method of lubrication.

17. All sprockets, rollers, or pulleys must have oil-impregnated bronze bushings or precision seal radial bearings (which are preferred). Bearings must be removable and replaceable and should allow a method for lubrication. A 6″ diameter pulley should be used whenever possible. Pulleys must be ⅝″ to 1″ thick and made of a durable material. Aluminum, steel, hard rubber, cast iron, or nylon are generally acceptable.

18. Standard Olympic bars are made of 1⅛″ or 1¹⁄₁₆″ diameter steel. They are 87″ or 2.2 meters long, and 20 kilos or 44 pounds in weight. The inside collar dimensions are 53″. In rare cases, Olympic bars have been made of 1³⁄₁₆″ diameter steel. When discussing the strength of the bar, it has become a common practice to refer to the term "tensile strength." The *tensile strength* refers to the force which is required to break the steel.[23,28] This never occurs in the weight room, since tensile strengths of Olympic bars range from 80,000 to 140,000 pounds per square inch, or more. In selecting an Olympic bar, a major concern is that the bar will bend and not return to its original straight form. This quality is determined by the thickness of the bar and by the composition of the steel.[23,28] The figure which represents this tendency is referred to as the "yield point" of the metal. If all steel were pure, the "yield" of any bar would be determined strictly by the thickness of the bar.[28] However, various steel alloys—carbon, chrome, vanadium, and others—have been created and can increase the yield of the steel.

  An Olympic bar is most likely to bend when it is loaded with a heavy weight and dropped on a weight rack, or, one end first, on the floor. To make sure that this does not happen, purchase a bar that is 1⅛″ in diameter and, if possible, find out what the yield of the bar is. The yield should be from 120,000 to 130,000 pounds per square inch. Bars with a yield above 130,000 pounds per square inch become much more expensive. So, buyer—beware! Dealers more commonly refer to the tensile strength, which is likely to be a higher figure and is *not* indicative of the more important yield point of the bar.

19. All Olympic bars should have oil-impregnated bronze or machine steel bushing sleeves. Oil-impregnated bronze bushings are preferable. More expensive bars have ball bearings which are, of course, even better, but the price is usually prohibitive.

20. There are two knurling patterns for Olympic bars. Power bars, which also have a 4″ middle knurling, have a 14″ knurling cut deeply, for a very coarse surface. Olympic bars have a 21 lines/inch knurling, or medium knurling cut not so deeply. In gyms or spas where the clientele is likely to be more sensitive, the medium knurling should be used.

21. Olympic plates are normally preferred with the 45 pound plates made 18″ in diameter with a notched rim. This usually results in a 45 pound plate which is approximately 1⅛″ thick. Thicker plates make it more difficult to fit higher amounts of weight on the bar.

22. Machine holes and machined back are recommended rather than straight casting.

Aesthetic Materials

23. One coat of enamel paint is acceptable for plates. When a more finished, or finer, look is preferred, a baked-on hammer-tone grey can be purchased.

24. All upholstery must be covered with top-grade Naugahyde and top-grade high-density foam rubber padding must be used. The foam should be no less than 1″ thick and 2″ in designated areas.

25. Upholstery anchors or staples should be on the bottom of the board. For a better appearance or more elite-type equipment, upholstery must be hemmed and sewn and pad boards must have rounded corners.

26. Normally flat benches, Olympic benches, inclined benches, etc., are 10″ to 12″ wide. The authors prefer 12″ for training purposes, although powerlifting competition size may differ.

27. All roller pads must be at least 6″ in diameter.

28. All painted areas must first be covered with an epoxy-based primer.

29. All machines and equipment areas must be painted with a polyurethane-based enamel from 3 to 4 millimeters thick or 1½ millimeters thick for power coating.

30. All paint used must employ catalytic hardener or powder coating.

In addition to the equipment specifications, it is advisable to require information about the equipment company itself and its procedures.

Checklist for equipment companies:

1. Does the company have a credible business record?
2. What business arrangement is required by the company?
3. How long does the company require to deliver the product?
4. If a specific color is requested, how much extra will it cost? Will it cause a delay in delivery?
5. How much will the shipping costs be?
6. What is the method of delivery? (Van lines and freight are much different.)
7. Will the company replace or repair pieces broken or scratched during shipping?
8. What kind of warranty or guarantee is offered on the equipment.
9. What, if any, service is available to help maintain or repair the equipment if it is broken?
10. What are the relative costs of replacement parts?
11. Contact several of the companies' past customers to see if they have been satisfied with the business relationship, the delivery time, the equipment itself, and the service. Check on any other factors which may have been sources of dissatisfaction.

The Selection of Equipment

The selection of strength training equipment should not be difficult as long as the procedures suggested in the earlier sections of the chapter have been followed: 1) the major objectives, minor objectives, and sub-objectives need to have been established; 2) the facility and equipment reviewing process needs to have been carried out; 3) the floor plan for the facility needs to have been drawn up; and 4) a wide range of strength training equipment needs to have been systematically evaluated, using the recommended specifications and a checklist procedure.

The selection process is performed by referring directly to the sub-objectives. One by one, the equipment needs expressed by each sub-objective are matched with the best available piece of equipment to satisfy that particular need. The sub-objectives relating to the number of persons using the facility and the strength programs to be administered were used to derive the floor plan. Thus, the floor plan can be used to determine how many of each piece of equipment will need to be purchased.

The following factors should be considered in making the final selection.

1. How well does the piece of equipment rate in consideration of the specifications, as compared to similar pieces from other companies? There is little need to purchase all equipment from the same company. An advantage in purchasing a large portion of the order, or several pieces, from one company might be found in reduced shipping costs, or in a volume rate on the equipment.
2. How well does the equipment satisfy the specific functional and practical needs defined in the sub-objectives? One machine may be capable of fulfilling more than one sub-objective. This question then arises, "Is the elimination of a work station in the given situation detrimental or beneficial?" For example, in a strength circuit, two persons can work simultaneously if two machines are available. In this case, even though one machine may be capable of both functions, two machines are preferred.
3. What size and strength are the people who will be using the facility? All equipment must be suited to fit the anticipated sizes and strengths. If a large range of sizes and strengths is expected, the equipment should be adjustable if at all possible. Are large male athletes, as well as beginning female athletes, to use the same machines? If so, the machines should be capable of heavy enough resistance for the bigger, stronger athletes and light enough with smaller increments for the weaker athletes. Women may need to be able to add increments of increase as small as 1½ or 2½ pounds. The equipment should function as well on heavier or lighter resistances. The recommended sizes of the structural materials for strength equipment to be used in various facilities is delineated in the equipment specifications.
4. What level of appearance does the facility require? The answer to this question calls for a subjective judgment to some degree. The most expensive spas may require all chrome-plated machines and weight stacks, and every affordable luxury. Collegiate weight rooms, while desiring some measure of luxury, may not want the facility to look too fancy or fine, since college athletes need to identify with toughness and hard work. High school and junior high school weight rooms are usually not trying to display luxury. They do need to be neat and clean, and it's beneficial if they are decorated to have a motivational effect.

5. How can the proper color combination be selected? As mentioned previously, the utilization of an interior decorator, the Graphic, or the Art Department is recommended. When selecting the paint for strength equipment, the brand of paint and a number which refers to the color can be sent to each equipment company. Automobile dealers and automotive suppliers can supply paint chip samples which show the proper paint for metal strength equipment. Upholstery color should be selected in a similar way. The upholstery brand and the grade of upholstery, with the color code, can be sent to each equipment company.

6. How much should the equipment cost? When each factor has been evaluated, the various brands of each piece of strength training equipment that best fulfill the required sub-objectives of the facility are compared. The specifications checklist should reveal very specific information about each product. This information will be very helpful but, again, prudent judgmental decisions will be required of the strength expert. *Caution:* Beware of equipment priced unreasonably more or less than the entire group of its competitors. There are, however, some smaller companies that are reliable and are able to produce elite lines of custom-built equipment for much less than the larger companies. If one of these companies is to be used, emphasis should be placed on the procedure recommended in Check List for Equipment Companies.

As the various pieces of equipment, and furnishings, are selected, the itemized budget can take shape. The budget should list proposed items to be purchased, in general categories. Possible categories:

1. flooring
2. recording and testing equipment
3. stereo system
4. free weight equipment
5. strength training machines categorized by vendor
6. interior decor and graphics
7. work shop equipment and tools
8. office furnishings

The budget sheet lists the following columns.

Item	Description	Vendor	Unit Price	Total Price
			Total Price	_____

The total cost for each category is tallied separately. Subsequently, the total cost of furnishings and equipment for the entire facility is determined by adding together the total cost figures from each category. When this has been completed, the budget is tentatively finalized and ready for approval by the administration or business office, whatever the case may be. After the budget is approved, the equipment can be ordered according to the procedure followed by the organization. In some cases it may be helpful to make selections and get approval in a specific category such as *flooring,* or *essential strength equipment,* to avoid late delivery.

SUMMARY

This two-part chapter contains a systematic process for designing and developing strength training facilities. The process is applicable to nearly any situation since the designer creates his or her own objectives by considering the goals and limitations of the particular situation. The equipment selection and evaluation is also dealt with in a systematic way. It utilizes a set of general specifications which have been developed to ensure that quality equipment can be found. Planning for the Illinois Football Strength Complex was used as an example throughout the chapter. Photographs showing the final strength facility that resulted from the process are shown in figures 20.7, 20.8, 20.9, and 20.10. Examples of the strength equipment that was specifically in adherence to the general specifications in this chapter can be found in the Appendix.

ACKNOWLEDGMENT

The authors would like to thank Severns, Reid & Associates, Architects, Champaign, Illinois, for the contribution of the blueprints and floor plans which they used in designing the University of Illinois Football Strength Complex.

REFERENCES

1. Arthur, M. 1980. "Strength Training Room Tips," *NSCA Journal* 2(4):26–27.

2. Bielik, Ed. 1988. "Equipment Utilization and Construction #4: Pull Cords," *NSCA Journal* 10(3):49–51.

3. Broyan, R. T. 1974. *New Concepts in Planning and Funding Athletic, Physical Education and Recreation Facilities.* Phoenix, AZ: Phoenix Intermedia, Inc.

Figure 20.7 Strength Facility

Figure 20.8 Strength Facility

4. Coe, Mark, et al. 1987. "High School Clinic— Helpful Hints #3 How Do You Equip Your Weight Room?" *NSCA Journal* 9(6):62–65.

5. Coker, Ed. 1987. "Weight Room Maintenance: The Olympic Bar," *NSCA Journal* 9(4):73–75.

6. Coker, Ed. 1987. "Weight Room Maintenance #3: Equipment Padding and Covering," *NSCA Journal* 9(6):7–9.

7. Coker, Ed. 1988. "Weight Room Maintenance #5: Repairing and Inspecting Welds," *NSCA Journal* 10(2):62–65.

8. Coker, Ed. 1988. "Weight Room Maintenance #6: Broken Plates," *NSCA Journal* 10(3):58–60.

9. Costello, George. 1988. Professor of Theoretical and Applied Mechanica, University of Illinois at Urbana-Champaign. Personal interview.

Figure 20.9 Strength Facility

10. *Design Manual: Roller and Silent Chain Drives.* 1989. St. Petersburg, FL: American Chain Association.

11. "Equipment Utilization #1: The Power Rack." 1988. *NSCA Journal* 7(4):58–60.

12. Fry, Andrew. 1986. "Equipment Utilization #2: The Bench Press," *NSCA Journal* 7(6):51.

13. Fry, Andrew. 1986. "Equipment Utilization: The High Pulley," *NSCA Journal* 8(1):64.

14. Fry, Andrew. 1986. "Equipment Utilization #4: Machine Bench Press Station," *NSCA Journal* 8(2):43.

15. Fry, Andrew. 1986. "Equipment Utilization: The E-Z Curl Bar," *NSCA Journal* 8(3):26.

16. Fry, Andrew. 1986. "Equipment Utilization: The Low Pulley," *NSCA Journal* 8(4):62.

17. Fry, Andrew. 1986. "Equipment Utilization: The Incline Bench," *NSCA Journal* 8(5):46.

18. Fry, Andrew. 1986. "Equipment Utilization: Hyperextension Bench," *NSCA Journal* 8(6):79.

19. Fry, Andrew. 1987. "Equipment Utilization: Vertical Leg Press," *NSCA Journal* 9(1):64.

20. *How to Build a Strength Training and Conditioning Program in Your High School: "Assessing your Facility."* Published by NSCA, September 1, 1986, p. 10.

21. Hurd, Jeff. 1987. "Weight Room Maintenance #2: Lubricating Equipment," *NSCA Journal* 9(5):69–70.

22. Hurd, Jeff. 1988. "Weight Room Maintenance #4: Cables—Inspecting and Replacing," *NSCA Journal* 10(1):81–83.

23. Juvinall, Robert C. 1985. *Fundamentals of Machine Component Design.* New York: John Wiley and Sons, Inc.

24. Kroll, Bill. 1988. "Business Management: The Development of the University of Illinois Football Strength Facility—Part II," *American Fitness Quarterly* 7:10–12.

25. Kroll, Bill. 1987. "Facility Considerations: The Development of a Football Strength Complex," *NSCA Journal* 9(5):28–30.

26. McClellan, Tim, and William J. Stone. 1986. "Research Technique: A Survey of Football Strength and Conditioning Programs for Division I NCAA Universities," *NSCA Journal* 8(2):34–36.

27. Morgan, J. S. 1977. "A Survey of Weight Training Facilities and Equipment of Major University Football Programs." Master's thesis. University of Kansas.

28. Offner, David H. 1988. Professor, Department of Mechanical and Industrial Engineering, University of Illinois. Personal interview.

29. Olsen, John R. and Gary R. Hunter. 1985. "Football: A Comparison of 1974 and 1984 Player Sizes and Maximal Strength and Speed Efforts for Division I NCAA Universities," *NSCA Journal* 6(6):26–28.

30. O'Shea, J. P. 1976. *Scientific Principles and Methods of Strength Fitness,* 2d ed. Reading, MA: Addison-Wesley.

31. Peterson, Dick. 1988. "Facility Design from Concept to Concrete: East Chicago (Indiana) Central High School," *NSCA Journal* 10(1):38–40.

32. Smith, Mark S. 1987. "An Open Letter to Equipment Companies: Improving the Design of Weight Training Machines," *NSCA Journal* 9(3):42–45.

33. Sochor, Dave. 1988. "Facility Design: The Weight Room at Doniphan High School," *NSCA Journal* 10(2):56–60.

34. *Wire Rope Handbook.* 1987. St. Louis, MO: Broderick & Bascom Rope Company.

35. *Wire Rope Users Manual,* 2d ed. 1987. Washington, DC: American Iron and Steel Institute.

APPENDIX

AEROBIC-ANAEROBIC PERFORMANCE CHART

(Mon.)	Dist.	Time	HR	(Wed.)	Dist.	Time	HR	(Fri.)	Dist.	Time	HR	Wk

Name _____ Max. HR _____

STRENGTH RECORDING SHEET

Date	Exercise & No. of Sets															
	Wt.															
	Reps.															

Appendix

Figure A.1 Olympic Bench

EQUIPMENT

The following are photographs and/or brief descriptions of some of the strength equipment used in implementing the programs in this text. The equipment described here adheres to the general specifications described in chapter 20. The intention of this section is to give the reader a general idea of some of the current strength training equipment used in the field of Strength Training for Athletics. It is in no way inclusive of the myriad of commercially available strength training equipment in a market that is currently expanding virtually faster than it can be categorized.

Bench

The Olympic bench should be about fifteen to eighteen inches high and from ten to twelve inches wide, with approximately an inch of padding. The rack for an Olympic bar should be wider than that for the standard bar. The rack should allow the bar to rest approximately three feet from the floor, in easy position to be removed for bench pressing.

The rack on the Olympic bench should have some type of high back on the cup that holds the bar. A standard Olympic bench is shown above in figure A.1. Various styles of benches have been created including racks that are adjustable in height and others that are very high and slant back in the direction of the spotter. This style has a number of pegs allowing the bar to be placed at various heights to accommodate individual differences.

Another method of bench pressing with the free weights is achieved by placing a bench in a power rack, as shown in the photos of the Self-Contained Power Areas.

Squat Rack

The squat rack for Squats and Military Presses should be adjustable, if possible; if not, the preferred height is about two inches to four inches below shoulder level.

In addition to the conventional squat standards, which consist simply of two upright posts with cups to hold the bar, several other styles of squat racks are available. Two examples, the "step-down squat rack" and the "S"-type rack are shown on p. 286. Just as in the case of the bench press, the power rack is also used for squatting.

Power Rack

The power rack can be used for a variety of exercises. The Military Press, Rack Squat, Rack Bench, and Rack Dead Lift are the most common. The exercise is done with the bar inside the rack. The pins in the rack can be adjusted so that the bar can be elevated to any level. By using two sets of pins, isometric exercises or partial isometric contractions requiring a minimum level of intensity can be done on the power rack. Power racks are shown in figures A.3 and A.4 (Self-Contained Power Areas).

SELF-CONTAINED POWER AREAS

In order to most efficiently and effectively utilize floor space and to provide the maximum number of free weight stations, the modular system of self-contained power areas can be employed. Suggested dimensions for the SCPAs feature rubberized floor space 14 feet measuring out from the wall and 8 feet wide. There should be at least 4 feet of floor space in between areas. Each area contains a self-standing power rack and a flat bench that adjusts to become a bench for the incline or seated military press, at a variety of angles. The power racks are of heavy duty construction and contain heavy, removable safety bars and heavy duty cups so that the barbells can be held at a convenient height inside or outside the rack. The rack can have 2 to 3 ft. inside dimensions and be 7 to 9 ft. high.

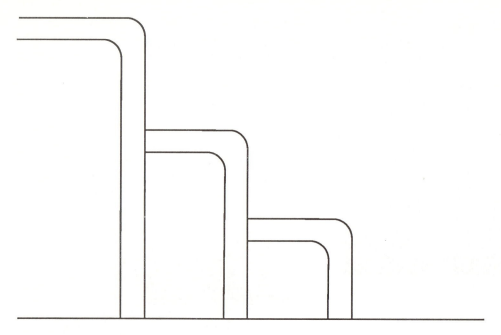

Step-Down Squat Rack (side view)

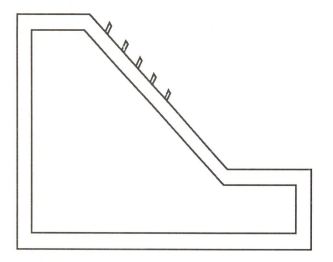

"S" Type Squat Rack with diagonal pegged rail and safety rack (side view)

Figure A.2   Squat Standards with Jack-Type Lift

Each "Self-Contained Power Area" (SCPA) can have a power bar, an Olympic bar, and a curl bar. Upright or horizontal weight racks should be positioned between the rubberized areas. If it is desired that every free weight exercise is to be performed in the SCPA, double-tiered dumbbell racks can be positioned adjacent to the tops of the areas. When this SCPA system is used in the room design, the strength machines most often used to supplement the free weights can be positioned more closely to the SCPAs. Machines used on a more limited basis are placed accordingly at a greater distance from the SCPAs.

Self-Contained Power Areas can be seen in figures A.3 and A.4.

High Angle Shoulder Machine   This angle shoulder machine is excellent for shoulder and upper chest development.

Shoulder Machine   This machine is particularly good for simulating the tackling arm and shoulder action.

Figure A.3 Power Rack

Figure A.5 High Angle Shoulder Machine

Figure A.4 Power Rack

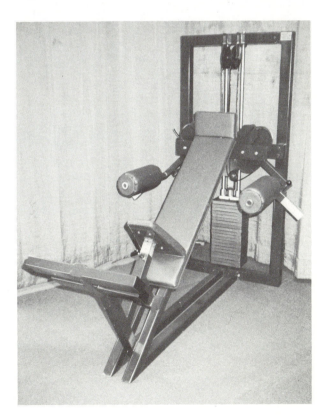

Figure A.6 Shoulder Machine

Figure A.7 Dumbbells

Figure A.8 Dumbbells

Dumbbells   Various types of dumbbells and dumbbell racks are available. The most inexpensive are solid iron dumbbells. The dumbbells shown in figure A.7 are "professional dumbbells" with chrome-knurled handles. It's usually best if professional dumbbells are welded on the ends to prevent them from being taken apart. The most expensive dumbbells are solid steel with chrome or nickel plating as those shown in figure A.8.

Figure A.9 Hip Flexor Machine

Hip Flexor Machine   The hip flexor machine is important for the leg drive and knee lift required by sprinters. The machine shown in figure A.9 is extremely heavy duty and is adjustable for height. It also works hip extension, abduction, and adduction as well as hip flexion.

Figure A.10 Hip and Leg Sled

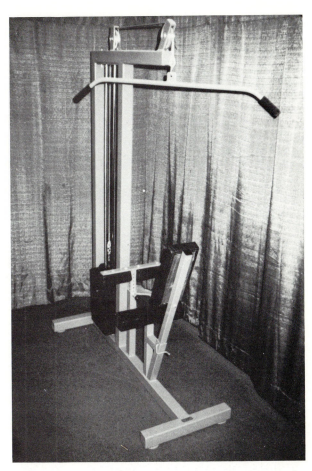

Figure A.11 Lat Pull Machine

Hip and Leg Sled   This hip and leg sled functions three ways—as a leg press, hack squat, and hip thrust. An outstanding feature is that it changes very easily and smoothly from one position to another (fig. A.10).

Lat Pull Machine   The unique feature of the lat machine is the removable back. This makes it possible to lean back and pull the lat bar down in the front of the head. The back rest can be removed making it possible to use the machine for Triceps Pushdowns (fig. A.11).

Lateral Deltoid Military Press Machine   This is an excellent machine that places the military press apparatus in the optimal position for comfort, back support, and shoulder development (fig. A.12).

Leg Extension Machine (Selectorized)   This leg extension machine adjusts in two directions: for thigh length and for calf length (fig. A.13).

Leg Extension (Plate Loaded)   Some coaches still prefer the plate loaded leg extension to aid in the prevention of knee injuries (fig. A.14).

Figure A.12 Military Press Machine

Figure A.13   Leg Extension Machine

Figure A.14   Leg Extension Machine (Plate Loaded)

Figure A.15   Neck Machine

Neck Machine   The cam in this neck machine seems to work downward movement of the head toward the chest at the optimal acute angle (fig. A.15).

Pull-Up Dip Machine   This apparatus is excellent for any athlete who cannot do chin-ups or bar dips. The angle is gradually increased over a period of weeks until, when working at the higher angles of the machine, the exercises can be done on the normal apparatus. This machine has a motorized winch. It is also available in lighter models with a crank winch (fig. A.16).

Vertical Bench   The vertical bench is a very popular machine. Bench presses can be done with individual arm action and with a much deeper (full) range of motion than regular bench presses. The machine also makes it impossible to cheat by raising the hips (fig. A.17).

Multi-Purpose Bench   The multi-purpose bench is a selectorized machine which can be used for numerous exercises. This is possible because of the second selector pin that allows the handle mechanism to be set at various heights. It is probably the best available shoulder shrug machine on the market and is manufactured in different styles by a number of commercial companies. It also can be utilized for Bench Presses, Military Presses, Incline Presses, Toe Raises, Upright Rows, and others (fig. A.18).

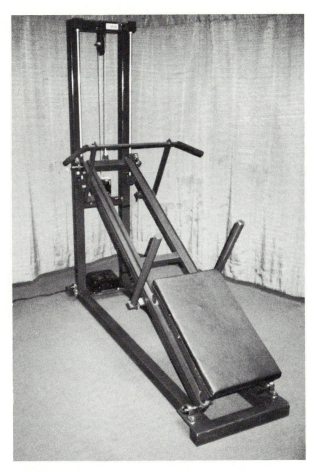

Figure A.16 Pull-Up Dip Machine

Figure A.17 Vertical Bench

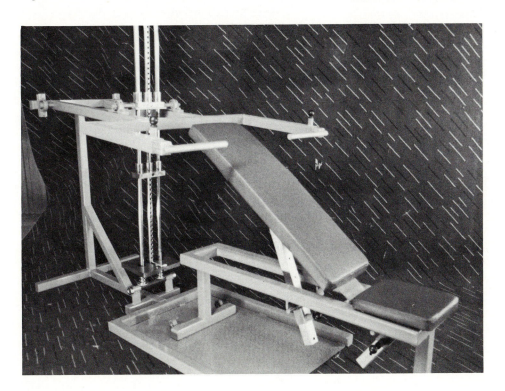

Figure A.18 Multi-Purpose Bench

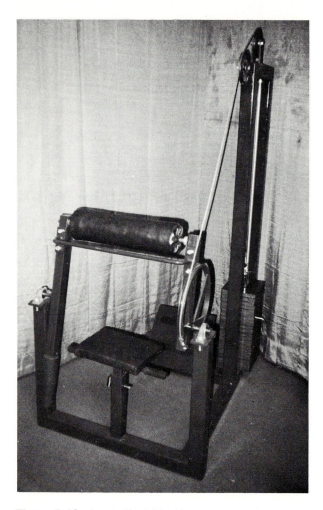

Figure A.19 Lower Back Machine

Figure A.20 Leg Curl Machine

Lower Back Machine   The lower back machine is an excellent way to develop an area that is involved in virtually every athletic movement. The lower back is one area that can be trained much more effectively with a machine than with the free weights. The secret is that the machine must be designed so that the entire range of spinal erector muscles are trained smoothly and with the proper relative resistance. A good lower back machine will greatly reduce the lower back tightness and can eliminate the soreness in this area that sometimes accompanies heavy squats (fig. A.19).

Leg Curl Machine   The leg curl machine is used to develop the muscles that flex the knee, the hamstrings. Two types of leg curl machines are shown: the prone "V" bench (fig. A.20) and the standing leg curl machine (fig. A.21).

Calf Machine   Various types of calf machines are available. The standard hinge type is sufficient. Many other types of equipment can be used for toe raises.

Neck Harness   The neck harness is a simple item that can vary greatly in quality. It is most important that the neck harness be comfortable, strong, and durable.

Pull Straps   These are usually about one inch wide and two feet long. They must be made of a tough cotton and/or nylon interwoven material.

Weight Belt   The weight belt is used to give needed support to the back and abdomen. The official competition weight-lifting belt can be no more than four inches wide at any point. In some cases athletes might wish to use a slightly wider belt since weight training for athletes, obviously, does not require that a competition size belt be used.

Figure A.21   Leg Curl Machine

INDEX

H

Hockey, 157
    programs, 158–59

I

Injury Prevention, 87
    exercises, 89–94
    rehabilitation exercises, 89–94
    training, 88
Interval training, 28
Isokinetic, 35
Isometric, 34
Isotonic, 35

L

LBW (lean body weight), 103
LME (local muscular endurance), 7
LSD (long slow distance), 26

M

Major exercises, 38
Maximal oxygen uptake (VO2 max), 116
Muscular
    contraction, 19
    endurance, 7
    fiber type, 18
    hypertrophy, 20
    strength, 7
    strength/endurance continuum, 41
    structure, 18

N

Nutrition (sports), 97
    athlete, 102
    basic food groups, 101
    basic nutrients, 99
    CHO (carbohydrate), 99
    CHO loading, 104
    defined, 97
    fat, 99
    pre-game meal, 107
    protein, 99, 106
    vitamins, 99
    water balance, 106

O

Olympic Lifts, 34
Overload, 36
Overtraining, 113

P

Percent body fat, 103
Plyometrics, 53
Position Statements, 11–13
Power, 8
Power Lifting, 34
PRE (progressive resistance exercise), 36
Pre-pubescents, 12

R

Repetition (Rep), 35
ROM (range of motion), 9, 59

S

Set, 35
Soccer, 145
    programs, 146–48
Softball, 173
    programs, 173–77
Specificity, 4, 37
Speed, 8
Sport fitness, 15
Sportsmedicine, 87
Strength
    defined, 7
    exercises, 221–57
    explosive, 8
    muscular, 7
    1RM, 7
    progression, 36
    recording sheet, 284
    tests, 118
    training, 33
Strength training
    assistant exercises, 38
    circuits, 47
    cycle systems, 47
    duration, 44
    essentials, 35
    exercises, 221–57
    frequency, 43
    intensity, 38
    major exercises, 38
    overload, 36
    plyometrics, 53
    progression, 36
    safety, 219
    set systems, 45
    specialty exercises, 39
    specificity, 37
    spotting procedures, 220
    supplementary exercises, 38